In the spring of 1204 the knights of the
F........ .... pos-

. ..   Greece. The reader
                ʻed among the
                ʻʻ how

CRUSADERS AS CONQUERORS

THE CHRONICLE OF MOREA

NUMBER LXIX OF THE

Records of Civilization: Sources and Studies

EDITED UNDER THE AUSPICES OF THE

DEPARTMENT OF HISTORY, COLUMBIA UNIVERSITY

CRUSADERS AS CONQUERORS

THE CHRONICLE OF MOREA

TRANSLATED FROM THE GREEK,
WITH NOTES
AND
INTRODUCTION, BY

HAROLD E. LURIER

COLUMBIA UNIVERSITY PRESS
NEW YORK AND LONDON 1964

Harold E. Lurier is Professor of Social Sciences at Pace College.

LIBRARY OF CONGRESS CATALOG CARD NUMBER: 62-9367

THIS TRANSLATION IS DEDICATED TO MY SISTER

JANICE

"Οὐ γὰϱ ἄμισθον τὸ εὖ ποιεῖν, κἄν μὴ
παϱαχϱῆμα τῆς εὐεϱγεσίας ἡ ἀντίδο-
σις φαίνηται."

Alciphron

ACKNOWLEDGMENTS

The author who undertakes the translation of a work already in print must face a special set of trials. Some of these I was able to avoid, since the text that I chose was both antique and anonymous. Yet there still remained the tedium and persistence of the mechanics of the translation. From these I soon learned that the translator needs spiritual sustenance rather than technical assistance from those to whom he turns for help. In this respect I consider myself most fortunate to have been first introduced to my labors by my mentor, Professor Kenneth M. Setton, whose exacting standards of scholarship provided me with a constant and sustaining goal.

I should also like to express my gratitude to the librarians and staff of the Public Library of Danbury, Connecticut, a small library not often thought of, perhaps, as a place of research, yet a library that offered me all its facilities and the friendly, even eager help of its staff through the long, otherwise discouraging, months that produced the main text of this book.

I must also thank Miss Elisabeth Shoemaker of the staff of Columbia University Press who read my manuscript with extraordinary skill and attention.

Finally, my deepest debt is to my sister Janice, who not only spent countless hours typing manuscript for me, but who was ever vigilant to correct my all too frequent errors. In the end her faith and trust in me produced this work, and to her I have dedicated it.

H. E. L.

October, 1962
Pace College

ABBREVIATIONS

H.   = Codex Havniensis (Copenhagen text of the Greek
            Chronicle)

K.   = P. Kalonaros, *Τὸ Χρονικὸν τοῦ Μορέως* (edited text
            of the Greek Chronicle)

L.   = *Livre de la Conqueste de la Princée de l'Amorée* (French
            version of the Chronicle, edited by Jean Longnon)

L. de F. = *Libro de los fechos, etc.* (Aragonese version of the
            Chronicle, edited by Alfred Morel-Fatio)

Lg.   = J. Longnon, *L'Empire latin de Constantinople*

M.   = W. Miller, *Latins in the Levant*

P.   = Codex Parisinus (Paris text of the Greek Chronicle)

S.   = J. Schmitt, *The Chronicle of Morea* (edited text of the
            Greek Chronicle)

Z.   = D. Zakythinos, *Le Despotat grec de Morée*

See Bibliography for full details on these works.

CONTENTS

INTRODUCTION

INTRODUCTION

HISTORICAL SYNOPSIS

On the morning of April 13, 1204, the knights of the Fourth Crusade found themselves in possession of the city of Constantinople. For the second time within a year this greatest prize of Christendom had bowed to its first conquerors. For three days the city was pillaged without mercy, but by Easter Sunday, April 25, some semblance of order had been restored. Even as the echo of the stately Latin chants still hovered above the Greek churches, proclaiming to the bewildered populace a new regime and a reunited Church, the leaders of the Crusade turned to the complicated problem of organizing their new empire.

In March the leaders of the Crusade, Boniface, marquis of Montferrat, Baldwin, count of Flanders, and the counts of Blois and St. Pol had met with their Venetian allies to determine the strategy for the assault and the division of the spoils. It was decided that the newly won empire would be given to an emperor chosen from candidates proposed by the Crusaders and the Venetians; the patriarchate and all its possessions would go to the loser. The booty was to be distributed fairly according to rank, and one quarter of the empire was to go to the emperor, the remainder to be divided equally between Venice and the Crusaders, with fiefs to be assigned one half in territory already taken and one half in lands yet to be conquered. This treaty was submitted for approval to Pope Innocent III who accepted its terms reluctantly.

As soon as the committee met to elect the emperor there appeared the factionalism that had brought dissension to earlier crusading hosts. After spirited wrangling, Baldwin of Flanders was elected emperor. His rival Boniface de Montferrat was offered extensive lands in Anatolia to assuage ruffled sensibilities and to keep peace among the Crusaders. As planned, the patriarchate and its possessions went to the Venetians, who assigned them to one of their aristocrats Tommaso Morosini, without any consultation with the pope, who felt an immediate chill of apprehension. At its very inception the Latin Empire of Constantinople had already established the pattern of dissension and competing ambitions that was to be its lasting weakness. But any forebodings were soon lost in the general excitement of the division of the staggering pile of booty. The emperor apportioned this fairly and then took a careful survey of the lands of the empire in order to make a just distribution of the fiefs.

Boniface, meanwhile, had married Marie, sister of the king of Hungary and the still young widow of the late Byzantine emperor Isaac Angelos. He asked the emperor to exchange his as yet unconquered lands in Anatolia for the kingdom of Salonika, either because he wished to be closer to his new brother-in-law, who might need his aid, or because he had ambitions of his own to establish a Balkan kingdom. Baldwin was suspicious but made the exchange. The rest of the empire was divided properly, and the fiefs were assigned. All thereupon rushed to conquer their new lands, the marquis marching westward with a large following of the best troops in the Host. In addition to his own vassals from northern Italy, his rank and reputation for bravery attracted Germans, like the count Berthold of Katzenelnbogen; Burgundians, like Guillaume de Champlitte and Othon de la Roche; Provençals, and even Flemings and Frenchmen, like Jacques d'Avesnes and Thomas d'Autremencourt. In addition he had a large Greek following that included a cousin of the late royal Greek house, Michael Komnenos Doukas. The marquis apparently was quite fond of him and put great trust in him, but as soon as he could, Michael deserted and with his brother Theodoros made his way to Epiros where he organized the local Greeks, the Albanians, and the Vlachs into a center of Greek resistance in the west.

The marquis reached Salonika without any trouble. In fact, he was greeted with joyous welcome everywhere by the Greeks. Leaving his wife in charge of the city's defense, he took her son by her former marriage, the young prince Manuel, and began a triumphant tour southward, displaying the boy everywhere. In Macedonia and Thessaly he was greeted enthusiastically, almost as a returning hero. The Vale of Tempe, Larissa, and other towns all paid him homage. He met no resistance until he reached Thermopylae. The explanation of this extraordinary passage lies in the fact that, even before it fell to the Latins, the Byzantine government had largely lost its control over Greece. Petty lords, pirates, local governors, and a few great feudal families had taken over the country for themselves and had crushed the people of the cities and the farms under an insupportable load of exactions. The fall of the city was the signal for a mad scramble for power among these petty leaders. It is no wonder that there was no will to resist another invader. In fact, the people of the land saw in the Latins a possible turn for the better. One of the local petty tyrants who had seized power was Leon Sgouros. His original holding was around the town of Nauplia, but he had expanded northward to Argos and Corinth, past Athens, where the valiant metropolitan Michael Choniates had put up too stiff a resistance, to Thebes and Larissa. As Boniface advanced, Leon withdrew to the mountains around Thermopylae to bar the entrance to central Greece. Then, losing his nerve, he fled to Corinth to protect the entrance to the Peloponnesos. The marquis, leisurely following, was welcomed by Thebes and Boeotia. Athens was not so hospitable but put up no resistance. Euboea fell without a blow. Finally he arrived in Corinth and besieged Sgouros in the fastness of the Acrocorinth, building a small castle called Mont Escovée to control the operation. Leaving Jacques d'Avesnes in charge, he then proceded south and laid siege to Nauplia. It was at this time that he received an unexpected visit that was to decide the history of Greece for the next two centuries.

Geoffroy de Villehardouin, nephew of the marshal of Champagne and chronicler of the Crusade, had gone directly to Syria and had not taken part in the assault on Constantinople. Like others who had done the same, as soon as he had heard of the establishment of the Latin empire, Geoffroy set sail for Constantinople, hoping to make his fortune. His ship was blown to the west by contrary winds, and he had to take refuge in the port of Modon in the south of the Peloponnesos. There he and his companions were approached by a local Greek archon who wanted to use this unexpected troop to expand his territories. The prospect of adventure and profit

ADRIATIC

SEA

ITALY

Strait of Otranto

ALBANIA

Durazzo

Ochrida

Lake Ochrida

Lake Prespa

Berat

Avlona

Kastoria

MACEDONIA

Vardar R.

Pelagonia

Melnik

Drama

Serres

Philip

Salonika

Chortiatis

CHALKIDIKI

Verroia

Kitros

Servia

Haliakmon R.

HAGION OROS

CORFU

Butrinto

Yannina

EPIRUS

PINDUS MTS.

Arachthos R.

Arta

Platamon

TEMPE

Kalambaka

Trikkala

Peneios R.

Larissa

THESSALY

SKIATHOS

CHILIODROMIA

Sporades

Prevesa

Vonitsa

Karditsa

VLACHIA

Velestino

Demetrias

Volos

IONIAN ISLANDS

LEUKAS

CEPHALONIA

Angelokastro

Acheloös R.

Pharsalus

Domokos

Thalassinos

Halmyros

Lamia

Spercheios

Neopatras

Sideroporta

Giona

Lidoriki

Grovia

Gardiki

Oreos

Ravennika

Boudonitza

Davila

Clisura

EUBOEA (EURIPOS)

Avlonari

Naupaktos

Galaxidi

Salona

Itea

Kephissos

Livadia

Orchomenos

Chalkis

Karditsa

Thebes

Phyla

IONIAN SEA

Patras

Cape Drepanon

Vostitsa

Livadostro

Eleutherae

Lirme

KARYDI

ATHENS

Achaia

Lissarea

Chalandritsa

Santameri

Kerpini

Perachora

Piraeus

ZANTE

Manolas

Lechaina

Klarentsa

Andravida

Palaeopolis

Chloumoutsi

Peneios

Vounarvi

Vliziri

Olena

Pondikos

Alpheios

Kalavryta

Corinth

SALAMIS

Megara

AEGINA

Akova

SKORTA

Araklovon

Prinitsa

Liodora

Hagionoros

Argos

Nauplion

Isova

Xenochori

Kopronitsa

Mountra

Karytaina

MESAREA

Nikli

Sapikos

Damala

HYDRA

Arkadia

Demetra

Makryplagi

Veligosti

Helmos

Arachova

Androusa

Nisi

Mistra

Lakedaimonia

TSAKONIA

Kalamata

Geraki

Eurotas

Avarino (Navarino)

Leftro

Methone

Korone

Messene

Gulf

MAÏNE

VATIKA

Helos

Passava

Monemvasia

Cape Maleas

Maïne

Cape Matapan

CERIGO (CYTHERA)

THIRTEENTH-CENTURY GREECE

UNDER FRANKISH DOMINATION

MEDITERRANEAN

SCALE OF MILES

0   25   50   75   100

BLACK SEA

THRACE

Adrianople

Xanthi

Christoupolis

Mesta R.

Maritsa River

Chorlu

CONSTANTINOPLE

Bosporus

Silviri

Chalcedon

Rodosto

Heraclea

Nicomedia

SEA OF MARMARA

THASOS

SAMOTHRACE

Gallipoli

Lampsacus

Dardanelles

Abydos

Cyzicus

Brusa

Nicaea

Athos

LIMNOS

Adramyttion

LESBOS

Pergamum

ANATOLIA

SKYROS

AEGEAN

CHIOS

Smyrna

Philadelphia

Karystos

ANDROS

ISLANDS

SAMOS

DUCHY

KEOS

IKARIA

TENOS

OF THE

MYKONOS

THERMIA

SIROS

PATMOS

ARCHIPELAGO

PAROS

NAXOS

SIPHNOS

COS

KIMOLOS

Cyclades

AMORGOS

MELOS

SIKHNOS

IOS

ASTYPALIA
(STAMPALIA)

Dodecanese

SANTORIN
(THIRA)

ANAPHE

RHODES

SEA OF CRETE

KARPATHOS

CRETE

SEA

Vaughn Gray

led Geoffroy to join the Greek, and together they conquered all of the western Peloponnesos as far north as Patras. These lands, it must be noted, had already been assigned to Venice. At this point the Greek died, and his son, distrustful of the Latins, closed all the cities to them and raised the Greeks against them. Finding himself in a hostile land and hearing of the arrival of Boniface in the Peloponnesos, Geoffroy rode in great peril across the peninsula to Nauplia to seek help. The marquis was delighted to see him and invited him to join his army. But Geoffroy found an old friend, Guillaume de Champlitte, in the host. He prevailed upon him to return to the west to conquer Morea and promised to become his liegeman for any lands that Guillaume might assign to him.

Thereupon, while Jacques d'Avesnes was at Corinth and the marquis at Nauplia, the two companions with about two hundred knights and four hundred sergeants began an astonishing adventure in the western Peloponnesos. With no trouble at all they took province after province, city after city, until they found themselves in the far south at Modon. They fortified the town and pushed their way into the mountainous regions of Messenia, Arkadia, and Lakonia. In short, almost all of the peninsula fell to them, and they made a great division of the land. Twelve major fiefs were created and assigned to barons and to each of these were assigned vassals, knights, and sergeants, each of whom was given a fief. The religious orders, the Hospitalers, the Templars, and the prelates, also received lands and for these they owed military service, but not garrison duty. In fact, the whole land was on a war footing and the vassals were expected to give military service all year round, four months in the field, four months in garrison duty, and four months at home on call, since no one could leave the land without permission. Even the Greek dignitaries had a place in the feudal order. Those who submitted retained their lands and had the same rights and duties as the Franks. The arrangements with the peasants on the land remained unchanged, but actually conditions for them improved as peace and order were restored and the crushing exactions of the Greek governors and tyrants were stopped. The moderation and tolerance of the new Frankish lords ensured the support of the Greeks, made the conquest easier, and brought about general prosperity. The new ruler of the land took as his official title the designation prince of Achaia, but he was popularly called prince of Morea, prince being a title unusual in the Middle Ages and unique in the Latin Empire. The prince and his barons held their lands by right of conquest, but technically Guillaume de Champlitte had asked leave of the marquis of Montferrat to go on his adventure, and the permission seems to have established some sort of suzerainty over Morea.

The marquis, meanwhile, was establishing the same sort of order throughout Greece. He gave Athens to Othon de la Roche who took the title duke of Athens, but he was commonly called by the Greeks Megas Kyr (great lord). Thebes was first given to an Italian, Albertino de Canossa, though it soon passed to Othon, who added it to his fief and to his title. Thermopylae went to another Italian noble, the marquis Guido Pelavicino, and became the famous marquisate of Boudonitza. The lands around Delphi, stretching to the Gulf of Corinth, were given to Thomas d'Autremencourt, who established the lordship of Salona there. The assignment of Euboea first to Jacques d'Avesnes, then to Ravan dalle Carceri, a noble of Verona, completed the arrangements for central Greece. Northern Greece was likewise divided among the many followers of the marquis, though many cities were kept by him as royal castellanies. Strangely enough, he never took the title of king. He was called lord of the kingdom of Salonika or simply marquis of Montferrat.

While the western part of the empire was being organized, Venice began to occupy the points that she had chosen for herself along the coasts of Greece and on the islands of the Ionian and Aegean seas. Baldwin, for his part, once crowned with pomp in the Church of the Holy Wisdom, led a swarm of Crusaders into Anatolia. The resistance of the petty Greek princelings in the area melted away before the superior tactics and determination of the western knights. A main center of Greek resistance, however, began to form around Theodoros Laskaris, son-in-law of the emperor Alexios III and hero of the defense of Constantinople. He was established near Nicaea, and leading Greek prelates and dignitaries began to join him there.

Once the lands were divided among the Latins, the problem of organization arose. Had the example of the Franks in Morea in their dealings with the Greeks been followed, all might have gone well, but unfortunately the new emperor Baldwin failed completely in developing a workable policy towards his Greek subjects. His natural hauteur and disdain led him to spurn all offers of assistance from the Greek nobles. Refused a part in the Latin feudal structure of the state, these outraged nobles became the nucleus of a Greek resistance and looked for help from the two free Greek centers at Epiros and Nicaea. They even looked to their ancient enemies the Bulgars for deliverance. As for the masses of the people, they were better disposed toward the Latins at first, and with them Baldwin displayed a more intelligent approach by allowing conditions on the lands to go on without significant change. But here again a spirit of Greek resistance arose, following the attempts of the new regime to force a union between the two churches. Already the Greeks identified their individual and communal liberties with the rites of their church. Though the metropolitans and bishops had fled their sees at the time of the conquest, the members of the lower clergy remained, and these the Latins attempted to bring under Roman control. The pope recognized the delicacy of the problem, and at times so did the emperor, but the Greeks increasingly resisted all overtures. They clung to their Church with a stubborn fervor and looked longingly to the same sources of deliverance that attracted their leaders. The situation was aggravated by a singular lack of tact and restraint on the part of many of the Crusaders, particularly the Venetians, who had taken Adrianople as part of their share of the empire. There an uprising broke out in February, 1205, and quickly most of Thrace fell into the hands of Greek insurgents. As the emperor proceeded westward with a fatally weak army made up mostly of his vassals called from their lands in Asia Minor, the Greeks called upon Kalojan, tsar of the Bulgars, for help.

This leader of the Bulgarians had sought before the Fourth Crusade to throw off allegiance to the Byzantine emperor and had turned to the pope for help. After a lengthy correspondence with Innocent III, who hoped to penetrate the Balkans and open a new route to Syria for the crusading movement, an agreement was reached in 1203. By its terms a Latin archbishop was made primate of Bulgaria in September, 1203, and in February, 1204, the pope recognized Kalojan as king of the Bulgars and the Vlachs. In the spirit of this *rapprochement*, Kalojan subsequently offered his services to the Crusaders in their conquest of the empire. They rejected his overtures in a particularly haughty and brutal manner and, treating him as a vassal, demanded that he do homage to the Latin emperor for his lands. In a rage, Kalojan threw off his friendship with the Latins and became their implacable foe. It was this man who now came to the assistance of the Greeks with a vast army, including in its troops over 14,000 Cuman mercenaries.

The two armies met near Adrianople, and the Latins were overwhelmed. The emperor was captured and later died mysteriously in prison. Remnants of the troops streamed back toward the capital, where the state was taken over by Baldwin's brother Henri de Hainaut. Henri's reign (1206-16) was crucial for the survival of the empire. With all of Thrace repeatedly laid waste by the Bulgars and Anatolia deserted by its Latin lords and falling bit by bit to Laskaris, Henri's position was desperate. In the east he allied himself with the Greeks who had established themselves at Paphlagonia and Trebizond under two sons of the late emperor Andronikos, and even with the infidel Turk, making an uneasy common cause against the common enemy, Laskaris. In the west his position was somewhat improved by the Venetians, who now began to take over their lands in earnest. Relentlessly they reduced all centers of resistance along the Greek coast, fighting Greeks, pirates, and Champlitte himself in the process. They sent fleets and armies to the Ionian islands, and a swarm of Venetians pacified all the islands of the Aegean. Ravan dalle Carceri did homage to Venice for his island of Euboea, and Crete, bought by Venice from Boniface de Montferrat, was invaded. In Greece the barons of Morea slowly pushed eastward, and in the north the marquis consolidated his holdings after the disastrous Bulgar invasions. Thus the west was made more stable, and the marquis and Henri cemented a treaty of friendship by the marriage between Henri and Agnes, daughter of the marquis. Marie, wife of the marquis, at this time produced an heir. He was named, significantly, Demetrios, after the patron saint of Salonika.

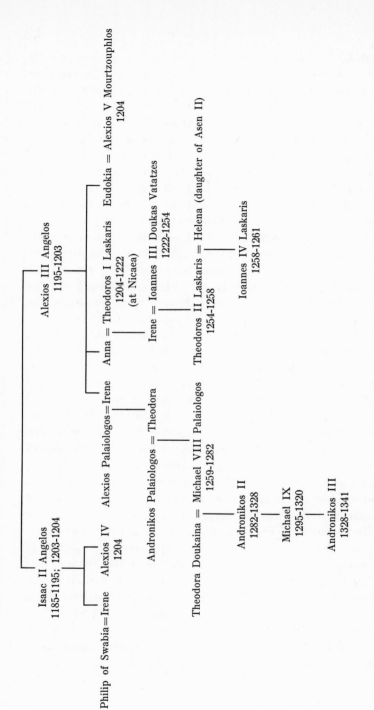

EMPERORS OF BYZANTIUM

Above all, Henri sought to conciliate his Greek subjects, who themselves now felt the heavy hand of the Bulgars and turned to their new emperor for help. The key to the situation was the religious question, and long, difficult negotiations between the Greek clergy and the Latins, led by Greek prelates from southern Italy who had accepted the suzerainty of the Roman pope, were carried on in the lands of the marquis and throughout the empire. Everywhere the Latins used a moderate tone of conciliation, and real progress seems to have been made. The stumbling block, however, was the question of Roman supremacy, and on this rock all negotiations shattered. The whole matter became academic after March, 1208, for at that time Laskaris saw to the election of a Greek patriarch in Nicaea, who promptly crowned Laskaris as legitimate Byzantine emperor. All the Greeks within the Latin empire immediately threw off any thoughts of reconciliation and union between the two churches and henceforth looked to Nicaea for deliverance and the return of their own patriarch.

Events meanwhile moved swiftly. Boniface was trapped by the Bulgars in 1207, and was killed, his head being cut from his still living body to be sent to his enemy Kalojan. But the days of the tsar were also numbered, and he died in his sleep on the eve of the feast of St. Demetrios (October 8, 1207). The Bulgar kingdom fell into anarchy and civil war and was thereafter slowly reorganized under John Asen. Thus it seemed that the crisis had been weathered. Laskaris had been fought back. The Bulgar menace was terminated. The lands of the Greek world were pacified. But there were many problems. Henri's Greek subjects could again indulge their resentment against the conquerors, though they were always fond of the emperor personally, for he favored them and had reopened the Greek churches. His barons and bishops were struggling over the age-old problem of ecclesiastical immunities. He put an end to this by forcing a compromise. In return for their independence, the prelates agreed to pay the traditional Byzantine land tax to the barons. The problem of defense was most pressing. New knights were attracted from western Europe, but they were never enough. Finally, there were tensions in the western part of the empire. The Greeks of Epiros were a menace and the barons of Salonika were restless under their infant king Demetrios. Henri called a parliament in Greece at Ravennika in 1209 to settle his problems. The result was a firmer control over Greece. But the most interesting feature of the parliament was the arrival in great pomp of the lord of Athens, Othon de la Roche, and Geoffroy de Villehardouin, the representative of Morea.

A curious sequence of events had been taking place in Morea during this period. Guillaume de Champlitte left his nephew Hughes in charge of Morea and set out for France in 1208, perhaps to claim his inheritance from his brother Louis who died there at this time. While in France he himself died, leaving his nephew heir in Morea. But he, too, died soon afterwards, and Morea was left without a legitimate lord. At this point Geoffroy de Villehardouin, the collaborator in the original conquest, emerged as the lord of Morea. It is hard to say whether this was because Guillaume had expressed the wish that Geoffroy eventually succeed him or because the barons preferred him to Hughes. In any case Geoffroy appeared at Ravennika, and there Henri accepted his homage for Morea and, as a signal honor, made him seneschal of the Latin empire. Furthermore, Henri supported Geoffroy in his negotiations with the Venetians, who had been given Morea as part of their share of the original partition of the empire, and who had begun a fight for it, as we have seen, in 1206. The Venetian-Moreot war was settled at a conference in June, 1209.

In the negotiations that took place and in the treaty that was signed, Geoffroy apparently did not use the title of prince of Achaia. The first such reference to him is in letters from Innocent III, dated March 22 and 24, 1210. He seems to have waited the customary term of one year and one day, or two years and two days, dating from the departure of Guillaume or from the death of Hughes, before claiming the title. In any case, by 1210 Geoffroy was calling himself "Prince of Achaia and Seneschal of all Romania." From this point on he set his roots firmly into the soil of Greece. He sent to France for his wife and son Geoffroy and established them in his castle in Kalamata, where his second son Guillaume, the most famous member of the whole family, was born in 1211.

The reign of Geoffroy I was of lasting importance for Morea. Acrocorinth, still in the hands of Leon Sgouros when Geoffroy came to power, fell to him after Sgouros' death in 1208. The mountainous valleys of Lakonia and Arkadia were pacified, and castles were built to defend the frontier. All in all, the principality was safe, and Geoffroy laid the foundation of a stable government as well. He encouraged the immigration of a constant stream of Burgundians and Champenois to swell the Frankish population, and there developed in Morea a culture which was famous even in France for its refinement and for the purity of its French chivalric traditions. Above all, this culture was a true transplantation. Slowly the Franks of Morea became true Moreots, speaking both French and Greek, following both French and Greek customs.

While Geoffroy was constructing the principality of Morea, Othon de la Roche was doing the same in the duchy of Athens. Slowly he pushed his boundaries southward to include Argolis and northward past Thebes, stabilizing the frontier and establishing friendly relations with his neighbors. He established his capital at Thebes. The Parthenon on the Acropolis at Athens, long the church of the Greek metropolitans, became the Latin cathedral of St. Mary. Othon founded monasteries and introduced western orders into older Greek monastic houses. A notable example is his invitation to the Cistercians to take over the great monastery of Daphne, a few miles outside of Athens. Here they built a cloister and an arcade in pure French style. He also established a French society in Athens, which was made up mostly of his many relatives and friends whom he encouraged to come to Greece from their Burgundian lands. The family emigrated to Greece throughout the thirteenth century. A nephew Guy, for instance, came and was enfeoffed with a part of Thebes by Geoffroy de Villehardouin. Another newcomer was Nicolas de St.-Omer, who arrived in Greece after 1208 and established himself and his family around Thebes. This family became as famous as the de la Roche line, intermarrying with them as well as with the Hungarian royal line.

While these vigorous princes were strengthening and consolidating their holdings, the emperor Henri was fighting against insurmountable odds. The last years of his reign are lost in obscurity. Until his sudden death at the age of thirty-nine on June 11, 1216, he strove to get help from Rome, from Hungary, from Bulgaria, but his efforts all failed. He did not even leave a direct heir of his body to succeed him, and his barons offered the crown to Pierre de Cour-

tenay, the husband of Henri's sister Yolande, with the hope that
he would bring armies with him from France. Pierre accepted but
never saw his empire, for on his way east he was captured and killed
by Theodoros, who had succeeded his brother Michael in Epiros. His
empress had gone directly to the capital by sea and arrived safely.
On her way she had stopped off in Morea and had given her daughter
Agnes in marriage to the elder son of Geoffroy I, the future Geoffroy
II. Soon after her arrival in Constantinople she bore a son, the
future emperor, Baldwin II. Before the year was over she died
and the barons again had to choose an emperor. This time they
chose Yolande's oldest son Philippe, marquis of Namur, but he sent
her younger son Robert in his stead. Thus in 1221 the weak, almost
idiotic Robert became emperor. A little later, Theodoros Laskaris,
wily and dangerous enemy of the Latin empire, died at the age
of forty-eight in 1222. But he was succeeded by his son-in-law
Ioannes III, Doukas Vatatzes, who for thirty-two years was to be
an even more dangerous foe, and against whom the Latin empire
could pit only the weakest of emperors.

The new emperor had lost all his lands in Anatolia, and now an
even worse disaster befell in the west. Theodoros Komnenos Doukas, with the help of the Bulgars and Greek families within the
Latin empire, attacked and captured the city of Salonika and all the
kingdom in 1224. His troops swept through northern Greece. Boudonitza, the lordship of Athens, and Morea alone survived the disaster.

Demetrios was in Italy trying to raise troops at the time and
eventually he died there in 1227, leaving all his rights to Frederick II.
Theodoros' victory was short-lived, for in his turn, five years later,
he was captured by John Asen, tsar of the Bulgars, blinded, and
stripped of almost all of his possessions. In the meantime Geoffroy I of Morea and the duke of Athens, in the face of the common
danger, strengthened their lands. Geoffroy pressed the clergy too
strongly for funds to build the castle of Clermont to protect the
plain of Elis, where he had established his capital. This brought
an excommunication from Honorius III, which was lifted in 1223.
Soon afterwards, Othon de la Roche returned to France, leaving
his nephew Guy in charge of the duchy. He died in 1234. Geoffroy,
his old companion, had died shortly after his departure, probably
between 1228 and 1230.

These years marked a turning point in the history of the empire. The old conquerors were all dead, and the states, now so few in number, were in the hands of younger men. In Greece Morea emerged as the focus of power, while in Constantinople Robert brought Henri's empire down in ruins. He lost contact with political realities and he withdrew into his palace with a young Frenchwoman whom he had married secretly. He never left the apartment where he had installed her and her mother. In disgust the barons broke in one night, drowned the old woman, and disfigured the young wife by cutting off her nose and lips. Robert in horror fled the realm and went to Italy to complain to Pope Gregory IX. He was persuaded to return to his empire but stopped on his way at Morea to visit his sister Agnes. There he took ill and died in 1228, unlamented by all but his sister, who apparently built a monastery in Morea in his memory.

The barons in desperation offered the crown to the aged hero, Jean de Brienne, who set sail for the east with a large army and arrived in Constantinople in 1231. The barons, however, were deceived in their hopes, for the new emperor, in spite of his troops and in spite of the help of Hungary and Morea, was able to do little. When he died in 1237, the realm was worse off than ever.

If the empire was in a state of crisis, Greece was enjoying a period of unparalleled prosperity. Under Geoffroy II, a humane, cultivated prince, the principality extended itself in all directions. The menace of the Greeks was removed in the north, because the capture of Theodoros by John Asen had precipitated a chaotic civil war in Epiros, and the prince of Morea, having received the vassalage of the lords of Cephalonia, Naxos, and Euboea, was the strongest power in the Latin East. By the time of his death, in 1246, Morea was a wealthy cultured state, able to finance the defense of the collapsing empire with money and fleets. The so-called duchy of Athens during the same period was equally prosperous. Guy de la Roche derived great profit from the silk industry of Thebes and attracted to his realm Venetian, Genoese, and other merchants, who vied with one another in purchasing trading privileges from the duke. At this time Bela de St.-Omer, son of that Nicolas who had settled in Thebes some years earlier, married Guy's sister Bonne and established his family as one of the most powerful in Frankish Greece.

When Jean de Brienne died, the new emperor, Baldwin II, was only nineteen years old. Born in the east, raised in a Byzantine atmosphere, Greek speaking, he was potentially a good ruler for the empire. Unfortunately, he was not of any marked intelligence or ability. Furthermore, he had inherited a situation that was hopelessly beyond remedy. His reign began in France where he had gone to find troops and money. For four years he wandered back and forth between Italy and his French estates, begging loans from the pope and King Louis which he hoped to secure by putting his lands up for mortgage. He sent one army eastward only to have it disrupted by his father-in-law's mortal enemy Frederick II. Finally, after the departure of the Fifth Crusade, he scraped together a fairly respectable army and led it across Germany, Hungary, and Bulgaria, arriving in his capital in 1240. His reign was one of desperation. At first he found respite in the rivalries between Vatatzes and Michael II of Epiros, who had reunited the despotate. Then he found help in alliances with the Cumans and other Turks. But he spent most of his reign in France and Italy seeking money to live on. Eventually he was reduced to selling the very lead from the roofs of his palaces. Constantinople simply waited until the Greeks were able to retake it in 1261.

The years which marked the decline of the Latin empire were the years of greatest achievement for the principality of Morea. From his capital of Andravida in ancient Elis, Guillaume II, brother of Geoffroy and prince from 1246 to 1278, commanded a state that included all central and southern Greece. In all the mountain valleys and at all strategic points along the coast he directed the maintenance of strong castles. Each of these was the center of the legal and communal life of the surrounding region, and in these castles Morea developed a civilization renowned throughout the world of the thirteenth century, memory of it lingering on into the fourteenth as well. The prince was a typical feudal lord, being *primus inter pares,* but the men of the Villehardouin family were so exceptional as individuals that their actual power was almost absolute. Guillaume II was the finest example of these princes. Born in Greece, he had been given the best education Morea could provide. He was expertly trained in arms, yet he was also an accomplished singer and writer of songs. Completely bilingual, he was equally at ease with the French *noblesse* and with his Greek subjects. As prince of Achaia, he was vassal of the Latin emperor, but he was suzerain of Morea. His power, however, was far from absolute, for his vassals of Morea always exacted from their prince a vow to maintain the privileges and usages of the principality before they would swear fealty to him. Even then he was constrained to take counsel with his barons. On the other hand, he had certain exclusive rights and privileges, such as the right to free serfs or grant charters to towns.

The prince was assisted by a few officials, the constable, the chancellor, the chamberlain, captains, and castellans. But Morea was primarily a military state, and the prince depended most on the feudal vassalage who held the many fiefs from him. There were two types of vassals, those of liege homage and those of simple homage. Both owed a full year's duty, garrison, field, and home alert, but the former was superior and had many privileges, including the right to hold his own court. The latter was considered inferior and was not allowed his own court, had to pay certain taxes, and received only common justice. The Greek magnates of the land were accepted into the feudal hierarchy as vassals of simple homage (as were the sergeants and bannerets). The chief members of the ecclesiastical hierarchy, as well as the Templars and the Hospitalers, all held lands in the principality, and for these only field service was due as for all ecclesiastical fiefs. There were, in addition, many towns that played a role in the life of the principality by furnishing the prince with money and troops in time of war, and occasionally burgesses were summoned to important meetings of the prince's council. The land was for the most part rural, thought there were some cities and some special industries, silk cultivation, for instance. Yet most of the people were on the land and were either free peasants, who lived singly or in communities and who held their land outright, or serfs who fell into the usual manorial patterns—they could not leave the manor, their wives became serfs of the lord, etc. All in all, however, their condition was probably improved under the Franks.

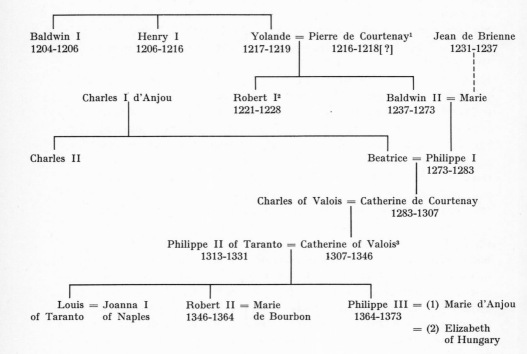

LATIN EMPERORS OF CONSTANTINOPLE

1. Pierre became emperor in 1216, but on his way east to claim his crown he was captured by Theodoros of Epiros and was murdered in prison, probably in 1218. Meanwhile, Yolande held the title until her death in 1219. The crown then passed to her son Robert who, however, did not arrive from France until 1221.

2. Robert I died in exile in 1228. The barons gave the crown to Jean de Brienne who arrived in Constantinople and was crowned in 1231.

3. Catherine married Philippe in 1313. He took over her title at this time and was known as emperor until his death.

Such, then, was the land that Guillaume ruled. In his early years he occupied himself with taking the last Greek outposts on the southeast coast and pacifying the Slavic tribes of the interior. He was successful and used wise restraint in his victory. He went on the Crusade of Louis IX to Damietta in 1250 and on his return to Morea he fought a bitter war with the Italians of Euboea. Allied with Michael II of Epiros, he was able to win this struggle and he established his suzerainty over that island and central Greece as well.

Meanwhile, the two Greek states were edging toward a new war. In Nicea Ioannes Vatatzes died leaving his throne to his son, Theodoros II Laskaris, who died soon afterwards, leaving an eight-year-old son under the regency of Michael Palaiologos, who soon usurped the throne for himself and, as Michael VIII, became the hero of the Greek *revanche*. Michael II, seeing these developments, strengthened his position by marrying one of his daughters, Helen, to Manfred of Sicily, and the other, Anne, to Guillaume of Morea. Thus the beautiful Anne, who took the name Agnes at the time of her marriage, came to Morea and in due time bore two daughters, Isabeau and Marguerite. The war finally broke out, and Guillaume led his troops north to join those the despot and Manfred had sent. The combined army made a brave parade through northern Greece and finally met the forces of Nicaea on the plain of Pelagonia in September, 1259. The result was the capture of Guillaume and much of the Moreot baronage. Two years later, on July 25, 1261, the city of Constantinople was reoccupied by a Greek army. Baldwin and his followers fled, sailing to Greece, whence the deposed emperor made his way in leisurely fashion to Italy and exile.

Guillaume remained in the custody of Michael VIII until 1261. He had signed a treaty with the Greek emperor by which he surrendered to the Greeks the key fortresses of Monemvasia, Mistra, and Maine. As soon as he was free he made new alliances with Venice and the Italian lords of the islands and prepared to renew the war. Michael sent his army to Greece, but after two serious setbacks it withdrew, having inflicted heavy damage in Lakonia and Arkadia. At this time the affairs of Morea were eclipsed by stirring events in Italy. Charles d'Anjou, invited into Italy by Urban IV to lead a crusade against Manfred, had defeated him in battle at Benevento on February 26, 1266, where Manfred and the Hohenstaufen hopes died on the field. Michael VIII, meanwhile, had suffered a stinging naval defeat, yet Guillaume still had need of a strong alliance in the west. Charles d'Anjou had begun to cast hungry eyes to the east. Pope Clement IV, hoping to control all these currents, invited all the principals to a council at Viterbo that met in February, 1267, and sat for five or six months. The most urgent topics were the union of the two churches and an alliance between Guillaume and Charles. Discussion of the first topic led to no permanent solution (though the negotiations gave Michael VIII a valuable respite). But the important treaty of Viterbo (May 24) was made between Charles and Guillaume, whereby a son of Charles was to marry Isabeau de Villehardouin and, though Guillaume would reign during his lifetime, upon his death the crown would go to the Angevins, for if the young couple did not produce a son, Charles himself was to inherit the crown. The prince of Morea remained in Italy to help Charles meet the attack of the young Conradin, last of the Hohenstaufen line, who was invading Italy to claim his lands. He was met at Tagliacozzo, and Charles, aided not a little by the barons of Morea, won a complete and final victory.

Back in Morea, the prince prepared to carry out the terms of the treaty. In May, 1271, Isabeau set sail for Italy, and she was married to the young Philippe on May 28, 1271. At this time, Charles's plans began to unfold. He sent troops over to Albania which sought to dominate Greece as a preprequisite step toward the domination of the whole Mediterranean. Morea was only one small piece in his great scheme, and a bitter war, fought just as hard in diplomatic maneuvers as in sea and land tactics, broke across the whole of Greece. The results were inconclusive, but Frankish Greece was badly shaken. One by one the outer fiefs began to crumble and break away. Desertions, betrayals, and defeats unnerved the Franks and Epirots alike, caught as they were in the middle of a war between giants. If in the last years of his reign Guillaume saw Morea spared the horror of total invasion, nonetheless he saw its most valiant defenders die, one by one, and already he could foresee the unhappy fate of his land. Under pressure from Charles, he began to prepare the country for the accession of the Angevin Philippe. But in February, 1277, this young prince died quite unexpectedly at the age of twenty-one. This blow must have weakened Guillaume fatally, for a year later, on the first of May, 1278, the most celebrated prince of Morea's history died after a reign of thirty-two years.

Morea now almost lost its identity as an independent principality and became an appendage of the Sicilian kingdom. Isabeau remained with the Angevin royal family in Italy and there Charles gathered the leading barons of Morea and the Latin empire. These barons served him well, but not always in the affairs of their own lands. For the administration of Morea, for instance, Charles sent as his bailli the seneschal of Sicily, Galeran d'Ivry, who was not a Moreot. All the feudatories of continental Greece and the islands, now greatly reduced in numbers, were ordered to make their oaths of loyalty to this man, but, interesting to note, they refused to take the oaths of fealty to the king, for these were to be made to him only in person, and agreed to swear only simple homage to his representative.

The war with the Greeks slowly turned much of Morea into a blighted no man's land. The Angevin armies, composed of a ragged assortment of mercenaries, foot-loose Sicilians, and freebooters, more interested in pillage and rapine than in the safety of the realm, did even more damage to the country than the enemy. Charles replaced d'Ivry in August, 1280, with Philippe de Lagonesse, marshal of Sicily, and conditions improved, but Moreot interests were always sacrificed to the grandiose schemes of the king in his struggle with Michael Palaiologos. Angevin troops, supplies, and moneys began to pour into Epiros, and after careful negotiations with the powers to the north, an attack was launched on Berat, as the prelude to an eastward advance on Salonika. It turned out to be a disastrous failure for Charles, who withdrew his forces to concentrate on fighting down the revolt that began with the Sicilian Vespers (at the end of March, 1282). Morea was left pretty much to its own resources. Agnes, widow of Prince Guillaume II, had married Nicolas II de St.-Omer of the duchy of Athens, and he now became bailli of Morea. The Moreot *noblesse* maintained as best they could the traditions of their land and were still known

in Europe for their bravery and their courtliness. Occasionally
Charles turned his attention to Morea to tighten up his holdings,
or to reward a faithful vassal, but on the whole the Angevins had
more pressing problems in the western Mediterranean. Charles
died in 1285, a bitterly disappointed and harassed man and was
succeeded by his rather incompetent son, Charles II, who was
faced with concerted opposition from other Mediterranean powers,
particularly Aragon. Though lacking in political ability, he was
a man of sensibility, and he took pity on the widowed Isabeau,
who had been at the Sicilian court for twelve years, and presented
her with large Moreot estates from his own domain. Later, on
the occasion of her marriage to Florent de Hainault, he turned over
the principality of Morea to her and her descendants. The return
of the principality to the Villehardouin heiress reflected the
ambitions of the house of Hainault-Avesnes, but even more the
longing of the barons for a stable government of their own which
would put an end to the evils of regencies.

Once Florent was established as prince of Morea, and had received
the oath of fealty and homage of his vassals, though those of the
duchy of Athens and of central Greece refused to accept him, he
set to work. He was not primarily a warrior, but rather a statesman
who hoped to restore Morea to a condition of prosperity by coming
to terms with its enemies. He made overtures to the Byzantine
emperor Andronikos II, who had now succeeded to his father's
throne, to settle the nagging war with the empire that had brought
so much ruin to southern Greece. Byzantium was under great
pressure from the Turks, the Bulgars, and the Greeks of the despotate of Epiros at this time, so it was not difficult to arrange an
extended peace. Greeks and Franks began to mix freely, each
pursuing his affairs, and Morea flourished. Difficulties arose,
however, from the prince's connections with the despot of Epiros,
Nikephoros, who was Isabeau's uncle. Taking advantage of the
peace in the south, Andronikos had invaded the despotate with
a large army which began a systematic pillage of the whole area.
Nikephoros called on his nephew for help, and Florent joined
him with a sizable force. The Byzantine forces were beaten and
forced to retreat eastwards, but the land had been further ravaged,
and all Greece was thereby weakened.

Two events occurred at this time which boded ill for the future of Greece. An Aragonese fleet appeared in Greek waters, attacked certain islands and ports and, after paying a friendly call on Isabeau and her court, sailed back to the west. Also, the Slavs of the central Peloponnesos rose and captured some Frankish castles, but were forced to return them by order of the Byzantine government. But these ominous matters were overshadowed at the time by an alliance which was to affect all the free states of Greece. Charles II arranged a marriage between his son, Philippe, prince of Taranto, and Thamar, daughter and heiress of the despot of Epiros. She received in dowry the chief places of Acarnania, while Charles conferred on his son all his rights in the east. Thus all Frankish Greece came under the suzerainty of Philippe, though Charles II remained his overlord during his lifetime. Charles obviously intended to simplify and make more efficient the administrative hierarchy in Greece, but actually, by bringing all the Frankish states under one head, he made matters more difficult, for bitter wrangling broke out over the feudal relationships among the various princes and dukes. Many times Charles had to arbitrate in these disputes, and though he eventually established the feudal hierarchy as he wished, nonetheless there remained bitterness and injured sensiblities. This was all the more dangerous since an increasing number of incidents was leading toward a resumption of the war with Byzantium. Before this happened, Florent died, genuinely mourned by his people, in January, 1297. His only heir was a three-year-old daughter, Mahaut.

Isabeau reigned for the next three years by herself, assisted by a council of the leading barons of the realm. She was occupied throughout this time with arranging marriages for her daughter, her sister Marguerite and, most important, herself. The young Mahaut was given, after prolonged discussion, to the young heir to the duchy of Athens, Guy, or Guyot, as he is commonly called in the chronicles. Marguerite had been left a widow in 1297 with a three-year-old daughter, Isabelle. Two years later it was arranged that she marry Richard of Cephalonia, the aged bailli of Morea. Isabeau herself went to Rome to celebrate the Jubilee called by Boniface VIII in 1300. There she acquired not only the many indulgences resulting from the pilgrimage, but a new husband as well, Philippe, the count of Piedmont, and nephew of the count of Savoy. She was over forty at the time, and he was about twenty-two. The marriage took place on February 12, 1301, and on the twenty-third Philippe was invested with the principality of Morea, or Achaia, as he preferred to call it. He set out for his new land with an entourage of Savoyards and Piedmontese, new barons anxious to make their fortunes in the east, which was indeed possible, but only at the expense of the older feudatories. The prince himself had spent great sums in winning Isabeau's hand and he fell on Morea with the rapacity of an Italian *condottiere*. The barons rose in protest, as did the Greek vassals. Furthermore, Morea now found that she could be drawn into a war by her own feudatories, for the duchy of Athens, at this point, went to war with the despotate, and the Moreot nobles had to go along. Charles II entered the war against Epiros in the interests of his son Philippe of Taranto. The prince of Achaia, still hungry for monies, accepted a bribe from the despina of Epiros not to fight. The outcome of these petty rivalries was inconclusive except insofar as it further illustrated that Greek affairs were now peripheral to Italian politics. The Angevins and the prince of Achaia-Savoy clashed over their North Italian lands, and it was there that the prince lost to Charles II and had to give up his titles in Greece. Isabeau refused to accept the loss of Morea as placidly as her husband did. She sought redress in French circles all through her remaining years, but her glamorous life came to an end after 1311 in bitter exile and disappointment. She was survived by her daughter Mahaut de Hainault, married to Guy II, the duke of Athens, and another daughter whom she had borne to Philippe in 1303.

Now began the final phase in the history of Morea, a sad story of rival claimants to the various fiefs, who sacrificed what was left of Franko-Greek power in Greece to their own ambitions. Guy II was named bailli of Morea by Philippe of Taranto in 1307, but he died in 1308, and with him died the de la Roche line itself. From now on the Angevins sent Frenchmen or Italians as regents, men who were unable to stem the gradual *revanche* of the Greek forces throughout the peninsula. It was at this time that Charles de Valois, brother of Philippe IV of France, decided to push the

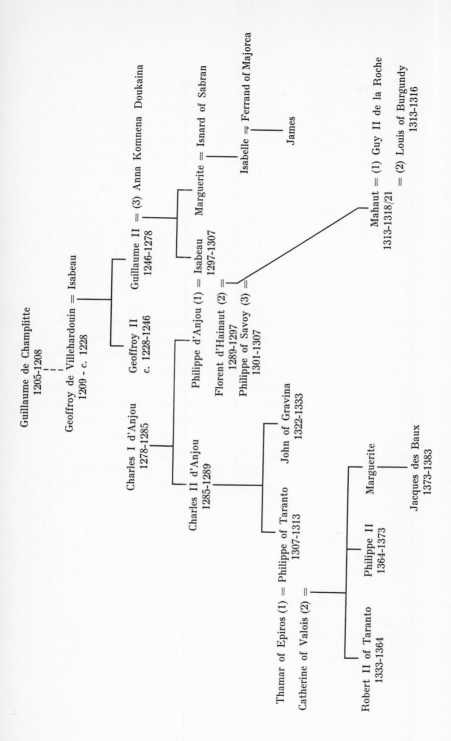

PRINCES OF MOREA

Guillaume de Champlitte
1205-1208

Geoffroy de Villehardouin = Isabeau
1209 - c. 1228

Geoffroy II
c. 1228-1246

Guillaume II = (3) Anna Kommena Doukaina
1246-1278

Marguerite = Isnard of Sabran

Isabelle = Ferrand of Majorca

James

Charles I d'Anjou
1278-1285

Charles II d'Anjou
1285-1289

Philippe d'Anjou (1) = Isabeau
1297-1307

Florent d'Hainaut (2)
1289-1297

Philippe of Savoy (3)
1301-1307

Mahaut = (1) Guy II de la Roche
1313-1318/21

= (2) Louis of Burgundy
1313-1316

John of Gravina
1322-1333

Thamar of Epiros (1) = Philippe of Taranto
1307-1313

Catherine of Valois (2) =

Marguerite

Jacques des Baux
1373-1383

Philippe II
1364-1373

Robert II of Taranto
1333-1364

claims of his wife, Catherine de Courtenay, titular empress of Constantinople. He thought of enlisting in his service the Catalan Grand Company. This was a group of adventurers who had fought in the Aragonese-Angevin wars in Sicily and who, when peace was declared there, had entered Near Eastern affairs by fighting in the service of Andronikos II against the Turks in Asia Minor. After breaking with the Palaiologoi, they entrenched themselves at Gallipoli, where they were a serious threat to Byzantium. Nominally, the company owed allegiance to Frederick II, king of Sicily, but he had sent his cousin Ferrand, son of the king of Majorca, to lead them and to further Aragonese interests in the east. However, undisciplined and restive, the company rejected him and chose their own leader. Ferrand eventually was captured by Thibaut de Chepoix, a French officer in the employ of Charles de Valois, and spent a year in an Angevin prison. Charles had sent Thibaut to hire the company, but this unhappy man found himself surrounded by a band of dangerous cutthroats, who had accepted his money, yet who were more avid in looting and pillaging Greece than fighting for the French. They had been ravaging Macedonia and Thessaly for months and then, with nowhere else to go, they turned southward and began to move into central Greece. Thibaut, meanwhile, had thrown up his hands, had slipped away from them and had gone back to the west. The company was then hired by Gautier de Brienne, duke of Athens, who hoped to extend his power among the various lordlings in Greece. Although the Catalans proved again their worth as a fighting force, Gautier soon wanted to have done with them, and when he fell four months behind in his payments to them, they threw off their allegiance to him and decided to establish themselves in Greece. The Franks united to expel the intruders, and the fateful battle was fought on March 15, 1311, not far from the ancient town of Chaeronea, where once before the fate of Greece had been settled in battle. The day was an irreparable disaster for Frankish Greece. The duke of Athens was killed and much of the Frankish chivalry was destroyed. Central Greece was lost as the Catalans moved into Thebes and Athens and became masters of the whole territory. They asked the king of Sicily to become their suzerain, and he gladly accepted, sending Berenger Estanyol as his regent.

The establishment of the Catalans in the duchy of Athens altered profoundly the balance of power in Greece. The Greeks, who held Salonika and Epiros, rejoiced to see their powerful Frankish rivals removed. The principality of Morea, moreover, reduced to about two thirds of the Peloponnesos, was menaced by this new power. Venice and the Angevins were also apprehensive about the fate of their Greek holdings. To the pope and western proponents of the Crusade the developments seemed to be a setback in their hopes to reestablish a Latin empire at Constantinople. Obviously there was need of a strong man to organize the Frankish defense and push western interests in Greece. Philippe of Taranto had already repudiated his adulterous wife Thamar and had thrown her into prison, where she died. Charles de Valois then arranged a marriage between his daughter Catherine de Valois, who had inherited the imperial claims of her mother Catherine de Courtenay, and Philippe, which was to be a union of all Frankish claims and titles in Greece, backed by papal and French power. At the same time Morea came into the hands of Mahaut de Hainault and her second husband Louis of Burgundy, a restoration which Mahaut's mother Isabeau had sought all through her years of exile. Morea had returned to the house of Villehardouin, though the new prince held it from Philippe, who was now titular Latin emperor, with his brother, King Robert of Naples, as his overlord. Mahaut set out immediately for Morea, but Louis was delayed for a time in Burgundy. He arrived, *en route* to Greece, in Venice in November, 1315.

This rearrangement had necessitated a great deal of shuffling of Burgundian and French titles and holdings. In general, those lords who went east gave up their claims in the west to other members of their families and were compensated with stronger holdings in Frankish Greece. All seemed to have worked out well when the most violent conflict in the turbulent history of Morea suddenly erupted. When Isabeau de Villehardouin died in 1311 her sister Marguerite made a claim to a part of Morea. Charles II did not recognize this claim nor would his successor Robert. Therefore, Marguerite sought help from Ferrand of Majorca, who had some connection with the east through the Grand Company. He married Marguerite's daughter Isabelle, in February, 1314. Mar-

guerite gave the couple as the bride's dower her claims to Morea.
She herself returned to Morea where Mahaut's regent arrested her,
threw her into prison, and confiscated her lands. The unfortunate
lady died soon afterwards. Ferrand immediately began preparations to invade Morea. Isabelle bore a son, James, on April 5,
1315, and died a few weeks later, leaving to her infant son all
her claims to the principality. Ferrand was supported by Frederick, king of Sicily, and the Catalans of Athens, and he landed
in Greece in June with a strong force. He quickly took the port
of Klarentsa (Glarentza) and the castle of Beauvoir (Pondikos).
Soon all of Elis was in his hands, and he began to move southward. Mahaut and her Burgundian troops arrived and a bloody
war broke out in which hundreds of knights on both sides were
killed. Eventually Louis was able to defeat and kill Ferrand,
and the war ended. Louis himself died rather mysteriously soon
afterwards, and Mahaut was left to rule an even weaker Morea.

All the surrounding states now sought to take advantage of
Morea's weakness to enlarge their own holdings. The Catalans
began by invading Euboea, which was under Mahaut's suzerainty.
Then Robert of Naples tried to arrange a marriage between Mahaut
and his brother John of Gravina to make sure that Morea would
come into his family's hands. Mahaut refused, protested to Pope
John XXII, and asked help of Venice. But Robert established
John of Gravina in Morea. The third brother, Philippe, was recognized as titular Latin emperor. Mahaut was thrown into
prison and spent the rest of her days there. But the dam had
burst. The Catalans began to cross the isthmus; the Greeks of
Mistra took over castle after castle in the south, inflicting damaging defeats on the Angevin and Moreot defenders. The only
reason that Morea still survived was that the despoilers began
to fight among themselves.

The principality struggled on for another century, but the old
Morea of the Villehardouins had disappeared. Of the original
twelve baronies, only the smallest remained. Most of the old
Frankish families of the conquest were gone. The country's de-
fenses, such as they were, were largely in the hands of mercenaries. New families, Italian for the most part, had settled in
the land, not as a feudal fighting aristocracy, but as a squirearchy,

paying taxes to the prince for their large estates. They turned from the prince to leaders who could better protect their interests, if necessary, even to the Byzantines. The Latin-Greek animosities of former times had subsided. Franks and Greeks had learned to live together, and a common culture began to emerge.

John of Gravina borrowed heavily from Italian bankers, especially the Acciaiuoli, and undertook some projects against the Greeks, but nothing important came of them. Gautier II de Brienne, who had married Beatrice, a daughter of Philippe of Taranto and Thamar, invaded Greece to reclaim his father's duchy of Athens from the Catalans. The famous castle of St.-Omer at Thebes was now destroyed. Gautier's expedition was a failure, and he returned to Italy in the late summer of 1332.

Philippe of Taranto had died in December, 1331, and left his titles to his son Robert. His widow, Catherine de Valois, forced John of Gravina to turn over Morea to her, as regent for her son, in exchange for money and lands in Italy. She attached herself to Niccolò Acciaiuoli, nine years her junior, a handsome and cultured member of the banking house, and turned over to him the affairs of her family in Greece. In 1338 Catherine and Niccolò made a trip to Morea and remained there for over two years. She attempted to familiarize herself with conditions there at first hand and to stop the steady decline of the principality, but in vain. When Catherine returned to Naples, the barons of Morea felt even more the inadequacy of Angevin rule and they offered the principality to James II of Majorca, son of Ferrand and Isabelle. He accepted the title but died before he could even visit Morea.

Robert of Taranto clung to all the lands and titles of his inheritance, but wars in France and in Italy kept him from going in person to the east. Morea was left to its own resources. Occasionally a governor came from the west, but more often the barons elected one of their own. The Turks were ravaging the coasts of the land, and no defense seemed possible. Now the most powerful man in Greece was Niccolò Acciaiuoli, to whom in 1358 Robert granted the rich castellany of Corinth and its dependencies. Robert died in 1364. His brother, Philippe, claimed the principality and began a fruitless war with rival contenders which dragged on until shortly before his death in 1373. He was succeeded by a nephew, Jacques des Baux, whose claim was immediately disputed by Joanna I of Naples. Another dreary war broke out. In 1376 Joanna leased the principality of Morea for five years to the Hospitalers, who appear to have held it for the duration of the contract.

A more important development occurred when the Navarrese Company entered the affairs of Greece. One of their commanders, ostensibly in the service of Jacques des Baux (d. 1383), took over and held the principality. Another, possibly in the employ of Nerio Acciaiuoli, adopted son of the great Niccolò, captured Thebes in the spring of 1379. A decade later, in 1388, Nerio took the Acropolis of Athens after a long siege, and the history of the Catalan duchy came to an end.

The Latin principality continued its feeble history for another two generations (until 1430), but most of Morea had come under the rule of the Palaiologoi, despots of Mistra, under whom there was almost a Greek renaissance. But the passing of every decade was increasing the power of the Ottoman Turks, who took Constantinople in 1453, and in 1460 brought to an end the despotate of Mistra.

Such, then, in its barest outline, is the history of the Latin empire of Constantinople and the principality of Morea. The story is told, into the fourteenth century, by the Chronicles of Morea, which have been the subject of curiosity and speculation for many years.

MANUSCRIPTS AND EDITIONS OF THE CHRONICLES OF MOREA

The Chronicles of Morea, as these have come to be known for lack of a better name, are a series of chronicles that have been preserved in eight manuscripts, written in Greek, French, Aragonese, and Italian. The Greek version is in verse; the others are in prose.

1. Codex Havniensis 57. Of the five Greek manuscripts, unquestionably the earliest and most authentic is the one in the Fabricius Collection of the library of the University of Copenhagen. This manuscript consists of 9,219 lines of political verse, written carefully in a legible hand and remarkably accurate in spelling. The text is written in small columns with wide margins and is marked with capitals in red ink. The first three leaves have been lost, and the manuscript begins with line 105 of the Codex Parisinus. The leaves are numbered both in Greek numbers, running only from δ to ρμέ (4-145), and by Fabricius in Arabic numerals, running from 4 to 237. In addition, the beginning of each quinternion (layer of ten leaves) is noted. One lacuna of two pages is indicated by the quinternion enumeration, but other lacunae are not so indicated, which shows that the manuscript was incomplete when it was copied. From notations on the cover, it is known that the manuscript passed from Thomas Bartholin to Johannes Grammius (1685-1748), who presented it to Johannes Fabricius as a Christmas present. After the death of Fabricius in 1736, the manuscript, along with the rest of his library, was acquired by the University of Copenhagen in 1775.

The first modern edition of the manuscript was done by J. A. Buchon, who presented the text without translation as volume II of his *Recherches historiques sur la principauté française de Morée et ses hautes baronnies* (Paris, 1845). This was followed by the outstanding edition of John Schmitt, *The Chronicle of Morea* (London, 1904), which contains in parallel the Havniensis and Parisinus texts, and in notes the variations in the Taurinensis. The most recent edition is by Petros Kalonaros, *Τὸ Χρονικὸν τοῦ Μορέως* (Athens, 1940).

2. Codex Parisinus grec 2898. This manuscript was originally in the library of Francis I at Fontainebleau. It was known to Ducange, who describes it correctly and who used it in compiling his *Glossary*. The manuscript consists of two parts: a Greek translation of Boccaccio's *Teseide* and, in folios 111-233, the Greek Chronicle of Morea. There are 8,191 lines, closely paralleling the Codex Havniensis, though little attempt is made to maintain its

metric qualities. The end of the manuscript is missing, and the text following folio 218 is written in a different hand.

The first modern edition was Buchon's *Chronique de la conquête de Constantinople et de l'établissement des Français en Morée, etc.* (Paris, 1825). This contains a French translation of the text, and only the prologue is given in Greek. Buchon then published the Greek text with a French translation in his *Chroniques étrangères relatives aux expéditions françaises pendant le XIIIe siècle* (Paris, 1840). The most recent edition is the one by Schmitt mentioned above.

3. Codex Parisinus grec 2753. This is simply a copy of the above, badly executed and valueless.

4. Codex Bernensis grec 509. This is another copy of the Codex Parisinus, though the handwriting is very bad and there are numerous mistakes in copying. It was not described by Buchon and was apparently unknown to him.

5. Codex Taurinensis B II. I. This manuscript was first made known by John Schmitt, who studied it minutely. In his opinion it is similar to the Codex Havniensis, but badly executed. He notes the special interest of the many almost illegible marginal notations and drawings, which give evidence not only of the many owners of the manuscript, but, more importantly, of the type of Greek which each spoke. They afford, indeed, an outline of the development of the modern Greek idiom.

THE FRENCH VERSION

The French version of the Chronicle survives in a single manuscript (Bibliothèque royale de Bruxelles, No. 15702) discovered by Buchon and published by him in 1845. It bears the following title: C'est le livre de la Conqueste de Constantinople et de l'empire de Romanie, et dou pays de la Princée de la Morée, qui fu trové en un livre qui fu jadis del noble baron messire Bartholomée Guys, le grand connestable, lequel livre il avoit en son chastel d'Estives. This manuscript, then, is an abridged version of one which was owned by Bartolommeo Ghisi before 1331. The scribe himself says he will relate his history, not as he found it written, but in its shortest form. The earliest edition appeared as volume I of Buchon's *Recherches historiques* (see above). The latest is that by

Jean Longnon, *Livre de la conqueste de la princée de l'Amorée: Chronique de Morée* (1204-1305) (Paris, 1911).

THE ARAGONESE VERSION

The Aragonese version of the Chronicle is unique in many ways. First, it is not a simple recounting of an earlier chronicle as are the other versions, but is rather a serious attempt at historical writing, using as a prime source the Chronicle of Morea, but incorporating the works of other historians as well. Second, it is the only manuscript which can be dated exactly. It bears the title Libro de los fechos et conquistas del Principado de la Morea, and we are told it was compiled "por comandamiento de Don Fray Johan Ferrandez de Heredia Maestro de Hospital de S. Johan de Jerusalem." It was completed on October 24, 1393. The manuscript was discovered by Count Paul Riant in the library of the Duke d'Osuma in 1880, and was edited and published five years later by Alfred Morel-Fatio (Geneva, 1885).

THE ITALIAN VERSION

The Italian version of the Chronicle is a badly executed translation of the Greek version, which appears as an appendage to Marino Sanudo Torsello's *Istoria del Regno di Romania*, and which was edited and published by Karl Hopf in his *Chroniques gréco-romanes inédites ou peu connues* (Berlin, 1873).

Dating the Chronicles

A question of basic importance in studying the Chronicle of Morea is the dating of the various versions. The Aragonese version, as stated above, bears its own date, so that it presents no problem. Likewise, the Italian version, since it is merely a faulty translation of the Greek, can be eliminated from this discussion. The French and Greek versions, however, since they are based on an earlier, lost work, present some difficulty.

THE FRENCH VERSION

It is stated clearly in its title that this version is based on a manuscript which was once in the possession of Bartolommeo Ghisi and which was in his castle of Thebes. We know that Ghisi was castellan of Thebes from 1327 to 1331. Therefore, the version we have may be assumed to have been written after 1332. Furthermore, a chronological table annexed to it relates events from 1304, the year the sequence in the Chronicle breaks off, down to 1333. On the other hand, Catherine de Valois is specifically mentioned as being still alive when the French version was written. Since she died in 1346, the French Chronicle must have been written between 1333 and 1346. It is probable, as Longnon suggests (*L'Empire latin*, p. 325), that it was written at her request during her stay in Greece from November, 1338, to June, 1341.

THE GREEK VERSION

The Greek Chronicle maintains a running account down to the year 1292, when it suddenly breaks off. Since the last leaves are missing in the Copenhagen text, we may assume that the account continued to the year 1304 as in the French version. As in the latter, however, events of a much later date are recorded in the Greek version. The account of the destruction of the Castle of St.-Omer in Thebes and all mention of the Catalans, for instance, are interpolations inserted by the scribe when the Greek version was composed. In lines 8459 ff. of the Chronicle, a genealogical passage discusses Erard III le Maure, lord of Arkadia, and his antecedents. The family was not of primary importance in Moreot affairs, and one feels that the chronicler must have had some special interest in recording the name in his chronicle. In line 8469 there is a specific reference to Erard III which gives the impression he was still alive at the time the chronicle was written. Since Erard died in 1388, it seems probable that the Greek version was written before that date, and that the chronicler had some sort of attachment to him. The Paris text, on the other hand, very specifically makes mention of Erard's death and pays tribute to him. The Copenhagen text, then, was probably written not too long before 1388, if we accept the evidence of line 8469 mentioned above (which is quite inconclusive), or at any rate very soon after; and the Paris text was definitely written after that date.

The Origin of the Chronicle

The most perplexing aspect of the Chronicle is its origin. Except for a reference in the Assizes of Romania and allusions in the Chronicle of Dorotheos of Monemvasia, which, itself, is to some extent derived from the Chronicle of Morea, the sources for the period that produced the Chronicle are completely silent. Moreover there are few statements in the Chronicle to enlighten us. The evidence, therefore, must be drawn largely from the language of the texts themselves, a method which by its very nature is incapable of producing absolute proof and which allows a wide range of possible interpretations.

THE PROBLEM

The problem is simply stated in these questions: 1. Is the French version the original Chronicle? 2. Is the Greek Chronicle a translation or a derivative of it? 3. Is the Greek Chronicle the original? 4. Is the French a translation and condensation of it? 5. Are both versions derived from an earlier work, now lost, written in Greek, in French, or in Italian? Adherents to each of these possibilities have not been lacking among the students of the Chronicle.

Buchon was the first to attempt to solve the problem. Unfortunately, his truly remarkable work on the Franks in Morea was marked with an excessive national bias. His primary purpose was to glorify French deeds in the past. Moreover, his aims were exclusively historical. He had little interest in philology and did little actual work on the Greek texts themselves. His edition, for instance, of the Codex Havniensis was not made from the manuscript, but from a collation of it made by Greek friends of his. His editions, therefore, are of little use for a study of the language of the Greek texts. It is not surprising that Buchon assumed that the French version was the original and that the Greek was a translation of it.

Hopf tended to agree with this view and observed that French was the language in general use at that time in Morea (*Geschichte Griechenlands*, I, 202). However, in his *Chroniques gréco-romanes*

(p. xlii), he is obviously uneasy about this view and promises to discuss it further, although he did not.

It is quite easy to reject the theory that the French version which we have is the original Chronicle. First of all, by its own statement this possibility is eliminated. It is very clear that it is an abridgment of an earlier chronicle. Schmitt, furthermore, examines the possibility in great detail (*Die Chronik von Morea*, pp. 41-75) and comes to the conclusion that the French version could not possibly have been the original.

It is also fairly easy to eliminate the Greek Chronicle as the original. First of all, the date of its composition precludes this. If, as stated above, it was written some time near 1388, it could not possibly be the original from which the French chronicle could be derived prior to 1332, nor, for that matter, one that dates from before 1346. Furthermore, the fact that the sequence of events moves in orderly fashion up to 1292, and presumably continued up to 1304, and that events of much later time are inserted out of chronological order, demonstrates clearly that the Chronicle is based on a work which goes up to 1304. Other evidence on this matter will be presented below.

It seems fairly obvious, then, that neither of the two Chronicles is an original text. It is certain, too, that the French text is not derived from the Greek text, which is of a later date. It is not quite so certain that the Greek text is not an expanded translation of the French version. However, the opinions of Schmitt in his *Die Chronik von Morea*, of Adamantios in his *Τὰ Χρονικὰ τοῦ Μορέως*, of Longnon in the Introduction of his *Livre de la Conqueste de la Princée de l'Amorée* and on p. 337 of his *L'Empire latin*, of Kalonaros in the Introduction and notes of his *Τὸ Χρονικὸν τοῦ Μορέως* and of all subsequent writers are conclusive. The Greek version is not a translation of the French, which, though an abridgment and much more straightforward, contains many facts which are missing in the other. The two are derived, rather, from a common source.

Evidence for this common source is also drawn from a curious reference in lines 91-92 of the Chronicle. Here it is stated: "as we have found written in detail in the Book of the Conquest." Actually, this refers to William of Tyre's *Historia*, which was not

called the Book of the Conquest. On the other hand, Article 3 of
the Assizes of Romania, speaking about Baldwin II, says: "as is
clearly told in the Book of Conquest." The Assizes is telling the
apocryphal story of Baldwin's marriage to "the daughter of Emperor Robert," and gives the identical details in almost the same
words as are found in the Chronicle of Morea. The reference, then,
is clearly to the Chronicle. But which one? Obviously it is not to
the Greek version, for it was written later than the Assizes. It is
not to the French version either, for the Assizes probably antedates
it, nor would the Assizes be based on an abridgment of an available
work. The allusion must be to a prototype, called by the title
given in the title of the French version, Le Livre de la Conqueste,
etc. The allusion in the Greek Chronicle, then, is explained by
assuming a prototype of that name, which was patterned after
William of Tyre's work, causing the writer of the Greek Chronicle
automatically to apply the name of the later work to the earlier
work on which it was modeled.

The problem of the language of this prototype, however, still
confronts us.

JOHN SCHMITT'S VIEWS AND A GREEK PROTOTYPE

John Schmitt, following the Marquis Terrier de Loray, rejects
vehemently the possibility of a French prototype. He presents,
perhaps in its strongest possible terms, the theory that the original
was written in Greek. One is forced, however, to keep in mind that
Schmitt's interests are wholly philological. His avowed enthusiasm
for the development of the modern Greek idiom and the beauties
of its literature has led him to place pivotal importance on the
Codex Havniensis as a milestone in this development. As he
himself states, the authority which he gives this text would be
badly shaken if it were a translation of the French version or
one might add, any French prototype. Other statements of his
indicate that, even though he may have stated no reservations in his
view, he was somewhat uneasy. For instance, on p. xxx of his
Introduction to *The Chronicle of Morea*, he states : "It [the proto-
type] may have been written in French, but as a more detailed
French Chronicle has not been transmitted, it was either lost or
it never existed, and we can prove neither the one nor the other."

He then goes on to say that the scribe who wrote the French version "either ... abridged a French Chronicle or translated with omissions a Greek Chronicle." It should be noted, however, that the scribe, who mentions so much, does not say that he is *translating* an earlier work. In another place (p. xxxi), stating that the Greek version is in every respect and in all narrations fuller than the French (true only with reservations), Schmitt goes on to say that "[the French version] can easily be explained as a mere extract of the Greek version; and the scribe expressly mentions it is an abridgement." This, as shown above, is not at all possible, and Schmitt himself does not really believe it, for he finally states that there was a prototype for both Chronicles, but one written in Greek.

His evidence for this is mainly linguistic. He points out that proper names in both Chronicles are given correctly in the form of the language in which they occur. Greek names are spelled correctly in the Greek version, French names in the French. Also French names in the Greek version are not badly mutilated, whereas Greek names in the French version are changed into French names (La Chacoignie = Tsakonia; La Glisière = Vlisiri, etc.). Thus, we can expect to find (1) all Greek and French names correctly written in their respective texts, and (2) names foreign to the texts rendered with more or less exactness. This is certainly true of the Greek text, especially the Havniensis. It is also true in the French text, but with certain exceptions (and this is the main point in Schmitt's theory). The fact, he believes, that some of the *French* names are mutilated in the French version shows that the scribe was not familiar with them and had to reconstruct them from the Greek text he was translating. "Thus, a number of French proper names contained in [the French version] can only be explained if we admit that they passed through a Greek medium."

Again following de Loray, he gives some examples. Tremolay is unusual for Tremoille and must reflect the Greek Τρεμουλᾶ; Anoée is unusual for Aunoy and derived from the Greek Ἀνόε where the α equals the *au* of the French and the όε equals the *oy*. Furthermore, Guillaume I is called Le Champenois in both texts, and his true name Guillaume de Champlitte is not given in either. In the French he is called *Guillerme de Salu* and also *de Saluce*, which, Schmitt states, must come from the Σαλοῦθε of the Greek.

Most important of all, d'Ivry becomes de Vry in the French text, and this must reflect the ντὲ Βρή of the Greek. (One might add another such example, which Schmitt significantly fails to mention. Enrico Dandolo is given the name ντὲ Ἄντουλος in the Greek text, which shows clearly that the writer automatically transliterated the name which he saw before him as a French name and wrote it accordingly, just as he wrote ντὲ Βρή for d'Ivry.)

The obvious weakness of this line of reasoning is, of course, the problem of where the names come from in the Greek text. Certainly they are not Greek; they must be corruptions of French names that the author either had heard or had before him when he was writing. I simply cannot see how Τρεμουλᾶ is a corruption for Tremouille any more than is Tremolay, or that Σαλοῦθε is one for Champlitte, especially if one follows Schmitt's own explanation of the rules the writer of the Greek text followed in transliterating French names. It seems so much more plausible that these forms of the names were the ones that the original chronicler used and that both later scribes simply adopted them. Certainly such evidence as this does not warrant the statement: "and thus the hypothesis of a full and complete form of the Chronicle in French is unfounded."

A few more examples of Schmitt's reasoning will suffice to demonstrate its inherent weakness. He points out with de Loray that the fact that five Greek texts have survived, whereas only one of each of the other versions has been found, tends to indicate the priority of the Greek manuscript. This indicates nothing of the sort. In fact, I have shown above that it is not true. Schmitt then asks why the Greeks would have any reason to translate into Greek such a violently anti-Greek document. He reasons that of course they would have no reason to do so. But, one might ask, then why write it in Greek in the first place? This question will be dealt with in more detail below. Schmitt's final line of reasoning, which perhaps is the most telling, deals with the honorific titles of address which appear throughout both texts. The French in the thirteenth century commonly addressed their king as *sire* and *monseigneur le roi*, both of which forms appear in the French version. But, certainly, such terms as *monseignor le saint emperor*, *je prie vostre saincte corone*, and *e puisque a sa corone plaisoit* which also appear are not typically French. Rather, they are translations of Byzantine titles. But does this necessarily indicate that the prototype was written in Greek? Cannot the presence of such terms indicate that the Latin Empire and its dependencies adopted the court ritual of the Greek basileus and that these terms were in general use in the East? The Latin court did adopt the Greek procedure for crowning the emperor, together with the imperial insignia, etc. (see ll. 984 ff. of the Chronicle), and one may assume they adopted the terms of address as well. Such words as ἄρχοντας, ἀφέντης, and βασιλεύς were in common use, and the more elaborate terms of address for the emperor would be all the more likely to persist, since they were all the more formal. This is, however, conjectural and, if it stood alone, would be inconclusive, but in conjunction with the evidence as presented below, it answers adequately Schmitt's contention.

Thus we find that Schmitt's arguments are inconclusive and open to embarrassing questions. The only possibilities that remain are that the prototype was written in either French or Italian.

A POSSIBLE FRENCH PROTOTYPE

As one reads the Chronicle in Greek, one is constantly aware of a definite insufficiency of Greek vocabulary. There is an almost ridiculous repetition of the same word over and over, especially when it is one that has struck the author's fancy. Along with this, there is an obvious lack of synonyms. Repeatedly the author uses the same word two or three times in a sentence, where the natural tendency would be to find a synonym. This is especially apparent in his attempt to maintain the poetic meter of the work. Whole phrases are repeated, sentences are inverted, unnecessary words are inserted, all to fill out the lines. These characteristics certainly betray a translation or adaptation rather than an original piece of writing.

Perhaps the clearest way to see this is to compare the Codex Havniensis (hereafter called H.) with the Parisinus (P.) and the Taurinensis (T.). It is immediately apparent that the violent anti-Greek bias of H., among the bitterest in any historical text, disappears in P. and T. The prejudice of the passages in lines 766-880, 1249-55, 3934-39, 4768, 4776-83, 4841-43, etc., is omitted

completely in P. The statements in lines 3995 and 5722 are miti-
gated. Those in lines 7133 and 7157 are altered. In line 1501
the size of the Greek army is reduced to 1,000. In lines 5379 and
5391 P. invents a massacre of the Franks. In line 7219 H. says
"great sorrow took place"; P. says "and sorrow to the Franks."
T. is even more ruthless in eliminating this anti-Greek bias (3723,
3983, 3772, 6541, etc.). These few examples, and many more, re-
move any doubt whatever that P. and T. were written by Greeks,
possibly over a century later than H. and undoubtedly for Greek
readers. Since this is the case, it is interesting to note the linguistic
changes that the author of P. makes in the text he is copying.
The first change is the elimination of many foreign words which
the author of P. obviously feels his readers will not understand.
Here is a partial list to illustrate:

line
227 ἐκατουνέψανέ τους becomes ἐδιόρθωσάν τους
1306 ἀππλικέψαν becomes ἀπεσκολάσαν
1378 κοντᾶτο becomes γονικόν
2938 ἐγκουσάτοι becomes ἐλεύθεροι
3025 ἐγκούσιον νὰ ἔχουσιν becomes ἀπάτητοι νὰ εἶναι
3191 κουρτέσικα becomes πολλὰ καλλά
3393 κουρτέσικα becomes καλῶς
3437 καπεροῦνι becomes σκέπασμα
4959 ἔχης ἀμαντίσει becomes σκεπάσης
5062 κούκουρα becomes ταρκάσια
6059 ῥοῖνες becomes ῥηγῖνες
7401, 7403, 7438, 7447 ἐπρεζαντίστη becomes ἐφάνησαν
8236 εἰς τὸν μποῦρκον becomes ἔξω τοῦ κάστρου
8244 μποῦρκος becomes ἐξώχωρον
8631-32 σιργέντων τῶν βουργησέων is omitted altogether

From this list it is apparent that the writer of P. is no purist,
simply trying to maintain pure Attic Greek—far from it, for the
grammar and vocabulary of his text are completely idiomatic.
He is simply trying to make the text understandable. Since this
is the case, it follows that H. would have presented difficulties to a
Greek reader. But if H. is representative of the Greek of the period
and was written for Greek readers, as Schmitt maintains, this
would not be so.

Another change that can be noted is the transliteration of foreign
words into Greek. For instance, κουγκέστα (1023, 1859) and

κουγκεστίζω (1382, 1510, 2567) in H. become κογκίστα and κογκίστω in P. Throughout H., the word ὁμά(ν)τζο appears for *hommage*. In P., this becomes ὁμάντζε. In lines 1964, 1968, and 7677 the word ῥουντζέστρο becomes ῥιτζίστρο. The king of Aragon in H. is called Ρόϊ Ραγκοῦ, but P. calls him ῥέ Ραγοῦ. A particularly telling example is the word προβελέγκιο or προβελέγγιο which is used throughout H. for *privilege*, with one exception. In line 7689 a reference is made to a "Frankish privilege," and here the word is spelled προβελέντζι, which is a close transliteration of the French word. P., on the other hand, always gives the word as πρεβελέτζι, προβελέντζια, προβελέζια. Schmitt derives the προβελέγκιο from the Italian dialectic *privilejo*, but this will not explain the use of the French spelling in line 7689. This can only be explained by assuming the author transliterated a word he saw before him. In line 2696 the word προβέντες appears in H. for the French *prébendes*; in P., to preserve the *s* of the French plural, the word appears as προβέντσιες. This is one of the few cases where a French *b* becomes a β in Greek, even though the β was already pronounced as a *v* at this time. The spelling βουργησέους for *bourgeoises* in line 2256 is another example. Everywhere else in the Chronicle either π or μπ is used. Obviously, in these cases, the author has made a visual error. He wrote the word in Greek as it looked to him on paper, not as it would have sounded.

The over-all impression, therefore, from this comparison is that the author of H. is transliterating a French document. The only other conclusion would be that he is working from a Greek document, which in turn was based on a French one—surely a needless complication. The author of P., on the other hand, by no means eliminating foreign words per se from the text, nor intending to use a classic Greek, has attempted to replace the French word that H. has Hellenized which would give trouble to Greek readers. He has also attempted to give correct transliterations to words that the author of H. has had difficulty with. This definitely indicates that all these words in H. were not part of the living Greek language of the period, but that they were words Hellenized as the author was translating a text from another language.

This becomes even more obvious when we look more closely at H. We notice immediately that the text is filled with foreign words. The actual number of these words gives no indication of their effect in the text, where they are repeated over and over. Most of them are given in transliteration with Greek endings, such as *πασσάντζο* (French, *passage*), *κουμοῦ* (French or Italian, *commune*), *τρι(μ)πουτσέτο* (French, *trébuchet*), *γαρνιζοῦν* (French, *garnison*), *ἀμιράλης* (French, *amiral*), *ἀβουέρης* and *ἀβοκάτος* (French, *avoué* and *avocat*). Quite a few of these foreign words, however, are first transliterated; then, because the author feels they might not be understood by his readers, or sometimes simply to fill out the line, they are immediately followed by the corresponding Greek word in apposition or attached by *καί*. Here is a representative list of such instances:

line
157-59	*πασσάτζο ... ταξεῖδι*
236-37	*καπετάνος, κυβερνητής, διορθωτής*
267	*καπετάνος καὶ ὁδηγός*
649	*κοῦρσος καὶ πλῆθος κέρδου*
1280	*χώραν ... ἀπλίκιν*
1359	*πέραμα καὶ τὸ πασσάτζο*
1362	*κεφαλῆς καὶ μέγας καπετάνος*
1622	*δράμουν ... κουρσέψειν*
1891	*παλιάτζο (balliage) ... ἀφεντίαν*
1904	*μπάϊλος ... ἀφέντης*
2190	*κόμιτας (comite de vaisseau) ... κύρης τοῦ κατέργου*
2340-41	*προβελέγγια ... συμφωνίες καὶ ἔγγραφα*
2256	*ἄρχοντας καὶ βουργη3έους (bourgeoises)*
2789-90	*ἔξοδον ... τὸ λέγουσιν πανάτικα*
2696	*προνοῖες ... προβέντες*
4341	*μαδίζη (mater) ... μάχην κάμνη*
4579	*καράβια καὶ ταρέτες*
5653	*δεσπέττο καὶ χολήν*
6882 8704 8765 8776	*τρέβα ... ἀγάπη*
6722	*γαρνιζοῦν καὶ φύλαξιν*
7706	*κουρτεσία καὶ χάριτα*
7724	*ὑπάπλωμα καὶ κουβερτάριν*
7795-96	*καπελλάνους ... ἱερεῖς*
7926	*ὀφφικιάλον καὶ ἀντίτοπος*
7937	*προβεούρης ... καστελλάνους* (which would more likely be known to the reader).

7992-8102   μπάϊλος (already familiar to the reader) καὶ βικά-
            ριος ντζενεράλ
9103   ὑποδρομή ... κοῦρσο

In addition to this practice, the author likes to coin Greek words based on French originals. For instance, we find διαφεντεύω and διαφέστερας for *défendre* and *défenseur*; ἀφροντισία for *franchise*; ῥεβεστίζω for *revestir* (but, significantly, for *se devestir* in l. 6479 we find ἐκδύνομαι, a literal translation); σκιβουρία for *eschiverie*. All these coined words have a Greek ring to them and are reminiscent of other words in the language.

Another habit of the author is to take purely French expressions and translate them straight into Greek, often with rather humorous results. *Seigneur naturel* always becomes φυσικός ἀφέντης; *surnoms* becomes ὑπονόμια (instead of ἐπώνυμα, l. 3149); *villainie* becomes χωριατία (l. 2534); *je m'angoisse* (?) becomes προσεγγι-ζαίνομαι (which really means "I approach," obviously absurd in the context of the passage, and which P. changes to προκρίνω "I prefer," l. 6104); *lieutenant* becomes ἀντίτοπος (l. 7926); *paroffrir* becomes παραοφρίζω (l. 7461); *vis-à-vis* becomes καταπρόσωπα (l. 8386); *incursion* becomes ὑποδρομή (l. 9103); *s'incliner* (meaning "to incline to an opinion") becomes πλαγιάζω (which means "to go to bed", though it is derived from a word meaning "slope" or "slant," l. 7582); *pardon* (name used for a jubilee of the Catholic Church) becomes παρτοῦν (l. 8590); *roi* always becomes ῥόϊ or ῥόε (ll. 1189, 6421, etc.); and, finally, *frères mineurs* (the Franciscans or Minorites) becomes φρεμενοῦροι (ll. 2659, 8622, etc.). An interesting Gallicism is the use of the French *ne...que* construction in the sense of "only." Insofar as I have been able to ascertain, no such construction exists in Greek. Yet we find in line 1406 οὐδὲν ... μόνον, in line 1730 οὐκ ... μόνοι,, in line 1792 οὐδὲν... μόνι, etc. This can only indicate a direct translation of a French text.

Perhaps the best evidence of this can be found in two or three of the most glaring mistakes that the chronicler makes in translation. In lines 1463 ff., in discussing the assault on Corinth, the chronicler speaks of Leon Sgouros, a particularly rapacious Greek archon. In this case, however, the chronicler is impressed by Sgouros' heroic defense of Corinth, calls him "great man" and "awesome soldier," and describes his protecting the women and children. Suddenly in line 1488 the Chronicle reads: Ὁ Σγουρὸς γὰρ ὡς φρόνιμος καὶ βέβηλος ὅπου ἦτον (now, Sgouros as the wise and *villainous* man he was. My italics—H.E.L.). This cannot be taken as facetiousness on the part of the author, for H. is singularly lacking in humor; furthermore, the praise of Sgouros in the passage is quite sincere. The only explanation can be found by examining the French text, which reads: *mais cellui Sguro qui appeleres et vaillans estoit.* It is obvious that the author of H. had difficulty in translating this passage, which, indeed, is somewhat confusing in the French version, and, falling back on the ubiquitous φρόνιμος, he completely misreads the word *vaillans.* He saw it not as *vaillans* but as *vilain,* which suggested the word βέβηλος very close in sound and meaning.

Another word that betrays a mistake in translation is σπήλαιον, which means a cave, grotto, or hollow between two hills. In lines 1697, 1773, 2804, and 3005 H. describes castles which are situated on hilltops or crags. To indicate this, the chronicler uses such terms as ἀπάνω στὸ σπήλαιον (on top of a cave) or εἰς βράχον σπηλαίου (on a cave's crag). Obviously, these expressions are perplexing. The explanation seems to lie in paragraph 115 of the French version, where the castle *estoit assis sur une pierre bise.* The Greek for this is: τὸ κάστρον κοίτεται ἀπάνω γὰρ στὸ σπήλαιον. Apparently the chronicler has misunderstood *pierre bise* and has mistranslated it. There seems to be no other explanation, especially since in line 5427 the word σπήλαιον is used correctly to translate the French word *cave.*

In view of all these peculiarities of the text, of the obvious marks of translation, and even of mistakes in translation, it is beyond doubt that H. is a translation from a French text. This is confirmed by a simple reading of the text—even by a nonexpert. The language flows well in some passages, especially those in which the chronicler interrupts his narrative to address his readers directly. Orations, obviously fictitious, also read well. But the narrative as such does not read well. The language is forced, twisted. Sentences are inverted to fill the meter. The word order itself is not natural. All too often it is patently French. This is apparent when one compares it to a French chronicle of the twelfth or thirteenth century.

The similarity is startling. Perhaps the best way to illustrate this is to give a few examples of corresponding passages in the Greek and French Chronicles of Morea. I have selected these particular passages because one of them (1) displays poetic imagery, rare indeed in the Chronicle; one contains what is apparently a French saying (2); one illustrates the use of a Greek word in apposition to a French one (3); one displays the slight difference between the two texts, but also their common origin (4); and the last contains a quaint phrase which must be derivative (5).

1. Lines 3618 ff.
   Ὅταν ἐπέρασε ὁ καιρὸς ἐκεῖνος ὁ χειμῶνας
   καὶ ἄρχασεν ὁ νέος καιρὸς ἀπὸ τὸν μάρτιον μῆναν,
   ὅπου ἀρχινοῦν καὶ κηλαδοῦν, τὰ λέγουσιν ἀηδόνια,
   καὶ χαίρονται, εὐτρεπίζονται τὰ πάντα γὰρ τοῦ κόσμου,
   ὁ πρίγκιπας γὰρ τοῦ Μορέως, ἐκεῖνος ὁ Γυλιάμος
   ὅστις ἦτον μακρύτερα παρὰ γὰρ τὸν Δεσπότην, ...
   Par. 273
   Quant cellui yver fu passés, et li noviau temps entra que li roussignol chantent vers l'aube de jour doucement, et toutes creatures se renovelent et s'esjoyssent sur terre, li princes Guillermes qui plus estoit lointains que le despot ...

2. Line 2387
   τὸν νόμον καὶ τὲς ἀγωγές, οἱ συμφωνίες τὲς κλειοῦσιν.
   Par. 167
   Li pat vainquent les loys.

3. Line 5653
   διὰ τὸ δεσπέττο καὶ κολήν, τὴν μὲ ὅποικε ὁ ἀνεψιός μου,
   ὁ ἀφέντης τῆς Καρύταινας, ὁ μέγας δημηγέρτης ...
   Par. 391
   Pour le despit de mon malveis nepveu, le seignor de Caraintaine ...

4. Line 4130
   ὁ πρίγκιπας, ὡς φρόνιμος, ρωμαϊκα τοῦ ἀπεκρίθη ...
   Par. 308
   Li princes Guillermes qui sages estoit et parloit auques bien le grec.

5. Lines 4478 ff.
   Μὰ τὸν Χριστόν, καλὲ ἀδελφέ, μὲ ἀλήθειαν σὲ τὸ λέγω,
   ἂν τὸ ἔμαθεν ὁ βασιλέας κι ἂν τὸ ἐπληροφορέθη,
   τὸ πῶς οὐδὲν τοῦ δίδομεν τὰ κάστρη ὅπου γυρεύει,
   οὐδὲν χρήζει τὸν πρίγκιπα μὲ τὸ ἄλας νὰ τὸν φάγῃ,
   ἀλλὰ νὰ ἐπάρῃ ὑπέρπυρα νὰ τὸν ἐλευτερώσῃ.
   Par. 327

Je suis certain que, quant li emperreor sauroit que nous ne voulons donner ces chastiaux pour sa raenchon, car il ne le mengera mie au sel, ainsi s'acordera pour monnaie.

It is evident at once that these passages are French. The Greek is nothing but an expanded translation.

One point alone remains to be considered in this discussion of the language of the prototype. Longnon has suggested that the original language was Italian. (See his Introduction to *Livre de la conqueste*, where he develops this theory, and his *L'Empire latin*, p. 317, where it is stated as fact.) His belief, briefly stated, is that a Venetian in the entourage of Bartolommeo Ghisi, or even Ghisi himself, wrote the Chronicle in Italian between 1327 and 1331. This, he points out, was the period in which the Italians were writing their histories, and the Chronicle of Morea was one of them. He also points out that the Venetian war with Frederick II is not mentioned in the Chronicle. No one has accepted this theory of Longnon, and it has been rejected out of hand by Adamantios. I think the main difficulty with it is that there is absolutely nothing about the Chronicle, beyond the reference to Bartolommeo Ghisi in the title of the French version, that suggests an Italian origin. Longnon, furthermore, has read too much into that statement. He assumes it means that someone in Ghisi's entourage wrote it, but the statement merely says that the Chronicle was found in a book once in the possession of Ghisi. It is impossible to read more into it than this. As for the absence of a reference to the Venetian war with Frederick, one can only say that there are many events far more important to the history of Morea which are also left out (the fall of the Latin Empire, for instance); no special importance may be attached to this isolated episode. The final refutation of the theory, I feel, is the following list of foreign words in the Chronicle.

This list is based on the Index and derivations of Schmitt. Some of these latter, however, are open to question. Many words which he derives from Latin may, though their ultimate derivation is from Latin, very well have come into the Chronicle by way of French (viz., κούκουρον from *cocure*, πανάτικα from *panatique* κούρτη from *cours*, etc.). Many words in the Italian column probably also came into the Chronicle from French (καλαφατίζω, etc.). I have marked such words with an asterisk.

FRENCH WORDS

ἀβοκάτος	*from*	avocat	μπαστάρδος *from*	bastard
ἀβουέ		avoué	μποῦρκος	bourg
ἀμαντίζω		amender	ντάμα	dame
ἀμιράλης		amiral	ντουάριν	douaire
ἀμπάρα		bars or Ital. barra	ὁμάντζο	homage
γαρνιζοῦν		garnison	παρλαμᾶς	parlement
διαφεντέβω		défendre or Ital.	παραοφρίζω	par-offrir
		diffendere	παρτοῦν	pardon
καπεροῦνι		chaperon	πασσάντζο	passage
καστελλανίκιον		chastellenie	πρεσαντίζω	présenter
καστελλάνος		chastelain	προβεούρης	porveor
καστέλλιν		chastel	ρεβεστίζω	revestir
κιβιτάνος		kievetaine (dial.)	ριτζίστρο	registre
κλέρης		clerc	ρόϊ	roi
κομεντούρης		comandour	σιργέντης	sergeant
κομεσίουν		comision	σκιβουρία	eschiverie
κουβερτοῦρι		couverture	ταρέτες	tarides
κουγκέστα		conqueste	ταρκάσιον	tarcois
κουρτέσικα		courtoisement	τριζουριέρης	trésorier
λίζιος		liege	τριμπουτσέτο	trébuchet
μαντάμα		madame	τσάμπρα	chambre
μισίρ		messire	τσαμπρελιᾶνος	chambellan
μπαΐλος		bailli	φαμελία	famille
μπαρουννία		baronnie	φιέ	fief
μπαροῦς		baron	φρέ	frère

LATIN WORDS

βικάριος	*from*	vicarius gene-	καπίστρι *from*	capistrum
ντζενεράλ		ralis	κασσίδια	cassis
βούκκινο		buccina	κάστρο	castrum
γαρδινάλης		cardinalis	κατοῦνα	cantonum
γιστέρνα		cisterna	κατσία	cattus
δεμέστικος		domesticus	κελλίν	cella
δηνέρια, δηνάρια		denarius	κιβοῦρι	ciborium
δοῦκας		dux	κόμιτας	comes
δρόγγος		drungus	κούκουρον	cucurum
ἐγκουσᾶτος		excusatus	κουμέρκι	commercium
ἐμπροστέλα		antela	κοῦρσος	cursus
ἴνδικτος		indictio	κούρτη	cortis
καβαλλικεύω		caballicare	κουστίζω	constare
κάμπος		campus	λεγᾶτος	legatus
κανόνικος		canonicus	μαΐστορας	magister
καπελλᾶνος		capellanus	μαντάτο	mandatum

μίλιν *from* mille
μίσεμμα missus
μισσεύω missus
μουλάρι mulus
μουρτεύω merda
ὄρδινας ordinem
ὁσπίτιον hospitium
ὀφφίκιον officium
ὄψιδα obses
παλάτι palatium
πανάτικον panaticum
πεδουκλώνω pedica
πόρτα porta
πορτάρης porta
πρίγκιπας princeps
πρωτοβεστιάρης vestiarius
ῥῆγας rex

ῥόγα *from* rogare
σαγίττα sagitta
σέλλα sella
σίγερον securus (?)
σκάλα scala
σκαμνί scamnum
σκουτάριον scutarium
σοῦβλα subula
στράτα strata
ταβέρνα taberna
τέντα tenda
τέρμενο terminus
φάλκονας falco
φάλκος falx
φλάμουρον flammula
φλασκί flasca
φουσσᾶτο fossatum

ITALIAN WORDS

ἀσεντζίζω* *from* asseggiare
βουργήσης* borghese
δεσπέττο* dispetto
καλαφατίζω* calafatere
καντσιλιέρης* cancelliere
καπετάνος* capitano
κόκα coca
κοντᾶτο* conte
κοντέσσα* contessa
κόντος* conte
κοντόσταυλος* conte and sta-
bulum

κουμοῦ* *from* commune
μαρκέσης marchese
ντζοῦστρα* giostra
πελεγρίνος* pellegrino
προβελέγκιο* privilejo (dial.)
προβέντα* prebenda
ῥοβολεύω* rugolare
σκαρελέτος* scarlatto
σκρόφα scrofa
τερτσέρια terzieri
τορνέσια tornese
φραγγίδα* franchigia

It is immediately apparent that, even when we assign to the Italian column words which might just as well have been derived from French words, there are still twice as many French words as there are Italian. Furthermore, many of these Italian words, especially those dealing with shipping and trade, were already in use in the Near East long before the Chronicle was written. It would be difficult indeed to demonstrate that any one of them is a transliteration from an Italian text.

The list makes it perfectly clear, rather, that French is beyond doubt the language of the prototype. Not only are there twice as many French words as Italian, but many of the words in the

Latin column should properly be numbered as French. All the rest of the Latin words are words that had come into the Greek language long before the Chronicle was written, especially terms dealing with government, religion, commerce, and warfare.

In summary, then, one can say positively that both the French and Greek versions of the Chronicle are derived from a prototype written in French. The former is a straightforward abridgment, written in prose, perhaps by a French cleric or a French knight, conceivably in the entourage of Catherine de Valois, between 1333 and 1346, and most probably between 1338 and 1341. The latter is an expanded, highly colored translation, written in political verse, probably by someone in the court of Erard III le Maure, a few years before or immediately after 1388.

The French Prototype

That the French prototype existed now appears to be beyond doubt, but to discuss it with exactness is a difficult task, for one must depend on evidence gleaned from its two derivatives. It is, however, possible to distinguish with some accuracy between the earlier work and later modifications, and thus to reconstruct the lost original. Obviously this method must depend largely on conjecture, but certain dependable conclusions may be reached.

THE DATE OF THE PROTOTYPE

A chronicler such as ours, a man of somewhat limited intellectual powers and educational background, can describe with accuracy only what he himself sees or what he learns from first-hand witnesses. Unless he depends on written sources, accurate in themselves, his accuracy must perforce diminish as the events that he describes recede farther into the past. It is immediately evident that our chronicler did not use written sources. He may perhaps have read William of Tyre, as the opening passages of the Chronicle suggest, but his description of the First Crusade is wholly inaccurate, even in broad outline. Nor is his account of the inception, course, and results of the Fourth Crusade close to the truth. It is obvious, though curious, that he did not use Villehardouin's account. His interpretations of the history of the happenings in the Greek states of the period further betray his total ignorance of the Byzantine historians. We can safely infer, therefore, that his only sources of information were his own eyes and the statements of witnesses, some of which came to him at first-hand and were dependable, and others of which came to him as hearsay and tradition. There is one exception to this—certain documents—which will be discussed below. Since this is so, it follows that the Chronicle cannot be far removed from the events it records. It is evident from the French Chronicle that the main narrative covers the years 1204-1304, with the latter half of the period described in detail. The chronicler, then, could not record an event with any exactness if he wrote more than a generation, let us say, after the event occured. The reign of Guillaume II (1246-78) is handled fairly extensively, with many vivid details, and we can assume that the chronicler spoke with people who had witnessed these events. This also explains why the reigns of Geoffroy I and Guillaume I are handled so summarily and inaccurately. The conclusion is that the Chronicle was written very soon after 1304. (It must be kept in mind that by the 1320s the Chronicle was apparently in circulation; it had at any rate come into the possession of Bartolommeo Ghisi.)

There are certain statements in the Chronicle which confirm this dating. In line 5738 we are told that children of the Turks who married and settled in Morea in 1265 were still alive when the Chronicle was written. This would be true of a time shortly after 1300, but not much after, in view of the appallingly high mortality rate in the war-torn Morea of this period. In lines 7421, 8071, 8110, and 8616 Nicolas II de St-Omer is called ὁ γέρος, the old man. But the Chronicler has mistaken the father for the son, Nicolas III, who died in 1314. This would indicate that Nicolas III was an old man and still alive when the Chronicler was writing. Thus the original Chronicle would seem to have been written between 1304 and 1314.

THE AUTHOR AND HIS WORK

It is surprising, but true, that there is not one statement in the Chronicle concerning the author himself. Yet his personality

emerges, though indistinctly and only by inference, from the
pages of his Chronicle. This has given rise to a variety of theories
among scholars, even as to his nationality. Longnon believed an
Italian wrote the original, a Gasmule the later Greek version;
Buchon and Hopf believed the original was written by a Frank,
the later one by a Greek; Kalonaros is not certain of the original,
though he believes it was written in French, and he believes the
later one was written by a Gasmule; Schmitt believes the original
was written in Greek by a Frank and that the later one is an accurate, if expanded, copy, etc., etc.

In my opinion, there is no doubt that the author was a Frank.
Why would a Greek write a violently anti-Greek document in
French? And why do we have to assume a Gasmule wrote it?
First of all, those who have suggested a Gasmule as the author
are not too clear in their distinction between the prototype and
the later Greek copy. Second, all that we know of the Gasmules,
the products of French-Greek marriages, in this period would indicate
that Gasmule feeling would be pro-Greek. The Gasmules were
welcomed by the Greeks and given high positions in the Greek
court and army. On the other hand, they were more or less rejected
by the Franks. It is difficult indeed to find a plausible reason why
a Gasmule would write a chronicle whose whole purpose is to extol
the glories of past Franks and to excite emulation among their
descendants.

For the Chronicle does just that. The object of the author was
not to write a factual history, as is instantly obvious to anyone
who attempts to annotate the Chronicle, but to produce a glowing
account of Frankish deeds of the past, to prod his listeners to
action in the days of Frankish decline in Morea. He wanted to
rekindle the warlike vigor of the reign of Guillaume II. Surely
such nostalgia and purpose indicate a Frank as the author.

In any case, the author was thoroughly French in his attitudes
and prejudices. The Franks are always placed in a favorable light.
Statement follows statement about Frankish superiority in arms,
morality, and valor. For effect, these are often put into the mouths
of their enemies, the Greeks. The typical anti-Greek sentiments
of the French Crusaders appear, though the violent diatribes of H.,
almost unsurpassed and unsurpassable in fury, were inserted by

the translator, for we find, for example, that those of lines 751-55, 816-19, 827-41, and 1249-55 are missing in the French version. The author was evidently a strong Catholic, though he was familiar with the Greek Orthodox Church and liturgy. He does not take the part, however, of the clergy in their struggle with the prince of Morea (ll. 2626 ff.). He was not a man of high station, for apparently he took no active part in any of the proceedings he describes. Furthermore, he seems almost in awe of high titles and never loses an opportunity to record them. He was definitely not a poet, for there are almost no imaginative, poetic allusions. Rather, he is extremely prosaic and speaks wholly to the point. There is, however, a dramatic quality to many passages, especially those dealing with court proceedings and clashes of personality. In these the speeches, though fictitious, have a ring of authority and indicate the character of the speaker. One feels that the person might very well have spoken just that way.

The most striking aspect of the author's personality is his intense interest in feudal customs and court procedure. True, he does describe battles and political developments, but always in a cursory way, and he has a tendency to cut such descriptions short. His main delight, however, is in the proceedings of the High Courts which fill a disproportionately large part of the Chronicle. Here he is on sure ground. His descriptions of procedure and law are minutely accurate. He has a wide and accurate knowledge of the law and states many of the stipulations of the Assizes of Morea. It is obvious that he has studied them. Furthermore, he seems to have studied the registry of the fiefs of Morea and to have used this as a source for his statements about the various castles, their founders, and their disposition. This is clear from his tendency to confuse father with son when they bear the same name—the distinction between them would not appear in most deeds unless both father and son signed the same document. The inference is, therefore, that he was a clerk or notary in the court. One further point, if somewhat oblique, tends to confirm this. He betrays a curious delight in cunning and loopholes, so long as they are on the part of Franks. He recounts, for example, with obvious relish the manner in which Robert was defrauded of his rightful inheritance. (See below, pp. 135-42). In the same category are the abduction and marriage of the "daughter of Emperor Robert" by Prince Geoffroy, the breaking of his treaty with Michael Palaiologos by Guillaume II, etc.

Thus the picture of the author of the original Chronicle slowly emerges. Alarmed at the decline and collapse of the house of Villehardouin, at the long series of disasters that had destroyed the prosperity of Morea, at the wars that had destroyed its fighters, at the foreign intervention that was threatening its very existence, this Frankish notary, of low birth, but of deep identity with his race and Church, undertook to shake his fellow-Franks from their apathy, to inspire them to repeat in their century the glorious deeds that had conquered Greece so easily the century before. In the tradition of the *chansons de geste*, he, too, produced a *chanson*, not a fanciful one of mythical heroes and dragons, but a factual one of Franks and their enemies. His chronicle is true, if understandably colored. It has the moderation of strength and power, realized and acknowledged. Magnanimous as the Franks it describes, it includes with its dislike a certain respect and tolerance for their enemies.

The Greek Chronicle

These characteristics are true, however, only of the French version of the Chronicle. The Greek Chronicle is another matter entirely. Though the original may still be discerned in its pages, the violent anti-Greek and anti-Orthodox bias of the Greek translation completely alters its tone. It is all too evident that a different type of personality is at work.

THE AUTHOR AND HIS WORK

Nothing at all is known about the Greek translator beyond the fact that he had a deep attachment to the Catholic Church and an equally deep hatred of the Greeks. Very little beyond this can be deduced from his insertions except that, as stated above, he may have been a member of the court of Erard III. It is usually assumed that he was a Gasmule, merely because he wrote in Greek. My reasons for doubting that the original author was a Gasmule are even more applicable in this case. Certainly towards the end of the fourteenth century, when it was obvious that the Greek resurgence was inevitable and permanent, when it was equally obvious that the days of Frankish rule in Morea were numbered, a Gasmule, eagerly welcomed by the Greeks, would hardly side with hitherto hostile Franks, though, of course, one might do so.

A more compelling explanation lies in an examination of the reasons why the Chronicle was translated into Greek in the first place. Schmitt has asked, Why translate such a chronicle into Greek? The proper question would be, Why not? The cultural assimilation of the Franks by the indigenous Greeks was astonishingly rapid. By the time of Guillaume II, who was of the first generation born in Greece and who spoke Greek fluently, a great part of the Franks was undoubtedly bilingual. Guillaume is specifically mentioned as speaking Greek (l. 4130). Significantly, the French Chronicle mentions this as something of an accomplishment; the Greek simply states it as a fact. Greeks, moreover, were often needed to act as interpreters. The next generation was wholly bilingual. French, however, remained a necessary and active language, for newcomers, who did not know Greek, were constantly arriving in Morea. (See l. 8320 where Geoffroy de Bruyères, a newcomer, has to use a Greek to write his letters for him.) Ties with Western Europe were still strong and there was continuous traveling back and forth. Thus, the Chronicle was properly written originally in French. In the course of the next hundred years, however, the situation altered drastically. The decline of Morea made it much less of an El Dorado. Few now came to make their fortunes. Intermarriages had increased many fold. The natural cultural assimilation had continued until it would be safe to say that Greek was the natural language of the Franks in Morea by the end of the fourteenth century. In the Chronicle there are three allusions to armies composed of Franks *and Greeks* as being of one language (ll. 3804 ff., 3986 ff., 4721 ff.). If these statements are part of the original Chronicle and date from around 1310, they are probably only further evidences of the author's pro-Frank bias. He simply overlooks the fact that Greeks were present, in order to keep emphasis on the Franks. (See below n. 66, p. 184.) If, however, these statements have been inserted by the later writer around 1388, a completely different interpretation may be placed on them.

In this case, since it was true that one tongue—namely Greek—was spoken by Greeks and Franks by that time, the chronicler has simply applied anachronistically to a time in the past a condition true in his own day. In either case, the fact remains that by the end of the fourteenth century there were more wholly Greek-speaking Franks than bilingual ones. In such a situation, if one wished to present a French Chronicle for the Franks, one would have to translate it into Greek. And that is exactly what our scribe did.

The reasons why he decided to make the Chronicle of Morea available to his contemporaries are not too difficult to surmise. They are exactly the same ones that prompted its original author to write it two generations earlier—with one difference, their intensity and tone. The developments which had alarmed him had become realities, some of them long since. The Franks in Morea had all but disappeared, as a people by assimilation, and as a nation by conquest and absorption. The later scribe desires the same ends as his predecessor, but his plea has an added note of despair. Notice the interjection in lines 8587 ff., where he foreshadows the coming of the Angevin control in Morea. Since he sees before him the obvious results of the decline of the power of the Franks, his characterization of their past glory is tinged with frustration and immoderation. To heighten his effect he turns the rather moderate anti-Greek feeling of the original into an almost hysterical denunciation. The brave, virtuous, invincible Franks are contrasted with the cowardly, deceitful, impotent Greeks. That the facts he presents do not always coincide with this portrayal does not deter him, and we find, for instance, that the Chronicle in one place (l. 4207) says of Michael Palaiologos, "like the wise and noble man he was," in another place (l. 1245), "Behold the iniquity and the sin the wretch committed." What has happened is apparent. Whereas the former writer sought a revival of Frankish power with some assurance that it could take place, the later writer has given up all such hope. He knows it is too late. He also knows that the Greeks are assured of final victory, hence his uncontrolled hatred. The irony of it is that he is reduced to using the language of these very Greeks so that the Franks will understand him.

Thus it seems to me that to explain the dual nature of the Chronicle and its internal inconsistencies we must assume that both

authors had similar aims in writing, but that the passing of over
two generations of turbulent, even disastrous, events in Morea had
produced a frustration and despair in the second author, resulting
in a distortion of the original Chronicle.

HISTORICAL VALUE

In spite of this dual nature, the Greek Chronicle must still be
considered an important historical source. Since the French version
is only an epitome, the Greek version is the only document we
have that gives a trustworthy running account of the establishment
of feudalism in Greece in the thirteenth century. It is, furthermore,
the chief Frankish source for Franco-Greek history. This and the
fact that it was written so soon after the events it describes took
place make it invaluable, even though as a historical work it is
far surpassed by Sanudo's work or that of the contemporary
Greek historians. However, the Chronicle should not be studied
primarily for its narrative, though this is our only source of any
kind for many events, but for the insight it affords us into medieval
institutions and social habits. Rather than discuss in detail the
merits of the Chronicle as a historical narrative, I refer the reader
to the historical sketch given above and to the commentary in the
notes. These and the text speak for themselves. Suffice it to say
here that the narrative is of very uneven quality. Parts of it are
completely false, parts are hopelessly confused, other parts are
somewhat dependable, while certain sections are wholly so. This
reflects the fact that the Chronicler relies on sources of uneven
quality. As a social document, however, the Chronicle is outstanding, almost unique. In its pages the feudalism of thirteenth-century
Greece is vividly portrayed. We see, almost step by step, how
feudalism was introduced into Greece, how the lands were distributed among the conquerors, how the castles were built. The
complicated relationships among feudatories, their vassals, and
their lords are illuminated throughout the Chronicle. We get a
clear picture of the relationship between Church and State in
Morea, and most important, of the one between Franks and Greeks,
and the resulting amalgamation of western and eastern institutions.
A fascinating aspect of the Chronicle is the detailed view it affords
of a feudal administration at work. We are present at many

deliberations of the High Court and can follow through all their technicalities the most important legal disputes that shaped Moreot history. We are eyewitnesses at councils of war, at jousts, at knighting ceremonies, at battles, at sieges, at parleys. We watch the investment of a vassal with a fief, the divestment of another. In short, the Greek Chronicle is a rich tapestry, portraying in all its vividness the social life of the Middle Ages.

Summary

To summarize, then, one can say that the evidence permits us to state definitely that a French *chanson de geste*, called La Conqueste de Constantinople et de l'empire de Romanie, et dou pays de la Princée de la Morée, was composed between 1304 and 1314, probably around 1310. This Chronicle was circulated in various versions, each prepared by a different person, who reflects in his handling of the original his own personality and prejudices, and who adds to it later events to bring the narrative down to his own day. The first of these that we know of was composed between 1333 and 1346, most probably sometime between 1338 and 1341. It is a concise, factual, straightforward abridgment, keeping closely to the original language of the text, providing a sort of extract of the facts of the history of thirteenth-century Morea, perhaps for the use of Catherine de Valois, certainly for some such personage. This version was not made for general use, but for the specific information of an administrator.

The third version of the work was composed around the year 1388 by a Greek-speaking French scribe, who translated the original into Greek idiom for the benefit of Greek-speaking Franks. It was written in verse, so that it could be either read or listened to in recitation, as is clearly stated in the Chronicle itself. The scribe has taken wide liberties with the original text, and his account is marked with many additions and omissions. His additions bring the narrative down to the year 1388.

A fourth version was made in 1393. This one, an Aragonese translation of the second version, is completely different from all

others in that it is a serious attempt at history, using various other
sources to correct or amend the Chronicle itself.

A fifth version appeared somewhat later than 1388, possibly a
century or more later, as Schmitt believes. This was made by a
literate Greek scribe, writing for a Greek audience. It is probable
that by this time the Greek translation of the Chronicle, in spite
of its content, was viewed as an important example of the Greek
medieval romances, written in popular idiom, whose development
was undoubtedly influenced by Western literature. This version
is a revision of the Greek translation and, in view of its audience,
a ruthless elimination of the strong anti-Greek bias of the earlier
work has been made. There is no attempt to continue the historical narrative, and the point of view is merely literary. This
version was followed at various times by at least four others that
we know of, one in Italian and three in Greek, but since these are
merely copies and a translation, all poorly done, they are of little
importance.

The Present Translation

Of the modern editions of the Greek Chronicle, the one published
by Schmitt in 1904 marks a high point, not only in the study of
the Chronicle of Morea, but in the editing of all medieval Greek
chronicles. His painstaking study of all the available manuscripts
of the Chronicle and his profound knowledge of the development
of Medieval Greek enabled him to give the definitive interpretation
of the text of the Codex Havniensis. His edition is the more useful
because it includes his excellent editing of the Parisinus and Taurinensis texts as well. However, the indexes at the end of the
volume are unfortunately not of the same caliber. The historical
identifications of people and places are based on nineteenth-century
scholarship and, as a result, are in need of much revision in the
light of more recent scholarship. Much more important, however,
are the limitations of his glossary of Greek words. This glossary,
curiously enough, in view of Schmitt's undoubtedly deep knowledge
of Greek, contains many misinterpretations and incorrect translations of medieval Greek terms. In general, Schmitt leans more

heavily on his knowledge of the classic Attic idiom and much less on medieval and modern idioms. Apparently his acquaintance with these was much more limited. In view of these inadequacies, therefore, a new edition of the Chronicle has been needed for some time, even though the text as presented by Schmitt admits of almost no improvement.

The edition by Kalonaros which appeared in 1940 was meant to fulfill this need. Much criticism of this work has appeared, some of it justified, most of it unjustified. Kalonaros has used with very little change the text as presented by Schmitt, which was only natural since Schmitt's work on the text was authoritative. The important contribution of the new work is its correction of Schmitt's glossary and indexes. Extensive work on the language of the Chronicle has been done since the late nineteenth century, especially by Greek scholars like Dragoumis, Adamantios, Phourikis, Hatzidakis, and a host of lesser known men, whose works have appeared in Greek journals not always familiar to American scholars. This work is of the deepest importance in the study of Greek texts of the Franco-Greek period. Kalonaros, who has read widely in this literature, has done a great service in bringing out an edition of the Chronicle which includes this new information in extensive footnotes. His identification of place names is especially important. However, the edition has certain unfortunate characteristics which limit its usefulness somewhat. First, for his historical facts, Kalonaros depends largely on older works, including those of Lampros, Sathas, and Paparregopoulos. His most recent authority is Zakythinos. Most regrettably he does not include the indispensable works of Longnon, who has completely revised the chronology of the whole period. Second, the edition is marred by a plethora of typographical errors which often make dates, page numbers, etc., very confusing. Third, there is a very faulty bibliographical apparatus. The bibliography contains only the standard works; it does not include the more recent works which are cited in the notes. These citations all too often omit date and place of publication, adequate page reference, and sometimes even titles.

In order to read the Chronicle with understanding in its original language, in view of the limitations of the two editions, one must use them both, with constant cross reference. Since a new edition of the work seems unlikely, this awkward procedure will in all probability remain necessary. It is the one I have had to follow in making this translation. Throughout, I have used both texts, with constant reference to the other versions of the Chronicle as well. In addition, since I felt that Kalonaros' notes were of great importance, and since they are not readily available to the reader not familiar with modern Greek, I have included in my own notes all of his that I was able to verify. In most cases I have not indicated this by the customary method, for I felt it would overburden annotation which was already extensive. The exceptions to this rule have been, of course, those places where I felt correction was necessary.

A few final words must be said about the translation itself. This particular Chronicle presents many difficulties to the translator. This would be true even of simple fourteenth-century Greek prose idiom, but it is especially true of this text, whose language is a mixture of classic Greek vocabulary, medieval Greek idiom, and medieval French. Furthermore, it is written in verse. (For an authoritative analysis of the versification, the reader is referred to the introduction of John Schmitt's *The Chronicle of Morea*, where the matter is thoroughly explored.) Above all, the text is thoroughly French in spirit and literary form; it is Greek, as Schmitt says (p. xliii), in language only. Confronted with such a text, the translator must be clear as to his purpose at the very start, so that he can maintain consistency throughout. My own controlling purpose has been to provide the English-speaking reader unfamiliar with Greek a translation as close as possible to the original text. This, I have felt, is of paramount importance, first, because the Chronicle is an important historical source that has never before been translated, with the exception of Buchon's very inadequate attempts, second, because it is a fascinating example of medieval Franco-Greek literature, and third, because its very language, as much as the social life it describes, illuminates the culture of the Middle Ages.

Therefore I have tried to reproduce in English, as exactly as I possibly could, the Greek text. This means that my translation is most emphatically not what I should consider to be a well-written English chronicle in verse. I am not, unfortunately, a Chaucer, but neither was my chronicler a Homer. His text is filled with repetitions, almost tedious redundancies. His grammar would be appalling to any Greek purist. Syntax has collapsed; the relative pronouns have almost disappeared; parataxis of the most startling kind occurs throughout, as does the magic καί (and); and punctuation has become the endless alternation of comma and semicolon with an occasional, reluctant period. But these are characteristics of the text, and I have felt that to change them, to correct the bad grammar, eliminate the repetitions, substitute synonyms—in short, to turn this badly but vividly written text into polished literature—would be to misrepresent it completely, one might even say to destroy it, rather than translate it.

The reader will find that the punctuation in this translation is not in accord with the best English usage. Nor is the style. Many passages are marked with startling, sometimes momentarily confusing, parataxis. I am well aware of these characteristics, but I have felt that only in this way would the flavor of the original emerge. To this end, I have weighed each word and have attempted to replace it with an English word of the same intensity and connotation. Technical words have been translated by their best English equivalents. Foreign words have been given in their original. Most important, for they are the most numerous, simple words have been given in simple English. Here the temptation to alter the original was perhaps the most powerful. The reader will also find that the usual mark of the translator, his insertions in brackets, has been kept to an absolute minimum. My aim throughout has been to make it possible for the reader unable to read the original in Greek to read an English equivalent, as close as I could make it. I hope that I have succeeded in some measure, for the pleasure of reading this Greek chronicle is unique and rewarding.

THE CHRONICLE OF MOREA

Codex Havniensis 57

THE CHRONICLE OF MOREA [1]

I am going to tell you a great tale, and if you will listen to me,
I hope that it will please you. When the year was the 6612th
since the creation of the world,[2] so much and no more, [the following events occurred] through the cooperation and zeal, great labor
and fatigue of Fra Peter the Hermit[3] of blessed memory, who set
out for Syria to worship in Jerusalem at the tomb of Christ. And
he found that the Christians, even as the patriarch who served
there at the holy grave, were being dishonored by the unbaptized
race, those Saracens, who were masters of it; when the patriarch
celebrated mass and raised aloft the holy things, they seized them
with violence and threw them down, and if he were so bold as to
speak out against them, they immediately threw him down and
tortured him severely. Seeing this,[4] that saintly hermit was greatly
troubled, he wept and grieved, and he said to the Christians and
to the patriarch: "As an orthodox Christian I swear to you and
say: if God and his glory grant that I get back to the West, I am
going to go in person to the most holy pope and to all the kings

---

[1] H. begins with l. 105 of P., the first three leaves of the ms. having been
lost. This and other lacunae in the text have been filled with the corresponding lines of P. in order to maintain a continuous narration. Each such inser-
tion is noted. The numbers in brackets at the top of each page indicate the
lines of text translated below.

[2] The creation of the world occurred in 5508 B.C. according to Byzantine chronology. The date indicated in the text would therefore be A.D. 1104. The
First Crusade occurred during the years 1096-99. This same mistake occurs
in L.

[3] Peter the Hermit (1050-1115) is alleged to have visited the Holy Places
in 1092 or 1093-94. After the Council of Clermont (1095), he wandered throughout northeastern France preaching the Crusade.

[4] The details of the First Crusade as given in ll. 18-104 are taken from the
account of William of Tyre.

to tell them what I see, and I hope in Christ's mercy to move them
to come with their armies to this place to expel the Saracens from
the tomb of Christ." Well, lamenting, he returned and went to
Rome; he related to the pope what he had heard and seen. And
the pope,[5] on hearing what he had related, wept long and hard
and he was deeply grieved; at once he ordered that letters be
written to all the kingdoms; he sent cardinals, legates, and bishops
to the kingdom of France and also to the other lands where there
were Christians and wherever they held sway; blessing and this
invitation did he send them: whoever went to Syria to the tomb
of Christ, however much he may have sinned since when he was
born, he would have immediate pardon for his sins.

As soon as they heard it, all the leaders of the West immediately
took the cross and swore by Christ to go to expel the barbarian
race. The mustering of the Christians was great; 88,000 knights
turned out and 818,000, their foot soldiers. They crossed over to
there by way of Constantinople; the territory of Anatolia[6] was
held by the Turks. Now, the basileus of the Romans, Alexios
Vatatzes,[7] seeing the multitude of the French, made an agreement
and an oath and he made treaties with the leaders: if God granted
and they expelled the Turks from the territory of Anatolia, which
was the hereditary estate[8] of the basileus, and if they surrendered
to him the land and the castles, he would go with them to Syria
in person and would have with him 12,000 knights. Now the
Franks, as truthful men in all things, believed the words of the
basileus and gave him their oath. The Franks, having sworn,
kept their oath; crossing into Asia Minor, they conquered the

---

[5] Urban II, who launched the First Crusade at the Council of Clermont.

[6] 'Ανατολή in the text. This is not modern Anatolia, but Grecian Asia
Minor. See S., Index of Geographical Names, p. 631.

[7] Alexios I Komnenos. The spelling of the names of persons and places
mentioned in the Chronicle has been a constant problem, especially since there
is a lack of consistency in every work I have consulted. I have followed this
general rule: Greek names are transliterated from the Greek; French names
are given in French; Italian, in Italian, etc. "Basileus," of course, is the Greek
word for "king."

[8] Τὸ γονικόν. K., Index, gives the meaning "inheritance"; Schmidt translates it as "feudal family estate."

land[9] and immediately surrendered it to Alexios Vatatzes, who was at that time basileus of all Romania.[10]

Now when he received the castles and the towns, he took sly counsel with his archons[11] as to what pretext they might find and withdraw from the Syrian expedition and not run any risks. Then the basileus met with the princes, the captains, and the commanders of the Frankish host and spoke thus to them; these things did he say to them: "First, I give thanks to God; second, to you, as well, who gave me help and I regained my hereditary estates. Then I beseech you, may it be with your will; give me a month's time that I may stay behind to provision the castles which you have won, that I may prepare my armies to go with me; I will make ready quickly to go there to find you." The Franks as Christians had no suspicion of deceit, they believed his statement and took leave of him; they passed Armenia, went to Antioch; and the basileus remained behind, he deceived the Franks, he failed in the oath that he had sworn, he broke it, and he did not go with them as he had sworn to them. Behold the crime this basileus committed; all the men of the world censured him. When the Franks went to Antioch, they underwent many hardships before they captured it.[12] Now when they took the city of Antioch, they wintered there until the month of March; and from there they went out into the places of Syria, plundering and capturing the castles and the towns; they fought many battles with the barbarian race, as we have found written in detail in the Book of the Conquest,[13]

[9] The Franks captured Nicaea on June 20, 1097, and surrendered it to Alexios.

[10] Romania refers to the Roman Eastern (Byzantine) Empire in Europe as opposed to Anatolia, which designates the empire in Asia Minor.

[11] The ἄρχοντας (demotic singular for classic ἄρχων) was a nobleman or court functionary. The term is often used in the Chronicle to indicate the Greek nobility of Morea, but is also given the more general meaning. I have preferred the form "archons" to "archontes" for the sake of euphony.

[12] Antioch fell to the Franks, after a long siege, on June 3, 1098. The victors were then themselves besieged in the city by the emir of Mosul, Kerboga.

[13] Buchon, *Recherches historiques...*, II, 5, n. 2, believes that this refers to William of Tyre's *Historia rerum in partibus transmarinis gestarum*. He further suggests that the Chronicle of Morea was patterned after the earlier history as a sort of parallel recital of Frankish exploits. If this is so, it is interesting

which was composed at that time in Syria. And indeed I am writing those things so that you may learn, but in summary, for I am trying to return to my story.

Now when they had penetrated well into Syria, they went straightway to Jerusalem; they besieged the town; they entered it. Now when they arrived at the tomb of Christ, they gave thanks and sang hymns to the Maker and Creator; the commanders took counsel as to whom they would make king; many were rivals [for the office], for they had great glory. But all the most prudent and the commons with them chose Godefroy de Bouillon[14] for king, because he was the most wise and virtuous of them all; they made him lord and king of Syria.[15] Now he, as a wise man, accepted the suzerainty; but by no means did he deign to have the golden crown placed upon his head, saying that he was not worthy, nor would it appear seemly that a sinful man be crowned with gold there where Christ was crowned with a crown of thorns.

Now after the seigneury of the Franks had begun to spread out in the kingdom of Syria, as I am telling you, and five or ten years had not wholly passed, from the kingdom of France, from

that William of Tyre's work is referred to as "The Book of the Conquest." He, himself, does not call it this. The inference is that the author of the Greek version of the Chronicle, having knowledge of a "Book of the Conquest" which was composed as a parallel to William of Tyre's work, has transferred the title back to the earlier work. The French version begins with the statement: « C'est le livre de la Conqueste de Constantinople..." This suggests the same reference to a "Book of the Conquest." It is my opinion that the Greek version, as well as the French, has been derived from this earlier volume. The Assizes of Romania (article 3), making an allusion to Baldwin II, says, "as is clearly told in the *Book of Conquest*." It then goes on to repeat the apocryphal story of Geoffroy II de Villehardouin's marriage to the daughter of Emperor Robert. The details are exactly the same as those given in the Chronicle in lines 2472 ff.; often even the words are the same. There can be no question that the "Book of Conquest" of the Assizes is a reference to the Chronicle of Morea, yet this chronicle is not known by that name. Therefore, it seems inescapable that the *Book of Conquest* is not the Greek version, nor the French version, though it uses the term in its title, but rather a prototype, on which both versions are based, and which was influenced, no doubt, by William of Tyre's chronicle.

[14] Godefroy de Bouillon (1058-1100), duke of Lower Lorraine, was elected Advocate of the Holy Sepulcher on July 25, 1099.

[15] H. begins at this point.

England, and from the various other kingdoms of the West, all those who loved Christ and were seeking piety, a multitude of poor and rich, [so dense] that troops [could] not make the crossing [for lack of ships], began to go to Syria to the tomb of Christ; they were going there with their families and settling, some for worship, and others for the glory.

Now when one hundred completed years had passed from when that crossing had taken place, the year was then the 6716th, I tell you, since the creation of the world,[16] such was the number of the year, those counts whom I name here met with one another and with still other great men of the West; they swore an oath together and took the cross to make the expedition together to the land of Syria, to Jerusalem to the tomb of our Lord.[17] The first

[16] A.D. 1208. This date is incorrect, as the early preparations for the Fourth Crusade began in 1199.

[17] The account of preparations for the Fourth Crusade, as given in the Chronicle, is confused and most often incorrect. The "council" of which the Chronicle speaks probably refers to the tourney, given by Thibaud III of Champagne (1197-1201) at Ecry-sur-Aisne on November 28, 1199. On this occasion Foulques, curé of Neuilly-sur-Marne, took the opportunity to fulfill the mission entrusted to him by Innocent III and preached a crusade against the Infidel, a "tournoi de Dieu." Among those who took the cross at that time were Thibaud of Champagne; Geoffroy de Villehardouin, marshal of Champagne; Geoffroy de Villehardouin, his nephew and later prince of Morea; and Louis, count of Blois. Later, on February 23, 1200, Baudouin IX (1196-1205), count of Flanders, joined the Crusaders. A meeting to discuss the Crusade was held at Soissons but, since nothing was decided, a second meeting was held at Compiègne, where a committee was appointed to make the necessary plans. Among those appointed was Geoffroy de Villehardouin, the uncle. The group chose Venice as the best point of embarkation, and they arrived there in February, 1201, to make arrangements with the doge. A treaty was signed whereby Venice was to have ready by the end of June, 1202, enough vessels to transport 4,500 knights, with their horses, 9,000 shield-bearers, 20,000 sergeants-on-foot, and supplies to support them for one year; in return for this the crusaders were to pay 85,000 marcs of silver. Egypt was decided upon as the destination of the Crusade, but this was kept secret. On their return, the plenipotentiaries found the count of Champagne gravely ill. He died on May 24, 1201. He had been considered by all as the natural leader of the Crusade, both for his lineage and his friendly relations with King Philippe of France, and his death was a serious threat to the successful launching of the Crusade. When the crusaders met at Soissons to elect a leader, Geoffroy de

was Baudouin, he was count of Flanders; the second was called the count of Champagne; the third was named the count of Toulouse.[18] Now the multitude of troops and bannerets[19] that were in that council and in that expedition, I have not the power to enumerate because of the excessive writing [it would require]. All the captains took counsel together as to whom they would make captain over the armies. Thereupon, they chose the count of Champagne because he was most mild of manner and skillful in arms; he was a young man of twenty-five; and at the invitation of all the leaders, he accepted the office; he took it eagerly. Then they decided in council that they would go, each to his own lands, to make ready for the expedition; in the following year, at the beginning of April, they would come together, to go to Syria.

And when they had separated, they went to their lands; a month or two had not fully passed when, from their sins, it came about that the count died, that outstanding man, the count of Champagne. Lamentation and grief broke out among all the pilgrims; and because of their great sorrow they were on the point of giving up the crossing and the expedition; behold the evil thing that befell, the death of the count!

Then since God wished the expedition to take place, and so that so many great men should not hesitate in doubt, stay behind and abandon such a good voyage, from among them there appeared an upright knight; he was a noble man, wise beyond measure, called Geoffroy, de Villehardouin the surname,[20] and he was grand marshal[21] of Champagne. He had been the adviser[22] and first

---

Villehardouin nominated Boniface of Montferrat and, after a long debate, the honor was conferred upon him.

[18] The count of Toulouse was, in fact, quite conspicuous by his absence. He was occupied at the time with the Cathari. The third count was Louis of Blois.

[19] Φλαμουριάρης, derived from φλάμουρον, "flag" or "banner" (Latin, flammula, dim. of flamma). The banneret, or knight banneret, ranked below a count but above other knights.

[20] Geoffroy de Villehardouin (1164 - c. 1216) is the author of the chief literary account of the Fourth Crusade, La Conquête de Constantinople.

[21] Μέγας πρωτοστράτορας. The πρωτοστράτορας was the hereditary marshal, who, in Morea, commanded the prince's troops and was supreme military judge. See Topping, Feudal Institutions, p. 123.

[22] Μαΐστορας (L. magister).

counselor to the count of Champagne of blessed memory, who had advised him to make the expedition; and when he saw the decree of fate, the death of the count, he took up the affair of that expedition. He reasoned, as a wise man, that it would be a sin if, because of the death of one man, the expedition and the salvation of the Christians were abandoned and it would be worthy of censure.

He took two of his knights from his council; he left Champagne and went to Flanders. He found Count Baudouin deeply sorrowed for the death that had overtaken the count of Champagne and, when the two had lamented together, Sir Geoffroy, as a wise man, comforted the count; and he knew so much to say and so much counsel to give that they determined anew that the expedition would take place. And after they had determined that they would carry it to fulfillment, the count of Flanders gave him a knight to accompany him to the count of Toulouse. They took to the road at once and went to Provence; they found the count saddened; he was excessively grieved, on the one hand, for the death of the count of Champagne, on the other, as he said, for the expedition which had been undertaken and was completely come to mischief. And then Sir Geoffroy, as the wise man which he was, began to comfort him and he informed him that Count Baudouin, the lord of Flanders, wished and had determined anew that the expedition would take place. "For this reason he has sent here this knight and myself, as well, with him, I tell you, to apprise you [of his wish] that, if you be willing, you two meet in any place you wish and that we write to the others bound by the same oath, that they too may come with you so that you all may meet together to determine the problem of what you are going to do."

Now the count of Toulouse as a wise man, hearing the words and proposal of Sir Geoffroy, immediately acquiesced and entered into his plan. Then they decided where they would meet. Why should I tell you the many details if perhaps you will be bored? The two counts met in Burgundy; they took counsel together with the pilgrims as to whom they should make captain over all the armies. Thereupon the wisest of all the pilgrims declared and agreed that they appoint Boniface; he was the marquis of Montferrat;[23] he was a great lord, indeed a celebrated soldier, the first of all Italy. He had formidable power and he had large armies; his sister happened to be the queen of France.

Thereupon, the two counts and also the various others, the leaders of the pilgrims, requested Sir Geoffroy to go to the marquis to urge him, to request him to consent to assume the leadership, to go up with them into Syria, to be first among them all, as head and commander of all the armies. The two counts gave him a knight apiece; they made him a promise that whatever he might arrange they would sanction and never revoke.

Thereupon, Sir Geoffroy said goodbye to them, he took the knights of the two counts and went directly to where Boniface was. They found him at Latsa,[24] which is a large town; and when they had dismounted and had found quarters, they went to the marquis; sweetly they greeted him on the part of those two noble counts and of all the rest of the pilgrims as well. First they presented to him the letters which they carried, and then that Sir Geoffroy spoke with him; he began to tell him this: that they, first he named the count of Flanders, second, the count of Toulouse, and then the nobles, the leaders of the expedition, all requested him to consent to become captain over them, commander of all the armies. All chose him as a wise and noble man, and they hoped in his prudence he would not fail them. The marquis, as a prudent man, answered them thus: "I thank the archons and all the counts, that they deigned to give me the office. Now, I cannot give an answer without the advice and consent of my lord the king, whom I have as lord and brother-in-law, the king of France, and likewise of the queen, who is my sister.[25] Therefore,

---

[23] Boniface I was marquis of Montferrat from 1192 to 1207 and king of Salonika from 1204 to 1207. He was about fifty years of age when he became the leader of the Crusade.

[24] Leopoldo Usseglio, after an exhaustive consideration of the problem, concludes convincingly that this refers to Castagnole delle Lanze, a castle in the neighborhood of Asti in Piedmont. See his *I Marchesi di Monferrato*, II, 179 ff.

[25] All the versions of the Chronicle make this same error, probably a result of a confusion between Boniface and Charles d'Anjou, who was the brother and also brother-in-law of Louis IX, king of France, as the two had married daughters of the count of Provence. Charles paid a visit to his brother

for love of him as for my honor, let them bear with me a little until I may go to them for advice and the answer that they will direct me to give, and afterwards I shall return and shall give them an answer."

The marquis made ready at once; he left Latsa and crossed the mountains which separate France from Lombardy. Now he traveled until he went into France; he found the king at Paris, likewise the queen; he greeted them together, since the two were there. They were very happy when they saw the marquis; the queen asked him: "What do you wish here, my brother? I am greatly astonished that you have come here; never have I seen you come to the kingdom of France to see us [when I was] ever in my life more lonely."

He related to both of them, in great detail he told them the reason, the problem, why he had come there to them: that the noble counts, who had sworn by Christ to go to Syria, had asked "that I go with them to the tomb of the Lord as captain and leader over the armies. And I would in no way give my answer without the advice and the consent of you whom I have as lords. For this reason I came to see you, to learn your will and what answer you command me to give." Immediately, the king of France answered him and he spoke thus to him, such words did he say to him: "I thank you, brother, Marquis of Montferrat, for the decision which you made to come and take advice from us whom you love and from your kinsmen. Now, it seems to me your honor is great when such great men appoint you and request you as lord, as captain and governor; you must give thanks to God and likewise to your good luck. As for me, it pleases me well and I advise you to do it, and do it boldly, with great eagerness; for I understand well, I know and recognize that it is because of me that they are doing this, so that you will have from me help and an army.[26]

for advice and consent before making his expedition into Italy at the behest of Pope Clement IV.

[26] This passage is somewhat obscure. The meaning seems to be that the king presumes that the leadership was offered to Boniface because, as a relative of the powerful king of France, he, and therefore the Crusade, would receive much assistance from the king. The whole episode is, of course, apocryphal.

Therefore, I say, brother, I command and like it; open my treasury
and take as much as you wish, and all those who wish and are eager
from all the kingdom, let them go with you into Syria, I wish it
and am pleased with it; for it is glory and honor to all your kinsmen."

Now on hearing this, the marquis, as a wise man, nodded his
head and gave sign of assent to the king. He gave thanks first
to God and secondly to him and he took whatever he gave him
of monies and troops; asked him for leave [to depart] and bade
him farewell; he embraced the queen and said to her, "My lady,
bless me that I may go with your blessing." Thereafter, he took
[leave] and returned to where he was lord, to the land of Montferrat, which he longed for greatly. At once, he wrote letters and
sent out messengers; he sent them to the count of Flanders and
to the count of Toulouse, [declaring] that he was returned from
France, where he had been with the king, and that he had the will
and eagerness to do what they asked of him, to go in their company
to the holy tomb where Christ was crucified for the human race.
Thereupon, they notified each other where they all should meet
to take counsel as to the point from which they might make the
crossing; they came together in Savoy and there they took counsel;
after they had deliberated, they came to an agreement among
themselves that they would make the crossing from Venice.

Whereupon, both counts, as well as all the others, the leaders
of the expedition, requested Sir Geoffroy, the leader of their council,
as a worthy man, the wisest of all the armies, to go to Venice to
arrange the crossing; they drew up written orders with hanging
seals for him, they gave him their power[27] and made him a promise
to ratify and fulfill whatever he might effect. The two counts
gave him one knight apiece; the marquis gave him another one;
Sir Geoffroy also had two others of his own and he took them [all]
and set out, crossed the mountains and arrived in Piedmont,
came to Montferrat, crossed Lombardy, and arrived in Venice;
he greeted the doge on the part of the marquis, and of the two
counts and also of all the others, the first and best, who had great
renown. Sir Geoffroy himself gave him the letters; afterwards,

[27] Power to act for them or in their name.

he spoke to him; by word of mouth he told him that they earnestly requested that he, as their friend and brother, arrange that they might have boats to pass over to the holy tomb of Christ, there in Syria; they required that 8,000 with their horses cross over and another 80,000, their foot soldiers. Now, the doge of Venice, Sir Enrico, he was called, Dandolo his surname, thus was he named[28] —he was a wise man and very charming—received Sir Geoffroy with honor; he became very pleased on hearing the message, for he expected and he suspected that Venice would receive honor and much profit from this expedition. He commanded that all the patricians gather, as did likewise the whole commons of the city of Venice; they entered St. Mark's and he began to speak to them: "Archons, friends and brothers, comrades, my kinsmen, look how the basileus of glory loves us; he has sent us honor and glory, profits [and has laid them] before us when the flower of France, the great lords, have come beseeching us in our own city, they to give their money and we our ships." When the archons, the leaders of Venice, and also all the commons, who were there with them, heard the words and the information which the doge had told them, they were overjoyed and thanked the doge for the advice and instruction which he had propounded to them; together they acclaimed him and ratified and sanctioned [his instruction], and said that it should be carried out without any delay.

And when they had ratified and sanctioned their policy, they called Sir Geoffroy and the knights who were there with him as his companions; Sir Enrico Dandolo, doge of Venice, gave them an answer, thus he answered them: that the thing which they sought was pleasing to Venice. They drew up stipulations, they put them in writing, they sealed them; they affirmed them with

---

[28] Enrico Dandolo (1120-1205) was elected doge in 1192. Before his election he had been sent to Constantinople as Venetian ambassador to the court of Manuel Komnenos. According to legend, while on this mission, he was blinded by order of the emperor, either by rays of the sun intensified by special mirrors or by hot copper, and because of this he had a bitter hatred of the Greeks. Actually, his blindness was the result of an illness and his motivation in diverting the Crusade from its original destination, Egypt, to Zara and Constantinople was not so much hatred of the Greeks as a desire to extend the possessions and trade of Venice.

great treaties to this effect: that if it should turn out that not enough Franks arrived to fill the heavy transports[29] which the Venetians would outfit for them, they would pay the cost of the ships which would have been left over and without delay or evasion.

And when they had completed these agreements, the Frankish knights took their leave; they bade goodbye to the doge and all the Venetians, they left Venice, journeyed across Lombardy, arrived in Montferrat, and found the marquis; in detail they described to him the affair and situation, and all that they had arranged with the Venetians. On hearing this, the marquis of Montferrat was very satisfied with what they had accomplished. Thereupon the knights said goodbye to Boniface, I tell you, that marquis; they crossed the high mountains of Lombardy and arrived in Flanders, where was the count, that all-wise Baudouin, I tell you. He questioned them in detail about what they had effected with the Commune of Venice, if they had found their satisfaction; and when they informed him of what they had effected and accomplished, it seemed to him extremely good, he was very happy. He ordered word be written immediately to all the kingdoms wherein were all those pilgrims who had taken the cross to go into Syria that they had arranged with the Venetians to outfit the ships so that they might make the crossing in the coming year, during the month of March.

And then, unfortunately, an obstacle beset the Franks, and all did not set out to go from Venice. The Provençals took counsel with the count of whom I have told you, the count of Toulouse, because it is on the coast and they had their own ships, to set out from there, because they considered it convenient.[30]

---

[29] *Πλευτικὰ καράβια.* Schmidt translates this as sseaworthy ships." Under *καράβιον* in his Index, he gives the explanation "a ship having the form of a *κάραβος*" (i.e., lobster). Zakythinos, *Le Chrysobule d'Alexis III Comnène,* pp. 53-54, claims that *καράβια* were merchant ships.

[30] A fleet under the command of Jean de Nesle set out from Flanders intending to join the others at Venice, but never arrived there. Others set sail from Marseilles, while still others left the road to Venice at Piacenza to go to Apulia with Gautier de Brienne and to set sail from Brindisi. Geoffroy de Villehardouin, the nephew, went with this last group, though the Chronicle makes no mention of this fact. This is no surprise since the Chronicle censures those who did not go to Venice and could hardly list one of its heroes in this

And when spring arrived, just as I am telling you, the count of Flanders and all the men from the places of France, and Boniface of Montferrat, the marquis, went to Venice to make the crossing. And when they saw that the count of Toulouse with his men and others from those lands were missing and that there were not enough men to fill the boats, there arose a great quarrel with the Venetians, and they would not let the Franks cross over until they fulfilled the agreements which they had [to pay] the cost of the ships that were left over. Now, the doge of Venice, as the prudent man that he was, strongly disapproved of this quarrel; he hastened and calculated how to quiet it.[31] Well, at the time which I am telling you about the city of Zara—it was there in Sclavonia— happened to be in revolt against Venice. He [the doge] called and said to the Franks, to all the captains, first to Boniface, the marquis of Montferrat, who was the commander in chief of the army over all, and second after him Baudouin, the count of Flanders, I tell you, who was first among all: "Archons, I say to you, if you wish the quarrel to come to an end and the dissension which exists in the army, if you are willing that it will happen and will promise to besiege with your force Zara, which is in Sclavonia and which is in revolt against us, and to surrender it into the hands of the Commune, then we will make you a gift of the cost of those boats which we are seeking from you."

Afterwards the Franks agreed, they sanctioned it, they drew up the treaties and their agreements; now the doge of Venice, together with his people, boarded those ships which had been left over and, raising anchor, they sailed from Venice. They went to Zara and seized the port. Then the Franks eagerly, with great

group. K., p. 20, n. on l. 395, claims that many of the crusaders refused to sail from Venice because the Commune had deflected the Crusade from its true goal for its own ends. This seems unlikely, since the aim to deflect the Crusade became apparent only when it was equally apparent that all the crusaders would not arrive in Venice.

[31] The following account of the events that caused the Crusade to be diverted to Zara and Constantinople is marked with strong bias and inaccuracy. The doge, far from disapproving of the quarrel, was only too happy to seize upon it as an opportunity to chastise the Christian city of Zara for its insolent manner toward Venice.

dispatch, disembarked from the galleys, attacked the city, captured it by sword, gave it to Venice, and redeemed their oath and pledge.[32]

Now, beginning at this point, I am going to turn from what I was recounting to take up something else: how there arose an obstacle before those pilgrims, and they abandoned their trip to Syria and went and conquered the city of Constantine.

At that time which I am telling you about, in those days the basileus of the city of Constantine, the basileus of the Romans, was Kyr Isaac Vatatses;[33] he had an evil full brother, Alexios they called him;[34] he blinded the basileus and seized the empire. Now the basileus Kyr Isaac Vatatses had by the sister of the king of Germany an outstanding son called Alexios;[35] when he saw

[32] The fleet set sail from Venice on October 1, 1202, and, after forcing the submission of Trieste and Muggia on the way, arrived before Zara on November 10. The city fell in five days.

[33] Isaac II Angelos, who was emperor from 1185 to 1195 and again in 1203-4 with his son Alexios IV.

[34] Alexios III Angelos ruled from 1195 to 1203. He was the younger brother of Isaac.

[35] Philip of Swabia married Irene, daughter of Isaac. The son Alexios was the brother-in-law, not the nephew, of Philip. Alexios III had seized Isaac and his son Alexios in 1195 and had thrown them into prison. The son escaped and fled to Germany in late 1201 or early 1202. He was, therefore, in Philip's court at the time that the final arrangements for the Crusade were made and it is quite possible that his presence and circumstances influenced all of them. It is known, for instance, that Boniface of Montferrat visited Philip before going to Venice. The matter is obscure, but it is certain that the interests of Alexios, those of Philip, who was fond of him and who may also have had aspirations in the East, and those of Venice, who certainly hoped for expansion there, would all be equally well served by the diversion of the Crusade. Alexios, in fact, had already opened negotiations with the crusaders while they were still in Venice—while they, in turn, had sent messengers to Philip's court to learn more details. The affair was further complicated by the position of the pope, who, no matter how strenuously he opposed the sacking of Christian lands, in theory and in practice, nevertheless could hardly oppose too adamantly the opportunity to heal the schism between the Eastern and Western Churches. A further element in the situation was the nature of the Crusade itself. Launched at a tourney as a "tourney of God," it had a flavor of romantic chivalry from the start. The picture of a dispossessed prince, cast out from his rightful inheritance, calling upon the chivalrous lords of the West for help to regain what was rightfully his and to cast out a usurping tyrant, most

that his father had been blinded, [he] quickly set out from there and went to Germany; he arrived before his uncle, the king of Germany; in detail he told him of the affair and situation, that his godless uncle had seized the empire. Now, the king, when he heard this, greatly sorrowed at it; he resolved, as a prudent man, to help him. Thereupon, he said to him: "My son and nephew, I do not have what will serve you in this that you are telling me; but I have heard reports—just a short time ago they were brought —that the host of Franks, who are on their way to Syria to the tomb of Christ, have arrived in Venice. Well, it seems to me that if you are willing to do it and are able to promise this [outcome] to the pope of Rome, that, if he orders the troops, those pilgrims, to abandon their expedition, the one to Syria, and to go to Constantinople to return it to you, to seize your empire so that you may have your dominions, to force all the Greeks to respect the pope, indeed to worship in the Church of Rome and be one with us in the Faith of Christ, in this way I hope and trust you will come into your majesty." On hearing those things, which I have been quoting, Alexios, the young Vatatses, promised all of them and vowed to do them. And the king, when he heard that he was eager to pledge himself, ordered messages to be written, letters to the pope; he instructed messengers and sent them to him, in great detail he made known to him all that I have been saying herein.[36]

Why should I tell you so much, if perhaps you will be bored? The pope, when he heard this, was overjoyed; he ordered that letters be written immediately to the pilgrims, he sent a cardinal

---

certainly appealed to the rank and file of the host. The full details of the diversion of the Crusade will probably never be known, but, in any case, in May, 1203, Alexios caught up with the pilgrims and signed a treaty with them. In return for their help in taking Constantinople, he promised to pay the money due Venice, provide the money and supplies needed for an expedition to conquer Egypt, send 10,000 men to help in this enterprise, maintain 500 knights to guard the Holy Land and, finally, to effect religious union with Rome. Needless to say, the account of this affair is completely distorted in the Chronicle.

[36] L. adds (§ 30) the detail that the king exacted a vow from Alexios and L. de F. (§ 32) states that Alexios, himself, went to Rome.

whom he made a legate. He sent his blessing to all and an invitation that, if they would abandon the expedition to Syria, to go to Constantinople to place Alexios, son, indeed, of the basileus Kyr Isaac, on the seat of majesty and to enthrone him, all those who died on this expedition would receive forgiveness and remission of their sins as if they had died at the tomb of Christ.[37] The cardinal that I am speaking of, that legate, took the commands of the most holy pope; he traveled from Lombardy, arrived in Venice, boarded a galley, and went to Zara. From the other direction arrived Alexios Vatatses; the king sent him from Germany. When they arrived in Zara, there was a proclamation to all the pilgrims to gather and hear the command of the pope. Thereupon, the legate spoke to them; he ordered the commands of the pope to be read.

In great detail, he showed them the campaign against the City,[38] that it was very different from the one against Syria, for it was far better to bring Christians into agreement and like-mindedness, the Franks and the Greeks, than to go into Syria with no hope [of success]. Some of the men in the armies who wished to go to the holy tomb became greatly alarmed; and, because their betters agreed to abandon the campaign into Syria to go to the City, a certain large number of clerics returned to France; because of the instruction of the legate and the blessing of the pope, the others developed a desire to go to the City.

Now when the doge of Venice saw this eagerness [to take up a new enterprise], as did likewise all the commons of Venice with him, they told and advised one another that they too should go to the City, since they had those extra boats of theirs; for if they were to return to Venice, it would be like a disgrace, a reproach to Venice. Thereupon, they came to an agreement, they resolved on this, that because of the forgiveness of the most holy pope, and secondly, for the honor of all Venice, they too would go there in the company of the pilgrims. And when all the members of the

---

[37] This account is completely false. Innocent III, in fact, had excommunicated the crusaders for their capture of Zara.

[38] Constantinople is referred to as the city of Constantine, Constantinople, or merely the City.

army were agreed, they left Zara, made ready and set out; they went straight through Romania and came to the City; the Franks quickly landed on the mainland, and the Venetians remained aboard the transports.[39] Now, let me tell you how the city of Constantinople lies; I may compare it to a ship's sail, for it is a triangle, two of the sides facing the sea and the third the mainland. Because the depth of the shore which lies around the City, as I have told you, is steep and great, equally so along the ocean as along the harbor, the galleys and also the cogs and the transports came up to the land as if they were rowboats.[40] The Venetians, as skilled craftsmen of the sea, with cunning and prudence and with great skill, built bridges upon the transports; with skill and prudence they threw these across to the walls, climbed onto them with their shields and swords and forced their way on to the walls of the City. Now as for the Franks, their battle was on the land, but they were in no way able to damage the City. Why should I tell you all so much if, perhaps, you will be bored? The Venetians entered the City first; the City was taken by the sword in just the way I have been telling you. That evil Alexios, the faithless basileus,

[39] The crusaders left Corfu by boat on May 24 and arrived before Constantinople on June 23, 1203. Astonished that the populace did not acclaim their "droit hoir" that had been brought home to them, the Franks decided to take the city by a typical medieval siege and assault. They quickly cleared the suburbs, stormed the tower of Galata, and encamped in Scutari, while the Venetians forced the chain lying across the harbor. The combined forces attacked from the land and sea on July 17, 1203. The usurper Alexios III, who had never been confident of his position, quickly lost heart and fled. Isaac was returned to the throne and on August 1 his son was crowned as co-emperor.

[40] This is a very obscure passage. The names used in the Chronicle for the various ships of the period are always a problem. The word κάτεργον is used throughout to signify "galley," a warship with oars and sail. The cog (κόκος; Lat., cogo; Fr., coque or coge) was a ship in use until the fifteenth century. According to Jal (Arch. Nav. II, 242 seq.) and F. C. Lane, Venetian Ships and Shipbuilders of the Renaissance (Baltimore, 1934), pp. 35-53, it was a round ship, wide at prow and poop, and quite short for its width, which rode high out of the water and was almost as deep as it was wide. It was apparently a warship, though smaller than the galley, but was later used as a merchantman. In the Chronicle, the word seems to be synonymous with καράβιον (transport), though this may be a misreading of the text. I have translated βάρκες (It. barca, barchetta) as "rowboats."

fled however he was able, crossed over to Scutari, left the City, and went into Anatolia.

Thereupon, the young archons of the City, seeing the great multitude of Franks who were coming in, quickly in haste ran to the prison where the basileus Kyr Isaac Vatatses was; they took off his irons and went to the palace; they seated him on the throne, blind as he was.[41]

Now, when the Franks learned about the basileus, they called Sir Geoffroy, their first counselor, and, afterwards, other archons and noblemen; in detail they instructed them to go to the basileus and to bring with them, indeed, Alexios his son; to discuss with him prudently the situation and the affair, the agreements that his son made with the pope, and whether he found them satisfactory and would sanction them.

Quickly the envoys went to him; they found the basileus seated on the throne, they greeted him respectfully on the part of the captains, told him in detail of those agreements which his son made with the pope of Rome and [asked] whether he liked them and wished to affirm them. Now, afterwards, the basileus, Kyr Isaac Vatatses, answered with prudence, as the basileus that he was: "Archons, friends and brothers, whatever my son has arranged, and with him my brother, the king of Germany, I desire it and find it pleasing and I ratify it with them; draw up orders and I shall put my seal to them."

Now, after these agreements had taken place, the leaders of the Frankish host decided, because it was the beginning of the season and winter was coming, to winter there in the city of Constantinople; and that in the following year, at the beginning of March, they would get under way together with the basileus, and would go into Syria according to their agreements.[42]

---

[41] Blindness would ordinarily have disqualified Isaac, for a Byzantine emderor had to be without mark or blemish. As a result, removing his eyes or tongue was a most effective method of removing a rival or a pretender to the throne.

[42] At the urging of the Venetians, the crusaders decided to spend the winter in the suburbs of the city. Alexios was not able to meet their demands, which were always increasing, nor could he satisfy a nationalist party which had sprung up within the city. Throughout the winter there was tension between

In accordance with the will and command of Kyr Isaac Vatatses, they crowned as basileus Alexios, his son. In this they took counsel with the basileus. Now, after they crowned his son Alexios as lord and basileus of all Romania, not even one full month passed —just as the Roman race[43] from the beginning [of time] is always found in much deceit and great infidelities—when some of the archons, the first of the City, went to the basileus, Alexios Vatatses, and spoke to him thus: "Sovereign, basileus, since God willed that you have your sovereignty, what persuaded you, our lord, to go into Syria? The distance is very great from here to Syria, the expenditures, the ships will cost a great deal; and even more important, perhaps we shall get lost on the seas of the ocean, or even on the mainland. These Franks that you see are undisciplined and lightheaded as well; whatever strikes them, they do. Let us let them go in God's curse and let us remain here in our estates."

The basileus, as a young man, and inexperienced in the ways of the world, quickly fell in with this advice. "And how is it to come about that we may be rid of them?" They said, "Let us leave them alone for still a month or two more, until they will have exhausted the provisions that they hold and thus we shall make a rebellion so that we may exterminate them." Just as they advised it, so did they carry it out. When the time was up in a couple of months—trusting to further their stupid plan— they closed the gates of the City and posted guards; the Franks

the Greeks and the Franks, with numerous inflammatory incidents, not the least of which was a fire, set by two Flemish looters, which raged uncontrolled for two days. Within the city rioting and street fighting led finally, in February, 1204, to a revolution led by the popular hero, Alexios Doukas Mourtzouphlos, son-in-law of Alexios III. Alexios was strangled in prison and Mourtzouphlos seized the throne. The Franks decided that only by seizing the city itself could they realize their great hopes, and in April the assault began.

[43] There is no satisfactory English equivalent for Ρωμαῖοι. The word itself means "Romans," but the Byzantine writers used it to designate the subjects of the Eastern Roman, or Byzantine, Empire, who belonged to the Orthodox Church and spoke Romaic (Ρωμαϊκά). Thus the Ρωμαῖοι were not exclusively Greeks, who continued to be called Ἕλληνες. None of the English equivalents in common use, such as Romaioi, Romaiotes, etc., appear satisfactory to me, and I have retained the original meaning, if not the spelling, throughout this translation.

who happened to be inside the City at that moment they put to the sword, they killed them all. Behold the impiety which the impious Romans committed to orthodox Christians and true men, who labored to put that king on the throne of the empire which he had lost. But God, the merciful, the just in all things, His Grace was pleased that in that massacre no nobleman of the wealthy Franks happened to be inside the City, but only poor men, hand-craftsmen.

Now the armies of the Franks that had remained outside the City, I tell you, exactly as I am telling it to you, hearing and seeing the alarm, the slaughterous skewering, the uproar and the screams of those who were being killed, quickly in haste armed themselves, foot soldiers and knights; they seized some of the Romans, asked them what was about, how the rebellion which the Romans were raising had come about, this perfidiousness which they were now committing against our troops. And those who knew informed them of the purpose and the excuse, the end for which they did it. On hearing this, the leaders of the Frankish army left the Venetians to guard the sea and a great many other troops, on the other hand, facing the mainland;[44] and the other remaining men of the multitude of the army blew their trumpets, unfurled their banners, and separated their squadrons,[45] both footmen and knights. They went away from the City and began to plunder the lands and all the villages, the places of Romania, reaching and plundering as far as Adrianople;[46] they made a five days' journey from the City. And when they had had enough of plunder and a great amount of spoils, they took stock and found that they had won more than what they had in the galleys and in all their ships; thereafter they returned and went to the City.

When the basileus Kyr Isaac Vatatses heard of these things, he cursed them mightily and was deeply grieved; he knew nothing

[44] To protect their flank facing the continental approaches to the city.

[45] 'Αλλάγια. The word indicates a small military detachment, but its meaning and origin are obscure. The maneuver of "separating the squadrons" is the prelude to every battle described in the Chronicle.

[46] Adrianople is on the Maritsa River in Thrace just under 150 miles from Constantinople. Alexios III had, by this time, rallied somewhat and had seized Adrianople.

whatever of that advice which those God-accursed, those lawless rebels, had given to his son, Alexios Vatatses. He ordered that his son Alexios be called; he dishonored him greatly, he was violently angry with him, and in tears he spoke the following words to him: "Tell me, God-accursed, are you not my son? How did you call to mind, unbeliever in God and the saints, this perfidiousness and rebellion which you have committed against those who made it possible for you to be basileus? You deserve from now on to be considered by everyone like that perfidious Judas Iscariot, who committed the betrayal of the Lord of Glory. I command you to tell me at once who advised you to commit such perfidiousness as you have done. You have dishonored the empire, the Roman people; from now on who will believe any Roman?"

The other, from his fear and from his embarrassment, had no way of denying it; he spoke and revealed those all-perfidious ones who had counseled him. Immediately, the basileus gave orders and they were brought before him; he took out their eyes and put them in prison; and then he called two noblemen, the first of the palace; he ordered letters to be written to the marquis and likewise to the other counts and captains. He declared to them as his excuse, with oaths he notified them, that he had never known of that perfidiousness which his son had committed with the rebels. "I beg you, archons, that the affair be smoothed over; let the quarrels come to an end, let nothing further occur. I am holding the perfidious ones here in prison; I have blinded them; take them; order that they be tried as rebels, unbelievers in God and the saints. Now, I consider the stipulations we have between us, the treaties and agreements, as being confirmed; I affirm that we will fulfill them without any fraud. Let the pillaging which you have done and the prisoners you have taken be compensation for the murder of your troops; and as for my son, a youngster and inexperienced in worldly ways, I beg you, archons, as brothers and friends, let him have your pardon, let him die with you; that he be like a brother to you from now on; let there be peace between us, love and harmony. Winter here together inside the City, and, in the spring season, go to Syria; my son will go with you in accordance with our agreements."

On hearing these words, the archons of the Frankish army took counsel among themselves and came to this agreement: that there be peace between them, just as there was before. Thereupon, they passed the winter, and the month of March arrived; the Franks made ready to go on their journey to the tomb of Christ. Then the basileus Alexios went to them and spoke thus to them, he besought them: "Archons, friends and brothers, beloved comrades, you know well the envy of the devil, that caused us so much trouble in the time of our youth. Well, I find myself a beginner in all my affairs and I do not have the things which I need, in the manner which I deem fitting for this expedition. And, furthermore, I tell you something else, be advised of it; because of the quarrel which took place, the Romans have not gotten ready to join with the Franks; for this reason, I say to you, I fervently beseech you, that I may have from you fifteen days' grace to prepare my armies and to catch up with you." Now the Franks sanctioned this, got started and left; they passed Herakleia,[47] always expecting the basileus Alexios Vatatses shortly.

Listen, all of you, Franks and Romans, all who believe in Christ and are baptized, come here and listen to a broad subject, the evilness of the Romans, their faithlessness. Who will put faith in them, believe in their oath, since they do not respect God nor love their ruler? They do not love each other except with guile.

When the Franks departed from the City, a certain rich man, an archon of the City, they called him Mourtzouphlos,[48] this did he have for surname, seeing that the old basileus had been blinded and that his son Alexios happened to be young, planned to seize the throne with guile. He called some relatives, friends, and neighbors, wretched and greedy men, and took counsel with them. Then they seized Alexios, the basileus, and murdered him; they

[47] Schmidt identifies this as Heraclea Pontica in Bythinia, which would place it on the coast of the Black Sea about 200 miles from Contantinople, though it seems more probable that it refers to the Heraclea which lies on the north shore of the Sea of Marmora, and would be on their route to Egypt, I cannot understand why they would have sailed into the Black Sea to get to Egypt.

[48] Alexios V Doukas, son-in-law and confidant of Alexios III. Mourtzouphlos, a reference to his heavy black brows, was a nickname.

found him alone and slew him and they crowned Mourtzouphlos, they placed the crown upon him and called him basileus, thus did they acclaim him. Now, afterwards, some men of the City, seeing this and hearing of the murder of the outstanding basileus, equipped a bark of fifty-two oars; they set sail and went forth, and reached the Franks there on their way to the places of Syria; in great detail they told them and informed them of the death of the basileus, that he had been killed and that the perfidious Mourt-zouphlos had seized the throne. Now the Franks, on hearing this, were very distressed; they then took counsel together as to how they should act. Why should I tell you too much and embellish it? On hearing these things, the archons of the Frankish host were greatly amazed, they were deeply grieved, and the most prudent of them began to speak, and to declare the Romans, with their self-esteem, to be devoid of honor:[49] "Who can have faith in a Roman, either in word or oath? They say that they are Christians and believe in God; berating us Franks, speaking out and censuring us, they call us dogs; for themselves, they have only praise; they say that they are Christians and they have been bap-tized; they, and they alone, say that they believe in Christ.[50] They sit with the Turks, they drink and eat and they say nothing [against them] nor do they censure them; if they should eat with us, they fall to bragging;[51] if a Frank happens into their church to go to mass, for forty days their church remains without masses being sung. Listen to the heresies which the Romans maintain; they, themselves, and only they, praise each other, and they berate us Franks, they

[49] It is curious that the most violent of these anti-Greek outbursts do not occur in P. Ll. 766-881, 1245 ff., 3932 ff., etc., of H. are represented by lacunae in the other codex. Individual lines of an anti-Greek or anti-Orthodox nature are also left out. Furthermore, these omissions all begin in the middle of a tirade or even of a sentence. This indicated that P. is the work of a later scribe who desired to tone down the violently anti-Greek bias of the Chronicle. H., on the other hand, is obviously the work of a scribe, either a Frank, as Kalonaros supposes (K., p. 34, n. 754), or a Frankophile. The French version of the Chronicle, it must be pointed out, includes few of the anti-Greek senti-ments of H.

[50] This line could mean "they say that they alone believe in Christ."

[51] Corrupt passage. Alternate readings are: "they sit as if they were walking on thorns"; "they sit as if on thorns"; and "they sit as if in privies."

censure us, who retain the faith and law of Christ just as the holy
apostles taught it to us. For the first apostle was Saint Peter whom
Christ enthroned as the leader of the whole world; He, Himself,
gave him the keys of paradise; He gave him the power to bind
and let loose; whatever he might do on earth, He would affirm
in the heavens. Now that apostle, as the wise man that he was
—and he had the favor of Christ and his command, as well—because
in those years the city of Rome ruled all the world, the whole
world,[52] indeed, and to cast down the idols, the disbelief of the
races, and to enlarge and strengthen the Church of Christ, he
went there and established the throne of the Church; there they
crucified him for his belief in Christ. And afterwards there followed a great many popes, who held the See of the Church of Rome.
Now, the Franks and the Romans maintained one faith; the bishops
of the whole world, Franks and Romans, the patriarchs and the
bishops, the leaders of the [Christian] world, each one received
ordination from him who was pope and bishop of the See of Rome.
Now, when many years had passed, those Romans, who had the
name Hellenes, thus they were named—they were very boastful
and they still kept it—took from Rome the name of Romans.
Because of this boastfulness and this haughtiness, they deserted
the canon of the Church of Rome and they stand as schismatics,
only bragging do they have. Look, good archons, at their perfidiousness; they say they are Christians and they do not maintain
truth; they do not maintain their oath, they fear not God; only
the baptism of Christianity do they have. Behold what their writing
and books command; the teaching which the twelve apostles taught,
the four Evangelists who enlightened us, the deeds that they
achieved at that time in the world when Christ was alive and walked
upon the earth, and, furthermore, the teaching that was taught
to us, that we are to maintain the canon of the Church; all these
they distorted when they separated from the Church of Rome,
which is our Catholic Church, and deserted ordination by the
most holy pope and now ordain by themselves their patriarch.
Well, since they do not respect the Church of Rome, why should
we go to Syria and why should we not return to take from the

---

[52] *Κόσμος* and *οἰκουμένη*.

faithless their dominions, since they strangled their lord, the basileus? And, furthermore, behold their faithlessness; the basileus
whom they had as natural lord, with envy and sedition, they
slaughtered and killed. Who will believe in them, in their oath
or in their word, who will consider them Christians as they say
and maintain? With words they are Christians, the deed is lacking
to them. Curse the Christian who will believe them." Now after
the Franks had mourned the basileus and had voiced their complaints and the deeds of the Romans, they began to take counsel
as to how they would act. Some of them said they should go to
Syria, and others, the wiser, said and advised, such counsel just
as I am telling you did they give: "Since the faithless Romans,
those rebels, have killed the basileus, their rightful lord, whom
they should have regarded second only to the Lord and have no
other rightful person to rule them, instead of going to Syria, which
we have not sought,[53] let us return to the City and let us all give
battle with our weapons. And, if God be willing and we take the
city of Constantine, let us keep the empire of all Romania."

Thereupon, all the leaders entered into an agreement, they as
well as all the commons of the Frankish host; they readied the
ships and reversed the sails. Why should I tell you too much?
Even I grow very weary. Our Franks returned to the City, and
when they arrived at the harbor, they surrounded the town by
land and by sea. The Franks planned their strategy as did the
Venetians; with them were the Provençals, together with the Lombards from Montferrat. They set up all the trebuchets[54] along the
land side of the City; they separated the divisions and began the
assault. Because of the great number of arbalests,[55] no man was
able to stand on the walls of the city of Constantinople. They also

[53] This is obscure. It may be read as "to seek what we do not have."

[54] Τρι(μ)ποντσέτο. The trebuchet was a catapult used to hurl stones upon
a besieged city.

[55] Τζάγρα and τζάγγρα. The arbalest or crossbow was an elaborate bow,
often made of steel, supplied with a crank or some other mechanical means
of drawing it. The arbalester often had to work the mechanism while lying
on his back and to discharge the weapon from this position. Though its arrow
had great penetrating power, its obvious drawbacks were its unwieldiness
and slow rate of fire.

had wooden ladders, well strengthened with iron; these they placed against the walls in order to climb into them. The knights dismounted from their chargers; seeing the ladders, they ran, and climbed up. Thus, just as I am telling you, the City was taken at that time. The Franks entered first from the mainland and then the Venetians entered from the transports, from there where they had set up the encirclement by sea. Be it known by you, then, that the City was taken, that is, when it was taken the first time by the Venetians, on the fourth day of November; and the later and second taking of the City took place in its turn on the fourth of April.[56] Because of the multitude of troops and the intensity of the assault, no one was able to flee by any means from the City. Now, they captured that faithless Mourtzouphlos[57] and brought him to the leaders for them to judge him. The noble counts were very happy at this; hubbub and dissension arose about what punishment he should suffer. A certain old man happened to be in the City; he was a wise man and very learned; on hearing that the Franks wished to punish that all-faithless Mourtzouphlos that I am telling you about, he ran to those who were the captains, who had authority over all the armies;[58] he began to tell them and to inform them that a certain basileus—Kyr Leo was his name;[59] he was a dread philosopher and made prophecies—had built many things there in the City; some things were fulfilled at the time they were to come about, and still others were waiting for their time to come.[60] Well, near the front of Saint Sophia he erected

[56] The first capture of the city took place on July 17, 1203, not November 4, and the second took place on April 13, 1204. The Chronicle significantly makes no mention whatever of the barbarous scenes that accompanied the second capture of the city, nor the enormous booty that was collected.

[57] Mourtzouphlos had first fled northward into Thrace, then, betrayed by his father-in-law Alexios III and harassed by Frankish troops, he fled to Asia Minor where he wandered forlornly with a small retinue until he was finally captured by the Franks some time in November, 1204.

[58] P. resumes at this point.

[59] A reference to Leo VI the Wise (886-912).

[60] A confused passage. The author is apparently saying two things at one time: Leo made many prophecies, some of which came true in their good time, while others had not been fulfilled as yet; and he also constructed many monuments in the city, one of which was the column in question.

an astounding column, it was wide and tall; and he had letters carved onto it which read as I tell you: FROM THIS COLUMN THERE WILL BE HANGED THE FAITHLESS BASILEUS OF THE CITY OF CONSTANTINE.[61] "And so, it seems, archons, the prophecy is to be fulfilled; since you have the column and the rebel, fulfill the prophecy of the philosopher." When the nobles heard this, they were greatly astonished; they took the old man to show them the column; and, when they came to it and had examined it, they were greatly astonished and pleased as well, for they had found a convenient way to deliver justice to the traitor; so they ordered him to be brought and there he was raised aloft; they cast him down from the top of the column; demons appeared, who took his soul.[62]

Now, after the execution of the rebel had taken place, all the great archons, the leaders of the host, went to the palace of the basileus; they took counsel together, small and great, as to how they should deal realistically with the dominions of the empire.[63] There were many words before they could decide the problems, but, in the end, they said and affirmed the following: since when they were on their way to Syria, the most holy pope, by a great mandate, had ordered them to abandon that expedition and to go to place Alexios Vatatses on the throne of the empire, and they had so placed him; and, since afterwards he was butchered and killed and done to death by his own people, the Roman race, and

---

[61] Lg., p. 69, identifies this as the Column of Theodosios in the forum of Theodosios II (Forum Tauri).

[62] This seems to be the way Mourtzouphlos actually met his death, as all the sources of the period describe the scene. "De haut homme haute justice," says Robert of Clari (XCII and CVIII-CIX).

[63] The disposition of the empire had already been settled in a treaty signed by the crusaders and Venice in March, 1204. This was submitted to the pope to obtain excommunication for those who would not observe its terms. By this treaty the Franks and Venice were to share the booty equally. A committee of six Venetians and six Frenchmen was to elect the emperor. The party that did not elect the emperor would provide the patriarch who would occupy Saint Sophia. The emperor was to receive one fourth of the conquered territory, of the remainder one half was to go to Venice, one half to the crusaders. Venice, furthermore, stipulated that all her trading arrangements in the East were to be preserved and that she was to receive a lion's share of the booty by way of indemnity for what was still due her for her expenses in the Crusade.

there was no one else from among them worthy of the sovereignty, "then let us keep it for ourselves and let us stay here; with right we took it, by the edge of the sword." Now, after they had come to this decision, just as I am telling you, they then held a council to elect an emperor.[64] They chose twelve archons, worthy men and most wise; six were bishops and six were bannerets; they agreed under oath to elect an emperor, with no evil intent or guile. They entered a small cell; there they were closeted until they would elect the emperor of the City.

They quarreled with each other with many words, because they were not in agreement among themselves on choosing an emperor; for some spoke for the doge of Venice and praised him highly as a wise and skillful man and declared that he was worthy of being emperor. And because of the many quarrels which they had with one another, someone went and told the doge of Venice. And he, all-wise and skillful in everything, quickly went to those twelve wise men, tapped on the door so that they would hear him, and he spoke thus to them: "Archons, listen! Someone has brought me a report, he came and delivered it, that some of you, from their excellence, as noble men and wise, are voicing their opinion; they speak words of me as one for the office of emperor, that I am worthy of becoming emperor of the City. Well, I thank them deeply as wise friends and brothers of mine; may God return to them what they have said and spoken of me, their brother. However, I, by God's grace and glory, do not find in myself, I say it to myself, so much lack of judgment as not to recognize that in the Commune of Venice there have arisen men of great knowledge and military experience, just as in other places, but none of them ever arrived to such glory as to be crowned with an emperor's crown. Therefore, I beseech you, as my friends and brothers; let the quarrels, the dissension, the words come to an end; and as for those who spoke of my becoming emperor, I take the words and shouts

---

[64] *Βασιλεύς* is the term used for "emperor" throughout the Chronicle, but I have used "emperor" to indicate Franks and have retained "basileus" for Greeks. Baldwin was elected on May 9, 1204, and crowned with full Byzantine ceremony on May 16 in Saint Sophia. The account of the election in the Chronicle is spirited, but apocryphal.

which they voiced and I, myself, place above them my own; and let us join the others to conduct, the twelve of us together, the balloting, so as to bring an end to the matter, and let us elect as emperor Count Baudouin, who is a rightful lord, the lord of Flanders; for he is worthy and noble, adept in all things and, among all those of the host, he is worthy to be emperor."

On hearing these words, the twelve whom I have been telling you about, who were all chosen to elect an emperor, thereupon came to an agreement and all endorsed it; they emerged from where they had been gathered and went to the palace of the basileus; they called for the whole army to gather to hear the solution which they had spoken and prepared, the election of the emperor and who he was to be.

And when the whole army had gathered in the splendid palaces of the basileus, one of the twelve, the wisest, made them a speech, he explained the affair, that with fear of God and with great care, they had chosen the count of Flanders to be emperor and king of the City and of the whole empire of Romania.

When they heard these things, all of them, small and great, the rich and the noble, the commons, the army, all were greatly pleased, they ratified and affirmed that Count Baldwin be emperor. The crown and the mantle were brought to the emperor, he was crowned and clothed as a basileus, I tell you, and he was acclaimed and glorified, as is the right and proper way.[65]

And when they had crowned him and he was become emperor, a quarrel and serious dissension broke out among the Lombards, I tell you, and also among the French, who desired and wished that the marquis become emperor, the marquis, indeed, of Montferrat, who was the captain of the army and the troops, as I told you before.[66] Thereupon, the all-wise doge of Venice, Sir Enrico,

[65] This is an attempt to describe the Byzantine ritual for crowning a new basileus. The mantle (σάκκος) was an emblem of royalty, and acclamation and glorification was the ritual of πολυχρόνιον whereby the populace wished their emperor long life and health.

[66] After celebrating Easter, which fell on April 25, the crusaders came together to choose the six electors. It became quickly apparent that Boniface and Baldwin were the chief contenders for the office and their partisans split the host into two factions. A compromise was worked out whereby the one

Dandolo his surname, tried, with various others, to snuff out the quarrels. He took with him the count of Toulouse;[67] he knew so many things to say to calm them so much and he spoke and explained, like the wise man which he was: "Archons, friends and brothers, since the election of the emperor has taken place and he has been crowned and it is over and done with—an ugly and unseemly thing, a great censure—that everyone should speak and hear all over the whole world, that, by the word and choice of such great men, the election took place and the emperor was crowned and afterwards you changed your minds, as it appears, because of envy. Therefore, I say to you, I plead with you that the quarrels disappear, it is not to our credit; since the count of Flanders has become emperor, let the marquis of Montferrat become king and hereditary lord of the city of Salonika, to rule with all that appertains and is owed thereto." On hearing these words, the troops, small and great, the rich and the commons of the Frankish host, cried out in a loud voice; all approved of them.

And when they had ratified it and had crowned Boniface, I tell you, the marquis, as king, the quarrels ceased and peace ensued. After this, they directed those twelve, who had selected the emperor, to make the distribution of the territory of Anatolia and of all of Romania, all that appertained to the empire of the City, I tell you, according to the rank and worth of each and every one and according to the number of troops each had in the conquest. By lots and with attention, the distribution was made; now Venice's share happened to be a fourth plus one half of a fourth, one eighth

of the two who was not chosen would be compensated with suitable lands in Asia Minor or Morea. The electors finally met on May 9, 1204. The deliberation was deadlocked for some time until the Venetians finally threw their support behind Baldwin, probably because they did not want to increase the power of their already formidable neighbor, the marquis of Montferrat. The day after the coronation, Boniface demanded that he be given the kingdom of Salonika, which he preferred to lands in Asia Minor, having just married the widow of Isaac II Angelos, Marie or Margaret, sister of the king of Hungary. Baldwin finally was forced to acquiesce.

[67] There was no count of Toulouse in Constantinople at the time. This is the second time that the Chronicle lists a count of Toulouse among the crusaders. It is probably the count of Blois who is meant.

others call it, of the city of Constantinople and of all Romania
just as the doge of Venice still records it in the documents and in
the evaluation of his suzerainty.[68]

Well, at the time that I am telling you about, in those days the
lord of Vlachia and of all Hellas, of Arta and Yannina and of all
the Despotate, was a man named Kyr Ioannes, Vatatses was his
surname.[69] And when he heard and learned and was informed that
the Franks had seized the rule of the City, and had crowned an
emperor, had taken the castles and had distributed the towns
of all Romania; quickly, in haste he sent word into Cumania;[70]

---

[68] In the fall of 1204, a new committee of 24, 12 Venetians and 12 crusaders,
was appointed to distribute the lands of the empire, excluding those already
given to Boniface, along the lines set down in the agreement of March. The
empire was considered in its various component parts, those already conquered
and those still to be taken, and each part was divided as they had stipulated.
Venice, of course, saw to it that she received lands that would strengthen her
trading interests. As a result she gained the most important share, if not the
largest in actual area. She also used her right to elect the patriarch and maintained through him a strong influence in the affairs of the Latin Kingdom.
The doge received and maintained until 1361 the title: "Dominus Quartae
Partis et Dimidiae Totius Imperii Romaniae."

[69] Vlachia was and is an area of indefinite boundaries in north central Greece,
comprising most of Thessaly and stretching northward into non-Greek territories. Arta, to the south, and Yannina (popular name for Joannina), in the
north, were the two principal cities of Epiros, slightly larger at that time than
today. Hellas was the name for the old Byzantine theme of central Greece,
which included Boeotia, Attica, Euboea, and parts of Aetolia. In the thirteenth
century much of this area was brought under the control of Michael Komnenos Donkas and his successors. Michael was the son of Sevastokrator Ioannes
Doukas, who had once been a well-respected governor of the region. The
Chronicle confuses his name, mistakenly given as Ioannes Vatatses, with
that of Johannitsa, who styled himself Tsar of the Wallachians and Bulgars,
but who is variously known as Kalojohn, Romaioctonos, Joanisa, John I Asen,
etc. He ruled an independent Bulgaria from 1197 to 1207. At first friendly
to the new Latin Empire, he soon found the Latins hostile to him and he
launched a barbarous attack on the regions around Salonika. He defeated the
Latins in the battle of Adrianople (April 14, 1205) and captured Baldwin, who
subsequently disappeared. Johannitsa was finally assassinated before the walls
of Salonika, by the patron saint of the city, St. Demetrios, himself, according
to popular opinion at the time.

[70] The land of the Cumans, a fierce, warlike people who inhabited the area
north of the Black Sea.

ten thousand came, all choice Cumans with choice Turkomans,[71] all on horse. They had good weapons, they carried jerids;[72] some held lances and others, clubs. He also mustered the troops of all his dominion, he amassed large and courageous armies, and he launched a vigorous attack to open war on the Franks; but not to fight in the field, face to face, but with cunning, as is the custom of the Turks. Now, when the one season passed, the other returned;[73] with cunning, he sent out his spies so that he might be informed at all times of what the Franks were doing. And when he learned of the whereabouts of Boniface, king of Salonika, thus they called him, he marched by night until he reached there.[74] He hid his troops in ambush in suitable places; and as soon as it was dawn and day was breaking, he directed two hundred of his light horse to rush in and pillage around his castle; they collected booty, took it and fled. Seeing this, the Lombards who were with the king quickly took up their arms and sprang into their saddles; the king, himself, went out together with them, like men inexperienced in the warfare of the Romans. Around fifty men rode back and forth; and those who had pillaged fled with the booty in order to bring them into the ambuscades. Thereupon, those who were lying in hiding leaped out of ambush on all sides and began to shoot arrows at the Lombards; the Cumans, who had pretended to be fleeing, rode around behind them and shot arrows at the chargers. And when the Lombards and Boniface, their lord, the king of Salonika, saw that they had encircled them and were shooting arrows at them, gathered themselves all together, to live and to die. But the Cumans and the Romans did not come close to them; they shot at them with their arrows from afar and in this way they killed them and did them to death. From that time on, as I am telling you, with deceit and guile, as

[71] An Asiatic people, neighbors of the Cumans, often used as mercenaries by Byzantine emperors.

[72] The jerid (djerid, jereed) was a short javelin used by the Arabs and Persians.

[73] I.e., when spring came.

[74] The chronology of the Chronicle is incorrect here. Actually, Boniface was killed by the Bulgarians on September 4, 1207, more than two years after the battle of Adrianople.

is their way, the Romans fought battles with the Franks, taking and losing them, as is the way of battles and campaigns everywhere, until three years had passed.

Now, when three years and more had passed, Emperor Baldwin wished to go to Adrianople, which is still a large city. And as soon as he went there, as I am telling you, someone reported it to the despot Kalojohn, I tell you, the lord of Vlachia; and he, as soon as he heard it and as soon as he was informed of it, quickly, speedily, and hastily, with great eagerness, he gathered all his armies from everywhere; he arrived at Adrianople speedily. Why should I tell you too much and perhaps bore you? For I too, like you, am bored in writing it but, for more brevity and short words, I tell and inform you, with truth I write it to you, that, just as it was done to the marquis, the king of Salonika, as I have told you, so was it done also to Baldwin, the emperor of the City; with ambuscades and intrigues, they were deluded and broke out into shouting and tumult, crying out and saying that the armies of Kalojohn, I tell you, the despot, were coming. The despot sent out fifty men, who rushed in and plundered the fields and lands around Adrianople, where the emperor was. Now, the emperor gave his orders to his marshal and the trumpets were sounded, they leaped into their saddles; he had six hundred Flemish and three hundred Franks, who were all hand-picked, rode chargers, and had splendid arms, as is the custom among the Franks. Alas, the destruction that took place that day to such noble men of the flower of France, that they were killed and died unjustly, because they were not at all familiar with the warfare of the Romans. Now the Adrianopolitan archons came and said to the emperor: "Our lord, despot, restrain your armies from marching out, because those, whom you see, who have come and are pillaging, have come as decoys, furtively to lure us out; and their armies are all hidden in ambush and are waiting for us to be led to them. Now they do not fight as you Franks do, to wait on the field to give spear thrusts, no, they fight with their bows as they flee. And take care, our good lord, not to go out against them; if they have taken sheep, horses, and cattle from us, let them take them as loans, which, by some chance, they may return."

On hearing this, the emperor reproached them for it, and in anger he ordered them not to say any more about it, for they were suggesting something which was a great rebuke. "For me to see with my own eyes right here in front of me my enemies damage, destroy, pillage my lands and I to stand like a corpse and suffer them it; I consider it better to die a death today than that rebukes be spoken elsewhere about me."

He ordered the trumpets to be sounded and blown; he separated his Franks into three squadrons, and the Romans into another three, and they went out onto the field. Now, when the Cumans who were pillaging saw that they had come out against them, they were overjoyed and pretended that they were fleeing with the booty which they had; and the Franks, like men inexperienced in that kind of fighting, began to pursue them to catch up with them; and they, again, as they fled, shot arrows at the horses and chargers which they were riding. They so led them astray and deluded them that they brought them into the ambush; quickly, the Turks and Cumans came out of ambush and began to shoot arrows at the chargers of the Franks. Now, the Franks expected to give them battle with spears and swords, as they were accustomed to do. But the Cumans fled and did not come close to them; they only shot arrows at them with their bows and they let loose so many that they killed them; for the chargers perished, the knights fell. They had Turkish *salives*[75] and clubs; with these they beat them on their helmets and killed the emperor and all his armies. Behold the destruction that took place on that day; one must grieve for every noble soldier, for they died unjustly without even a chance to fight. Now, the Romans who were with the emperor near Adrianople received few wounds, for when they saw that the emperor had been killed, they fled, returned to and entered the town; they dispatched messages to the city of Constantine that the Turks had destroyed the emperor. Now, the doge of Venice happened to be there;[76] he quickly mustered armies,

---

[75] A kind of Turkish weapon. Perhaps the word signifies a mace, derived from Gr. σαλεύω , "to shake."

[76] Doge Dandolo, in fact, was still alive and in Constantinople at the time. He died a few days after the battle and was buried in Saint Sophia. His tomb remained there until 1453 when it was destroyed by the Turks.

went to Adrianople to help the troops safeguard the city; at the same time he quickly dispatched an envoy to Sir Robert, full brother of the Emperor Baldwin.[77] He held suzerainty over towns and castles in Nymphos;[78] he had strong armies and bannerets with him. And as soon as he heard and learned, and as soon as he was fully informed that the Turks had destroyed the emperor, he provisioned his castles and went to the City. Now, the doge of Venice returned; from all sections, he sent word everywhere to the leading bannerets who were then ruling in Romania. And when they had gathered and had met together, they enthroned as emperor Robert, brother of Emperor Baldwin. Now, the emperor, Sir Robert, had a son, whom they also called Baldwin,[79] who became emperor and lost the empire; his daughter he sent, a few years later, to the king of Aragon[80] for him to take as his wife; the galleys took harbor at Pondikos,[81] which is in Morea[82] and is a splendid castle. Sir Geoffroy, lord of Morea, happened to be there, he who was the older brother of Prince Guillaume;[83] with cunning and slyness, he seized and married the daughter of the emperor Robert. And the emperor was greatly disturbed when he heard

---

[77] Baldwin's brother and successor was Henri de Hainaut (1206-16), who is not mentioned in the Chronicle. Yolande, their sister, married Pierre de Courtenay and had by him a daughter, also called Yolande, who married Andrew of Hungary. When Henri died he left no direct heirs, and the succession reverted to his sister. Andrew was considered for the office, but it was offered to Pierre. He accepted, but on his way to the east, he launched a campaign in Epiros in which he disappeared. Yolande continued on to Constantinople and took up the regency for her missing husband. After two years Pierre was assumed dead and in 1219 the crown was offered to Yolande's oldest son, Philip, who declined in favor of his younger brother, Robert de Courtenay, who is the Robert mentioned here in the Chronicle.

[78] Nymphaeum, near Smyrna in Asia Minor.

[79] Baldwin II (1228-61) was Robert's brother. He came to the throne at the age of eleven. John of Brienne was regent for him until 1237

[80] King James II?

[81] See below, p. 117, n. 24.

[82] The word Μορέα is used in the text to indicate both the whole principality of the Peloponnesos and the district of Elis. Here Elis is intended.

[83] Geoffroy II de Villehardouin (1228 [or -30?]-46) was the older brother of his successor Guillaume (1246-78). For details about the marriage, see below, p. 144, ll. 2476 ff. and n. 89.

it, but, afterwards, they came to an agreement, as you will learn here in this book further on in another passage.

Now, I stop at this point and I wish to finish what I was speaking of in order to take up something else, to tell you a story, a great tale, what the Romans did when they fell out of and lost the empire of the city of Constantine. Therefore, I shall begin at this point: listen that you may learn. Now, at the time and in the season when the Franks captured Constantinople, as I have related, seeing this, the Roman archons, the first of Romania, there in Anatolia where they had prestige, elected as their lord and enthroned as their basileus Kyr Theodoros, Laskaris he was called; he was the son-in-law of Basileus Kyr Isaac Vatatses and had his daughter as wedded wife.[84] And when he had been crowned and made basileus, he provisioned his castles and hired armies, Turks, Cumans, Alans, Zychoi,[85] and even Bulgars. He began, with great eagerness, to make war on the Franks who were in the territory of Nicaea, there in Anatolia where Philadelphia is, where Sir Robert of Flanders was and ruled;[86] and their war lasted around three

[84] The Chronicle at this point begins to discuss the rulers of the Empire of Nicaea. Theodoros I Laskaris (1206-22) married Anna, the daughter not of Isaac Angelos but of Alexios III. His third wife was the daughter of the Empress Yolande, Maria de Courtenay. He was succeeded by a son of his second wife, an Armenian princess, Ioannes III Doukas Vatatses (1222-54). He in turn was succeeded by his son Theodoros II Laskaris, who is the Theodoros referred to in the Chronicle. He died in 1258, affected in mind and body, at the age of thirty-six, leaving his son, Ioannes IV Laskaris, barely eight years old, in the care of a regent, whom the nobles would not accept and whom they replaced by Michael Palaiologos, a direct descendant of the Angeli. Michael was named regent, then despot, then finally in 1259 co-emperor. Ioannes was kept in the background and, when Michael entered Constantinople as Michael VIII, was blinded and cast into prison.

[85] The Alans were a nomadic people, living in the Caucasus region. The Zychoi, or Uzes, lived on the shores of the Black Sea.

[86] When the empire was partitioned by the Latins after the capture of Constantinople, large portions of Asia Minor were assigned to Emperor Baldwin I. He, in turn, granted large fiefs in this territory to his followers. Among these were the Duchy of Nicaea, assigned to Count Louis of Blois, and the Duchy of Philadelphia, assigned to Count Stephen of Perche. Neither of these new dukes ever took possession of his lands, and after repeated attempts by the Franks to establish dominion over Asia Minor, the lands fell to the

years and more, until the time when Emperor Baldwin was killed
and they crowned Robert as emperor. Now the basileus Laskaris
lived as many seasons and years as wished the Basileus of Glory;
and, when there came to him the common fate of this world, to
die—and he had a son, a young lad who was a minor—he ordered
them to summon Kyr Michael Palaiologos, I tell you, the first
man of Romania, since he was an honest man and the wisest of
all the Romans; first, he surrendered to him that son of his and,
then, the suzerainty of all the empire. Under oath, he received
what was surrendered to him; father, indeed, of the basileus, it
was ordered he be called. And as soon as the basileus died, the
Palaiologos gave orders that the castles be provisioned; he placed
good guards, who took their oath of allegiance in his name; he
received the oath of all the captains and likewise of the commons
of all the empire. And, when he had received all the suzerainty,
he honored the archons of all the empire; to some he granted
gifts, to others he gave towns; and, as soon as he had satisfied
all their desires, he strangled and killed his little lord, the son,
indeed, of the basileus Laskaris. Behold the iniquity and sin
which the wretch committed, to strangle his lord, to seize his sovereign power; who will hear of it and say that men who keep neither
to the truth nor to an oath believe in God? Why, the unbaptized
races, should they make you an oath, according to the customs
which they have and to the law which they adhere to, would receive
death rather than commit perjury. But the Romans, who say
that they believe in Christ, the more they swear to you and affirm their oaths, the more they plot against you to deceive you,
to take of your possessions or to slay you.[87] Alas, and what do
they gain by sinning against God? And how completely has the
sin which they commit dazzled them, that it has plucked them
out of their estates and they have become slaves of all the world.
What other people exists in the world today that is sold as slaves

Greek emperor of Nicaea. Robert of Flanders did not rule at Philadelphia,
though this may be a reference to Henri, Emperor Baldwin's brother, who
did lead a campaign in Asia Minor in 1204-5. Robert is confused with Henri
throughout the Chronicle, as in l. 1221 above.

[87] This passage (ll. 1249-55) is missing in P.

other than the Romans? But as each man does, so shall he receive.

But the story which I began to recite and to write, I am going to continue until I finish it. After Kyr Michael Palaiologos killed, I say, his little lord, the son, indeed, of the basileus Laskaris, and received the suzerainty over all the empire, he gathered armies, Turks and other nations, and he undertook a war to fight the Franks in Asia Minor, where he had the advantage. Now the emperor, Sir Robert, was not alive at the time I am telling you about, for he had been killed a few years earlier and his son Baldwin was ruling, he who lost the empire with his bad management.

Thereupon, Palaiologos came to an agreement with the Commune of Genoa and he gave them Galata, which is near the City, across the harbor; they built a quarter there and a large establishment;[88] they swore an oath and signed treaties with the basileus: that they be exempt from the *commercium*[89] in all of Romania, that they help him with galleys in all his battles, that they have their wages as mercenaries and their extra gifts.[90] Palaiologos equipped sixty galleys: he commanded that war be launched against the Venetians, because they were helping Baldwin; they held the entrances to the sea and the sea routes so that provisions

---

[88] *Ἀππλίκιν*. Schmitt derives this from Latin, *applicare* (*castra*), "to dwell or take up quarters." The word is used in the Chroni le elsewhere with this meaning (*viz.* ll.5047, 6435), where it means "to provide quarters." Here the word is used in apposition to χώρα ("town" or, as here, "quarter"). However, *ἀππλίκιν* may signify a landing place, this being derived from a second meaning of *applicare*, which is "to land or moor a ship." *Applicare* often means "to land" in fourteenth-century Latin (cf. Antonino Mango, *Relazioni tra Federico III di Sicilia e Giovanna I di Napoli* [Palermo, 1915], doc. L, p. 116, and Sp. P. Lampros, *Ἔγγραφα...* [1906], pt. 1, doc. 45, p. 83). The harbor referred to in this passage is the Golden Horn.

[89] *Ἀκουμέρκευτος*. The κουμέρκι (Lat. *commercium*) was a commercial tax, levied both as a sales tax and as a customs duty. It is discussed at length in Zakythinos, *Le Chrysobulle*, pp. 54-59. The treaty was signed at Nymphaeum on March 13, 1261. By its terms commercial supremacy in the Levant passed from Venice to Genoa.

[90] *Τὴν ρόγαν τους καὶ τὴν φιλοτιμίαν τους*. Ρόγα (Lat. *roga* from *rogare*) seems to be "a soldier's pay" and the verb ρογεύω means "to hire mercenaries." The φιλοτιμία seems to be some sort of largess or bonus, but apparently one that was included in the contract.

could not be brought into the City from anywhere. And he again crossed over to the neighborhood of the City with as many armies as he was able to muster; he shut in the City by land and by sea. And seeing this, the Romans who were in the City quickly came to terms with Palaiologos; they swore an oath, signed treaties, and showed him in. And, when Emperor Baldwin saw that the Roman people had betrayed him, he fled to the old palaces[91] with all the Franks who were with him, and there the Turks and Romans attacked him. Now, when Emperor Baldwin saw that they had closed him off in the old palaces—he had a peerless transport; it was large and splendid—he boarded this with three thousand others; they left the City, sailed across the sea, arrived in Monemvasia, and landed the ships there; they disembarked and arrived in Elis. Prince Guillaume was there at that time and, hearing that the emperor had come, went to meet him, for he honored him highly as the emperor which he was.[92] The emperor hurried to go to the West, hoping and expecting that the pope, with the Church, and the king of France would help him, would give him armies and great assistance so that he could return again to the City.

Thereupon, many of his troops remained there with Prince Guillaume with the expectation that the emperor would find them there on his return, which he hoped to make from there. These whom I now name remained. The first was Sir Ancelin, his surname was de Toucy, who was full brother of the then caesar of the City and who took to wife the mother of Sir Geoffroy de Tournay and remained in the land.[93] After him, there was

---

[91] Baldwin first took refuge in the palace of Blachernae, then, seeing the city, in flames, he fled across the city to the Great Palace, the Bucoleon, from whose small port he finally set sail from the city.

[92] The fugitives landed first in Euboea, then they went to Athens, then sailed from Piraeus and Monemvasia, and finally left for Apulia. Prince Guillaume throughout this period was a prisoner in the hands of Michael VIII.

[93] Ancelin de Toucy was the brother of Philippe de Toucy, *bailli* of the Emperor Baldwin. The title "Caesar" was usually reserved by the Byzantines for princes of the blood, but appears to have been used by the Latins for the *bailli* of Constantinople. Ancelin was captured at Pelagonia, but was released by Michael, who hoped to use him in his attack on Constantinople. For a detailed discussion of his capture, see Deno Geanakoplos, "The Battle of Pe-

Sir Vilain, his surname was d'Aunoy, who was at that time marshal of Romania; the prince gave him Arkadia as a benefaction.[94] The de Plancys and the de Brices remained. The d'Abys were four brothers and the d'Agnys, another two. Another was de l'Espinas and there remained many other esquires,[95] as well as Roman archons, whom I do not name for you because of the much writing it would require.

Hereafter, I will, from this point on, bring a halt to what I have been telling you, the deeds which were done by the Emperors Palaiologos and Baldwin, because I am trying to return to my subject, as I undertook it at the beginning of my discourse, and therefore bring an end to the beginning of the Prologue.[96]

How the Franks Won the Land of Morea

If you are learned and understand what I am writing to you, and versed in writing to grasp the meaning of what I am saying, you must have understood the prologue which I spoke in the beginning of my book, and told so minutely—as a beginning of the fundamentals, I told you the story of Syria, that of Asia Minor, and that of the City, how the Franks conquered those places—so that I shall now come, bearing you with me, to tell you minutely how the Franks, in like manner, conquered Morea as well.

And, if you have a desire to hear the deeds of good soldiers, to learn and be instructed, perhaps you will attain your wish. If you know letters, start reading; if, on the other hand, you are illiterate, sit down beside me and listen; and I hope, if you are wise, that you will benefit, for many who have come after them

lagonia," *Dumbarton Oaks Papers*, No. 7 (Cambridge, 1953), Appendix B, pp. 137-41.

[94] Vilain d'Aunoy was a cousin of Guillaume de Villehardouin and received from him the fief of Arkadia, carved out of the prince's domains. Arkadia is the medieval name for the ancient and modern Kyparissia, an important town on the gulf of that name.

[95] See below, p. 128, n. 59.

[96] In Buchon's edition, the Prologue ends with l. 1332, but Schmitt adds six lines in order to end it with the phrase indicating the end. The next line, 1339, is used as a title for the next and main part of the Chronicle.

have made much progress because of the tales of the old-timers.[97]

Therefore, I shall begin at this point, and listen to what I tell you. The wonderful count of Champagne—of whom I spoke to you in the beginning of this book, who began that crossing and expedition with the various other noblemen to go into Syria to the tomb of Christ—was chosen as leader and great captain over the armies which the pilgrims had at that time and he fell ill and died, as I have told you.[98] He had two other brothers, younger than he. And, when they heard and learned that those Franks, who were going to Syria with the blessings of the pope, had abandoned their trip, had gone to the City and had conquered Romania and were become lords, they took counsel together, these two brothers; one of them was to remain in their patrimonial estates and the other to go to Romania to win land.

Well, as are the fortunes of human comeliness, and brothers do not resemble one another in appearance nor in charm, the younger of the two brothers was somewhat the more skillful and prudent of the two. And the two brothers agreed that the elder would remain in his country, that of Champagne, and the younger of the two (Sir Guillaume, he was called, he had a surname of his own, they called him de Saluthe) would find as many armies as he could to take with him, and he would go to Romania to conquer some castles and towns to have as his estates.[99] Now,

[97] This whole passage is obscure. I cannot, however, understand the interpretation of Schmitt (S., xxxvii). In order to indicate that the author of the Chronicle was in contact with people who were alive during the period covered by the Chronicle, Schmitt declares that 1. 1344 *seq.* "does not so much refer to the accounts of the old conquerors as to those of the old men who came μετὰ ἐκεινῶν, *with them*, which in medieval Greek can also be interpreted *after them*...." This may very well be true, but no matter how one twists the sentence, it is impossible, so far as I can see, to derive from it the significance that Schmitt finds there. The phrase in question reads too easily to be as complicated as he finds it.

[98] Thibaud III. See above, p. 71, n. 17. Guillaume was not his brother, but a distant relative.

[99] Eudes, le Champenois, de Champlitte, and Guillaume, his brother, were sons of Eudes, son of Hugues of Champagne and Elisabeth of Burgundy. They received the name *Champenois* from their origin and the name *Champlitte* from the place to which Elisabeth fled when she was repudiated by her husband. The name *de Saluthe*, according to Schmitt, is a corruption of *Champlitte*. It

the count handed out to him all the money he had and he said to him: "Little brother, since I am staying here as lord in our castles and in our patrimonial estates, you take our money and all our common possessions and go with my dear blessing and with that of our father, as well, and I hope that, with God's mercy, you will have good fortune."[1]

Thereupon, he gathered and hired troops; he sent into Burgundy and many from there went with him, some taking pay as mercenaries to go to him; others, who were themselves bannerets and who were wealthy men, went with him, each to conquer what he could for himself. He sent word into Venice that ships be prepared, and as many as he wished and needed were quickly made ready. In the month of March they went there and crossed over from there and arrived in Morea on the first of May; they docked[2]

occurs in all the versions of the Chronicle and Schmitt argues that the French version must therefore be derived from the Greek, for a Frenchman, if he had written the original Chronicle, would have been familiar with the name *Champlitte*, whereas he might not recognize it in its corrupted form. But can we be sure that *Saluthe*, *Saluce*, and *Salut* are really corrupted forms of *Champlitte*? Was there not perhaps some such name by which he was known, which is lost to us?

[1] The arrival of Champlitte in Morea occurred under completely different circumstances. Guillaume had, in fact, gone to the East with the Fourth Crusade. He was with Boniface, king of Salonika, when he marched into Greece to claim his kingdom and subdue the penninsula. In the fall of 1204, a contingent of troops arrived in the East from the West, and it is possible that the author has confused this arrival and that of Geoffroy de Villehardouin, nephew of the chronicler, who arrived by accident in Morea at about the same time, with the arrival of Champlitte and Boniface in Attica. Geoffroy became involved in local Moreot affairs in the fall and winter of 1204 and, seeing a great opportunity in the unsettled state of the area, he rode to meet with Champlitte, who was taking part in the siege of Nauplia at the time, and to convince him to return with him and lead a conquest of Morea. Champlitte agreed and returned with Geoffroy.

[2] Ἀποσκάλωσαν. This word is derived from σκάλα (Lat. *scala*) which means a ladder or flight of steps Schmitt also gives it the meanings *station* and *mountain pass* This latter, he derives from the Κακὴ Σκάλα, a pass called the "Evil" or "Difficult Stairway" for obvious reasons. (See l. 3260 below.) The word is used in reference to a pass only in this sense and its meaning cannot be extended to include "pass." Zakythinos (*Le Chrysobulle*, pp. 51-52) indicates that a σκάλα was a landing place. The word ἀποσκαλώνω

at a place called Achaia, which is around fifteen miles this side of Patras;[3] they immediately built a castle, all of brick. Now, at the time of which I speak and in that season, all the land of Morea, which comprises what they call the Peloponnesos, thus they call it, had throughout its breadth only twelve castles. Well, when they disembarked at Achaia, they brought the horses out from the transports and they stayed there a couple of days until they might rest them. And afterwards they rode out and went to Patras; they surrounded the castle, as well as the town, set up the trebuchets around on all sides, placed the arbalesters, and began the battle; and from the multitude of troops and the courageousness of the battle, on the first assault, they broke into the outer town. And, after they had taken the town, those who were in the castle quickly came to an agreement also and surrendered the castle on terms and condition that they keep their property, each his house and what was his.

And, when they had captured Patras, they placed guards, provisioned the castle and likewise the town with troops and arms, as was right and fitting; and, from there they returned to Achaia. They took counsel with the local Romans, who knew the places and the condition of each one, and these spoke and advised them that Andravida was the most splendid town in the plain of Morea;[4] it lay in the plain, an open town, having no towers nor walls what-

---

would then mean "to dock" or "to disembark," not "to stop at a station." There was a Byzantine maritime tax called the σκαλιατικόν, which further strengthens this meaning of the word.

[3] The Achaia here referred to is the modern Kato-Achaia, which lies to the west of Patras. I have translated the phrase ἐδῶθεν τῆς Πάτρου as "this side of Patras." The word ἐδῶθεν means "from here" or "hence"; thus the passage might be read "fifteen miles from Patras, further from here": i.e., "the other side of Patras." But in line 3167 we find the statement that "Geraki is ἐδῶθεν of Helos." Helos borders on the coast; therefore Geraki, which is to the north, must be "this side of" Helos and not "the other side of Helos," which would place it in the sea. This confirms the theory stated in the Introduction that H. was probably written in the Arkadian court, which did lie between Patras and Helos.

[4] Andravida was the principal city of Elis and lay in "the Plain of Morea," the region through which the Peneios River flows in its lower reaches. The city became a favorite of the princes of Morea and their capital.

ever around it. Thereupon, they set out for there, straightway they went, and they unfurled the banners of each army; and after they had come close to Andravida and the Andravisaioi[5] learned that the Franks were coming, the archons and the commons of the town of Andravida went out with the crosses and the ikons and went to do homage to the Champenois.[6] And he, as an all-prudent man, received them well, and he swore and promised them he would not act unjustly towards them, nor would they receive damage to their estates, but would have honor, gifts, and great beneficences; all swore to him that they would die his slaves.[7]

And, when he had gratified the town of Andravida, he took counsel with them as to where he should march. Thereupon, the counsel was given him that they go to Corinth, for it was a formidable castle, the finest of Romania, and was the capital which governed all of the Peloponnesos, which is included in Morea. For, if God were to grant that Corinth do homage, all the other castles of the land of Morea, without sword and battle, would do homage.

And, after this counsel which I am telling you was given, he appointed troops to be left in Andravida, others in Achaia, and

[5] The people of Andravida are still called by this name. Longnon (*Livre de la conquête de la princée de l'Amorée. Chronique de Morée: 1204-1305* [Paris, 1911], p. xcix) contends that the name Andravida is Slavic and means "place of otters" (*pays de la loutre*). Dragoumis, however, questions this. (*Χρονικῶν Μορέως, τοπωνυμικά* ... [Athens, 1921], p. 6, note.)

[6] This was the customary Byzantine manner of greeting an overlord. The people of Greece, oppressed by the local lords and tired of their constant petty wars, welcomed the Franks as deliverers. The state of affairs in Attica at the time of the arrival of Boniface is graphically described by Michael Choniates (Acominatus) in a memorial to Alexios III (*Τὰ Σωζόμενα*, ed. Sp. Lampros [Athens, 1879-80]), and his brother Nicetus Choniates (Acominatus), historian of the period, observes bitterly that Boniface was received by the local Greeks "as someone who is returning to his home after a long absence" (*Historia*, in Migne, *PG*, CXXXIX, ch. 9, pp. 805-6). The Chronicle refers to Champlitte hereafter as *Καμπανέσης*. The French version calls him "le Champenois."

[7] *Δοῦλοι*. Perhaps "slaves" is too strong. The verb *δουλεύω* in this period seems to have been the Greek way of expressing the performance of feudal service or the position of a liege man. *Δοῦλοι*, then, is perhaps better translated as "vassals."

a third group in Patras, and he ordered the ships to put out to sea and he, with the rest of the troops of the army, set out from Vostitsa[8] and went to Corinth. And after they had arrived at the town, they set up tents around it and encamped.

Now, the castle of Corinth lies upon a mountain crag (it is a hill made by God and what man shall praise it?) while the town lies below on the plain, well enclosed, indeed, with towers and walls. Well, there happened to be there, at the time that I am writing to you about, a certain great man and formidable soldier, and he held Corinth and also Argos and Nauplion; as governor and rightful lord, he held them on the part of the basileus of the Romans—he was named Sgouros,[9] this was his surname—and when he was informed that the Franks were coming, he led out of the town the women and children, as well as the little people who carried arms, and led them up into the castle of Corinth; and he remained in the town with all those who held arms to defend it.

Now, after the Champenois had arrived,[10] as I have told you, at the town of Corinth, he stationed his armies and surrounded it. He allowed them to rest that day; but on the following morning, as soon as day broke, they blew their trumpets and began the battle. They fired the trebuchets from all sides at the towers, and the arbalests did not allow a man to lean forward out through the

8 Vostitsa is a port on the Gulf of Corinth, east of Patras.

9 Leon Sgouros was a petty tyrant who was plaguing the towns of Greece during the disorders attendant upon the Fourth Crusade. His father was some sort of lordling, theoretically a governor of the basileus, in the town of Naupaktos. Leon, succeeding to the power, took advantage of the fall of the capital and extended his power to Corinth and Argos. The energetic metropolitan of Athens, Michael Acominatus, repelled his attack on Athens, but he moved on to take Thebes. When Boniface began his march into Greece in 1204, Leon Sgouros decided to resist him at Thermopylae but, as Nicetas says bitingly, at one look at the Franks, he turned and ran. He retreated into the citadel of Corinth where he held out until 1208, when he committed suicide in desperation by leaping with his horse from the walls of the castle.

10 The assault on Corinth was begun by Boniface himself, who built a small fortress, which he named Mont Escovée, to help in the siege, which he later entrusted to Jacques d'Avesnes. It was during the early days of the siege that Geoffroy de Villehardouin arrived to procure the help of Champlitte.

teeth of the wall to see who was shooting. They placed their ladders
against the walls, and they entered immediately and captured
the town. Those who surrendered found mercy; those who continued to fight were killed by the sword. Sgouros, indeed, prudent
and villainous man[11] that he was, fled and went up to the castle.

And, after the Franks had captured the town of Corinth, the
Champenois ordered a proclamation drawn up, declaring that those
of the towns in the neighborhood of Corinth that would do homage
and would receive him for lord would have honor and beneficence,
a fine reception; but those who resorted to war would not find
mercy. On hearing this, the archons and likewise the commons
began to go up, small and great, from the town of Damala and
from as far away as Hagion Oros;[12] all who heard of it went with
great eagerness and swore to the Champenois to die his slaves;
and he received them with great joy. Far and wide the report
then spread that the Franks had captured the castle of Corinth
and that they had an outstanding lord, whom they called Champenois.

In that year and season when the Champenois went and landed
in Achaia, as I told you before (it seems to me that I wrote you
in the prologue of the book that, only one year, indeed, after the
capture of Constantinople, the Champenois went to conquer

[11] Βέβηλος. In Attic Greek the word has the meaning of "profane" or "stained
with crime," which latter is the meaning given by Schmitt. This sudden and
complete reversal of opinion about Sgouros, who is called "great man" in l.
1464, "rightful lord" in l. 1466, and is thoughtful of the women and children
in l. 1470, can only be explained by examining the French version, which
says at this point: *mais cellui Sguro qui appeleres et vaillans estoit....* Βέβηλος
in the fourteenth century was pronounced as *vévilos* and K. suggests inade-
quately (p. 63, n. 1488) that βέβηλος is derived from *vaillans*. It seems obvious
that what has happened is that the author of the Greek Chronicle, transcribing
or, as I believe, translating, the original Chronicle, mistook *vaillans* (valiant)
for *vilain* (villain) and that the sound of the latter suggested *vévilos*, which
would also correspond in meaning. P. goes one step further, drops βέβηλος,
and substitutes πονηρός (evil). Schmitt seems to have missed the significance
of this word completely.

[12] Damala, ancient Troezen, near the end of the peninsula of Argolis, was
an important episcopal see in the Middle Ages. Hagion Oros, now called
Agionorion, lies to the south of Corinth about halfway to Argos.

Morea, as I have told you), well, as the report spread and was being heard, Boniface, king of Salonika, happened to be in Vlachia with his armies; and there was with him that praiseworthy man who was called Sir Geoffroy, Villehardouin, his surname.[13] Thereupon, they agreed, on hearing the report, to go to Corinth to see the Champenois; as they had decided it in council, so did they carry it out and they went to Corinth and found the Champenois; they held a great celebration when they met there, for they had been very eager to join one another.

Afterwards, they decided in council to go to Argos; they took their armies and went there. The castle lies on a hill and is well fortified, whereas the large town of the city of Argos[14] lies in a plain like an opened tent; arriving there, they gave battle and entered within.

Now, Sgouros, that laudable soldier, who was in the castle of Corinth, seeing that the Frankish armies had departed, came down during the night and entered the town with as many men as he could bring with him. He caused great havoc, a massacre among the Franks, who, full of confidence, happened to be in the town; indeed, those who were healthy in their bodies and had time to arm themselves, these gave battle, and those who were sick and were lying in delirium, all these were butchered at once, not one was spared.

That same night, the report sped to the Champenois, I tell you, there where he was in Argos; he was very sadly grieved for the sick who had been slaughtered in their beds; he left the town of Argos well provisioned; good soldiers remained to guard it, and he returned to Corinth. And, after he had returned there, he tarried with the king of Salonika, Sir Boniface; around six or eight days, indeed, they stayed there. Then, the king sought to take

[13] This account is, as the reader has more than once been warned, a muddle of inaccuracy.

[14] In the Chronicle, the word χώρα is used throughout to mean "city" or "town." Occasionally, as here, the word is used with the word πόλις, the classic word for "city." The expression χώρα τῆς πόλεως must mean the town of the city, distinguishing town from castle. However, the word μπούρκος (bourg or burg) is also used in this sense (ll. 1687 and 8236). The expression χώρα τῆς Πόλεως (ll. 532, 583, etc.) means simply "the city of Constantinople."

leave. Thereupon, the Champenois asked of him a boon, that he afford him an aid and provision, that he help him in some way from his kingdom. And he, indeed, as the nobleman and king that he was, gave him and granted him the homage of the lord of Athens (Great Lord he was called, thus they named him who was then lord of Athens—they had, indeed, this name from the Hellenes)[15] and he likewise gave him the three homages of the lords of Euripos and also that of the lord of Boudonitsa, which the marquis held, that they might hold them from him and consider him their lord.[16] Now, the lord of Athens was from Burgundy; the three lords of Euripos that I speak of were from Verona, from Lombardy.[17] The king ordered that they be written to go to the Champenois; and after they had gone to where the Champenois was, the king, himself, released them to have the Champenois as lord, and afterwards he bade them farewell and went his way. Now, Sir Geoffroy, who had come with the king of Salonika, when he was about to depart, spoke to him and besought his permission to remain there with his lord, whom he considered his rightful lord, the Champenois, I tell you, whom he was very eager to see, to join, and to remain with.[18]

[15] The title μεγασκὺρ or μέγας κύρης is entirely medieval in origin and has no reference whatever to ancient Greece. The supposed classical origin of the title was, however, assumed by both Dante and Boccaccio, who apply it to Theseus, legendary hero of ancient Attica. See Schmitt, "La Théséide de Boccace et la Théséide grecque," in Etudes de philologie néo-grecque, (Bibliothèque de l'École des Hautes Études, 92d fas.), Paris, 1892.

[16] Thi account is incorrect. Boniface made no land grants to Champlitte whatever. Later, in 1210-12, Othon de la Roche (lord of Athens 1204-25) assisted Geoffroy de Villehardouin in his campaign to subdue the Corinth-Argos region and in return was granted the suzerainty of Argos and Nauplion, thereby becoming Geoffroy's vassal. Boudonitsa and Euboea came under the suzerainty of Geoffroy II much later, in 1236.

[17] As Boniface marched through Greece in 1204, he distributed lands and castles to his followers. The area around the pass of Thermopylae was given to Marquis Guido Pallavicini, whose successors retained the rank of marquis of Boudonitsa. Athens and Thebes, with surrounding territory, were given to the Burgundian noble, Othon de la Roche, who took the title "Megaskyr" and the rank of duke. The land of Euboea (Euripos or Negroponte) was divided by Boniface among three Veronese nobles, who were thereafter called the terzieri or "triarchs" of Euripos.

[18] The Chronicle here again confuses Geoffroy, the Chronicler, with his

And so, after the king of Salonika had departed and Sir Geoffroy had remained, as the shrewd man that he was, he asked the archons, the local Romans, who knew the places, the castles, and the towns of all of the Peloponnesos that is included in Morea, to explain to him the circumstance of each one; and as soon as he had inquired fully and had been informed, he called the Champenois and said to him: "Lord, I, as a stranger, indeed, to this land, have questioned the archons who are with you; and as I was informed by them of the truth, so did I see with my own eyes the castles of Corinth, of Argos and of Nauplion and the strength which they have. If you were to stay to besiege them, you would lose what you have undertaken and would be ruined; for the castles are strong, well-provisioned, and you will in no way be able to take them by assault; but, as I have been informed by good men, from Patras on as far as Korone[19] the towns are more spread out and there are fields and wooded places, so that you may pass freely with all your armies. And, when you capture the towns and they do homage to you, should the castles remain, how long can they hold out? So order the ships to go by sea and let us all go by land; and after we arrive there where you have your troops in the land that you have taken, I hope, by your destiny and by God's mercy, that you may derive great profit."

Hearing this, the noble Champenois thanked his marshal broadly; he ordered that the town of Corinth be provisioned; he left good armies to guard the land; and just as Sir Geoffroy had said and had advised, so did he carry it out and they went to Morea. They went out from Patras and arrived in Andravida, where were the archons of the plain of Morea. And then Sir Geoffroy, as the wise man that he was, gathered the archons together and said to them: "Archons, friends and brothers, and, henceforth, comrades, behold and gaze upon this lord, who has come here to your lands to take

nephew. There also seems to be a slight allusion in the phrase "considered his rightful lord" to Champlitte as a claimant to the county of Champagne, perhaps as the younger brother of the count of Champagne, as the Chronicle mistakenly calls him in ll. 1379-80.

[19] Korone lies at the entrance of the Gulf of Messene on the southern coast of the Peloponnesos.

possession of them; think not, archons, that he has come for booty, to take clothes and animals and then to depart from here; I tell these facts to you as the wise men I see you to be; behold his armies and his noble bearing; he is a lord, an emperor, and he has come to conquer. You do not have a lord to protect you; and if our armies should advance to plunder your land, and your towns be captured and your men slaughtered, afterwards, what will you do when you will have repented? Therefore, it seems to me better for you that we come to terms whereby murders, lootings, and the taking of prisoners will not take place in your patrimonies and you, who are wise and know the others, who are, I say, your relatives, friends and comrades, will prevail upon them to do homage."[20]

When the archons heard this, all did homage to him and sent their envoys to all the places in which they knew there were friends and relatives of theirs; they disclosed the matter to them and informed them of it; they sent them a statement of leniency[21] from the Champenois; all those who wished to go to do him homage would keep their patrimonies and he would give them others in addition; all those who were worthy and proved useful would have great honor.

And when the archons and also the commons heard this, they began to come in and all did homage; and when they had gathered in Andravida, the archons of Elis and of all Mesarea,[22] they made an agreement with the Champenois that all the lesser archons who had fiefs would retain, each one of them, the homage and military service consonant with his rank, so much would remain to him, and the rest, the greater part, the Franks would divide among themselves and the peasants of the villages would remain

[20] In other words, in return for having their patrimonies spared, the archons of Elis must prevail upon the other archons of the Peloponnesos to do homage to the Franks.

[21] Ἀφροντισία.

[22] Note that the Chronicle draws a distinction between the archons of Elis and those of the central Peloponnesos. Mesarea is the medieval name for Arkadia. See A. Meliarakes, Μεσαρέα. Ἱστορικαὶ ἔρευναι περὶ τοῦ ὀνόματος τούτου ὡς γεωγραφικοῦ (Athens, 1893) and G. N. Hatzidakes, Περὶ τοῦ ἐτύμου τῆς λέξεως Μεσαρέας, in Ἀθηνᾶ, VI, 3-64, and XII, 205-6.

as they had found them. They appointed six archons and another six Franks, who distributed the lands and the fiefs.[23]

And, when they had settled this that I have been telling you about, the marshal Sir Geoffroy came into the council where they sat and said to the Champenois; "Lord, you must perceive and have it understood that you are far away from your patrimonial estates; you have here many armies which are in your pay; the ships cost more than the troops; for this reason, I tell you and I advise you not to lose your time and your troops. I have been informed by your archons; here, close to us, lies the castle of Pondikos,[24] which is on the coast; let us go there; beyond this is Arkadia,[25] and after this Korone,[26] and just a bit further on is Kalamata[27]. Those four castles which I have named are on the coast and I say this, lord; as long as we have the ships, let us go there to take those castles, which have harbors in places which suit us and we find convenient."[28]

When the noble Champenois and all the rest of the other leaders of his council heard these things, they praised Sir Geoffroy and approved of his words; they readied their armies and likewise their ships; they arrived at Pondikos and attacked it. The castle was low-walled; by sword, they took it and placed good troops within

---

[23] L. states that the assessment and distribution was assigned to Geoffroy de Villehardouin "and many other nobles, as well as to noble and wise Greeks of the land."

[24] Πονδικοῦ τὸ κάστρον. This castle, standing in ruins outside the modern seaport of Katakolon, is today called Pontikokastro or Mouse Castle. Greek historians of the period give the name as Ποντικόν, as does L. de F. (§ 110). This latter work adds the information that the castle was an ancient one repaired by the Franks and renamed Belveder or Beauvoir. L. calls it Beauvoir (§ 75, § 178, etc.). In the Greek Chronicle, the name is given variously as Πονδικοῦ and Ποντικοῦ in H. and Ποντικόν and even Μποντικόν in P.

[25] See above, p. 106, n. 94.

[26] See above, p. 115, n. 19.

[27] Kalamata lies at the head of the Gulf of Messene. It is still one of the principal towns of the Peloponnesos.

[28] The punctuation of this passage as given in Schmitt and Kalonaros makes it obscure. I have translated the singular Τὸ μέρος as "places." However, the meaning may be "to take those castles, which have harbors, at whatever time it suits us and we find convenient."

it as guards; and when the castle of Pondikos had been provisioned, his ships set sail and went by sea, while he arrived at Arkadia by land; they found the sea rough and there was no harbor for the ships to take and come to anchor.

Thereupon, they decided in council not to attack the castle then, that time they went there, but, as long as they had the ships, to go to the castles which were on the coast and had harbors. However, some of their infantry ran forward and fought their way into the bourg;[29] and as many as they caught they put to the sword on the spot; and as many as were able to flee entered the castle.

Thereupon, they fitted out the ships and went straightway to Methone,[30] they found the castle deserted, it was completely destroyed; the Venetians had destroyed it earlier, because the Romans used to keep their ships there and had been stopping and looting ships of the Venetians. And then they set out and went to the castle of Korone, and they found the castle with low walls and towers; it lay upon a precipitous crag[31] and was fortified; but, arriving there, the ships encircled it all around. The knights and the foot soldiers began the battle; they set up the trebuchets and struck repeatedly at them therein; indeed those Koronians who were inside the castle had no possibility whatever to stand

---

[29] Μπούρκος.

[30] Methone, often called Modon, lies on the southwest point of Messinia. Villehardouin in his history states that when Champlitte and Villehardouin, the younger, left the army of Boniface, they advanced as far as Methone, which they found in a state of ruin. They improvised immediate repairs in the walls, for Michael Doukas, the first ruler of Arta, had stumbled upon them and was preparing to attack. The Franks met the Greeks after one day's march, defeated them, and brought rich spoils back to Methone. After this they received Korone by treaty and finally Kalamata. (*Conq. de Const.* § 328-30.)

[31] Εἰς βράχον σπηλαίου. This expression is obscure. The word σπήλαιον obviously does not carry its ordinary meaning of "cavern" here nor in ll. 1770, 1773, 2804, and 3005, but signifies a cliff or steep rock. Schmitt makes no note of this in his Index, but Kalonaros equates the phrase to the *pierre bise* of L. The use of the genitive here in l. 1697 offers a hopeless redundancy (lit. "upon a rock of a steep rock"). P. reads εἰς βράχον ἦτον, σπήλαιον, which indicates that the υ of the genitive is simply an error for the ν of the accusative.

upon the walls; seeing the multitude of troops and the boldness
of the attack, they cried out and asked that they be pardoned,
that they would surrender the castle to them, with the proviso
that they would swear to them that they would have their houses
and likewise their patrimonies. The marshal Sir Geoffroy heard
this; quickly he promised them; the battle was stilled; the Franks
entered within and received the castle; they placed provisions
within and troops of their own, and on the following day they set
out and went to Kalamata. They found the castle dilapidated,
it was being used as a monastery; arriving before it, they attacked
it and took it by the sword; the defenders surrendered it on terms,
as the others had done.[32]

Now, as soon as the Romans in Nikli,[33] those of Veligosti,[34]

---

[32] Villehardouin states (Conq. de Const. § 330) that the castle of Kalamata
was strong and splendid and that it was captured by the Franks only after
a long and difficult siege. The word Kalamata is given as Chalemate by Villehardouin, Calemate in L., and variously as Kalommata, Kallomata, Kalomata, etc., in the Greek versions. N. Polites has maintained (in Λαογραφία,
Σύμμεικτα A, pp. 142-45) that the name Kalamata is derived from the forms
Kalomata and Kalommata, which in turn are derived from some eikon of a
Madonna of the Beautiful Eyes (Παναγίας καλομάτας), but this seems un-
necessarily far-fetched, as variations in the spelling of proper names occur
throughout the Chronicles.

[33] Nikli or Amyklion lay in Arkadia in the plain of ancient Tegea. This
passage would indicate that the town predates the Frankish conquest. However, Dragoumis in a complicated analysis ('Aθηνᾶ, XXIII, 393-412) insists
that Nikli was originally an episcopal see, then a castle in the time of Guillaume
de Champlitte, and finally a town built by Guillaume II Villehardouin in 1248-
50. He suggests that it was located near the present town of Steno, north of
Tripolis. It was destroyed in 1296 (see L. de F. § 267, 485) by the Byzantines
and replaced by two castles in the hills, "Mucli and Cepiana." Dragoumis
identifies these as Tsipiana, west of Mt. Artemesius, and Palaeo-Mouchli,
on the north slope of Mt. Parthenus. Lognon places Nikli at modern
Palaeo-Episcopi; Kalonaris puts it at Piali. In any case, the very involved
discussion of Dragoumis notwithstanding, the town can be placed at best
close to ancient Tegea or modern Tripolis.

[34] Veligosti (Veligourt in French). According to the research of Buchon
(La Grèce continentale et la Morée [Paris, 1843], pp. 480 seq.), Veligosti lay to
the west of Leondari and close to the town of Samara, which, in fact, has been
called Veligosti since 1918. Dragoumis has questioned this identification in
Χρ. Μορ. Τοπ. .., pp. 69-84.

and those of Lakedaemonia[35] learned of it, they all gathered together, foot soldiers and knights; their foot soldiers came from
the zygoi of the Melings;[36] they came from the villages of Lakkos[37]
and arrived at Chrysorea, where they heard and learned that the
Franks had come, and they marched out from the villages and
began to plunder and said and planned that they would defeat
them. They were led to the place called Kapeskianous, to a spot
which bears the name "at the olive grove of Kountoura." There
were four thousand of them, foot soldiers and knights. Now,
when the Franks learned of this, again from the Romans who
were with them and who knew the land, they led them there and
they went and found them and they waged battle, the Franks
and Romans.[38] And the Franks, foot soldiers and knights, were
only 700 in number, so many were they reckoned. The Romans
began the battle with eagerness, because they saw them so few;
later, they repented. Why should I tell you the many details and

---

[35] Lakedaimonia (Lakodaimonia, Lakkodaimonia). Medieval Sparta.

[36] Οἱ ζυγοὶ τῶν Μελιγῶν. The original meaning of ζυγός is "yoke,"
but here it means "defile" or "ridge." The Melings were one of the most important tribes of Slavs in the Peloponnesos. They are mentioned as early as
the tenth century by Constantine VII Porphyrogenitos (De admin. imp., III,
pp. 220 seq.) when he is discussing events of the eighth and ninth centuries.
The territory they inhabited stretched across the northern half of Lakonia
and down the Taygetos Mountains from Mistra to Passava. The Chronicle
seems to include the peninsula of Maine in their territory. Dorotheos of Monemvasia (Pseudodorotheos) confuses ζυγοὶ τῶν Μελιγγῶν with Maine. (Βιβλίον ἱστορικόν, etc. [Venice, 1814], p. 476.) Maine undoubtedly included
the whole peninsula south of Mistra at that time.

[37] Schmitt in his Index quotes Buchon, who identifies Lakkos as either a
valley in Messinia extending from Makry-Plagi to Kalamata or a vast plain
near Makry-Plagi. From the context here, the latter identification seems the
correct one. I have not been able to identify Chrysorea, though the Chronicle
states here that it lies somewhere between the villages of Lakkos and Kapeskianous, which with its nearby olive grove is also impossible to locate exactly,
though according to the Chronicle it lay within a day's march of Kalamata.

[38] This battle was the only pitched battle of the Frankish conquest and
decided the fate of Greek Morea. The Moreot Greeks, aided by their ally
Michael I, ruler of Arta, were decisively defeated. Though Villehardouin
states (see above, p. 118, n. 30) that the battle took place before the capture
of Korone and Kalamata, the Chronicle is probably correct in placing the battle
after these events.

what would be my gain? The Franks won the battle at that time; they killed them all, few escaped them. That was the only battle that the Romans fought during the time that the Franks conquered Morea.

And, after the Franks had won Kalamata, they saw the land was fertile, spacious and delightful with its fields and waters and multitude of pastures. The Champenois gave orders to all his ships, each one of them, to come there where he was; for the Roman archons informed him that he would need them no longer. So he ordered that provisions, many weapons, and also arbalesters be taken out of the transports. And, as they were crossing the land of Kalamata and he was resting his horses as well as his troops, he took counsel as to where to go and where to ride. Thereupon, the Romans and the leaders of his council said they should go to Veligosti and from there to Nikli, for these were the chief places in all Morea; both of them lay in the plain and they would take them quickly; and from there, furthermore, they should go to Lakedaemonia. And then the marshal Sir Geoffroy said and advised that they go to Arkadia and seize the castle so that the land might grow broader, and that they send troops against Araklovon, which commands the *drongos* which is called Skorta;[39] it was a small castle but sat upon a rocky hill and was well fortified; it was said that one of the Voutsarades was holding it, his name was Doxapatres[40] and he was a great soldier; "and after we have

---

[39] Araklovon or Oreoklovon ("mountain-cage"?) lay north of Karytaina. The district of Skorta (δρόγγος τῶν Σκορτῶν) is a mountainous country lying chiefly in western Arcadia. Within it lay the two castles of Karytaina and Akova. The word δρόγγος presents many problems to the translator. According to Schmitt the original meaning was: (1) "a military detachment" and (2) "a heap," "a group" (Lat. *drungus* from the Germanic *throng*). He, however, gives it the meaning of defile. In the Chronicle (l. 2993) it is used synonymously with ζυγός. The two words apparently mean a mountain ridge, or defile between mountains and, by an extended meaning, a territory comprising many such ridges or defiles. Araklovon lay within the δρόγγος strategically placed to command communication between the upper and lower valleys of the Alpheios. The Frankish name for the castle was Bucelet.

[40] The Voutsarades were one of the great families of Morea and were in possession of Araklovon before the conquest. Doxapatres became one of the

taken that place also and our territory is widened, then let us go to those other places." Just as Sir Geoffroy advised, so did the Champenois, himself, determine it would be. He ordered that all their trumpets be sounded and, straightway, they mounted, set out, and departed. They arrived at Arkadia at the hour of noon; they set out their camps and set up their tents in the field; they demanded the castle, but they would not cede it, for the castle lay at the top of a cliff and they had a strong tower, dating even from the time of the Hellenes; they had abundant supplies and hoped to withstand the battle and the assault and not surrender.[41] That day passed and the next dawned; the Champenois ordered the trebuchets to be set up and they began to fight up around the castle. From the one side, they attacked with the trebuchets; while behind and in front were the arbalesters. When the Arkadinoi who were in the castle saw that they could not withstand the strong attack, they sent up a strident cry that the assault be halted; they agreed to surrender the castle; and immediately the marshal Sir Geoffroy ordered the generals to halt the attack. The Arkadinoi asked that he pardon them and that with their dependencies they be granted immunity; they quickly swore an oath and surrendered the castle.

And, after the Champenois received the castle, they tarried there only two days; and then certain envoys arrived there; they held letters which they brought from France, and they gave them to the Champenois and bowed before him; he bade them by their mouths "to declare the messages." And mournfully with tears in their eyes they said to him: "Know, our lord, your brother has died, he who was your elder brother, the count of Champagne.[42] The archons of your domain, all the bannerets, likewise all the common people who are your chattels urge and beseech you to go there quickly, for they have no other rightful lord but you. The

heroes of the Greek resistance. L. de F. states that he was most powerful, bearing the heaviest of armor and a fearsome club (§ 111).

[41] The Franks had bypassed the castle of Arkadia on their march down the coast. (See ll. 1679 *seq.*) L. calls its walls "the work of giants" (§ 115).

[42] Louis de Champlitte, older brother of Guillaume, died in 1209. He was not "count of Champagne," but lord of the castle of Champlitte in Burgundy.

king of France, from whom you hold your fief, is very desirous and impatient that you arrive at once; your relatives and all the nobles of the West, all write to you and beseech you to go there quickly."

When the noble Champenois heard these words, he was greatly sorrowed as a prudent young man and wept a great deal, I tell you, and entered deep grief and then he ordered that the leaders of his army and his first counselor, Sir Geoffroy, be called and he spoke to them as a wise man and said to them: "Archons, friends and brothers, comrades, soldiers, I place God as a witness to the sorrow which I have for the death of my lord and brother. Furthermore, I am also grieved and I feel great uneasiness for that which I have undertaken, for I came to Romania to receive glory and honor and to conquer land; and though I undertook it and was pursuing it to the end, I have lost my hopes and they are dashed to the ground, and the opposite has come to me in both my intentions. However, as I have always heard from old men,[43] who tell us and instruct us—those of us who suffer misfortune—to have patience and in this way we shall profit; therefore, I say to you, I beseech you all to counsel me as is fitting and seemly so that I may do the proper thing as will befit your honor and so that non will find fault with you who are my followers."

Thereupon, this is the counsel that was given and whis is that was done: that Sir Geoffroy be the marshal and that, together with two bishops, two bannerets, and five more archons he divide the lands, giving to each man according to the rank that he held and the troops and arms that he had in the army.[44] Thereupon, these ten men alone sat together and made a list of the troops and the leaders of the army. Then, after they had listed the lands and had distributed them, those ten of whom I am speaking brought the lists and gave and presented them to the Champenois; and when they had read them aloud and had disclosed them, all praised them, as did the Champenois, himself; because there was written in that distribution

[43] Ancients?

[44] The Chronicler here seems somewhat confused, for earlier he states that the lands were divided by a committee composed of six Greeks and six Franks under the direction of Villehardouin. (See above, l. 1649.)

nothing for Sir Geoffroy, his marshal, he was greatly astonished
and he declared and praised him for his arrangements, his wisdom
and his graces. Thereupon, he spoke to him: "Sir Geoffroy," he
said to him—before everyone, he called to him and spoke to him
aloud—"I have been informed, with truth I say it to you, that
you gave the initial impetus and advice at that time to my lord
and brother for the Syrian expedition, and he was made captain.[45]
And, when it happened, by great misfortune, that my brother died,
you would by no means suffer that the expedition be abandoned
and you all went to Romania and captured the City. Indeed,
all the achievements and the great deeds, you counseled them
and arranged them, and when you heard that I was come here
to Morea, the share which was your due to take from the conquest,
the emperor Baldwin and all your comrades, all these you left
behind and came to me; and it would be a sin, a great reproach,
were I not to reward you as is proper and seemly. Therefore, I
wish to give you to hold as your patrimonial estate Kalamata and
Arkadia with the land around them."[46] So he invested him on
the spot with a gold ring and, when he had been invested and had
done him homage, he called him again and said to him: "Sir Geoffroy, henceforth you are my liege man, for you hold your land
by my suzerainty, and it behooves you to be truthful to me in
all things, and me, on the other hand, to entrust to your care all
my affairs. Well, since I have to go to France, I request and command you for love of me to receive and hold the land which I have
won here in Morea and to safeguard it for me; you will be my *bailli*
in such manner and motive that you will hold the suzerainty

[45] Here again is the Chronicler's confusion between the two Villehardouin
and between Thibault, count of Champagne, and an elder brother of Guillaume
de Champlitte.

[46] Villehardouin in his History claims that his nephew was given Korone
(§ 330), but as Longnon points out (Lg., p. 73, n. 3), Kalamata was of the two
the more appropriate fief with which to reward Geoffroy for his important
role in the conquest. He further points out that if Villehardouin's statement
be accepted, then we have to assume that after the Venetians captured Korone
in the campaign of 1206-7, the Villehardouin were then given Kalamata, for
they remained the lords of that fief throughout the Frankish occupation
(Lg., pp. 73, 90).

as I myself would do. And if, on the one hand, it should please me and occur to me to send another of my men from among my relatives within one year, you will surrender to him the land and the suzerainty and you will then hold your land from him. And if, on the other hand, the time passes, the time limit of one year, and no one comes here to take over the suzerainty, it is my wish and desire and I hereby give you my word that you will remain lord after me, lord by inheritance."[47]

Thereupon, Sir Geoffroy, as the wise man that he was, bowed before him and he spoke and thanked him for the honor and praise to which he bore witness and, secondly, for the gift which he had made him; thus the bailliage of Morea and the suzerainty of the land, these he received according to the terms set forth by the Champenois; he ordered that the documents containing those agreements be written; these were drawn up with oaths and then the bannerets, the bishops, and the leaders of the army put their seals to them.

And. as soon as they had arranged these agreements, the Champenois made ready, set out, and departed; he would take with him only two knights and twelve squires; he made the crossing by galley and went to Venice and he passed straight over to France, to Champagne; and Sir Geoffroy remained in the land as lord.

Now, after Sir Geoffroy had remained as *bailli* and lord of Morea, as I have been telling you, he ordered that there gather in Andravida his troops which were at that time under the jurisdiction of the lordship, as it was; and as soon as the gathering of small and great was met, he called for the book in which was written the share of each man and that which had been allotted to each to hold and administer by the Champenois. Therein were listed all those who were enfeoffed.[48]

---

[47] Guillaume left for France some time around 1208 and died a short time later. Before leaving he formally appointed as his *bailli* his nephew Hugues de Champlitte, not Villehardouin. Hugues, however, died soon after and Geoffroy became *bailli*. He was probably elected by the local barons and not appointed by Champlitte as the Chronicle would have us believe. He became *bailli* some time before May, 1209, for he appears at the Council of Ravennika as the representative from Morea and there Emperor Henry affirms his fief and office (see Lg., p. 111).

[48] Here follows the register of the twelve major baronies of Morea, often called

The first who was listed was Sir Gautier, de Rosières was his surname, thus was he named; he held twenty-four knights' fees; he was given a holding in Mesarea; he built a castle there and named it Akova, thus it is still named.

Next there was likewise given to Sir Hughes, de Bruyères was his surname, a holding in the *drongos* of Skorta; he was given twenty-two knights' fees. When he received his fiefs, he built a castle there and it was named Karytaina, as it is still called. He had a son, Sir Geoffroy, lord of Karytaina, thus was he named, who was a famous soldier in Romania.[49] Next was listed a third baron, Sir Guillaume he was called, he had the surname Aleman; Patras was listed for him to hold and to rule: with all its appurtenances it was given to him to hold.

Next was assigned the barony of Sir Mathieu, he had de Mons as his surname, thus was he called; the castle of Veligosti and four knights' fees he was to hold, and he was to bear a banner.[50]

Next there was listed another Sir Guillaume to have the castle of Nikli with six fees.[51]

After him another was next listed in the book; Sir Guy, he was called, de Nivelet, his surname; he was given six fees to hold in Tsakonia; he built a castle there which he named Geraki.[52]

the Domesday Book of Morea. There is much disagreement among the various versions of the Chronicle as to the number of knights' fees assigned to each fief.

[49] Akova and Karytaina were the two principal fortresses of Skorta or Arkadia. The latter was not built by Hughes, but, as is correctly stated in l. 3155 below, by the son Geoffroy. Akova, called Mategrifon ("Stop-or-Kill-Greek") by the Franks, stood on the small river Ladon, and its remains may still be seen near the present village of Galatas. A general discussion of Frankish castles in Greece may be found in K. Andrews, *Castles of the Morea* (Princeton, 1953), in A. Bon, "Forteresses médiévales...," *Bul. de cor. Hellénique*, LXI (1937), 136-208, and in R. Traquair, "Mediaeval Fortresses," in *The Annual of the British School of Athens*, XII (1905-6), 258-76, continued in XIII (1906-7), 268-81.

[50] Mathieu de Walincourt de Mons was his full name.

[51] This was Guillaume de Morlay.

[52] Geraki was built, not by Guy, but by his son Jean. (See l. 3365 below.) Its ruins still stand and contain some beautiful Byzantine frescoes. Tsakonia was then far more extensive than the area in Arkadia called by that name today. It extended from the Parnon Mountains of Arkadia southward to Vatika, thus including Geraki and Monemvasia. Tsakonia was often used as a name for medieval Lakonia. The Tsakones themselves were a warlike people of

Sir Othon de Tournay was enfeoffed, also, to hold Kalavryta with twelve fees.

Next was likewise listed Sir Hughes de Lille to have eight knights' fees in Vostitza; he dropped his surname and he was named de Charpigny.[53]

To Sir Luc were given only four fees to hold, the neighborhood of Gritsena and the Lakkos valleys.[54] To Sir Jean de Neuilly was given Passava and four fees to hold and he was to bear a banner, to be marshal and to hold this as a hereditary office.[55] Sir Robert de Tremolay was given four fees; he built Chalandritza and was called lord.[56] To St. John of the Hospital were given four fees; to the Temple were given another four and it was to raise a banner; and, likewise, to the Germans were given four fees to hold in the territory of Kalamata.[57] The metropolitan of Patras,

disputed origin who appear in the sources from the time of Constantine Porphyrogenitus. Slowly decimated and scattered, they are represented today by a small group who still speak a dialect unlike any other of Greece. They were certainly not Slavs, and their language has been called "New Doric." See M., p. 4. For the Tsakones and their language, see the works of Deffner, cited by Miller; the Νεοελληνική Γραμματική of M. Triantafyllidis (Athens, 1938), I, 303-8; Amantos "Τσακωνία - Sclavonia" in Ἀφιέρωμα εἰς Γ. Χατζιδάκιν (Athens, 1921) and also his "Σάλωνα-Τσάκωνες," Ἑλληνικά, X (Athens, 1938), p. 211, where he derives the word from ἔξω Λάκωνες; and also C. Lehman-Haupt, "Τζάκωνες," Εἰς μνήμην Σπυρίδωνος Λάμπρου (Athens, 1935), p. 353, who derives the word directly from Λάκωνες.

[53] Vostitsa is in Achaia, on the Gulf of Corinth, east of Patras. Kalavryta lies in eastern Achaia, south of Vostitsa. It became customary for the higher barons to drop their French titles and to replace them with the titles of their new estates in Morea.

[54] For the valley of Lakkos, see above, p. 120, n. 37. Gritsena was a city somewhere in the valley, perhaps on the southern slopes of Mt. Taygetos. This Sir Luc is mistakenly called Luca de Serpi in the Italian version of the Chronicle.

[55] Passava or Passavant was a formidable castle built on the coast of the Gulf of Lakonia, about half way between Maine and Helos. The name Passavant is supposedly derived from the password of the troops of Champagne, Passe avant!

[56] Schmitt gives his name as Andebert de Tremolay. Chalandritza was a small town, just south of Patras.

[57] These, of course, were the three great religious orders of knights: the Order of the Knights of St. John of the Hospital (later of Malta), the Order of the Templars, and the Teutonic Order of Knights.

with his canons, was given eight knights' fees to hold; the bishop of Olena was given four fees and the bishops of Methone and Korone, with their canons, were each given four, as were those of Veligosti and Nikli; all had four each, as did the bishop of Lakedaemonia.[58]

All these whom you hear me mention by name were the ones who, in the days of the Champenois, were listed in his register and who were enfeoffed. The knights, who had one fee each, and also the squires[59] who were enfeoffed, I do not name because of the amount of writing it would require.

And after the register had been read, Sir Geoffroy asked counsel of the captains, the archbishops, and the bishops as to how to establish and arrange the regulations governing how those who held the fiefs with which they had been enfeoffed would perform their service so that they might maintain arms and protect the

---

[58] There were four ecclesiastical provinces in Frankish Greece: Patras and Corinth in Morea, and Athens and Thebes in continental Greece. The archbishop of Patras, primate of Morea, had four suffragans: the bishops of Olena, whose see was at Andravida; Korone; Methone; and Kephalonia. The archbishop of Corinth had as suffragans the bishops of Argos; Lakedaemonia; and of Monemvasia, while it was under Frankish control. Under the archbishop of Athens were the bishops of Thermopylae, whose see was at Boudonitsa; Salona; Davlia; Negropont; Aegina; and Andros. Under the archbishop of Thebes there were only two suffragans: the bishops of Kastoria and Zarakoria.

Of the four, the archbishop of Patras was without question the most powerful. In fact, sometime around the middle of the thirteenth century, he acquired from Guillaume Aleman the barony of Patras, whose twenty-four fees, added to the eight he already had, made him the leading feudatory of all Morea, which fact is evident from the frequent appearance of his name in the documents at the head of the list of the Moreot nobility, or as their representative and spokesman. See Lg., pp. 205 *seq.* and Z., II, 270-309.

[59] Σιργέντες. The word sergeant signifies someone just below the knight in the feudal order. I have translated the word as squire, signifying a shield-bearer, throughout, except in l. 1988 where I have retained the phrase "sergeants of the conquest," as it seems to have some significance as a title to the Chronicler. Ll. 1985-90 and secs. 67 and 89 of the Assizes of Romania (ed. Recoura, pp. 206-7 and 219) indicate that two squires equaled one knight in assessing feudal dues. The wording of the passage above (l. 1965) would indicate that all the knights received a blanket enfeoffment of one fee each, but that only some of the "sergeants" were enfeoffed. The sections of the Assizes mentioned above speak of "sergeanties," fiefs which owe the service of one sergeant or squire.

land, for if the land, which they had won by arms and campaigning, were not protected, they would lose it again.

Thereupon, with a public council and great discernment, it was debated, and arranged and established that all those who had four fees each would hold banners and be bannerets and that each of these would have to have, besides his banner, one knight with him and twelve squires, and that those who held and had more than four fees, for each fee, would give and furnish two squires on horse or one knight. And the knights who held one fee each, each one of these would be obliged and required to serve in person as his obligation; likewise, those who were called "sergeants of the conquest," each of these would furnish service with his body.

They declared and arranged that, since they were at war, the one part of them would protect the lands they had won and the other would conquer those that they did not have, and that the obligatory service for the whole year, I say, would be scheduled in the such manner and arrangement as I herewith catalog: that out of the twelve months which the whole year has, each man would spend four months in general garrison duty[60] wherever the lord wished; that in the next four months he would go in an army wherever the lord of the vassal had need and wished; and in the third four months of the year, the feudatory would be bound to be where he may desire.[61] With respect to what they declared,

---

[60] *Γαρνιζοῦν καθολικήν.*

[61] This division of the year corresponds to article 70 of the Assizes of Romania, where, concerning the third four months, it states: "and he shall remain for four months in his house, or in any place where it shall appear to him to be more necessary in order to fulfill his service in the aforesaid Principality" (Topping, p. 51). L. adds the phrase *sans passer mer* (§ 130). L. de F. states that a vassal could leave the principality to make a pilgrimage, but still had to return within a year and a day or else lose the income of one year, or within two years and two days or lose the fief completely (§ 140). The Assizes is quite explicit about the absence of a vassal (secs. 36, 55, 60, 82, 101, 111). In general, if a vassal leaves without permission, and his heir to the fief presents himself to the lord within a year and a day, the lord may invest the heir. However, the vassal has the right to request to be absent and the lord is generally required to give permission. Under these circumstances the vassal usually has two years and two days to return to his fief. It is to be

that there be service throughout the year, it was up to the preference of the lord, whoever he was, to take out of the twelve months whichever ones he wished. The bishops and the Church and the Temple and Hospital were not obliged to furnish garrison duty; but they were obliged to be in all ways like the feudatories in military aid, in raids, and in battles, wherever the lord had need and the need of the country required.

Likewise was this principle resolved: that the heads and bishops of all the churches would hold banners in the event of war; in the council, moreover, of the lordship and in trials of the land, they were obliged to be themselves like the other bannerets, with the exception, of course, of murder trials and inquests, which bishops under no circumstances should judge.

And, after all these affairs that I am telling you about were settled, Sir Geoffroy ordered that small and great, all should get ready to march out, that they might subdue the lands with which they had been enfeoffed and so that they would conquer those which they did not have. And as soon as they marched out, they took the route and went straight to Veligosti with the counsel of the Romans, who knew the territory and who delivered them there; at that time the castle lay on a low hill; they took it by assault and few did homage.

Next they crossed straight over to Nikli, which lay in a plain. Now, seeing the Frankish armies and those of the Romans that were with them, the archons of Nikli fortified the towers with whatever troops and arms that they had with them. The walls were high, all were well mortared; they met the assault with great eagerness, and for three days they withstood the assault on the castle and by no means would they surrender. When Sir Geoffroy realized this, he ordered wood to be brought in to make scrofas[62] and also

noted that the various versions of the Chronicle disagree in the enumeration of the fiefs and the duties of the feudatories. L. de F. gives more details, especially concerning the position of the ecclesiastical hierarchy in the feudal organization of the principality (§ 117-140).

[62] Σκρόφα from Italian scrofa ("sow"). A common name for the bore and its wooden shelter which was used to undermine walls during a siege. See Charles Oman, A History of the Art of War in the Middle Ages (N. Y., 1923), I, 133.

trebuchets; he swore by his oath that he would not leave there until he had taken the castle of Nikli by the sword and that, if he took it by the sword, he would not have mercy on a single soul. When the Romans who were with the Franks and who had relatives inside the castle heard this, they quickly called to them and informed them that, if they did not cede the castle and surrender and it was taken by sword, all would be killed. And, as soon as all the Nikliots heard this, they took counsel together and surrendered the castle; they ceded it with agreements that they would keep their patrimonies.

And as soon as Sir Geoffroy received Nikli, he ordered it to be provisioned, as was proper and seemly; and then, he set out from there and journeyed straightway to Lakedaemonia, which was a large town with towers and good walls, all well mortared; they were, indeed, very determined not to surrender. For five days the Franks surrounded the city with unceasing assault, night and day, and they set up the trebuchets, which they had brought from Nikli; and as soon as they began to suffer losses and the towers were damaged, they quickly surrendered, in terms and with oaths that they would keep their houses and the fiefs that they held.

And after the Lakedaemonites had surrendered, Sir Geoffroy, himself, took quarters there; he gave orders to his armies to begin marauding in the land of Tsakonia as far as Helos and in Vatika and in Monemvasia.[63] Thereupon, the archons of Lakedaemonia, as well as those of Nikli, who held their fiefs in Tsakonia and in the other places where those armies were raiding, came and spoke to Sir Geoffroy and asked him to order his armies to stop their raiding and that the villages would do homage and have him for

[63] Helos is the district in Lakonia, around the mouth of the Eurotas and bordering on the Gulf of Lakonia. Vatika is the promontory that ends in Cape Malea. Monemvasia lies on the east coast of this promontory, slightly to the north. Monemvasia was one of the most important towns of Morea during the Middle Ages. Not only was its fortress, built on a huge rock in the sea and approached from the mainland only by a narrow isthmus, considered impregnable, but its harbor was excellent. It was the chief port of entry for Byzantine commerce in the Peloponnesos. Monemvasia, of all the Moreot cities, put up the most heroic resistance and was starved into submission only after a siege of three years. (See below, ll. 2930 ff.)

lord. And he, reasonable in all things, heeded the archons and ordered his army to return.

Thereupon, he ordered that the leaders of his council come before him, those of the soldiers who had enfeoffed the towns, and then that there be put in writing in the registry all that had been won and had been conquered since the Champenois had departed. He called the archons, the leaders of Morea, and asked them to inform him exactly which castles remained that had not done homage. And they answered him and gave him this information: " You are still lacking four castles, our lord; the first is Corinth; the second, Nauplion; the third, Monemvasia; the fourth, Argos; these castles are very strong and well provisioned; you can never take them by assault. Well, if our lord wishes to capture the castles and that we, the race of Romans, shall die his slaves, this we ask, and bid you grant it to us by your oath in writing so that we and our children will have it: that, from now on, no Frank will force us to change our faith for the faith of the Franks, nor our customs and the law of the Romans."

Hearing this, Sir Geoffroy received the words well and he established it for them with oaths and put it in writing.[65] And after Sir Geoffroy had settled all the affairs of the Franks and the Romans, each man's desire and the problems within their fiefs, they all loved him so much, small and great, because he was estimable and just to all that the most prudent among them took counsel as to how the suzerainty of the land of Morea might remain in his hands, for he was a good man, wise in all things, "rather than that there should come from France some plunderer, inexperienced and indiscreet, to throw us into confusion." Thereupon,

---

64 'Εκεῖνοι ὅπου ἐπρονοιάζασιν τὲς χῶρες τῶν στρατιώτων, "those who had enfeoffed towns by means of the soldiers" or "...towns to the soldiers" (?).

65 A tolerant attitude by the Franks toward the Moreot Greeks characterized the conquest. Greek feudatories were allowed to retain their estates (ll. 1642-48) and their privileges. Here above we learn that they were undisturbed in their faith, customs, and law. This attitude is reflected in the Assizes of Romania (secs. 71, 138, 178, 194), where Greeks and Franks are more or less equals under the law. Along with this, of course, went equal obligations, and we find constant references in the Chronicle to Greek troops and nobles campaigning with the Frankish armies.

they went to him and delivered their words to him; he shrank from the evil deed and would in no circumstances do it; however they spoke to him at such length, they urged him so much, that they ripped him from his discretion; he fell in with the plan that it take place and the affair be accomplished.[66] Thereupon, they

[66] Here follows a romantic, though entertaining, story, intended to surround the elevation of Geoffroy to the rank of prince with a suitable legend. In point of fact, as was pointed out above, p. 125, n. 47, Guillaume de Champlitte left his nephew as *bailli*, not Geoffroy. Hugues died a short time later, perhaps within three or four months, and the principality was without a lord. These facts are known from letters of Innocent III (Letters, XIII, 170, *PL*, III, 342). Though the matter is not clear, apparently Geoffroy became *bailli* for the heirs of Champlitte after the deaths of Guillaume and Hugues. Certain it is that he was acting as head feudatory of Morea by May of 1209, for in that year he appeared at Ravennika in that capacity and there the emperor ratified his new station. In the words of the Chronicler Henri de Valenciennes: *Et la devint Geoffroy l'homme de l'empereur Henri; et l'empereur lui accrut son fief de la sénéchaussée de Romanie* (H. de V. § 670). In other words Henry recognized Geoffroy's legal holding of the fief of Morea and added to it the office of seneschal of Romania. Geoffroy thereby became the direct vassal of the emperor. Furthermore, in the following month, June, 1209, Geoffroy entered into a treaty with Venice which brought to a halt the tension that had existed between the Commune and Morea since 1204. By the terms of this treaty, Geoffroy recognized in theory that he had received all of Morea as a fief from Venice. In other words, be became a vassal of Venice for the same land he already held from the emperor. Up to this point, he had still not officially taken the title of Prince of Achaia, so it may be assumed that he still acted as representative of the heirs of Champlitte. Some time in the fall of 1209, in September, 1209, according to Longnon (p. 113), or early in 1210, he became prince in name as well as fact, for letters from Innocent III sent between May 22 and May 24, 1210 are addressed to him as Prince of Achaia (Letters XIII, 6, 23, 24, 25, *PL*, III, 201, 221-22). The letter of May 22 is also given in Potthast, *Regesta*, etc. (Berlin, 1874-75), where it is numbered 3939. And he, himself, first uses the title in a document dated 1210 (quoted by Longnon, p. 115). Apparently, Geoffroy waited for the legal limit of a year and a day and when no heir appeared to claim the fief, he either took possession or was elected by the barons as prince. It is quite unlikely that the emperor would have sanctioned such an open fraud as the Chronicle describes, nor would Venice have entered a treaty with a man whose claim to his title was based on such a patently illegal act. However, a shred of truth seems to linger in the story. Philippe d'Ibelin comments in the Assizes of Jerusalem (*Rec. des hist. des Croisades*, ed. Beugnot, *Lois* II, 401) on advisable procedures to be followed during the minority of heirs, because of the danger that may befall

schemed as to how they might arrange to impede with some base
plan him who might happen to come from France and that he be
prevented by some means from arriving before the end of the
time limit that the Champenois had established. Thereupon, Sir
Geoffroy, as the sensible man he was, sent out a knight whom he
had as confidant, and he went to Venice straightway to the doge.
There was friendship, love, and attachment between them, and
he sent him gifts and warmly besought him to do something to
delay him whom the Champenois might happen to send. Now,
he also sent another knight to France to the friends and relatives
that he had in Champagne.

Now, at this point, I am going to interrupt what I have been
writing and telling about Sir Geoffroy so that I may tell you minutely of that noble count of Champagne[67] and how well he fared
when he arrived there after he journeyed to France to his patrimony.
Now, after the Champenois set out from the land of Morea and
journeyed to France, he arrived in Champagne, which he had
much desired.[68] His relatives received him well; and after he
had rested for about a fortnight, he set out and journeyed to the
king of France. He found him in Paris with his archons; they
were celebrating Pentecost in the usual manner[69] of the Franks;
the king was very happy with the count, for he saw that he had
returned from Romania and so, too, were all the noble dukes and
counts, who were his comrades and relatives. And as soon as
they had exchanged gifts with one another there, he performed
the homage to the king for his estate and, asking his leave, he
returned to Champagne. And as soon as he went to his land and

them "as befell, in fact, in Morea the children of the Champenois from Sir
Geoffroy de Villehardouin, in whose hands it remained." This may indicate
that a specific heir was evicted, or it may simply be a comment on the fact
that Guillaume's heirs were too young to take possession at the time of his
death, and that Geoffroy took the title and kept it. (For a full discussion,
see Lg., pp. 111-15.)

[67] Of course, the count of Champagne here is Guillaume de Champlitte.

[68] There is half a line missing in H. at this point, and the phrase "which
he had much desired" is taken from P.

[69] Pentecost, or Whitsuntide, the seventh Sunday after Easter, was when
the French king customarily assembled his vassals at the *cour plénière*.

became lord, while putting his land and his affairs in order, eight months went by, so many were they in number. And then be remembered the agreements he had with Sir Geoffroy concerning the land of Morea; he had strong hope and great confidence in him that, if he were to send him one of his kinsmen, he would receive him as his lord and would surrender the land to him. Thereupon, he took counsel with his kinsmen as to whom he should send into Morea as lord and his man. He had a certain cousin, who was called Robert; he was a young man, beyond comparison in all things. The count of Champagne called him and invested him; he gave him the suzerainty over the land of Morea; he ordered put in writing all the privileges and liveries of seizin that he was to take with him; he gave him much money and, with it, a retinue of four knights and twenty-two squires. He left Champagne at the beginning of November;[70] and when he came to Savoy to cross the mountains, he found the snows heavy and very thick on the peaks which separate France from Lombardy, and he could in no way pass through. Therefore, he was delayed there a month and more, and as soon as he was able to get over the mountains, he came out of Lombardy and traveled to Venice, where he arrived at the beginning of January, hoping to find a galley to make the crossing.

Now, when the doge of Venice was informed that Robert, cousin of the count, had come there—he was coming from Champagne to go to Morea—he called his admiral and told him secretly of the affair and the plan to impede him and that he was not to give him a ship to go to Morea. Then the doge called Robert to him and showed him great honor and a countenance of friendship so that he would put confidence in him and he might deceive him, and he held him so long with his pretty words, wiles, pretexts, and false excuses that he tarried in Venice for around two months and more. But finally he gave him an armed galley which happened to be going to Crete and he ordered the *comitas*,[71] the master

[70] K., (p. 92, n. on l. 2158) suggests that, Guillaume having died on his voyage homeward or soon after his arrival, his widow sent someone as her representative in Morea, perhaps a certain Robert de Pontallier. Hence, the appearance of the name Robert in the Chronicle.

[71] Κόμιτας (form of Latin *comes*). Schmitt translates this in his Index as

of the boat, to abandon him when they had crossed over to Corfu.
Well, the affair came about just as I am telling you; and as soon
as he brought the galley to the castle of Corfu, the *comitas* called
Robert and said to him: "The galley is damaged below and I must
caulk it in order to repair it; therefore, my good brother, let us
take your baggage off so the galley will be lightened so that I may
caulk it."

And the other, believing him to be speaking to him truthfully,
ordered that his baggage be removed to the castle, while he settled
himself at the inn. And, when most of the night had passed and
the cock was crowing, the galley's crew blew their whistle and,
at once, they went quite away; and when morning came and Robert
became conscious and awoke, he was told that the galley had left.
And as soon as he was informed of it he began to grieve; then did
he perceive completely the betrayal done him and as soon as he
was informed of it and had comprehended the fraud, he sought
and found a boat that he might charter; and the captain of Corfu,[72]
because he had been sent abroad by the lord of Morea, Sir Geoffroy,
ordered that the owner of the boat be called. He ordered and
enjoined him, on pain of bodily harm, not to take Sir Robert
across under any circumstances.

Meanwhile, the galley which was on its way to Crete dropped
a man off at St. Zacharias, the spot where the town of Klarentsa[73]
is today; he carried letters from the doge of Venice to Sir Geoffroy,
the lord of Morea, informing him in writing about Robert: when
he had arrived in Venice and how he had been delayed two months
and more and, furthermore, how the Venetian galley which was
on its way to Crete had dropped him off on the island of Corfu.

a shipowner. However, I believe it signifies simply a ship's captain. Its
equivalents are *comite de vaisseau* and *patron de gaillie*.

[72] *Καπετάνιος* or *καπετάνος* (It. *capitano*) and *κιβιτάνος* (Fr. *chevetain*
and *kievetaine* in dialect of Picardy) are the two words used in the Chronicle
to indicate the commander of a castle. (See l. 2229 for *κιβιτάνος*.)

[73] Klarentsa or Glarentsa (Fr. *Clarence*) was the seaport of Andravida,
lying on the Elian coast, on the site of ancient Kyllene. It was built by Geoffroy
I de Villehardouin and became the principal port for trade with Europe.
St. Zacharias perhaps alludes to an abandoned church or monastery lying along
the shore near where the town arose.

Sir Geoffroy was at Andravida at that time; and when the Venetian brought him those letters, he paid him great honor and gave him gifts, and he called his *chevetain* of Andravida; he gave him detailed instructions as to how he should act when Robert would cross over and come there. And then he left Andravida and went to Vlisiri to wait until he should hear some news about Robert.

Now, when Robert perceived the manner of fraud with which the Venetians, I say, were deceiving him, as I have been telling you, he made great haste to find a boat to cross over and arrive in Morea within his time limit, where, by chance, a boat from Apulia was going. He managed to board the boat and it brought him as far as St. Zacharias; he asked that he be told where the *bailli* was and someone answered him that he was in Andravida. He sent a sergeant to bring him horses; the latter journeyed the footpath until he reached there; he did not find Sir Geoffroy, who had gone elsewhere, but he found the *chevetain* of the town of Andravida. Thereupon, he spoke to him and told him his message, that in St. Zacharias was Robert, the cousin and relative of the count of Champagne, "who has come to be your lord, you Moreots; send him horses that he may come here."

And the *chevetain*, immediately on hearing the message, took with him all the troops that he had under his command and the archons and burghers[74] of all of Andravida; he took all the horses that were needed and he went straightway to St. Zacharias; they displayed great joy on seeing Robert and showed due signs of respect and that they were very pleased that he should come to be their lord and that they should live in his service. Thereupon, they took him with great joy; they went to Andravida and there they lodged him; and he displayed great elation and good humor and received everyone and addressed them with fine phrases, assuming and believing that he had them as vassals and that they, in turn, held him to be their lord.

Thereupon, someone appeared and informed him of the understanding and agreements that the Champenois had with Sir Geoffroy, the *bailli* of Morea; if the time of the term of one year, in which he was to meet Sir Geoffroy and assume the suzerainty,

---

[74] *Βουργήσης, βουργησέους* (It. *borghese*) are freemen in the towns.

should pass, then his efforts were in vain and he had lost all that he came to seek.[75] When the noble Robert heard this, he asked the *chevetain* of the town to give him horses, so that he could go immediately to the *bailli*, and that he also have a guide to lead him; and the captain was obligated to do his will. He found for him as many horses and escorts as he wished; he, himself, went with him as far as Vliziri,[76] saying and expecting that they would find the *bailli* there. Now Sir Geoffroy, when he had heard the report that Robert had arrived in St. Zacharias, had left there quickly and had gone to Kalamata; and again, when he heard that Robert was coming, he departed from there and went with his retinue straightway to Veligosti, where they arrived at noon. Now those who were with Robert brought him straightway to Kalamata and from there they took the horses and went back. So Robert was left there all alone; he called the *chevetain* of the castle of Kalamata and spoke and requested him to give him horses that he might go to Sir Geoffroy, the *bailli* of Morea. And he gave him as many horses as he could, and he also gave him guides to lead him; and he went to Veligosti and he did not find the *bailli* there; but he was told that he had gone to Nikli. The people of Kalamata returned, they went back to their houses in Kalamata. So Robert remained there at a loss, for he could not find horses to take with him. However, the *chevetain* found horses for him, as best he could, and gave them to him and he went to Nikli.

And after Robert had arrived in Nikli, messengers went to Lakedaemonia, where Sir Geoffroy was, and informed him that the cousin of the count of Champagne, said Robert, as he was

[75] L. de F. adds that one of the friends of the Champenois then advised Robert in secret to present himself before the *chevetain* of Andravida and, in the presence of many witnesses, to register, in public and in a written deed, the fact of his arrival in Morea before the expiration of the stipulated term, which act Robert performed (§ 166-167).

[76] Vliziri (Fr. La Glisière) was, according to l. 5248, less than a day's march from Andravida. It lay to the southeast, and was a short way to the northeast of Pondikos. (See below, l. 2484.) L. tells us that it became the favorite summer resort and place of recreation for the princes of Achaia (§ 836, 837, 957).

called, had arrived in Nikli.[77] And Sir Geoffroy, on hearing the report, shrewdly took with him small men and great, all, in fact who were in his company and went quickly to meet Robert; he met him with honor and proper signs of respect and displayed great joy in the presence of all. And after they arrived in Lakedaemonia, he ordered that he be lodged in the lordship's manors.[78]

Now the cousin of the count of Champagne, with the expectation of acquiring the suzerainty, on the following morning, as day was breaking, ordered that the *bailli* Sir Geoffroy be called and he spoke to him thus: that he have those who were in his company, the leaders and the most worthy, come and see the commands of the count of Champagne, the orders which he had brought with him from him. Thereupon, Sir Geoffroy gave his order and, as soon as all, every one of them, had gathered and had seated themselves to hear what the count had written, he had a clerk whom he had brought with him arise[79] and he directed him to read the privileges which he had brought. Then he read them and explained the words, that the count gave him suzerainty over the land, all the Peloponnesos that is included in Morea. And next he displayed and also read the orders and commands to all the captains to receive Robert as their lord. And as soon as those documents were all read, Sir Geoffroy arose in the presence of all and he humbly bowed to the authority of the count's orders; and he quickly ordered brought forward the privileges which they had and the agreements and documents which he had from the count, that he surrendered to him the land of Morea to hold and protect and to be his own *bailli*, and if, within the term of a year and a day, the count or some other member of his family should come, he was to surrender the land and the suzerainty to him. But, should the time pass, the term of a year, and no one of them

---

[77] L. concurs with the Greek in the route that Robert supposedly followed. However L. de F. differs somewhat. It mentions other towns he stopped at and states that they met in Lakedaemonia after eight days of cat and mouse (L. de F., § 168-71).

[78] Τὰ ὁσπίτια and Τὰ σπίτια in 1. 2300 are both derived from the Latin *hospitium*.

[79] L. says: *Et puis après fit lever .j. clerc nés de Paris, liquelx estoit moult sages et bien parlans* (§ 163).

should arrive, as I have been telling you, then the land and the suzerainty would remain, without fail, in the hands of Sir Geoffroy as heir.[80] And after those documents had been read, the agreements which the count of Champagne had made, Sir Geoffroy arose and said to the bishops and the bannerets: "Archons, you have heard the agreements and commands of my lord the count, which he left with me. Therefore, I say to you, I beseech and command you,[81] by the oath which you have sworn to the count and to me, as Christians, fearful of God and the truth, to debate and judge the right in this matter. Likewise do I also beseech Robert, as a noble and my lord, that we stand on the right; judge the right, as is fitting and seemly.[82] My lord would never do anything unjust, therefore, with fear of God, judge the two of us."

When the noble Robert heard this, he quickly fell in with the suggestion and bade them consider the affair; and however they decided and declared with fear of God, he would indeed accept it and would submit to it. When the bishops and all the knights heard these words, they took up the documents and read them from the beginning, minutely and with great care. Then they reckoned the year's term and found that the limit was fifteen days past when Robert happened to arrive to present the documents of the count of Champagne to his *bailli*, Sir Geoffroy, that

---

[80] This is the first of the many occasions that the chronicler takes to give lengthy details of court procedure. His great fondness for courtroom rhetoric and his sure knowledge of legal customs suggest that he himself was trained in the law, or, at least, had gained intimate familiarity with it as a court clerk. It might also be pointed out at this point that his style improves considerably in these passages, especially in the speeches that he gives as direct quotations. Throughout the Chronicle, in fact, one finds that all the speeches have a dramatic vividness that is wholly lacking in the purely descriptive passages concerning places and events. The chronicler apparently had a keen interest in personalities, apart from legal procedure, for it is certain that he has far greater feeling for character delineation than for history.

[81] The editions of both Schmitt and Kalonaros read at this point παρακαλῶ καὶ ὁρκίζω ("I beseech and swear"), but this makes no sense. I believe it should read παρακαλῶ καὶ ὁρίζω ("I beseech and command"), which does make sense. Either Schmitt (for, in general, Kalonaros follows Schmitt's edition exactly) or an earlier scribe mistook the one for the other.

[82] This last phrase is missing in H. and is inserted from P.

he might give him the land.[83] Thereupon, they called the two of them and said to them: "Archons, we find in these documents of the count, who effected these pacts, which we have examined, and to which are attached his seal and, with it, those of us all, that, with design and purpose and with solemn pacts, he left Sir Geoffroy as his representative here in the land. So, since it was by pacts that he left him the land and the term has passed, you do not have the right, for, wherever there are Christians in all the world, pacts confine the law and lawsuits."

Whereupon, Robert, on hearing this, from the grief and bitterness that were in his heart, could make no answer whatever. But Sir Geoffroy got right up; he thanked them all humbly and with care, as is the custom in the courts of lords, where those who deliver justice are thanked.

After the judgment and verdict was given that the suzerainty of the land of all the Peloponnesos, which is called Morea, should remain Sir Geoffroy's, he did Robert great honor and he spoke to him thus: "My lord and brother, try not to be grieved by what the judgment has produced; justice requires it and this is the way of the world. If you wish and desire to stay with me here in the land of Morea, I shall hold you as my brother and of whatever we win together you will take what is your due." And he, because of his grief, did not accept.

Thereupon Sir Geoffroy sent out a general invitation and invited everyone, small and great, and gave a *chamotsoukin*,[84] as the Romans call it; and they ate and made merry, and they jousted; they held dances and games past counting. Now, he whom I call Robert of Champagne called Sir Geoffroy and said to him: "Since I have seen that I do not have the suzerainty, give me horses and escort that I may take my leave." Likewise he asked of all the captains,

---

[83] L. states that Robert arrived over a week late, but that some believed he arrived in time to receive the suzerainty. However, the committee found against him because "agreements take precedence over laws" (*Li pat vainquent les loys*, L. § 167). L. de F. adds more details, including the witnessed statement of his arrival that Robert drew up for the *chevetain* of Andravida (L. de F. § 170 f. and 177-81. See above, p. 138, n. 75).

[84] Χαμοτσούκιν. A party, probably in the open, where much drinking took place; a symposium.

the bishops, and clever men who were in the council and who had delivered the judgment and verdict that they draw up a document for him, to which they would put their seals, stating how they had decided and declared the judgment which they had given, and including a copy of the pact which had been concluded between the count of Champagne and the most noble Sir Geoffroy that he might take it with him to France to show to the king and all the captains who were then in France and to the count of Champagne, so that they would not consider him stupid in the affair. Gladly they drew it up and all put their seals to it.[85]

Then Sir Geoffroy gave him many and sundry gifts and presents; humbly and with propriety he made him promises that he was at his command and that he would always be his man.[86] And after this he guided him and kept him company; he, himself, went with him as far as Andravida, and from there, he boarded a galley and journeyed to France.

And after Robert had set out from Morea and Sir Geoffroy had remained as lord, he ordered that he be called Lord of Morea. The lands and affairs that had been his to regulate, he set on a different footing, now that he was rightful lord; he always took pains and struggled to increase them. Well, as is natural that all must die, there came also to him the time to leave this world. He called his captains and all the bishops, and he drew up a mighty will, wise man that he was; he determined all his possessions, wrote them down and put his seal to them. Now, he had two sons: the first was named Sir Geoffroy, as he was called, the name of his father; the second was named Guillaume, as he was called, and the surname of Sir Guillaume was de Kalamata; he left him as lord of the castle of Kalamata with the rest of the territory of the castellany, because this was his own property from the hereditary land of the conquest.[87] He directed and with sweet

---

[85] This right to a written, sealed statement of the court's verdict and a copy of the evidence introduced during the hearing is expressly stated in Articles 168 and 191 of the Assizes of Romania.

[86] Somewhat obscure, but probably merely polite phrases of parting.

[87] The original fiefs distributed immediately after the Conquest were always in a special category. The holders, for instance, were able to bequeath them as they wished, whereas the later fiefs were subject to the terms of the individual

appeal he besought the captains, the bishops, and all the knights, that they accept Sir Geoffroy as lord by inheritance and that they remember always his principles of government, the labor he expended that Morea be won, and the compassion and love for his fellow man that he felt towards everyone. And as soon as he had settled these matters and many others, he died, as a Christian; may God grant him forgiveness.[88]

And as soon as he died, as I am telling you, great lamentation broke out in all Morea, for they had considered him of great worth and they loved him deeply for his good rule and for his wisdom. And after they had held his funeral and their grief was somewhat calmed, all took counsel, small and great alike, and crowned as their lord Sir Geoffroy, the younger. And as soon as he received the glory of the seigneury, he began to go forward as a wise soldier; he was most devoted and philanthropic toward all and he strove mightily to increase his honor.

grant. Soon after Geoffroy became prince, he sent for his wife Isabeau and his adolescent son Geoffroy, who had remained in France. They arrived some time early in 1210, for she is mentioned in a document of that year (Lg., p. 115). L. de F. states that the second son, Guillaume, was born in Kalamata (§ 187-88) and P., in l. 2449, makes the same assertion. He was born in 1211.

[88] The traditional date given for the death of Geoffroy is 1218. However, Longnon maintains that the Geoffroy involved in the struggle with the Church during the years 1219-23 (see below, ll. 2658-80) was Geoffroy I and not his son, Geoffroy II. He correspondingly places his death sometime between 1228 and 1230 (Lg., pp. 164-66, where he summarizes much that he states in his "Problemes de l'histoire de la principauté de Morée," *Journal des Savants* [1946], pp. 157-59). There is no question that great confusion exists in the Chronicle. Geoffroy II, for instance, is stated as attending the second council at Ravennika, whereas this was obviously Geoffroy I (ll. 2598 f.). The conflict with the Church comes later in the Chronicle and it is quite possible the same confusion persists. It is interesting that L. de F. claims that Geoffroy I died around the same time as Guy, the great lord of Athens. This statement has always been considered false on two counts: first, the great lord in question was not Guy, but his uncle Othon, and, second, Othon died in France in 1234, whereas, it was believed, Geoffroy died in 1218. If Longnon, however, is correct, then the statement is not quite so far-fetched as has been generally assumed. Othon left Athens some time during 1225 and he was dead by 1234. If Geoffroy died between 1228 and 1230, then they did die around the same time and the only serious error in the statement is the confusion in the names Guy and Othon.

Shortly thereafter, it happened, listen to what I am going to tell you, that the Robert, emperor of the city of Constantine, who was then lord and emperor of Romania, with an eye toward a marriage alliance, made treaties and agreements with the king of Aragon, king of Catalonia, that he take as his wife the daughter of the emperor; he placed her in two galleys with great honor; and knights and archontesses accompanied her.[89] They went to the castle of Pondikos, which is in Morea,[90] near Andravida, and stopped there. And as fate would have it, Sir Geoffroy, lord of Morea, happened to be nearby at the town called Vlisiri. Quickly, reports were brought to him in the castle from Pondikos, as it is called, for this is still its name, that two galleys had put into the harbor of Pondikos, as I said, which were carrying the daughter of Emperor Robert, and which were on their way to the king of Catalonia. On hearing this, Sir Geoffroy went there with all speed; he dismounted from his horse, went aboard the galley and greeted the daughter of the emperor, and he invited her and urged her to go ashore and to enter his castle to refresh herself, to rest there two days and then to continue on her way. And she, as a noble lady, gladly went ashore with her suite and entered the castle. That day passed and another dawned; some of his followers and counselors spoke to Sir Geoffroy and gave him advice: "Lord, you are here in Romania and hold the land of Morea, of which you are lord; and if you do not produce a son to inherit it, of what use are these things to you and why should you worry about them? Nowhere is there a woman worthy of you; and, since God has so

[89] This curious story, already alluded to in ll. 1186 seq., has almost no truth in it whatever. The lady in question, not named in the Chronicle, is Agnes de Courtenay, daughter of Pierre de Courtenay and sister of Robert, who had no daughter. On their eventful journey from Brindisi to Constantinople in 1217, Agnes and her mother, Yolande, stopped at Pondikos, where they were feted graciously by Geoffroy I. Yolande, duly impressed by what she saw, agreed to Geoffroy's request for the hand of Agnes for his son. The two were married before the mother left for Constantinople. The king of Aragon at the time was James II, who, in 1217, was nine years old. L. de F. refers to Agnes sometimes as sister and sometimes as daughter of the emperor, but does not name the emperor (§ 193-200). Article 3 of the Assizes of Romania contains the same story, with identical details.

[90] Elis is meant.

ordained and has sent her here, she who happens to be the daughter of the emperor, take her and marry her and make her our lady. And, if, by chance, the emperor, her lord, should become somewhat angry and grieved, still he will accept it."

They so pressed him and so urged him that he summoned the wisest of his followers and asked all of them to give him counsel, and all together declared and counseled him: "Lord, to us it is pleasing; do it freely."

The bishop of Olena[91] conversed with the daughter of the emperor and suggested to her that she take Sir Geoffroy as her man and husband; he pointed out to her many wise and clever reasons why this relationship by marriage[92] would turn out to be more beneficial for their lord than for the king to whom they were taking her in Catalonia. Why should I tell you the many details, lest you should be bored? They said so many things to her, urged her so much, that she agreed and the marriage took place; and after they were wed and had celebrated their nuptials, the emperor's galley returned to the City. In detail, the knights who were aboard told him what had happened, and the emperor was very grieved when he heard it; if he had had the power and if it had been at all possible, he would have shown Sir Geoffroy clearly that he had committed an ugly deed, a great villainy, by marrying his daughter without his consent, for it upset his plans to establish the marriage ties and his agreements with the king of Aragon, that he, in turn, might have troops, armies, and assistance from him in his war with the Romans, and now he had thwarted him and he found himself duped.

[91] See above, p. 128, n. 58. The see of this bishopric was originally, perhaps, at Olena, a town northeast of Pyrgos in Elis, but in Frankish times it had been moved to Andravida, whose bishop retained the name in his title.

[92] Συμπεθερία. This type of relationship has always had a more solemn importance in the East than in the West. By convention, all members of the groom's family become related to all members of the bride's family, and this extends far beyond the immediate family, to cousins and second cousins, etc. Another such relationship is called συντεκνία in the Chronicle. It is exactly the same kind of tie between two families, except that it arises from the baptism of a child. It is a much stronger relationship than our own godparentage.

Now Sir Geoffroy, lord of Morea, clever, tactful, and experienced as he was, did not stand around, losing his time; quickly, he wrote letters and sent messengers to the emperor who was in the City, asking him and beseeching him to forgive him for what he had done and had become his son; he had not done it with evil intent nor with arrogance, but had done it with the desire and the right good intentions of a man who finds himself in Romania far from his kinsmen and patrimonial estates and who had not found by any means a woman to marry, as befitted him and was his due according to the rank which he had; he should consider and realize that he too was in Romania and had great wars with the Roman people, as did the emperor; and he did not have an overlord to command him; with his sword he won the land which he held. Therefore, if the emperor were willing, he would do this as reparation for what he had done by taking his daughter as his wedded wife: he would bind himself as his liege and would hold from him the land and his suzerainty over the Morea, and, if he should have need of his armies as well as his own person, whenever he might command and be in need, he would be at his command and would stand by his side and together they would sustain the war and conquer the Romans with their armies.

On hearing this, Emperor Robert would by no means return an answer until he had taken counsel with his [vassals]. He called the leading captains of his council; in detail he told them the story and showed them the letters, all that he was given notice of by Sir Geoffroy of Morea. Now the captains and the emperor debated a long time and considered the affair. Thereupon the wiser spoke and counseled that, since the lord of Morea avowed and promised to become the liege man of the emperor of the City and to hold his land in vassalage from the emperor, and that he and the emperor would join forces to fight together all their opponents wherever they might find them, this was enough and sufficient for there to be peace and friendship between the two lords of Romania; for this relationship by marriage was more advantageous than the one with the king of Aragon, who was so far away; since he even bound himself in service to the emperor to hold from him the land which he had won. Thereupon, an answer was given to Sir Geoffroy that they should meet in Vlachia to hold a council and there to settle once and for all the affairs they had to settle.

Thereupon, the emperor went to the castle of Larissos and Sir Geoffroy, lord of Morea, journeyed there by way of Thebes and took with him the man who was then ruling Athens, who was called great lord, and from whom, indeed, he held the land and the suzerainty which he had in Romania, and all the bannerets who were in Morea. All traveled with him into Vlachia and they joined the emperor in Larissos;[93] they held great celebrations after they were met, and amidst these they conversed together and debated and resolved these points which I now list for you.

First, the emperor gave him as a gift and as a dowry all of the Dodecanese to hold them from him; second, he honored him to be called prince; third, he made him grand domestikos of all Ro-

---

[93] This meeting is undoubtedly a reference to the parliaments held at Ravennika by Emperor Henri in 1209 and 1210. Henri had marched into northern Greece to enforce imperial authority over the rebellious nobles, largely Lombard, of Thessaly and Thrace. Finding that a full-scale campaign was developing, he called to his aid the nobles of central and southern Greece. Geoffroy I de Villehardouin and Othon de la Roche were engaged in the siege of Corinth when they received the summons, which they answered immediately. It was largely in return for this loyalty that Henri recognized Geoffroy as prince of Morea and appointed him seneschal of the empire. The meetings were of prime importance for the emperor, for he was able to assert imperial authority over the barons of Greece. They were important for Geoffroy in that his claim to Morea was formally recognized and he was appointed to one of the highest imperial offices. Out of the meetings there emerged a concordat, furthermore, signed in May, 1210, that was designed to protect the interests of the Church in the empire. By its terms, the barons were to return to the Church any Church property illegally seized by them, and the clergy, in turn, agreed to hold the property as lay fiefs and to pay land taxes, etc. Suzerainty over the Cyclades (called the Dodecanese in the Chronicle) did not figure in these meetings, but was granted to Geoffroy II much later, in 1236, by Baldwin II in return for services rendered. The right to coin money was also granted much later, in 1250, by Louis IX of France to Guillaume II of Morea. I have not been able to identify the castle of Larissos. Henri did occupy the castle at Lamia (Zitoun), which had belonged to the Templars, and earlier he had attacked the stronghold of Larissa. The chronicler has apparently confused these names. I believe that Larissa was uppermost in his mind, for, whenever the word is used in the Chronicle, Larissos, which has a masculine ending, always appears with a feminine article.

mania; and, fourth, that, in the lands which he held, he exercise the right of the coinage of *tournois* and *denaria*.[94] He became thereafter the liege man of the emperor to hold from him the land which he ruled.

Next, he gave him in writing the Customs which the emperor maintained at that time in all his empire, though his brother, Emperor Baldwin, had obtained them from Jerusalem.[95] And when they had established these matters which I am telling you, they took leave, each from the other; the emperor journeyed straightway to the City, and Sir Geoffroy returned to Morea with thanksgiving and jubilation, for he had effected the peace which he wanted and desired and was most eager to obtain. And after Prince Geoffroy went to Morea, and his excellent wife, the princess of Achaia, daughter of the emperor, learned that the prince had come to an understanding with the emperor, she praised God first off and was very happy.

Then the prince, Sir Geoffroy, called his captains to give him counsel as to what was to be done and what was to take place about the castles which the Romans still held in the principality, Corinth, Monemvasia, Argos, and Nauplion.[96] Thereupon, the leaders of his council answered him: " You know, my lord, that the churches hold close to one third of Morea, of the whole principality; they sit and take their ease and give not a thought to the war which we are carrying on with the Romans. Therefore, lord,

94 The δεμέστιχος (never spelled δομέστιχος in the Chronicle) was a military officer of the Byzantine court. In the Chronicle μέγας δεμέστιχος is equivalent to seneschal. The *tournois*, or *denier* of Tours, was the model on which Guillaume patterned his own coinage. He located his mint in the castle of Chloumoutsi, which soon came to be known as Castel Tornese, from the Italian name for the *tournois*. Δενάρια is apparently the French *deniers* and is synonymous with *tournois*.

95 The Customs here referred to are the Assizes of Romania, while "those of Jerusalem" refers to the Assizes of Jerusalem. Article II of the Assizes of Romania claims that Baldwin and his advisers sent to the king and patriarch of Jerusalem for their "usages and assizes" to help them rule the new empire of Romania. This story is highly suspect.

96 Corinth, Argos, and Nauplion were taken by Geoffroy I during the years 1210-12. Monemvasia was the only castle left in Greek hands when Geoffroy II became prince.

we declare and give you this advice, that you bid them come with arms to help us that we may take the castles which are holding out against us; and if they do not do so, seize their fiefs."

And when the prince heard this, he approved of it highly; he ordered that they be called and they all went before him. He asked them for aid, and that all of them help him with troops and armies with weapons, that he might protect the land and attack the castle of Monemvasia. And they answered him that they owed him only honor and homage, as a prince which he was, and they declared that what they had and held, they had from the pope. The prince became enraged and ordered that all the lands and fiefs wherein they had holdings be seized. And he would not take anything at all for himself from the incomes of the fiefs of all the churches, but he ordered that the construction of Chloumoutsi be begun; the bishops excommunicated the prince forever.[97] Now, for three years, the prince held the lands of all the churches, I tell you, of the principality, until he finished the castle of Chloumoutsi, and they excommunicated forever him and all the barons of the principality. And when it was finished as he wished and desired, he sent Minorites and two knights to the most holy pope in Rome, declaring and avowing that he was at war and was fighting the Romans in Romania. For this reason, he had asked the prelates who were metropolitans and bishops, the Temple, and the Hospital to help him in any way whatever in the war he was waging. And they would not help him at all; he had the lands

[97] From the settlement at Ravennika in 1210 up to 1218, the conflict between the clergy and the barons became increasingly bitter. The prelates claimed that Geoffroy I and the other barons occupied their lands in spite of the concordat they had signed, whereas the barons claimed that the prelates abused their power to confer orders by ordaining anyone who wanted to escape his feudal obligations. The matter came to a head in 1218 when the cardinal-legate to Morea excommunicated Geoffroy I and Othon de la Roche. This was confirmed by the pope on January 21, 1219. It is possible that the reasons for the struggle as given in the Chronicle have some validity. We know that Chloumoutsi (Clermont) was built during this period, for it first appears in the documents in 1224. (See Lg., pp. 164-65.) The Chronicle, of course, like many modern historians, is quite incorrect in assigning these events to Geoffroy II. L. omits the whole episode, but L. de F. relates it, though briefly, and assigns it to Guillaume de Villehardouin.

and fiefs which they had and held throughout the principate seized and he did not wish in the least to take anything from the taxes and the *corvées* of all the churches, but had a strong castle built which would guard the coast and the harbor of Morea.[98] If, by chance, the Franks were to lose Morea, they would win it back with this castle. "For this reason, he begs of you, as most holy pope, that he may have your love and that you pardon him, for if the Romans had taken the land of Morea, they would not by any means have allowed the churches of the Franks to remain."

And the most holy pope, as soon as he was informed of this, straightway sent absolution to Prince Geoffroy. When the prince saw the absolution of the pope, he was very happy and glorified the Lord. Then he sent word for the metropolitan whom they call the metropolitan of Old Patras to come, and also the bishops who were of his see, the commander of the Templars, and him of the Hospital.

He showed them the decree, the pope's absolution, and then he ordered that the lands which he was holding be returned and upon this, he entreated them prudently and peacefully: "Fathers, by what I did when I took your fiefs, I did not wrong you; no, by Christ, you are more at fault, for you should have known and have heard that if the Romans should have seized—God forbid !— the lands which we have here in Romania, they would not have allowed you, because you are of the church, to hold your fiefs here and to have prebends; but, rather, they would have murdered and disinherited you the same as us, the laymen who are soldiers. Well, I do not ask you, nor are you required by right, to do garrison duty like the fief holders; but, in other matters, for the guarding of the land or for the relief of a castle which is besieged by our enemies, you must help us, as also on a foray when we go for plunder.

---

[98] Morea here means Elis. Chloumoutsi or Clermont lay on the coast, south of Klarentsa. (Schmitt incorrectly states that it was built by Geoffroy II. See his Index.) It was built, undoubtedly, as a stronghold against the forces of the despot of Epirus, just across the gulf from Morea. It was the finest fortress in the principate and became the residence of the prince. For Chloumoutsi, see Buchon, *La Grèce continentale*, p. 510, and P. Kalonaros, "Khlemoutzi, le château franc de Clermont," *Hellénisme contemporain* (Dec., 1936), pp. 174-80.

And in other affairs for the defense of the land, we must stand together to protect our land, for you, without us, are as nothing. And if I seized the lands of the church, I took nothing to receive as my own profit; I built, you will notice, a castle for the salvation of the land; for you and for us, I built it, to be a key to the land. If, by chance, we were to lose the land of Morea, we would win it back by means of the castle of Chloumoutsi. Therefore, I beseech you as fathers of the church, let me have your pardon as I have from the pope, and from now on let us have harmony; cooperate with me in arms as is fitting and seemly, and I, in turn, will help you in whatever way is necessary." Thereupon, they forgave him and made peace and they promised henceforth to be at his command.

Now after this which I have told you took place, Prince Geoffroy did not have the good fortune to produce any son to leave as his heir. As is the nature of the human race, that all who are born must die some death, the prince fell into the delirium of death. And when he saw and understood that he was going to die, he called his brother Guillaume and spoke thus to him, beseeching him lovingly: "My most sweet brother, my beloved brother, I have now fulfilled the years of my life and you remain after me as lord by inheritance of all that our lord and father conquered with difficulty and heavy labor, as all men know. Well, my beloved brother, I had in mind to erect a church and to found a monastery in which I might place the holy remains of our lord and father, and, due to my sins, I did not accomplish this. Therefore, I ask of you, I beseech and charge you, since I was not able to accomplish it, you do it, little brother, to have my blessing and that of our much-tried lord and father; let his remains be placed in the tomb and then, in turn, let mine be placed beside them. And see to it, good brother, that the monastery has cantors and celebrants, and that they have their livings, so that they may commemorate us unto eons of eons.[99] And after this, brother, I say and advise that you take to yourself a woman to be your wedded wife so that you

---

[99] The language of this passage is reminiscent of the Greek Orthodox liturgy. One might almost suppose that the chronicler has Greek cantors (ψάλτες) and celebrants (λειτουργοί) in mind.

may produce with her children and heirs that they may inherit
the land of our father." Now, after Sir Geoffroy had set in order
all the matters that, as a wise man, it was his duty to arrange,
he surrendered his soul and the angels bore it away; and all you
who hear me now, say GOD REST HIS SOUL.[1]

So, thereafter, the bishops and all the bannerets crowned as
prince Guillaume, brother of the prince Sir Geoffroy, who, further
more, turned out to be a skillful man, wise and hard-working for
all men born in the territory of Romania; and he also loved his
fellow men, and everybody loved him. And after he received the
suzerainty of the land, he found that the Romans still held the
castle of Monemvasia, that of Corinth, and also that of Nauplion,
which is near Argos, the which castles had the best harbors, and
to which the ships of the basileus of the Romans came bringing
provisions and men-at-arms.[2] Seeing this, the prince was very
disturbed, saying that so long as he did not have those castles,
he should not be spoken of as prince of Morea. Thereupon, he
came to a conclusion by himself, then, he asked the counsel of
others, who agreed with him, that if he did not have ships to control
the sea, so that supplies would not reach the above-mentioned
castles, he would never command them nor win them. He sent
messengers to the doge of Venice and offered to come to terms
with the Commune with the following agreements: that the Commune should afford him, until he should capture the castles of
Monemvasia and Nauplion, four good galleys with their full equip-
ment; that he should give to the Commune the castle of Korone
with its villages and the land around it and, likewise, Methone
for the Commune of Venice to hold as an inheritance; and also
that, from that time on, having taken the castles, Venice should
always give for the protection of the land two, and only two, galleys

[1] Geoffroy II died in 1246. Guillaume was about thirty-five years of age
when he became prince. The church with monastery in question is the church
of St. Jacob (St. James) at Andravida, in whose crypt the three Villehardouins
were indeed buried. Excavations of the site in 1890 produced only slight traces
of the church and a few bones. See K., p. 315, n. on l. 7790.

[2] Again it must be noted that by this time only Monemvasia remained in
Greek hands. The chronicler is discussing events of the reign of Geoffroy I,
which he assigns to a later period.

with full crews and the prince would pay all their expenses, which are called *panatika*, excepting, however, wages.[3]

And in like manner, while the prince was arranging this, he also arranged for the siege of Corinth to take place. In this, he ordered that the lord of Athens—great lord, they called that lord— be written to come to help in the siege of Corinth.

Next he sent word to the duke of Naxos and to the three lords of Euripos and to all those of the islands to come with a force of arms and armies; and after they had joined his army, the prince arranged their siege.[4]

Well, while the hill of the castle of Corinth is wide and high and formidable and the castle lies on its top, there happens to be to the south of that castle a certain small hill, a rocky crag with a cliff. Here, the prince ordered a castle to be built on top and it was named Mont Eskouvé,[5] as it is still called; and, on the other

---

[3] The πανάτικα (Lat. *panaticum*) were the provisions given troops to maintain them on a campaign. Apparently, the meaning here is that he would feed the men, but would give them no salary in cash. Korone and Methone had been in Venetian hands from 1206 to 1209, during which years the Commune had expelled the small garrisons of Franks left there during the initial conquest of the peninsula. Possibly the statement in the Chronicle indicates that Guillaume gave up all claims to these places and recognized anew Venetian claims in return for the galleys.

[4] Under the terms of the original partition of the Greek Empire, Venice received title to all the islands of the Aegean. However, unwilling to incur the expense of occupying them, the Commune left this task to its enterprising private citizens. Accordingly a group led by Marco Sanudo sailed among the islands and by 1207 had subdued at least seventeen of them. Marco kept Naxos for himself and distributed the rest among his relatives and other followers. Euboea, originally conquered by Jacques d'Avesnes in 1205, was after his death divided into three large fiefs, which Boniface de Montferrat granted to three Veronese nobles, the *terzieri* or triarchs. Shortly afterward, however, one of the three, Ravano dalle Carceri, remained as sole lord. In 1209, moreover, he recognized the suzerainty of Venice over his fiefs, and after his death in 1216 Venice became the ruler of the island, in fact if not in theory. The siege of Corinth described in this passage is, of course, the siege of 1210, conducted by Geoffroy I.

[5] Μοῦντ 'Εσκουβέ. Longnon (p. 71) calls this castle "Mont Escovée (*mont dénudé*)." Schmitt (Index, p. 638) gives the Greek form and says the name corresponds to the French proper name Mont Esquiou or Esquieu. He also suggests a connection between this name and the curious word σκιβουρία

side, called the northern side, the great lord built a castle of his own. They placed in these provisions and shield-bearing arbalesters, and they closed the Corinthians in so tightly that they did not have leave to bring in even a piece of wood, nor could any provisions come in to them from anywhere; only the plentiful water of the springs and wells which are on the hilltop, inside the castle, this they had in abundance, and who could take it from them? Well, if I were to write you in detail all that happened at the siege of Corinth, those who heard it would be very bored. But, when those who were within saw that they could not have help from any quarter because of the great closeness of the siege, they capitulated and gave up the castle, but on oath and treaties that they were to retain their fiefs, even as the rest of the Romans of the whole principality.

Now after Prince Guillaume had won the kingly castle of Corinth, he ordered that a great supply of men and arms be placed in it, as was fitting and seemly.

And then he called first of all the great lord and then everyone, all the captains, and he spoke to them thus, with great wisdom; "Comrades, friends and brothers, we must give thanks first to the glory of God and, second, to that of the Theotokos for the favor which they have bestowed upon us and we have won the finest place of Morea, and now only a little is lacking to us; the castles of Nauplion and Monemvasia, these two we are lacking and I say that, if you are of like mind, now that we find ourselves together, let us have a discussion and let us take counsel together as to the manner and campaign with which we should fight to win them as well."

Thereupon, the wisest declared and affirmed that "since both castles lie on coastal promontories and have harbors, we must lay siege to them both by land and by sea."

(haughtiness) which appears in l. 7907 of the Chronicle. W. Miller (p. 36) calls the castle Montesquiou. Dragoumis, in a long passage (Χρ. Μορ., pp. 49-64), discusses this castle at length. He derives the name from the old French word *eschiverie* (*esquiverie*: haughtiness, disdain), which is the σκιβουρία mentioned above, and gives the form Mont Eschivée. The modern name Penteskouphes or Penteskouphia is a corruption of the French name, influenced by the Italian *scuffia* (cap), and means Five Caps.

While they were still seated in that council, messages were brought to Prince Guillaume by envoys, who were come from Venice and who brought the treaties, drawn up entirely as the prince had sought them, as he had wished and desired; the four galleys had come to Korone. When the prince heard this, he was overjoyed, and likewise did all the captains approve of it. With his council the prince called for those Venetians who had brought the treaties. He sent a knight to Korone; he surrendered the castle that the Venetians might hold it together with all the dependency included in Methone; that the doge of Venice might hold and govern whatever villages there were which the court held at that time, with the exception of the lands and fiefs which the feudatories held.[6]

And after the Venetians received at that time the castle, the surrounding lands and the villages of Korone, the galleys went straightway to Nauplion; they laid siege to the castle from the sea, and the prince with all his armies, from the land. Summer passed, winter came, and there they wintered on the land and on sea. And when the second season came and summer arrived and those within saw that the castle of Nauplion was closed in and that they had no help of any kind coming, they made a treaty and surrendered the castle. Now Nauplion happens to be a castle on two crags; therefore, they negotiated that the first be surrendered and the other, the weaker one, the Romans would retain; they made the treaties with oaths and vows.

And after the prince received Nauplion, he promptly presented it to the great lord, to hold with Argos as hereditary fiefs.[7] The gift of Nauplion together with Argos, which the prince presented at that time to the great lord, was in return for the aid which the great lord, I tell you, gave in the capture of Corinth and also because the prince expected him to help him in the taking of Monemvasia as well.

[6] Korone and Methone, not far apart geographically, are usually mentioned together in the documents. In this passage they seem to be treated almost as one fief.

[7] Nauplion and Argos were captured in 1210-12 by Geoffroy I. He presented not only these two fiefs to Othon de la Roche, but also an annual charge of 400 *hyperpyra* upon the tolls of Corinth (see M., p. 62).

Well, after they had taken the castle of Nauplion, the prince set forth with the great lord; and then they separated, the great lord went straightway to his town, which is called Thebes, and, the prince went to the territory of Morea. And when the season called winter had passed, Prince Guillaume sent out messengers; he wrote and invited first the great lord, the three lords of Euripos, the duke of Naxos, and also all the other lords of the islands, the count of Cephalonia[8] and all the captains of the principality of Morea, small and great, to come with arms and heavy provisions; he wished to go to the castle of Monemvasia; since it was unassailable, he wished to besiege it by land and by sea and to set up a blockade and siege, until he would take it.

And when the season opened, beginning in the month of March, the armies came from everywhere; in the meadows of Nikli, there in the fields, the mustering of the armies took place, and from there they went straightway to Monemvasia. The four Venetian galleys went and stood off the coast and seized control of the sea; the prince arranged his siege; Monemvasia was then enclosed exactly the same way as the nightingale by its cage. Those of Monemvasia, who knew in the castle that the prince was coming to besiege them, had collected their provisions according to their means and were not of the opinion that the Frankish armies, having small expectations of success, would tarry long in the siege they were laying against them. Now the prince, seeing such arrogance, swore on his sword in fury and anger never to leave there until he had taken the castle. He ordered the trebuchets, and around three were set up, and they fired unceasingly, night and day; they destroyed the houses and killed people. Why should I tell you all the details and when shall I have time to write all that the prince did at Monemvasia and, again, how

---

[8] Cephalonia had already been lost by the Greeks twenty years before the Frankish conquest. When the Normans had invaded the peninsula from Sicily, their admiral Margaritone of Brindisi occupied Cephalonia, Zante, and Ithaka. At the time of the Fourth Crusade, these were in the possession of Maio (Matthew) Orsini, a member of the Roman family, but himself probably an Apulian. He and his son Robert, who succeeded his father, ruled the Ionian islands throughout the thirteenth century.

the Monemvasiotes conducted themselves?[9] But for the sake of more brevity and to shorten it for you, the prince acted in accordance with his oath that they would never leave Monemvasia until the hill as well as the castle were taken.[10] To this end, they remained there three years and more; the people of Monemvasia had nothing to eat and they ate the mice and cats; then they had nothing more to eat except their own bodies. And when they saw their plight and that death stood before them, they took counsel together to surrender. They asked a treaty of Prince Guillaume: that they always remain there, with their inheritances together with their goods, as privileged Franks, owing no *corvée* but the use of their boats and having their stipend and largess.[11]

The prince put into writing and sealed the treaties and promises which they asked of him; and as soon as they received their copies of the oaths, three of their archons took the keys of the castle of Monemvasia and brought them to the prince; one was a Mamonas, the other a Daemonogiannes, and the third was a Sophianos, thus was he named.[12] These were the most noble families which

[9] All authorities seem to agree that the siege lasted for three years and that the castle fell in 1248. However, Zakythinos (p. 21) gives the years 1245-48; Longnon (p. 217) says Guillaume began the siege after he became prince (1246) and captured the castle in 1248; Kalonaros (p. 122, note on l. 2923) gives the dates as 1248-50; the *Cambridge Medieval History* (IV, 440) merely gives the date as three years after Guillaume became prince. There is an extensive literature on Monemvasia and its capture. In addition to the works already cited, see Adamantios, Χρον. Μορ., p. 566; Kalonaros, Δουλούδια τῆς Μονεμβασιᾶς καὶ τοῦ Ταϋγέτου (Εἰκόνες απὸ τὴν Πατρίδα μας) (Athens, 1936), pp. 50-57.

[10] There is a lacuna in L. corresponding to ll. 2932-3023 of the Greek Chronicle (§ 205 ff.).

[11] Φράγκοι ἐγκουσάτοι. Ἐγκουσάτος is derived from the Latin *excusatus*. Schmitt in his Index (p. 605) discusses the word at length and gives its meaning as "exempt, enjoying immunity or certain special rights granted by privileges." The Monemvasiotes owed only service with their boats and for this service, moreover, they were to receive a salary and largess as though they had been hired as mercenaries. For "stipend and largess" see above, p. 104, n. 90.

[12] These three great families are prominent in Moreot affairs throughout the Frankish period and after. The Mamonas family, in fact, is still extant in Greece, and Sophianos is a fairly common family name. The history of the Mamonas family from 1248 to around 1900 was written by Anthony Miliarakes in his Οἰκογένεια Μαμωνᾶ (Athens, 1902).

were in Monemvasia and which are still there; they did homage to the prince, and he received them well, as the prudent and discriminating man that he was to all men; sweetly he welcomed them and with great honor and he bestowed upon them gifts of horses and chargers, robes, all of gold, and scarlet ones as well, and he enfeoffed them, furthermore, in the district of Vatika.[13] And after Prince Guillaume received the famous castle of Monemvasia, he placed within it abundant provisions, men-at-arms, weapons and rations, of which it was in need.

Now when the outlying districts, the territories of Vatika and Tzakonia, which were in revolt, heard that it had submitted to Prince Guillaume, they began to come in at full speed to do homage to him; and the prince, as a wise man, greeted them all and received them sweetly in accordance with the rank that each held.

And as soon as Prince Guillaume had set in order the castle of Monemvasia and the surrounding districts, he ordered that all his armies be dismissed and likewise the galleys which belonged to Venice, and then he returned to Lakedaemonia. He called his captains to give him counsel, and they answered and advised him that, because they had made a great effort on land and sea during the three years that they had stayed at Monemvasia, they should have leave, small and great, to go to their homes to have a vacation; and that the prince with those of his household should stay in Lakedaemonia to pass the winter. Thereupon, small and great departed and the prince remained, as I am telling you, and thus, he went riding with his retinue and strolled among the villages in the neighborhood of Monemvasia, and to Helos[14] and to Passava[15] and to the lands in that direction; with joy he went around and passed his time.

And when he had sought in all those places, he found a wonderful hill, cut off from the ridge as a peak, a mile or more above Lakedaemonia. Because he was eager to build a stronghold, he ordered that a castle be built out on the hill, and they named it

[13] See above, p. 131, n. 63.
[14] *Ibid.*
[15] See above, p. 127, n. 55. These were lengthy strolls, for the towns were twenty to forty miles from Lakedaemonia.

Mistra, because the place was called this; they made it a splendid castle and a great stronghold.[16] Well, because the people of the place told him that the *zygos* of the Melings was a great *drongos* and had strongly fortified passes and large towns and arrogant people who respected no lord, he pondered a great deal as to how to control them. To this end, his council said to him that now that the castle of Mistra had come into being and stood above the *zygos*, the *drongos* of the Melings, he should erect another somewhere around those mountains so that they might control the area. Thereupon, the prince himself made a tour on horseback, following the directions of the people of the land, and he passed Passava and journeyed to Maine; there he found an awesome crag on a promontory. Because he found it very pleasing, he built there a castle and named it Maine, as it is still called.[17]

[16] Myzethras, or Mistra, as it is usually called, was built on a spur of Taygetos, about three miles from Sparta. It was intended to control the approaches to the defiles of the Melings, whose fierceness is quaintly described in the Chronicle of Dorotheos of Monemvasia (p. 476). The derivation of the name has been of great concern to scholars. Hopf considered it of Slavic origin (quoted in M., p. 100), though no Greek scholar has yet agreed with him. The usual interpretation of the word is that it is derived from the word μυζίθρα, a kind of cheese still very popular among Greeks. Schmitt (Index, p. 638), Longnon (p. 218), and Miller (p. 100) tend to agree with this interpretation and they give many references to the literature on the subject. Kalonaros also agrees and adds the opinion that the name had been applied to the site even before the castle was built (p. 125, n. on l. 2990). In this footnote he adds three more references from the long bibliography on Mistra.

[17] It is quite difficult to locate exactly the castle of Maine (Fr. Grand Magne). Though possibly founded as early as the time of Justinian, the first appearance of the Byzantine fortress in the sources occurs in Constantine Porphyrogenitos (*De Administrando Imperio*, ed. Gy. Moravcsik with English translation by R. J. H. Jenkins [Budapest, 1949], pp. 236-37), where he gives some vague references to the location of the castle and the fierce character of the inhabitants, a reputation they have persistently maintained to the present day. Based on this passage, an article by P. A. Phourikis (Παρατηρήσεις εἰς τὰ τοπωνύμια τῶν Χρονικῶν τοῦ Μορέως, Ἀθηνᾶ, XL [1928], 26-59) attempts to locate Maine and also derives the name from an Albanian word meaning "to build." D. Zakythinos in an article in Ἑλληνικά, III (1930), 258-59, easily refuted this etymology, and Kalonaros in three works claims to have corrected the geographical location ("A travers le Magne. Les châteaux francs de Passava et du grand Magne," *Hellénisme contemporain,*

And as soon as the archons and the leaders of the *drongos* saw that the Franks had built those two castles, they took counsel together as to how they would act. Thereupon, the leaders, who also had the wealth, said that they should stand firm rather than submit to vassalage. However, the mass of the troops and all the commons said and gave counsel that they should do homage but that they should have honor and not perform *corvées* as did the villages which were in the plains; "for, since those two castles have come into being, and we do not have leave, so much have they closed us in, to descend to the plains to carry on trade to live, we do not have the power to live in the mountains."

Now the archons and the leaders of the *drongos*, seeing that the commons desired that they do homage, had nothing else to do but to fall into step; they sent messengers to Prince Guillaume requesting a treaty whereby they would have exemption, that they would never in all their lives perform *corvées* nor pay levies, just as their parents had never done in all their lives; they would give homage and service at arms, as they likewise had given to the basileus.[18] Prince Guillaume affirmed the agreements and put them in writing, hung with seals.

And after the *drongos* of the Melings had done homage, some of them said to Prince Guillaume that, if he wished to have the whole *zygos* under his will, he should build a castle on the coast close to Gisterna. And the prince believed him who told him this; he ordered that it be built, and it was named Leftro.[19] And so,

V [Nov., 1939], 275-380; Ἐθνογραφικὰ Μάνης [Athens, 1935], and Λουλούδια τῆς Μονεμβασιᾶς). He places it on the small peninsula of Tegani (so called from its shape of a frying pan), near the harbor of Megapon. As far as I can ascertain, this places it not far to the north of Cape Matapan and on the *western* coast of the peninsula. (Schmitt, in his Index under Μέλιγγοι, also locates it at the southwest corner of Maine.) Longnon and Miller, on their maps, however, place it on the *east* coast. See Zakythinos, pp. 22-23, and a very long footnote in Kalonaros, p. 126, n. on l. 3004. Also see Miller, p. 100 and n. 2.

[18] Constantine Porphyrogenitos (*De Adm. Imp.* III, 224 ff.) says of the inhabitants of the *drongos* of the Melings that they were: αὐτόνομοι, αὐτοδέσποτοι, μὴ δεχόμενοι, οὔτε ἄρχοντα παρὰ τοῦ στρατηγοῦ, οὔτε ἄλλην τοῦ δημοσίου δουλείαν ἐκτελεῖν. The Maniotes, therefore, were asking for a continuation of their customary status under the Byzantine administration.

[19] Schmitt, following Buchon and Phillipson, has mistakenly located Gisterna

after they had built the castles which I have named for you, Leftro, Mistra, and Old Maine,[20] he subdued the lands of the Slavs and had them under his will, and he walked throughout the principality and rejoiced in it all, as if he had conquered it and was lord of it all.[21]

Now from this point on, I am going to stop speaking about Prince Guillaume of Achaia and I am going to tell you about the basileus Kyr Theodoros of Laskaris, basileus of the Romans, who was in Anatolia during those years, for in the City there was a Frankish emperor and he was called Baldwin, thus he was named. You have heard here above in the book about the times when Kyr Theodoros Laskaris was basileus over the Romans and how death came to him, and he left his son, who was a minor child, to be raised by the man named Kyr Michael, the great Palaiologos, because he was the foremost of the archons of Romania. And he, because he would commit a sin, strangled and killed his little lord and seized the empire of all of Romania.[22] When Angelos Kaloioannes, Koutroules was his surname, despot of Hellas, heard how Palaiologos had acted and what he had done and had murdered

close to Cape Matapan. (See his Index under Gisterna and Leftro, pp. 634 and 637.) Kalonaros, in a very long and detailed footnote (p. 128) quoting all the sources, gives the correct location and points out how the error originally arose. Gisterna (the Byz. Kinsterna) was a *theme* lying in northwest Lakonia, with its western boundary along the coast of the peninsula, south of Kalamata. Leftro (called Beaufort in French) lay on the coast, near the present Lefktro, south of Kalamata. It is correctly located on Longnon's map (pp. 200-1) though he is vague as to its location in his text (p. 218). L. states that Leftro lay on the coast "between Kalamata and Grand Magne" (§ 207). Therefore, Leftro lay on the western coast, north of Grand Maine, which in turn was north of Matapan.

[20] The terms "Old Maine" and "Grand Maine" are both used in the Chronicle. Kalonaros points out (p. 129, note) that the two terms are synonymous, and do not, as some scholars have thought, indicate two separate towns. L. uses only one term throughout—"Grand Maigne." The terms "Grand Maine" and "Old Maine" came into use to differentiate Maine, not from another town of the same name, but from the town of Mikromane (Maingne) in Messenia. (See below, ll. 8069 and 8094.)

[21] This passage is obscure. Perhaps it should read: "he walked in the good will of all the principality, as if...."

[22] These events are described at the end of the Prologue, ll. 1210-44. See above, p. 102, n. 84, for true chronology and names.

the basileus and had taken the empire, he was angered and enraged
and greatly did he grieve for it; he made a firm oath never to
consider Palaiologos as basileus nor to have him for lord; since
he had seized the empire of the Romans by a rebellious plot, he
did not have to consider him his lord nor his friend nor indeed his
relative.[23] When the basileus Palaiologos heard these things, he
was greatly incensed, angered, and enraged and said that if he
had a road whereby to cross over to the west, he would in short order
grieve him in good measure, but because Baldwin happened to
be emperor in the City at that time and held sway, he did not have

[23] Angelos Kaloioannes Koutroules is a fictitious personage, for no ruler
of Epiros bore any of these names. Apparently the chronicler is again confusing the Kaloioannes of the Bulgars with the lord of Epiros. (See above,
p. 97, ll. 1030 ff. and n. 69). The establishment of the Komnenos Doukas line
in Epiros is the subject of an article by Lucien Stiernon, "Les origines du
despotat d'Epire," *Revue des Études Byzantines*, XVII (1959), 90-126, where
he shows that the early rulers were lords, but not despots. The work of
Michael I, after his death in 1214, was continued by his brother Theodoros I.
Relentlessly expanding his dominions at the expense of Bulgar and Frank,
he finally put an end to the kingdom of Salonika in 1224. Feeling that his
state, now including almost all of continental Greece, parts of Bulgaria, Vlachia, and Thrace, was equal in size and power to an empire, he decided to
assume the title of basileus. This precipitated an immediate and bitter rivalry
with the emperor of Nicaea. Though in a truly powerful position, Theodoros
was led by ambition to attack the Bulgarian tsar John Asen II in 1230. In the
battle that ensued, he was defeated and made prisoner. His brother Manuel
seized the empire, but in 1240 Theodoros, released from captivity, led a revolt
against his brother and placed his son Ioannes on the throne. This feeble would-
be monk, however, was no match for the surging power of the Nicene emperor,
and in 1246 Salonika fell to Ioannes Vatatzes, second basileus of Nicaea. Meanwhile, in Epiros Michael II, bastard and only son of Michael I, had revolted
in 1237 against his uncle in Salonika. He set up an independent lordship
which included Epiros, Corfu, and Thessaly. He married the extraordinary
Theodora Petraleiphas, later canonized, and had by her a son Nikephoros and
two daughters, Helene, who married Manfred of Sicily, and Anna, who married
Guillaume II de Villehardouin in 1259. This alliance involved Morea immediately in Greek rivalries and when war broke out in the north between
Michael II and Michael Palaiologos, Guillaume led a Moreot force to help his
new father-in-law. The resulting battle of Pelagonia in 1259 was disastrous
for Morea. This defeat, with the captivity of Guillaume, marks the turning
point in the history of Morea and is the prime cause of all the subsequent disasters that overtook the Franks in the Peloponnesos.

the power to cross over to the west. But after he had conquered the city of Constantine and had crossed over to Galata and had possession of the empire, he took action and made war on land and on sea and launched a fearsome attack against the despot of Arta. And he, because he was wise, applied himself well; he engaged as mercenaries the Franks, Prince Guillaume and the lord of Athens, and also the Euripiotes; he was helped by them and he went off to battle.[24]

Thereafter, there occurred the death of Kyr Ioannes the despot and he left as his heir Kyr Nikephoros, his son; to him he bequeathed all of his despotate.[25] He had another son also, but who was illegitimate, to whom he left a good portion in Vlachia, towns and strong castles for him to rule; Kyr Theodoros they called him, Doukas, his surname. Now he turned out to be courageous in arms; he was a marvelous soldier, wise and skillful. And when he saw that his father, Kaloiannes, had died and that there remained his brother, Nikephoros, who was not wise as his father had been, he wished and desired to seize Vlachia and to seize, indeed, half of all the despotate. He built a strong castle, which is called New Patras, and began a fierce struggle with his brother, Kyr Nikephoros, I tell you, the despot.[26] And because the Franks were helping the despot, Kyr Theodoros went to the basileus, to Kyr Michael, I tell you, the great Palaiologos. He promised and vowed to do many things: he vowed to surrender to him his brother, the despot, bound like an archtraitor, and to do him homage. He made him sevastokrator of all Romania and he gave him his armies to have under his command, to battle and to bring to justice

[24] The chronology here is, of course, confused. Constantinople fell in 1261. The campaign was launched by Palaiologos in 1258. As was pointed out in the previous note, Guillaume went as an ally, not a mercenary.

[25] This Kyr Ioannes is really Michael II, who died in 1271. His legitimate son Nikephoros succeeded him and ruled until 1296. His illegitimate son, John (Ioannes), called Theodoros in the Chronicle, received the title of Sevastokrator and ruled over Vlachia and Neopatras from 1271 to 1295. The Franks, confused by his name Komnenos Doukas, referred to him as duke of Neo Patras. The story of this fratricidal war and the intervention of Palaiologos is wholly fictitious.

[26] New Patras (Neopatras, the modern Hypate) lay in Thessaly, a short distance to the west of Lamia.

the despot, his brother; he honored him greatly and gave him bene-
factions.[27]

And when the despot heard at that time the news that Kyr
Theodoros, his brother, had risen in revolt against him and had
gone over to the basileus, who was his enemy, he was deeply grieved
and lost courage completely. He called on his archons to give
him counsel; and all advised him to give his sister as lawful wife
to Prince Guillaume, for if he had the prince as an ally and brother,
he would defy the war of the basileus, such as it might be. And
when he had taken counsel with his archons, he sent messengers
to Prince Guillaume. They were shrewd men and they quickly
brought him to terms; they made the agreements over the dowry
and the wedding. Quickly, they returned to the despot; they
told him all, by word of mouth they reported to him, how they
had arranged the marriage. Sixty thousand *hyperpyra*[28] was the
dowry which the despot gave at that time to the prince for his
excellent sister, I say, and this apart from her robes and gifts.
Nor did they delay at all in holding the wedding, which took place
in Old Patras. And since the prince and the despot had become
in-laws, they now loved one another very much and were as one,
and when it would happen that the despot had need of armies and
men-at-arms from the prince, as many as he needed and wished,
he had at his command.[29]

[27] Sevastokrator seems to have been an honorific title coined from the
words σεβαστός (august) and αὐτοκράτορ (emperor). Gibbon (*Decline and
Fall* [Mod. Lib. ed.], II, 854-55), quoting Anna Comnena, claims that Alexios
Komnenos originated the title and reserved it for princes of the blood. The
rank seems to have entailed no specific duties in the court, but was conferred
as a great honor to the higher nobility.

[28] The ὑπέρπυρον (Lat. *hyperperum*) was the standard gold coin of Byzantium.
It was previously known as the *bezant* and the *solidus*, and had a value, at its
proper weight of gold, roughly equivalent to the English pound.

[29] Actually, Michael Palaiologos sought to avoid the conflict with Michael II,
but the latter, encouraged by his recent alliances with Manfred and Guillaume
and covetous of the crown, was not in a conciliatory frame of mind. Guillaume
entered this alliance to please his Greek subjects and possibly because of aspirations of reviving the kingdom of Salonika. Anna was, in the words of the
Chronicle of Dorotheos of Monemvasia, "without arraying herself in vestments,
already arrayed in her beauty and loveliness, for she was as superbly lovely

At this point, I am going to pause for a bit in discoursing and speaking about the despot of Arta to tell you and recite about the prince of Morea, Sir Guillaume. Now, after Prince Guillaume captured the castle of Monemvasia, his dominions were extended; indeed, he had no reason to fight with any man in the world. The bannerets of Morea, together with the knights, began to raise castles and strongholds, each in his own territory making one of his own; and as soon as they had erected these strongholds, they put aside their surnames, which they had from France, and they assumed the names of the territories which they took.[30]

Thereupon, the first to begin was a certain great lord, Sir Geoffroy, he was called, his surname de Bruyères, who was lord of Skorta, both of the *drongos* and of the territory; he built a fortified castle, a handsome stronghold and named it Karytaina and he was dubbed lord of Karytaina, the famous soldier. The second was known as Sir Gautier, de Rosières, he was called, this he had for surname; he built an awesome castle in Mesarea and named it Akova and he was lord. A certain other was called by the name of Sir Jean, de Neuilly his surname, who was also marshal of the principality of Morea, and he held it as a hereditary office; his lordship built a castle and called it Passava. Another was de Nivelet and had the name Sir Jean; his lordship built a castle and called it Geraki, which is in Tzakonia, this side of Helos. And likewise with the others who held seigneuries, the knights and bishops and all the bannerets, each built a stronghold in his land; they wished and desired the pleasures of the world and they all rejoiced during the time that they had.

and charming of head and all her body as a second Helen of Menelaus." It has been suggested that she was the model for Helen in Goethe's *Faust*, as was Guillaume for Faust in the second part, at least, and that the Sparta of Menelaus in the third act, second part, is a description of the medieval Frankish principate of Morea. For varying opinions of this, see Schmitt, Introduction, pp. lviii-lxvi; Baronne Diane de Guldencrone, *L'Achaie féodale* (Paris, 1886), where this interpretation of *Faust* was first made; and G. Moravcsik, "Zur quellenfrage der Helenaepisode in Göthes Faust," *Byz.-Neugr. Jahrbücher*, VIII [1929-30], 41-56.

[30] There now follows a repetition of the information from the register given in ll. 1911-50.

At this point, I am here going to stop speaking about them and
I return to telling you how the war began between the prince of
Morea, Guillaume, and the lord of Athens, Sir Guillaume by name,
de la Roche his surname, thus was he named. You have heard
me tell you earlier in my book about the time and season and
those days when Boniface, the marquis of Montferrat and king
of Salonika, came to Corinth to the lord of Morea, the Champenois;
and because of the great love which they had for one another,
the Champenois asked help of the marquis. And he granted him
the homage and liegedom, first, of the lord of Athens, and of the
three *terzieri* of Euripos, and in addition, fourthly [*sic*], of the
marquis of Boudonitsa.[31] And during the wars which Prince Guillaume, and also his father, Sir Geoffroy, and likewise Sir Geoffroy,
his brother, had waged, they had all spent their time *courtoise-
ment*. Well, as soon as Prince Guillaume became lord over the
principality of Achaia and had it in his power, he asked the great
lord to do him homage, and also the lords of the island of Euripos,
and likewise the marquis, the lord of Boudonitsa. And they met,
all five together; they took counsel with one another and made
him an answer that they only recognized him as their peer; as

---

[31] These apocryphal details are given in ll. 1553 ff. See above, p. 114, nn. 16
and 17. The real cause of the struggle between Guillaume and Guy de la Roche
(not Guillaume de la Roche, as stated in l. 3177) and the other lords of central
Greece is to be found in a dispute over an inheritance. The second wife of
Guillaume was Carintana dalle Carceri, who was related to the leading family
of Euripos and baroness over the northern third of the island in her own right.
When she died in 1255, Guillaume claimed her barony as heir. The local barons
and the Venetians opposed his claim and declared war. Guillaume was taking
vigorous and successful steps to defeat them when the struggle spread to the
mainland. Guillaume de la Roche, brother of Guy, great lord of Athens, though
a vassal of the prince of Achaia, joined forces with the Euripotes and prevailed
upon his brother to refuse Villehardouin's call for assistance. Being his vassal
for Argos and Nauplion, Guy was obliged to respond to his lord's call and his
refusal constituted a crime. The struggle became a baronial rebellion against
the aspirations of the prince of Achaia. The issue was settled in 1258 at the
battle of Mount Karydi, where Guillaume de Villehardouin was victorious.
Guy de la Roche was captured and forced to go to France to stand trial before
the king of France. While Guy was in France, Guillaume was taken prisoner
during the Battle of Pelagonia (1259) and the whole situation in Frankish
Greece was altered. See M., pp. 102 ff.

for the homage which he mentioned, they owed him nothing, nor would they ever condescend to to him homage.

The prince was enraged on hearing these words, which seemed to him improper; he held his council, and his council advised him to make a campaign and that he march against them to make war on them as rebels and traitors, which they were against him.

To this end, he ordered that everyone of the principality be written, the bannerets, the knights, all the bishops, the Temple and Hospital and all the burgesses. He charged them to gather at Nikli on the twentieth of May, with no excuse. And when the great lord heard and learned that the prince of Morea was preparing to come against him for war with all his armies, he sent out a summons everywhere, wherever he had a friend, requesting and pleading that they come to help him against the prince, who was coming to make war on him. His best friend and relative at that time was the most valiant lord of Karytaina, before whom they trembled in all of Romania; he had his sister as wedded wife.[32] The great lord wrote to him, notifying him and pleading with him, as his true brother, not to fail him on this occasion and in this his need, for in him did he have hope and all his confidence.

On hearing what his brother asked of him, the most valiant and famous lord of Karytaina paused and pondered well how he should act, to whom he should first go to help, the prince, who was his liege lord and blood relative—he happened to be his uncle—or the great lord, his wife's brother. And as much as he pondered, he took the worse as his choice, that which was not to his honor. He said that he considered it better to lose his honor than to fail his wife's brother. Now this is the reasoning that he had in mind at that time: that, if he failed the prince—he was, after all, his uncle—he would have his pardon, and he would take it lightly. Thereupon, he hastily gathered together strong armies, and this was heard everywhere, and all were amazed at it. And the prince, when he heard of it, was overjoyed, believing and hoping that he would come with him. But he hurried to go to the great lord and

[32] Geoffroy de Bruyères was married to Isabeau de la Roche, daughter (not sister) of Guy de la Roche. His mother was a sister of Guillaume de Villehardouin.

took his army and went to Thebes; he found the great lord gathering an army. And when he saw that his brother-in-law had come there, it seemed to him that he was gaining half the world; he was very happy; later, he repented. And the prince, when he heard of the action and deed of his evil nephew, the lord of Karytaina, it seemed to him very regrettable and he was deeply grieved; first of all, because of the reputation he had in the world of being the best of all the soldiers that were in Romania in those years, and again, because he was related to him and was his nephew and had betrayed his lord and had gone over to his enemy. However, as he was wise, he consoled himself and ordered his armies and they went to Corinth; they forced the "stairway of Megara" and won this pass by battle.[33] The great lord learned of it and was very disturbed, for he learned that the prince had passed the defile and had entered his lands and was out looking for him. He took his armies and went out to meet him and they met at Mount Karydi. They began the battle on top of the mountain; as God is a judge and judges on the right, he cast for the prince, and he won the battle.

The one banneret killed there in battle was called Sir Guibert, de Cors was his surname, who had as his wedded wife the daughter of Sir Jean de Passava; and after him, she took as her wedded husband Sir Jean, called de St.-Omer, this was his surname; and together this couple produced an outstanding son, the wonderful Sir Nicolas de St.-Omer, lord of Thebes and grand marshal of the principality of Achia.[34] Likewise, there were killed in that battle sergeants and knights without number.

---

[33] The road that crosses the isthmus and leads along the coast of the Saronic Gulf towards Megara is still called the κακὴ σκάλα ("evil stairway"), because of its narrow and rocky nature. The pass of Mt. Karydi (Walnut Mountain) lies about midway on the road from Megara to Thebes.

[34] The opening phrase of this sentence should perhaps read: "There was killed there in battle a certain banneret called...." Marguerite of Passava was the daughter of Jean II de Neuilly by a daughter of Gautier I de Rosières, lord of Akova. Her third husband was Jean de St.-Omer. Marguerite's father was hereditary marshal of Morea and the title passed through his daughter to her husband, then to her son Nicolas III de St.-Omer, lord of Thebes.

The great lord fled, going to Thebes with as many as followed him and went with him; the lord of Karytaina went there with him. Now, after Prince Guillaume had defeated the great lord in the battle which took place at Karydi, the great lord fled, going into Thebes; the lord of Karytaina was there with him, as were Sir Nicolas de St.-Omer with his brothers, Sir Jean de St.-Omer and Sir Othon,[35] and also the great lord's three brothers, who were all praiseworthy soldiers and knights, each bearing his own banner; and the lord of Salona, Sir Thomas;[36] the three lords of Euripos and the marquis, all of whom carried banners; but the other knights who were in the battle with the great lord, I do not list here because of the much writing it would require.

And the prince, seeing that he had won the battle, routing and killing his enemies, prudently pursued them with his armies to Thebes and blockaded them. He ordered that the armies pitch their tents all around it; they plundered the suburbs and captured them. Now, when the chiefs of the army saw that their relatives there whom they loved, the great lord together with the others who were with him, were losing their villages, the metropolitan of Thebes and certain others from there set themselves to mediate to come to some terms with the great lord and those who were with him, and they so endeavored that they came to terms with

[35] Sometime between 1230 and 1240, Bela de St.-Omer married Bonne, sister of Guy I de la Roche. She brought as her dowry one half of the seigneury of Thebes. The other half remained in the hands of her brother. Their sons were Nicolas II, co-feoffee of Thebes and *bailli* of Morea 1287-89; Othon, co-feoffee of Thebes; and Jean, who became marshal of Morea on his marriage to Marguerite of Passava.

[36] The barony of Salona was established by Boniface de Montferrat in 1205 on his initial invasion of Greece. He granted it to one of his followers, Thomas de Stromoncourt (or d'Autremoncourt), who built in Salona, the ancient Amphissa, lying at the western foot of Parnassos, a magnificent castle (La Sole), whose remains are still quite impressive. The barony, at its height, stretched roughly from Salona southwards to the coast of the Gulf of Corinth between Itea and Galaxidi in the east and Naupaktos in the west. The curious Chronicle of Galaxidi compiled in 1703 tells us that the name Amphissa was changed to Salona in honor of Boniface, king of Salonike, and second founder of the town (*Chron. Gal.*, ed. Sathas [Athens, 1914], pp. 207 ff.). The Thomas referred to here is Thomas II, son of the former. The Chronicle of Morea calls him simply "lord," whereas the Chronicle of Galaxidi always calls him "count."

them. The great lord swore to the prince at that time to put an end to his raiding and destroying; and, on his oath, he would go to Corinth and in the town of Nikli, would do him homage, and for whatever wrong he had done him, whatever felony he had committed against him, for the arms he had raised against the prince, he would make restitution as justice required. The banner-ets entered as guarantors and guaranteed that the great lord would go to Nikli within a term, which they then prescribed. And as soon as they had established this which I have been telling you, the prince set out and went to Corinth and from there he journeyed straightway to Nikli. And the great lord immediately made ready and took with him his noble bannerets and all the knights that had followed him; honorably and nobly, he then set out and went straightway to the town of Nikli, where Prince Guillaume was waiting for him.

And as soon as the great lord arrived there at Nikli and had joined with all the archons of the principality, they all went with him before the prince. He fell on his knees and all pleaded with him to forgive what the great lord had done, for he had taken up arms in battle against him. And he, noble and prudent man that he was, courteously forgave the great lord at that time; thereupon, he did the homage that he owed and kissed him upon his mouth and they were reconciled.[37] After this, in the presence of the cap-tains, he ordered him, as redress for the felony he had committed and had taken up arms in battle against him, to go before the king of France and be judged by him. And the great lord im-mediately promised him that he would fulfill what the prince had commanded.[38]

And after they had finished with this matter that I have been telling you about, the bishops, together with all the others, in-

[37] This description of the act of homage agrees with the form prescribed in the Assizes of Romania, chapter 3 (Recoura, pp. 151-53).

[38] Actually, it was Guillaume's baronial court that made this decision. Impressed by his retinue and perhaps understanding the suspicions and re-sentments that had caused him to resist Guillaume's aggressiveness, they declared that since they were not his peers they were not able to try Guy and that he would have to appear before the court of Louis IX for judgment. Guillaume was bound to accept this verdict. See M., p. 106.

cluding the great lord, took Sir Geoffroy, the lord of Karytaina, with a halter around his neck and went before the prince. Pleading on their knees, all prayed that he be merciful and forgive him. And the prince did not wish to and opposed them vigorously, giving them as his reason, and it was the truth, too, the wrong which he had committed by leaving and going over to his enemy, I tell you, the great lord; he deserted him, his rightful lord.[39] However, they urged him and pleaded with him so much, the bishops and the archons and all the captains, that they won the prince over, and he became merciful toward the lord of Karytaina, his nephew. Thereupon, he gave him pardon in this way: he returned his land to him to hold from then on as an inheritance for direct heirs of his body, should he have any; as a new grant he gave it to him to hold from then on.[40] Now, after these agreements had taken place, the young knights held a celebration; they held jousts, broke lances, and had a fine time. And when they had celebrated well, they set out from there; the great lord and the lords of Euripos asked leave of the prince and they departed.

And because the winter season was approaching, the great lord remained to spend the winter. And when the new season arrived in the month of March, he equipped two galleys, boarded them, and crossed over to Brindisi and landed there.[41] He bought

[39] Article 167 of the Assizes of Romania states that "when a person deserts his lord in battle and flees before the battle has been lost, he deserves to be disinherited of his land by judgment of the court of his lord" (Recoura, p. 265).

[40] The original fiefs carved out of Morea at the time of the conquest were granted to the first holders, the *bers de la conqueste*, with full rights of inheritance: i.e., they could be inherited by any heir named by the lord in his testament. However, later fiefs were granted with limited rights of inheritance: i.e., they could be inherited only by direct blood-heirs and if there were none the fiefs reverted to the lord who had granted the fief or to his heir. Thus, in this case, Guillaume took away Geoffroy's fief for his crime and then returned it to him as a new fief to hold for his lifetime and with the right of bequeathing it only to a son or daughter. L. says, *lui rendi sa terre par tel maniere que, de lors en avant, ne la deust tenir de conqueste ne a tous hoirs, ançoys lui randi de novel don, et aux hoirs de son cors* (§ 241).

[41] L. says that as soon as spring arrived the great lord set out with two galleys from Rivadostron (Rivedostre) and went to Brindisi (§ 244). L. de F. informs us that he left his brother Othon as his *bailli* in Thebes (§ 224). Rivadostron was the port of Thebes during this period. Its modern name is Livadostro,

saddle horses[42] and took to the road; he traveled so well that he arrived in Paris. He found the king there; it was the high holiday which is called Pentecost and the king was celebrating.[43] The great lord bowed submissively before the king, and he received him with great honor, for he had learned that he was coming from Romania. The prince had sent word in writing with one of his knights about the situation that the great lord had brought about. The knight had made obeisance to the king and had given him the letter from Prince Guillaume. And the king received it and ordered it to be read; and after the king understood fully the deed which the great lord had committed at that time against the prince, he shrewdly perceived therein that the prince of Morea had sent the great lord there to him because of his honor before the world.[44] For this reason, therefore, he ordered that the captains who were then in Paris for the holiday come before him; he asked of all of them that they counsel him good counsel. At great length and in detail, they discussed the felony that the great lord, I tell you, had committed against Prince Guillaume. And as soon as they had spoken at length and had found the truth, they called the great lord and also the knight; they gave their answer to both of them. Orally they declared it to them and presented it to them in writing as well; and the great lord stood and listened to the words. A baron pronounced the words of the court; he called the knight and said to him: "Listen, my friend and brother,

and it lies at the eastern end of the Gulf of Corinth on the Bay of Livadostro, more commonly known in Greece as the Alkyonian Sea.

42 *Ἄλογα τοῦ δάου*. The δάος was a type of pack horse or saddle horse. According to Schmitt (see his Index) the word is derived from the Turkish *dagh*, which means "mountain." Dragoumis, p. 78, says that δάος is equal to ἀγγάριος or "a beast of burden."

43 See above, p. 134, n. 69.

44 Louis IX was overlord to neither Guillaume de Villehardouin nor the great lord for their fiefs in Greece. The decision to send the latter before him was therefore an act of courtesy and a tribute to the reputation of Louis as the great dispenser of justice. A meeting of the French *cour-plénière* did take place at this time (spring, 1259), though principally to settle eastern affairs in general, and it is possible that the great lord's affair was settled at that session. Guy is known, furthermore, to have been in France at this time. See Buchon, *Rech. hist.*, I, 115, n. 1, and M., pp. 106-7.

understand the words with which the court of France answers you.
If the great lord had done homage here to his lord, Prince Guillaume, and thereafter had taken up arms against him and had
fought in the field with him face to face, then the law would order,
and judgment demand, that he and his descendants be disinherited
from whatever land and suzerainty he holds from him. However,
since the document which you brought here declares, and you told
us with your own mouth the same in the presence of the court,
that the great lord never did homage to your lord the prince of
Morea, the felony does not bring the matter to the point of disinheritance; however, since the great lord knew and he himself
recognized, and it had also been the command of his former lord,
the king of Salonika, that he should do him homage, it should
never in any way have come to pass that he take up arms nor
wage a war with his lord. Therefore, since Prince Guillaume sent
the great lord, and he has come here to the court of our lord, and
he came by himself, eager to make reparation, and he has come
at great expense, with trouble and fatigue, and his voyage has
been a long one, which is only the truth, for him to come from
Romania here to France, and, furthermore, for the honor of such
a great lord as is our lord, the king of France, this of itself is suitable
as redress; let him be pardoned."

And when the baron had completed this speech which I have
recorded for you, the great lord stood before the court, removed
his *chaperon*, and answered prudently;[45] he thanked the king and
after him the court. And after this, entreating, he requested the
king to write to the prince the findings of the court, the judgment
which it passed and its decision. And the king, as a noble man,
so ordered, and it was done.

And after the papers had been drawn up and the task was finished, the king, himself, then called the great lord and spoke thus
to him with sweetness of mind: " You have come here from your
land, from Romania, with trouble and expense, here to my kingdom, and it would not be seemly for you to return without receiving from me some compensation and gift. For this reason

[45] The *chaperon* (*καπερούνι*) was a medieval head covering worn by both
sexes. The term was especially used for the hood worn by a knight in full dress.

I say to you, ask me boldly; whatever you should like from me, I shall bestow upon you."

Hearing this, the shrewd great lord made obeisance to the king and thanked him ten thousandfold; he pondered a little bit and then he answered: "I thank your crown and your majesty,[46] O lord, for having the desire to grant me a beneficence. Therefore, I say, my lord, to your holy majesty, that the seigneury of Athens, which I have and hold, whoever held it in olden time was called duke; now, let it be by your word and command that from now henceforth I shall be called duke." And the king, when he heard this, approved of it highly; he ordered that he be invested within the palace.[47]

Now from this point on, I am going to stop talking about the king of France and the duke of Athens, and I am going to tell you and recount to you how the prince of Morea, Guillaume, was captured in the battle of Pelagonia, he and his troops.

As you have heard here above in my book, the despot Koutroules made a treaty with Prince Guillaume of Morea and gave him his sister as wedded wife.[48] Out of this in-lawship, the love

---

[46] Such expressions as εὐχαριστῶ τὸ στέμμα σου, τὴν βασιλείαν σου (ll. 4294, 6454), etc., are typical Byzantine expressions prescribed by court ceremony. These also appear in L. (cf. *je prie vostre saincte corone, puisque a sa corrone plaisoit*, etc.). Schmitt declares that, since the common term of address for the king among the Franks was simply "sire," the presence of such elaborate "periphrastical titles," so common in the Greek language of the day, in the French text indicates that the French must be a translation of a Greek prototype. However, in my opinion, this is not a necessary conclusion. It is enough to conclude that such terms had come into general use among the Moreot Franks through their close contact with the local Greeks, as had such words as βασιλεύς, ἀφέντης, ἄρχοντας, κύρ, etc. See Schmitt, *Introduction*, p. xxxiii; and Adamantios, *Tὰ Xρον. τοῦ Μορ.*, p. 610.

[47] This allusion to an ancient precedent for the title is false. The Latin word *dux* was often used by the Byzantines as the equivalent of στρατηγός (general), but there was never an official at Athens with that title. (See M., p. 107.) It is unlikely that Guy was invested with the rank of duke at this session of the court, but after his return from France, he may have been addressed as "sire" and may have used loosely the title "duke." (See Buchon, *Rech. hist.*, I, 116, n. 3 and II, 385-87.)

[48] Ll. 3050-3137 above. The despot Koutroules and Theodoros Doukas are Michael II and his natural son, Ioannes, lord of Vlachia. It is to be noted again

between the prince and the despot grew stronger; in fact, they and their troops loved one another as much as if they were all from one mother. Well, when the war with the basileus, which Kyr Theodoros Doukas, the sevastokrator, was fighting constantly at that time against the despot, grew in intensity, the despot planned to inflict a blow upon the basileus and to undo him.

And when the prince heard this and was informed of it, he took his knights and bannerets. Straightway he traveled to Old Patras; at the same time, the despot arrived at Epaktos[49] and crossed over from Drapanon and went to Patras and met with his brother-in-law, the prince. They and their troops held a splendid celebration; and when they had celebrated as much as they desired, they sat down together with their captains and all the wisest counselors whom they had with them. Thereupon, the despot began to speak and to voice complaints of the damage he suffered from the sevastokrator, his brother. And when he had finished with his complaints, all the wisest of the despotate gave cunning advice—afterwards they repented—that the two brothers, the despot and the prince, should march out with all their armies, pass through Vlachia[50] and enter Romania and overrun and plunder all of Romania; and, if they should chance upon armies of the basileus, or if the sevastokrator, himself, should meet them, then they should give battle in the field, for they would be victorious over them.

And after they had held counsel, as I have been telling you, the despot returned to Arta; he sent everywhere to gather armies.[51]

that this account of friction between Epiros and Vlachia is completely false. See *Chron. of Galaxidi*, pp. 142-52 of the Introduction and pp. 209-10 of the text.

[49] Epaktos is the medieval name for Naupaktos, a town lying on the northern shore of the Gulf of Corinth, opposite Cape Drepanon. Drapanon is the medieval form of Drepanon. The straits between the two points and then the whole Gulf of Corinth came to be known as the "Sea of Paktos" from the name Epaktos (cf. below, 1. 3626). Today a busy ferryboat connects the two points.

[50] Vlachia here indicates the lands of Ioannes (called Theodoros) Doukas, also known as the Duchy of Neo-Patras.

[51] L. states (§ 260) that the despot asked for 400 mounted knights from Apulia. It is certain that his son-in-law, Manfred, sent this number of knights,

And the prince returned to the town of Andravida; he sent word everywhere that all should equip themselves with arms, small and great, foot soldiers and knights; and in the spring of the year, with winter passed, after they had Eastered together in the month of April, that all should come straight to Andravida to cross over and invade the territory of Romania. Now the despot and the prince expended moneys to hire mercenaries; they hired as many armies as they were able to procure.[52]

At this point, I turn from what I have been telling and I am going to take up other matters, to tell you and to relate about the basileus. Just as there took place the meeting, which I have told you about, which the prince and the despot held in Patras, where they met and took their counsel to invade together the land of the basileus, to do battle with the basileus, to plunder his land and to overrun the sevastokrator's Vlachia; so, too, the sevastokrator, when he heard these reports, provisioned his castles and strongly fortified them with troops and food, that they might dwell in them and guard them; he ordered and instructed that the common soldiers who were in the villages go into the castles, as many as there was room for to go in and to bear arms, and the others to go up into the mountains with their animals to protect themselves there.

Now, Kyr Theodoros, the one that I am telling you about, had three outstanding sons, who held arms; the first was called Komnenos, the second, Doukas, and the third was called Angelos, thus were they named.[53] He arranged that the first, Komnenos,

and there is even a suggestion by the historian Gregoras that Manfred himself came with them. See M. Dendias, "*Le roi Manfred de Sicile et la bataille de Pélagonie*," in *Mélanges Charles Diehl* (Paris, 1930), I, 55-60. Runciman, *The Sicilian Vespers* (Cambridge, 1958), p. 299, n. to p. 47, discounts this and gives references for the battle.

[52] L. adds that Guillaume instructed Othon de la Roche, *bailli* and brother of Guy, who was still in France, and his other feudatories to be ready for a spring campaign (§ 262).

[53] These three names are the dynastic names of the Byzantine emperors of the eleventh, twelfth, and thirteenth centuries. The family of the lord of Epiros bore two of them. The expedition of Michael Palaiologos against Michael II of Epiros was led not by Ioannes, son of the latter, but by Ioannes Palaiologos, brother of the basileus.

be lord and governor in the land of Vlachia, and he ordered that small and great pledge themselves to him; and as soon as he had made all his preparations, he took all those who wished to go with him and went to the basileus who was in the City; in detail he described to him the situation, that they had made ready with their armies, and that the prince of Morea with the despot of Arta were hiring mercenaries everywhere, hurrying to gather armies to come with the new season to invade Romania, "wishing, as they declare, to seize your empire and to disinherit you and us your followers." Hearing these things, the basileus, the aged Michael,[54] though he was great in wisdom and in bravery, yet did he become fearful, and, on hearing it, he lost heart almost completely; he was afraid of the prince because he had the Franks. So he ordered that all the wise and noble captains who were in his kingdom be called. He began to tell them and to relate to them that the prince of Morea with the despot of Hellas had taken to the field and were coming straightway into Romania. "Therefore, I wish and beseech that all should give counsel as to what we should do hereafter and how we should act." Many were the words which they said and spoke, but in the end they agreed and gave one counsel.

The first who spoke and addressed the basileus was the sevastokrator, Kyr Theodoros; and he said to the basileus and to the captains: "Despot, holy basileus, your majestic compassion, if you expect to protect the land of Romania with the troops that you have alone, I inform your majesty that you are ruined, you lose your empire and you disinherit us. Order, then, that your treasury be opened and spend your money and hire Germans; send word to the king of Hungary to help you with troops, and also to the king of Serbia, who is your neighbor, to come himself if he is able

---

[54] Michael VIII was born in 1234 and was therefore only twenty-five at the time of the battle of Pelagonia. In fact, one of the most notable aspects of his career is the early age at which he achieved his successes. This designation of him as "aged" can only mean that the chronicler was alive during the closing years of his reign and therefore knew of him as "the aged Michael" or that his informants so knew of him. Schmitt in his introduction to the Chronicle discusses such expressions and allusions (pp. xxxvi-viii), but apparently he overlooked this particular one.

or to send his troops; send word to Anatolia to the armies which are experienced in fighting with the Turks to come. And after these whom I have mentioned and named have come, I hope, first in God and then in your blessing, that we shall protect your land from the enemy and that we shall destroy those who threaten us."

When the basileus, the aged Kyr Michael, heard the speech and the counsel of the sevastokrator, he thanked him deeply and commended him warmly, for it seemed to him good that in this way his land would be protected, and he would ruin his enemies. Thereupon he ordered that letters be written to all the lands which Kyr Theodoros Doukas had mentioned and had counseled; messengers went to Germany; they hired three hundred, all knights who were all select, all hand-picked. From Hungary came fifteen hundred, who were all choice mounted archers. Kral, king of Serbia, sent him six hundred on horse, all good archers. Countless numbers came to him from Anatolia, and they brought with them five hundred Turks. And when the new season came in the month of March, in the neighborhood of Adrianople in the broad field these armies gathered. And the basileus, a prudent man, was still worried and he sent for two thousand Cumans, mounted archers very nimble in battle, and they came. And after all his armies had gathered, he called Kyr Theodoros, his sevastokrator, and he made him captain over all the armies; he surrendered them all to him and enjoined them all to accept him as captain and representative of the basileus, and to fulfill his command as if he himself were commanding them. At this point, I am going to turn from what I am saying and relating to return to telling you about the despot and the prince of Morea, Guillaume, and what they did and how they acted in the battle which they began.

When the winter season passed and the new season began with the month of March, when the birds called nightingales begin to warble and all creatures of the world rejoice and are renewed, the prince of Morea, Guillaume, who was farther away than the despot, sent into Euripos and all the islands and gathered from everywhere all his armies. He crossed the sea of Paktos at Pyrgos,[55] and he traveled straight to where the despot was; at Arta the

55 This Pyrgos refers to Psathopyrgos, a town near Cape Drepanon.

armies met and joined forces, and they tarried no more than one day only; on the second day they set out and went by way of Yannina and entered Vlachia and there they waited a short time until there should arrive the troops of Euripos, the islands, Thebes, and Athens and the lord of Salona. They had passed straight through the Sideroporta and came upon the prince in Vlachia; they joined together on the plain of Thalassinos.[56] And then after all the armies were joined together, all the great lords took counsel together as to how they should effect their advance and from where they should start. Some of them said they should set their armies to besiege Patras and Zetouni[57] and to attack the weaker castles. But the wiser, experienced in the ways of warfare, did not agree with this counsel; for if the troops set themselves to attacking the castle, they would fail to accomplish anything. "The better and more advantageous thing for us to do is to go from here into Romania, plundering and destroying the lands of the basileus, and if we should come upon the basileus waiting in the field, we shall with God's strength give him battle. And if God is pleased to give us the victory, we shall capture very easily the territory of Salonika, and on our return, we shall take all of Vlachia; we shall then winter here; and then we shall see that when the troops within the castles of Vlachia hear that we have fought and have been victorious, all the castles will quickly surrender to us."

And the leaders of the armies came to an agreement on this plan. Thereupon, they separated a thousand horsemen and three thousand foot soldiers to accompany them to go ahead plundering the lands. They drew them up in three groups and gave them instructions: they were to march all day, plundering the lands and

---

[56] Sideroporta (Iron Gate), the ancient Heracleia, is a fortified spot lying in the mountains that separated the duchies of Athens and Neopatras, near the present village of Eleftherochorion, on the Athens-Lamia highway, in the province of Phthiotis. The remains of the castle (Siderocastro) that protected the spot may still be seen. The plain of Thalassinos probably lay near the present Lianokladi, a village near the Hellas (Spercheios) River, between Lamia (Zetouni) and Hypate (Neopatras). See K., p. 156, n. to l. 3634.

[57] Undoubtedly Neopatras is meant here. Zetouni (Fr. Gripton or Giton) was the medieval name for Lamia. For Zetouni and Neopatras consult the Index of M.

when evening came and night arrived, they were to gather together in one spot, all of them. Next they separated all their divisions and set themselves on the road and began to march, plundering and destroying the land of Vlachia, and always their raiders marched one day's distance in front of them, by so much were they ahead of them.[58] And when they had plundered the places of Vlachia, they crossed the boundary which separated the land of the basileus from Vlachia at a place called Katakalon,[59] and they entered the lands of the basileus to plunder. There they found a castle, which is called Servia;[60] they captured some troops from this castle. They asked them to tell them what information they had learned and they answered them and informed them "that the sevastokrator with all the armies of Kyr Michael the basileus, who were waiting for you near Adrianople in the broad fields, happen to be on their way here looking for you; we expect they have crossed over to somewhere near Salonika."[61]

On hearing this, the prince and also the despot then made clear their great joy to their troops and that they wished and desired to give battle. They took counsel immediately as to what they should do, and their council advised them to go with all directness to where those armies were, to fight with them, and, they hoped, to be victorious; and if luck should be with them and they should win the battle, they hoped to remain lords of Romania. And they rode until they arrived in the district of Pelagonia, as it is called and named.[62]

[58] Obviously this whole passage is false, since the prince of Morea came to Vlachia as a friend, relative, and ally.

[59] Katakalon was a fortified spot, perhaps a pass, on the boundary between Thessaly and Macedonia, probably not far from the present town of Sarantoporos. The name owes its origin to land owned in the neighborhood by some member of the great Byzantine family, the Katakaloi. This is probably also the origin of the Katakalon of Elis. See K., p. 158, n. on l. 3674.

[60] The ruins of this castle may still be seen in Servia, which lies west and slightly north of Olympos.

[61] This is a particularly obscure passage, but this reading seems to make the most sense.

[62] Pelagonia is a district in northwestern Macedonia, whose principal city is Monastir. Originally a lake-filled basin, like Ochrida and Prespa, its waters

Kyr Theodoros Doukas of Vlachia, who was sevastokrator of all Romania, renowned in warfare and esteemed in all things, when he heard that the prince and the despot were coming, readied his army and separated the squadrons, and he expounded to each of his captains the campaign strategy which he intended to pursue. He had in his following two thousand Cumans, and because they were the most nimble of all the armies, they were to ride ahead to reconnoiter the place. Next were to come the three hundred Germans; he readied the Hungarians and they were to be the next division, and after them were to come the Serbs and the Bulgarians; and then he was to come with the Romans and the Turks. And when he had separated all his squadrons, there were twenty-seven mounted divisions.

Shrewd and sly that he was in all things, he sent orders to all the villages for the peasants to come in with their mares, bulls, and cows and whatever pack asses they had, and they brought them all in; they rode them all up onto the mountains and from afar they appeared to be knights. And every evening, each one lit a fire for himself, and the mountains and the fields all seemed to you to be on fire. And next he further ordered small and great, his armies as well as the peasants, to let loose with one voice a tumultuous roar, and it seemed to you as if claps of thunder were shaking the earth. Next, again, he instructed some of his men to take clothes and horses and to slip out and go to the prince of Morea and also to the despot and to tell them lies, things they had neither seen nor heard. They praised the troops of the basileus

have been drained by the upper Cherna River, leaving an area of broad fields. In these fields, at a spot near Monastir called at present Vorilla Wood, the battle of Pelagonia took place in October, 1259. Monastir in the Middle Ages was a metropolitan see and the metropolitans bore the title "of Pelagonia." Apparently this title was then applied to the area as a whole. (See K., p. 159, n. on l. 3694.) The battle itself has been well covered by contemporary and later Greek historians, including Acropolites, Pachymeres, Gregoras, and Sphrantzes. See also M., pp. 111-12; Z., pp. 15, 19, 42; and the study by Dendias, *Le roi Manfred*, etc. The best recent works on the subject are those of Deno J. Geanakoplos, especially his *Emperor Michael Palaeologus and the West* (Cambridge, 1959), pp. 59 ff. S. Runciman gives a picture of the battle in *The Sicilian Vespers*, pp. 39 ff.

inordinately and they exaggerated their numbers, declaring 500 for each one, and they dropped so many false reports that all the despot's followers became very frightened.[63]

Next after this, he called a man of his council and offered and promised him fiefs and much money to pretend to desert and go over to the despot. He gave him a document to give to the despot in secret, stating that he was to believe whatever he might tell him orally. He took his letters and took to the road; he walked rapidly and went to the despot, and secretly he went up to him and called him aside.

The sneak was sly and exceedingly crafty; feigning tears, he began to speak to the despot; "Lord, my master, your brother, sent me here to tell you his secret, his advice to you. It is the truth, my lord, and he bears witness to it, that you two have fallen into discord and hostility because of men's malice and envy and compulsions; you seek Vlachia, and he, the despotate. And from this cause arose the struggle between you two brothers, which has been a great censure, that you two brothers should fight one another. Therefore, good my lord, when you attacked him to take Vlachia, my master, your brother, had not the where-withal to arise and to fight back, and he sought refuge with the basileus, who is your opponent. And then the basileus learned that you were raising armies, that you made the prince of Morea your brother by giving him your sister as wedded wife and that you took him as your ally with all his armies.[64] You received bad counsel; and who gave it to you, to leave your lands and ease to go into Romania to the lands of the basileus? Who are you, my despot, to make war on the basileus? How many like you does he have under his command? Well, my good lord, hear, and believe me, that many armies are coming here to meet you; he has a good five hundred select Germans and thirteen thousand Hungarians, all with bows; he has around four thousand Bulgarians and Serbs; he has here all the Romans from Romania, and those from Turkey and Anatolia are past counting; for every one which

[63] These strategic devices are also given by George Akropolites in his history (*Historia*, Vol. I of the *Opera*, ed. Heisenberg [Leipzig, 1903], chs. 165-70).
[64] This last phrase is taken from P.

the prince and you have, there are two hundred with the basileus for every one of yours. For this reason, my despot, my lord your brother says that, though you have been fighting because of the demon's malice, he has no better friend in all the world, and just as he loves you a great deal, so does he very much pity you. And you know another thing, my lord, how hostile the basileus of Romania Palaiologos is toward you; and if you enter battle against so many armies, first, it is possible by misfortune that you will lose your life, and second, far worse, if you should fall into the hands of Basileus Palaiologos, being so hostile toward you as he is, you will never again gaze upon Arta nor the despotate. Therefore, my lord, my master your brother, has this to say to you: make some plan to flee with all your council to save yourself, you and the young archons of the despotate, and go to your land and protect your castles. And besides, if you should lose any of your foot soldiers, since you will have the suzerainty and will be in the despotate, armies will still not be lacking to you, and you will have all you want."[65] Now this godless one who was saying these things said them weeping all the while and, weeping, he told his story. And as soon as he had finished these words and many more besides, he saw clearly and recognized that the despot had lost heart; he asked leave that he might withdraw. But the despot held him until he might talk with the prince that he might learn the messages. He called two of his pages and spoke to them aside: "Go to the prince and tell him for me to come here immediately, that I have need of him at once." And they hurried off and went quickly to the prince to tell him what they had to announce from their lord, the despot; quickly he hurried to where the godless one was in the despot's tent. A second time he spoke to the prince in great detail and related everything to him, as he had done to the despot; and after he had related to the prince what he had to tell, they gave him leave and he returned whence he had come. In

---

[65] This account also appears in L. (§ 282-84) and in L. de F. (§ 263-64 *seq.*). The story is also to be found in Gregoras (*Byz. Hist.*, Bk. III; chs. 5, 36), where the details are quite different. According to him, the spy prevailed upon Michael to desert his allies in the middle of the night by telling him that he was in danger from these very allies.

detail he related to the sevastokrator what he had accomplished with the despot and that he had promised him to depart that very night.

When Kyr Theodoros heard this, he was very happy, he called the wisest counselors that he had in his armies; he told them the whole story, and they were jubilant. But the despot, I tell you, he of Hellas, was not happy; he had great sorrow. He called the prince; the two took counsel as to what they should do together and how they should act. They called their captains, the foremost in the army and they had them swear to keep secret their council. Now after the oaths of the captains were done and they had all sworn to keep secret what the despot of Arta was going to tell them, the despot then began to speak and to relate to them in detail the messages which had been spoken and related by that traitor who had been sent by Kyr Theodoros Doukas, the despot's brother, all in wickedness.

When these, the foremost archons of the army, heard these things, some believed right away and said it was the truth, others said that the betrayer had told lies. The celebrated lord of Kary-taina was ashamed when he heard of the proposed flight, and he was very much alarmed and said that the villain who had come and had related these things to the despot had told lies; they were all words, invented opportunely, boastings of the Romans, who, everyone of them, vaunt themselves and censure their enemies. "But let us halt here in these fields and, should they come against us, let us receive them by giving battle. Do not be at all afraid because they are more than we; any troops which are heterogeneous and of several tongues can never have good agreement among themselves. Now we, even though we are small in numbers in comparison with them, we are all as brothers and we speak one tongue, and soon we shall demonstrate whether or not we are soldiers."[66]

[66] This statement that they were of one tongue is a curious one, for the Chronicle itself indicates that there were Moreot Greeks in the ranks of the Franks, to say nothing of the Greek troops from the despotate. Kalonaros has suggested that the statement is an anachronism on the chronicler's part. Apparently, and there is ample evidence for this, by the time the Chronicle of Morea was written, the Franks had become Greek-speaking. The chronicler

Most of them from their fear did not heed the lord of Karytaina at all; rather, in the end they declared and decided this: that when night came and the moon was risen, and the common troops were asleep, so that they would not grasp what they were doing, the most secretly and quietly that they were able, they would make a moonlight dash to get away and to flee, as many as were able, to escape their peril. And as soon as the council decided that they would flee, each one went to his quarters.

Thereupon, the most valiant lord of Karytaina, that outstanding and laudable soldier, felt heavy sorrow and his heart was grieved. He was ashamed of the proposed flight, and he also grieved for his troops and he pondered, as a wise man, how he might help them so that they would not be lost blamelessly and he be guilty of a great sin. He stood in his tent, holding in his hand a staff, and he struck the tent post with the staff and said to it: "My post, hold strong the tent which covers me and tell her for me that she should never disbelieve that I love her well and that I do not require her to be in peril. We have taken counsel, the prince and the despot and the foremost of the army, to flee this evening and leave to their peril the common troops. For this reason, I say to you, my beloved tent, do not by any chance think that the matter stands otherwise; consider how you may escape your peril."

has simply projected into the past a condition that was true in his own day. This explanation is more plausible, I believe, than to suggest that as early as 1259 the Franks and Greeks could be spoken of as "speaking one tongue," which is patently absurd. If Kalonaros is correct, however, the statement indicates an astonishingly rapid assimilation of the Franks. He goes one step further, moreover, to state that the Chronicle of Morea, originally written in French, had to be translated into Greek so that the Franks could understand it. This whole line of reasoning is somewhat weakened by the fact that, in the passages beginning with ll. 3986 and 4721, their enemies are described as polyglot and heterogeneous, whereas they speak of themselves as being "one race." Obviously this would not include both Greeks and Franks, no matter how much intermarriage had occurred. This suggests the possibility that the statements are due to the Chronicle's excessively pro-Frank bias, evident throughout. The chronicler may mean that they all spoke French, overlooking the Greek contingents in his desire to emphasize Frankish deeds. See K., p. 165, note on l. 3840.

When the troops who were with him heard this strange novelty, the like of which they had never seen in all their lives, they all became terrified and were deeply shaken; the thing spread from man to man. When the prince heard it, he was very angry; immediately he ordered that the lord of Karytaina be called and he said to him in anger: "Was that a good thing that you did, to openly betray the oath which we made and our council as well and to give us away? You did not act discreetly; it was an act of great misconduct."

The lord of Karytaina answered the prince: "I am guilty of no misconduct and whoever has censured me, I am ready to defend myself and to give battle to whoever said that I erred, with the exception of your lordship, who are my liege lord, and I may not offer you resistance. Those who said we should flee and abandon our troops I consider fools and unfortunates, who ought not to be lords nor hold arms nor be called soldiers."

When he heard this, the prince understood and was ashamed; he repented deeply all that had happened; he called the marshal and gave him orders, telling him to have his crier announce that no one should give any heed nor be in the least frightened by the rumors that were being spread in the armies and that no one should believe them, they were big lies. But let them hold this to be the truth, let no one disbelieve it, that on the morrow, if God be willing, they would give battle.

When all the Moreots heard this report being announced and confirmed, that gave the lie to the rumors, and that on the next morning they would give battle, all rejoiced and were much in favor of it. And the archons of the despotate, when they heard it, were exceedingly disturbed; all of his grandees went to the despot and secretly they said to him in private: "Lord, what are you doing? Do you wish us to die here unjustly with you? Do not listen to the unfortunate Franks of Morea, who did not lose heart at the great numbers of the armies of the basileus which are coming against them, but who, instead, are steeling themselves to fight them." The despot answered them and said to them: "I hold to what we said and the counsel which was given; let the Moreots speak and do what they wish. Have one of you go through the army of the despotate, I tell you, to make an appeal, and when evening comes, as soon as the moon has come out, let all get started at once with great quiet and let us go straight to our estates; and whoever has a good will and desire for battle, let him stay here tomorrow and he will find what he is looking for."[67]

Thus did those Romans of the despotate act; when night had fallen, they slipped out of the army. Behold the evil deed that the despot committed at that time, to come and bring out of the Morea Prince Guillaume with the flower of the nobility of Morea, who were enjoying ease and undisputed power, and they went to his assistance in his war; then did he deliver them into the hands of his enemies and fled, traveling in God's curse. Who will hear of this and ever believe a Roman, either for love or friendship or for any relationship? Never believe a Roman in whatever he may swear to you; when he wants and desires to betray you, then he makes you godfather of his child or his adopted brother, or he makes you an in-law so that he may exterminate you.[68]

Now it is the natural custom of the world that no one can keep bad news secret. That all-faithless one, the great betrayer who cooked up all these things that I am telling you about, when he saw that the despot was fleeing in haste, he quickly sped to the army of the basileus and reported to the sevastokrator that the despot had fled with the armies which he had brought from the despotate and that the prince remained alone. When the sevastokrator heard this he was very happy; he quickly made ready his squadrons and they began to move out and hastened to go straight-

[67] The reasons for the sudden defection of Michael on the eve of the battle are obscure, since the sources are not always in agreement. The fullest and most probable interpretation is given by Pachymeres, who maintains that the trouble arose out of a quarrel between Ioannes, Michael's bastard, and Guillaume de Villehardouin. Ioannes complained that his wife had been insulted by some Frankish knights and when he received insulting allusions to his birth in reply, he deserted to the enemy. His father, warned of what his son was planning, fled to his own lands (Pachymeres, I, 83). Miller (p. 111) accepts this interpretation.

[68] As usual, this diatribe against the Greeks has been omitted from P., where ll. 3931 and 3934-39 are missing. For the practice of blood brotherhood or adopted brotherhood (ἀδελφοποιΐα), see S. Kyriakides in the Great Greek Encyclopaedia (Μεγ. Ἑλλ. Ἐγκ.), I, 569-70.

way to Pelagonia. They moved on Saturday and advanced toward the prince; on Sunday morning they set out to give battle.

And when the prince saw that the despot had fled and he recognized from his information the deed he had done to him, and that he remained in Pelagonia abandoned thus with only his armies, which he had brought from Morea, and he knew that the squadron of the basileus was coming with the sevastokrator to do battle with him, like the wise and noble man that he was and soldier, he called his captains, the foremost in the army, and all the knights, both Frank and Greek, and began to speak to them and to address them ; sweetly he exhorted them and consoled them : "Comrades, friends and brothers, you who are like my own offspring and children, God and his glory know how stricken I am by this which my brother the despot has done to us and has abandoned me like a child and has brought me to this. I, for love of him and again for my own honor, seeing the death and disinheritance with which he was threatened by the sevastokrator, his brother, who, having taken from him Vlachia, was seeking the despotate, I took my armies, you, my men, and I came as his ally to help him. And as soon as he had brought me here into Romania, he delivered us to his brother, just as Judas did Christ to the Jews. Therefore, I say to you, I beseech you all; now that this sin has brought us here to our enemies, you know that we are far distant from Morea, and, if we were to flee, we should accomplish nothing, and it would be an ugly thing for this to be said about us all over the world, that, though we are soldiers, we fled like women. Rather, let us stand like men, experienced soldiers; first of all, to save our lives, as is imperative, and second after this, to save the praise of the world, which is loved by all those who bear arms. Those who are coming here to give us battle have all been picked up everywhere from several nations;[69] and I want you to know, let no one disbelieve this, that troops that are a motley crew and gathered from many places never have good agreement among themselves. We, on the other hand, though few in numbers in comparison with them, we are all acquaintances and men of one essence and we must

---

[69] L. at this point reads: *se il sont plus de nous, il sont frapaille et chetive gent et de maintes generacions, et nous nous sommes bonne gent eslite* (§ 294).

all love one another as brothers. For if we have love among us, as is fitting, each one of us will be worth two hundred of those who are coming here to give us battle. I am not worried about any others except the Germans; they are only three hundred and have a lord called the duke of Carinthia, thus is he named.[70] And I have been informed that the Germans will constitute their first squadron that will go into battle. Well, if we make an attack as wise soldiers to counter the momentum of the Germans' attack and if God, our fortune, and the blessing of our parents grant that we scatter them and beat them completely, we shall have all the others like the falcon, the partridge. Therefore I say to you, let us make our first division the best one, all of chosen men who know how to fight and are mindful of world opinion; and let there be over them as captain and lord my nephew the lord of Karytaina. And I hope, first in God and then in his military prowess, that he will act prudently and as a good soldier."

As the prince said, so was it done; they separated their squadrons and their regiments. In the grouping of their squadrons and the regiments which they drew up, Prince Guillaume and all the Romans took the field at Pelagonia.[71] Their first division was that

---

[70] The duke of Carinthia is referred to three times in the Chronicle: here as leader of the Germans, in ll. 4021 ff., where his death is described, and in l. 7103, where he is pictured as one of Conradin's companions at the battle of Tagliacozzo. Schmitt assumes that these lines all refer to the same man, though he does not explain his appearance at Tagliacozzo nine years after his death at Pelagonia. Buchon (Rech. hist., I, 135, n. 3) identifies him as Ulrich III of Carinthia, but, as Kalonaros points out (p. 171, note to l. 4021), this man is known to have been alive as late as 1269. Kalonaros in the same footnote puts forth his own interpretation of the title "Duke of Carinthia." He claims that the duke of Carinthia present at the battle of Pelagonia was not a real person at all, but a synthetic character, created by the chronicler as a symbol of extraordinary bravery. He points out that the name for the lord of Karytaina in L. is seignor de Caraintaine. In the passage corresponding to the one here in question (chs. 207 ff.), there exists a confusion between the lord of Karytaina, who is called sire de Carinée, and this duke of Carinthia, who is called duc de Caraintaine. The duke of Carinthia, then, in his view, is a fictitious person, given this title under the influence of the more familiar name Karytaina.

[71] There is a break in H. following l. 4015. This sentence is taken from P., where it constitutes ll. 4016-18. Immediately after the break in H. is a detached phrase, καὶ διὰ καὶ ἐσὺ καὶ οἱ Ρωμαῖοι ἐδῶσαν εἰς τὸν κάμπον,

of the Germans; now, when the renowned lord of Karytaina saw them, he set out straight towards them and they set their lances in position. The first whom he encountered and gave a lance thrust was he who was called the duke of Carinthia; he struck him in the breast upon his shield and with his steed knocked him to the ground dead; then he struck two others, who were his relatives. The lance which he held broke into three pieces; and at once, he quickly put his hand upon his sword and began to fight the Germans; all those who came against him to give him battle, all those he mowed down like grass on a meadow.[72] And when the others who were with him saw, all bravely rallied around him and they slaughtered the Germans and killed them.

And when the sevastokrator saw from where he was observing that the Germans had scattered and were seized with panic, quickly he sped to where the Hungarians were and ordered all of them to let fly their arrows at the squadron that had become entangled with the Germans and he said to them boldly: "Take no heed whatever of the Germans because they are our men, for as I see and observe, that dragon the lord of Karytaina presses them badly, and if you were to shoot only against the Franks, you would never succeed in breaking up their attack; rather, all together shoot into their battle to kill their horses which they are riding, so that the knights on their steeds may fall, so that we may overthrow them before they kill us. And should the Germans die together with them, it is better that they alone be lost rather than all the armies; let the sin be mine; do as I order you."

And the Hungarians, as they were ordered, so did they do; they began to shoot their arrows at Franks and Germans; and from the other side came the Cumans, and together they shot their arrows at the Frankish people. Why should I tell you all the details and how shall I tell them minutely? All the horses and steeds of the Franks and Germans, all were slaughtered, and the

which, though it is meaningless by itself, seems to parallel the sense of the corresponding line in P. I have omitted this phrase. The reader should note, however, that the sense of the phrase would indicate that the chronicler is addressing himself to an audience of Franks, not Greeks.

[72] This picturesque phrase also appears in L. (§ 297) and L. de F. (§ 276).

knights fell. There fell also the wonderful, the pride of the soldiers, the lord of Karytaina, together with his steed. And then the sevastokrator, when he saw and recognized him, let fly a sharp little cry and ran to him, lest anyone else shoot an arrow at him and into his body. And he said to him: "Sir Geoffroy, lord of Karytaina, before they kill you, brother, surrender to me; on my dear soul you will find no guile." He swore to him upon his sword, and then he surrendered. After the wonderful lord of Karytaina, the renowned soldier, surrendered, his banner fell where they seized him; the sevastokrator, himself, picked it up and took it and gave it to someone of his retinue to hold it carefully and to guard it for him.

When the prince saw the wickedness which the sevastokrator committed at the beginning of the battle, that, when the lord of Karytaina and the Germans, I say, had intermingled and were slaughtering each other, he had set the Hungarians, and the Cumans as well, to shooting their arrows at them to slaughter their horses, he took a squadron with him and rode towards him to help him, if he was able, so that they would not overwhelm him. But the great numbers of Romans and the mass of archers[73] slaughtered the horses, and the knights fell; and after they found themselves foot soldiers amidst the armies, they could do nothing, whether they wanted to or not. Before they should die an unjust death in this world, they all surrendered, as did the prince himself.[74] None saved themselves except the mass of the poor; as many as

---

[73] Σαγιττολάσι. Schmitt (Index, p. 617) translates this word as "a shower of arrows," deriving the ending λασι from the verb ἐλαύνω. Kalonaros, however, points out (p. 212, note to l. 5087) that this is incorrect. The ending, he maintains, really corresponds to the French ending ace or asse, indicating great numbers, as in such words as populace, paperasse, and filasse. The ending appears in other medieval Greek words, one of the more common being γυναικολάσι.

[74] The three principal Greek sources for the battle, Akropolites (p. 170), Pachymeres (I, 86), and Gregoras (I, 75), give a more detailed account of Guillaume's surrender. When he saw that the battle was lost, he sought to save himself by hiding in a haystack or in some deep woods, but he was discovered and captured by some Greek troops, who recognized him from his prominent front teeth. This last was a well-known characteristic of his, so much so that he was often called "Long-Tooth." Others of the Frankish horsemen were captured as far away as Platamon and elsewhere.

were able fled and escaped by way of Vlachia; some foot soldiers saved themselves and went into Morea, and the Vlachs captured others in Vlachia, and the rest, moreover, they killed and plundered. And as soon as the battle was over and the Franks had been defeated, the sevastokrator ordered that the tents be set up. The tent of his quarters had four posts; and after it was set up and he had entered, he ordered that all his archons and captains come, and then he ordered that Prince Guillaume, the lord of Karytaina, and all the knights be brought in. Respectfully he took the prince by the hand, greeted him sweetly and seated him beside him. "Welcome, my brother; welcome, my brother-in-law; how desirous I have been to see you, just as I see you now." With his other hand, he took the lord of Karytaina and respectfully he had him sit by his side. And when they were seated together and the crowd of knights and all the archons filled the tent, the sevastokrator began to speak to the prince: "Now, by Christ, good brother, prince and my brother-in-law, you ought to have thanked God and the saints a great deal when God granted that you and your descendants be lords of Morea and to have such glory, and you ought to have stayed in comfort in your dominions and not to have sought to disinherit others. Tell me, how did I wrong you, what evil did I do to you, that you came against me to seize my patrimony? And furthermore, it did not suffice you to come against me, who am your neighbor and you have my sister, but you came against my lord, the holy basileus, to seize his kingdom and to become basileus. In this matter, you ought to have heard and comprehended that he is a far better man than you and a Christian with truth. And God, who is judge and judges upon the right, brought you into his hands and he has you in his power; and since you sought to disinherit him, he will put you out of Morea, to which you have no right. He is the hereditary lord of Romania; and should you be released from prison, go to France, where lies your rightful patrimony."

And as soon as he had finished what I have been telling you, the prince, as a wise man, answered him in the Roman tongue:[75]

---

[75] Ρωμαίϊκα. L. reads: *li princes Guillermes, qui sages estoit et parloit auques bien le grec...* (§ 308).

"My lord sevastokrator and brother of my wife, to a high degree do you have great preference over me to speak and to act, for I am in your custody. Even if it were to happen that I should die on the spot, yet would I not refrain from speaking even one part of the truth. The noble man should not boast nor be reproachful should he have an enemy whom fate delivers to him to hold in his custody, as you hold me. And again, another thing and worse is that one should find fault with a situation for which he himself is to blame and bears the responsibility. If I, brother, tried to increase my honor, my wealth, and my glory, you ought to praise me, for the man who bears arms ought to increase his wealth and his honor, so long as he does not act unjustly, take from his relatives and disinherit those of his body and the friends of his body. At any rate, I am a prince, a small soldier, and you have not seen me attack a relative of mine, nor a poor neighbor of mine to take what is his; but I did attack a basileus, who is a great lord, who has power and great suzerainty in the world and is famous for bravery above all soldiers, and it is to my honor and pride that I should come to grips with him, for he is a basileus and I, a small soldier. And furthermore, he is of the race of the Roman people and I share with him no relationship whatever. Now, you who are brother to the despot in such manner and means as you yourself know, it did not suffice you that he gave you from his patrimony for you to hold in lordship the land of Vlachia, which is the best portion of his kingdom, no, you wanted to disinherit him completely and to take what he held and all of the despotate, and that he be a miserable wretch[76] and alone in the world. And you committed even more, a very evil deed, for you were not satisfied to fight with him as a neighbor and relative and in the way accepted all over the world, no, you ran to the basileus, who is a great lord—you went to him because he has him as his foe and has enmity with him—so that he might give you aid and strength of armies, so that you might ruin him completely and disinherit him. And it was not seemly for you, brother, nor to your honor, because sin

---

[76] Τζάγδαρος. Sathas derives this word from *jactarius*, a javelin-bearing foot soldier. The word takes the meaning "wretched" or "miserable" (Sathas, Ἕλληνες στρατιῶται, Ἑστία, XXX [1885], 523).

and the fortune of war have brought me to fall into your hands
and I am in your custody, to reproach me in so ugly a way, unjustly and without reason, for things and schemes which have
nothing to do with me, here in the presence of such noble men
and to divest yourself of the affairs and your responsibilities and
place them on my head, things which have nothing to do with me."

And when the sevastokrator heard the prince's words and that
he answered him with great arrogance and paid no heed to the
fact that he was in his custody, he was very distressed and deeply
grieved. Indeed, he became very angry with Prince Guillaume;[77]
and had it not been for his feelings of shame before the noble men
who happened to be there, Franks and Romans, he would have
spoken and acted towards the prince in an ugly way. Now, when
the nobles who were there with them saw the mien and fury of
the sevastokrator, they undertook with speeches and with kindly
ways to calm their words and they brought peace between them.

And after the sevastokrator and his armies had rested at Pelagonia—they spent two days in burying the slain, and all those
who were wounded, in treating their wounds—he readied his armies
and they set out to go straight to Constantinople where the basileus
was.[78] He brought the prince with him in a respectful manner;
he rode by his side and he slept with him; and they traveled until
they reached the City. And after they had dismounted and had
taken quarters, the sevastokrator took Prince Guillaume and,
holding him by the hand, they went into the palace. The basileus
was seated on his throne; all around him were the lesser archons
and in their midst, the basileus. The prince on his knees greeted
the basileus, and the basileus, as the wise and noble man that he
was, took him by the hand and raised him up; "Welcome, O prince,
with your suite." He bade him sit with him for a little while and
then the basileus ordered that he be led away from there; they
placed him in prison with great honor. The lord of Karytaina

[77] Ll. 4183 and 4184 are taken from P.

[78] This is obviously an error on the part of the chronicler, for Constantinople
at the time (1259) was still in Frankish hands. Akropolites (I, 73) offers the
information that the wounded were treated at Lampsakos (Lampseki), on the
Dardanelles, in the presence of the basileus.

and the other bannerets were placed with the prince so that they might share, as their consolation, with equal honors the prison which they had by the majesty of the basileus. And when they had spent a week in prison, the basileus ordered that the prince and all the knights who were with him be brought to where the basileus was within the palaces; and the basileus, himself, said to the prince: "Prince, you yourself see and observe that you are in prison and that I have you in my power, whether I want you to go free, or whether I want you to die. And I give you this piece of information, disbelieve it not; if you were in Morea, there where you were lord, and you had a war with me like the one you undertook, you would not be able to withstand me very long before I should throw you out of there by land and by sea and conquer your land, which is my dominion by inheritance. Well, now that you are here in my prison, and all your troops are here with you, if I were to send my armies there now, send them to cross the sea by galleys and then again by land to go by way of the mainland, since your land is stripped of its armies, they would take it easily and you would lose it. Therefore, I say to you, prince, and I give you this advice; since your parents struggled and spent much money to conquer Morea, and you have done the same after them, instead of losing what you hold and remaining disinherited, take of my money—I will make you a present of a great deal— you and your knights who are here with you, and I shall release you and set you free; and go and buy towns in France so that you and your children will have for always and leave to me Morea, which is my patrimony. For if I released you from my prison, and you remained in Morea, as you were before, you and your children would never have peace and respite in which to eat your bread."

The prince heard the words of the basileus and pondered how to answer so as not to make any mistake. And as soon as the basileus had spoken and had finished with what he was saying, the prince, in turn, began to speak to him: "Despot and holy basileus, I entreat your power, foreign and inexperienced man that I am, that I may have your permission to give answer. Since, despot, the power of your majesty commands that I surrender to you the land and suzerainty which I hold in Morea, my lord, in

return for which you will give money to me and to my comrades
who follow me and that we go into France, which is our patrimony, and buy lands and remain upon them, and that Morea,
which is your patrimony, remain to you, it is in my power to answer,
and I can only give you the answer which I am going to give you,
and receive it as truth, for if you were to keep me in prison for
fifty-five years, never could you have from me anything other
than this which I am able to tell your majesty. Now this land of
Morea, my lord, I do not hold as my patrimony, nor as land inherited from my grandfathers to hold it with the power to give it
away and make a gift of it. This land was conquered by those
nobles who came here to Romania from France with my father
as his friends and comrades. They conquered the land of Morea
by the sword and they divided it among themselves by the weights
upon the scales; each was given according to his rank, and afterwards all of them together elected my father, as the most honest
and prudent man among them, and made him commander over
all. By stipulations and agreements which they put in writing,
he had no power to judge by himself, nor to do anything at all to
the people without the counsel and will of all his comrades. Therefore, lord basileus, I do not have the power to give away one jot
from the land which I hold, for my progenitors won it by the
sword in accordance with our usages, which they stipulated among
themselves. However, as is the custom that is followed by soldiers,
whomever they capture in battle and keep in prison they ransom
for *hyperpyra* and money. My lord, let the power of your majesty
decide according to the rank of each of us who are here what each
may give to ransom himself and emerge from your prison. And
if the power of your majesty favors this, despot, each of us will
make such efforts as he can and is capable of to pay it and to
ransom himself to emerge from your prison; if it seems to you
better, my lord, not to act towards us in this fashion, here you
have us in prison, and let your will be done."

Hearing these words, the basileus was much enraged and he
said to the prince in great anger: "Prince, it is very evident that
you are a Frank, for you have the same arrogance that the Franks
have; for their arrogance always leads the Franks astray and
leads them to the loss of their expectations, just as your arrogance

brought you, too, to fall into my hands here in my prison. And you say and expect in your arrogance to get out of my hands and out of my prison. I swear to you by God as a basileus, and hold it as truth, that never in your life will you leave here in return for *denarii*, sell yourself for money, nor leave in return for wealth."

The basileus immediately gave orders that he be seized and carried back to the prison where he had been, just as you are hearing me say it and tell it to you. When they heard the basileus, all the Varangians and Romans who stood before him and who guarded him seized the prince with arrogance and cast him into the prison where he had been. He spent three years there with all his men, making great efforts to ransom himself with sums of *hyperpyra*.[79]

And when he saw and recognized, he and his men, that never for *hyperpyra* nor for wealth would he be freed and emerge from his imprisonment, with the counsel and will of the lord of Karytaina and of the other bannerets, he made this agreement: that he give to the basileus for their freedom the castle of Monemvasia and that of Great Maine and a third one, and the most beautiful,

---

[79] Discouraged by the three years of prison life and by the fall of Constantinople in 1261, at the end of 1262 Guillaume was determined to procure his release at any price. By this time Michael's attitude had softened somewhat, so in that year a treaty between them was drawn up. This treaty, which had a lasting effect on the subsequent history of Morea, has been discussed in detail by Zakythinos (pp. 15-25). According to its terms, Guillaume ceded the following: the three castles of Monemvasia, Great Maine, and Mistra, as all the sources state; Corinth, which L. de F. states was promised but not surrendered (§ 307); Geraki and "all the theme around Kinsterna," added to the list by Pachymeres. Guillaume, furthermore, became the vassal of the emperor and was to be given a title as a sign of his vassalage. In return for all this, Guillaume was granted his liberty and the rank of domestikos, or "grand marshal" as stated in L. de F. (§ 305). A second agreement seems to have been drawn up to regulate the future relations between Morea and the empire. Though somewhat vague, its terms seem to have established the suzerainty of the basileus over Guillaume and Morea. The treaties were strengthened by protestations of eternal friendship, and Michael made Guillaume the godfather of his child. Thus, Michael gained a firm foothold in Morea for the eventual reconquest of the peninsula by the Greeks. Note in l. 4319 the mention of the Varangian guard that had probably been reestablished at Nicaea after 1204. See Geanakoplos, *Emp. Mich. Pal.*, p. 43 and n. 57.

the castle of Mistra, with the design and understanding that he would be released with his men, with all who were with him, small and great. And as soon as these agreements were determined, they were put in writing and sworn to.

The basileus had a young son to have baptized; he asked the prince that they become related by this baptism. In the agreements that they made, there was also this included: that never would they have war, but would maintain peace; and should anyone attack one of the two and despoil him and make war on him, the other would help him with all his power.

And after they had established these things which I am telling you, the prince and the others who were with him together directed the lord of Karytaina, himself, to go into Morea in person to surrender the castles which I have written here to the agents of the basileus, whom he would bring with him. Now, these agreements that I am recounting to you, the prince with his council made at that time with this design, purpose and intention: that as soon as he would be released from his imprisonment, he would do something with adroitness and skill to win back again the castles which he had surrendered; for, since they were valid for no other purpose than that he and his men get out of prison, those oaths which he made in the prison where he was did not bind him to be accounted a perjurer, according to what the Church stipulates and wise men say. The lord of Karytaina, that famous man, left the City with the representatives of the basileus, who were being sent to receive the castles. They traveled from Romania by land, passed through Vlachia and went to Thebes, and there they found that the great lord had arrived at that time from the kingdom of France—where Prince Guillaume had sent him, as you heard here—with the honor and rank given to him by the king, to be addressed and spoken of as the duke of Athens. And when the duke saw that his brother-in-law the lord of Karytaina[80] had arrived, which thing he had greatly desired, he was very happy, as the brother that he was to him. And when he had asked and had been informed by him that Prince Guillaume, to get out of the prison of the basileus, had agreed to surrender the castle of Monemvasia, that

---

[80] Actually he was his son-in-law. See above, p. 167, n. 32.

of Grand Maine, and also that of Mistra to the basileus to hold,
he disapproved of it greatly and was deeply grieved. He cried
out in a loud voice and told him plainly that in no wise at all did
it please him that the basileus receive those three castles; for
the basileus would then have great power and would send armies by
land and by sea and would put us out of Morea and would take
it for himself.

The lord of Karytaina stayed with the duke; he spent a week
there in Thebes, where they conversed and celebrated like men
who had great longing, each to see the other, and to celebrate
together; and after this both of them set out together. They crossed
from Corinth and went to Nikli; there they found the princess
with all the ladies of all the Peloponnesos, which is called Morea,
who had come together to take their counsel[81] concerning the
reports which they had heard about those three castles which
the prince was giving to the basileus to get out of prison, he and
all his troops, all the men of Morea, all the bannerets and the
knights with them, who were there in the City. For this reason
the archontesses, their wives, were with the princess in the castle
of Nikli, holding a parliament and taking their counsel; and they
had no other men with them except Sir Leonardo, who was the
logothete, and the wise Sir Pierre de Vaux, who was the wisest

[81] According to Longnon (p. 229), Guy de la Roche, on hearing of the disaster
at Pelagonia, left France in haste and arrived in Greece in the spring of 1260.
He assisted the princess at the council, which she had convened, *avec une
sorte de commandement militaire*. Miller, however, puts the situation differently (pp. 114-17). After Pelagonia, the Princess Anna Komnena Doukaina
wrote to Guy, while he was still in France, and offered him the position of
bailli of Achaia, which he accepted. When he heard the news of Guillaume's
agreement with Michael, he convened a parliament, as was his duty, to discuss
the matter. In either case, a parliament was convened in 1262, apparently
under the presidency of the princess (Z., p. 20) and composed, with two exceptions, entirely of women. This last fact is a startling instance of the absence
of Salic law in Morea, for the ladies were there as heirs or representatives of
the lords killed and captured at Pelagonia. This ladies' parliament and its
significance are discussed in all the histories of the period and most enter-
tainingly in Marquis Terrier de Loray's "Un parlement de dames au xiii[e]
siècle," *Acad. des Sciences, Belles-Lettres et Arts de Besançon* (Besançon, 1881),
pp. 205-11.

man in all the principate. These two were present at that parliament.[82]

And when the two lords, the duke of Athens and the lord of
Karytaina, arrived, they immediately took quarters in the town
of Nikli and then went directly to see the ladies, who were all
in the palace with the princess. On seeing them, the princess
greeted them sweetly; she began to question the lord of Karytaina
about the health of the prince and his followers in the prison of
the basileus and about the deed they had committed in order to
get out of prison and to return to their homes. The lord of Karytaina began to recount how the prince and all his bannerets had
made great efforts to get out of prison by giving money; and the
basileus had sworn to them on his soul that they would never
get out of there for gifts of money. And they, anxious to get out
of his prison, came to an agreement and gave him the three castles
and these alone, the castle of Monemvasia, that of Grand Maine,
and also that of Mistra, to hold as his own; they made a strong
peace and also a relationship by baptism and, with oaths, affirmed
they would never go to war.

Thereupon, the great lord, himself, answered and said to the
princess and all the bishops that were in that parliament I am
telling you about: "It is the truth, as small and great know, that
I got into difficulties with my lord the prince because I said that
he was requiring me illegally to become his liege man and hold
from him the land and lordship which I hold as my patrimony.
I took up arms to make war on him. But afterwards I recognized
that I had committed a felony against him, and I made reparation
as he himself stipulated. For this reason, perchance, some of you
may think that I am hostile to my lord the prince in this that

[82] Leonardo (Lenart) of Veroli was chancellor of Morea and a hard-working
servant of his prince. He represented Guillaume at the council of Viterbo in
1267 and witnessed the treaty; he took an active part in the celebrated case
of Marguerite of Passava; and he arranged the treaty of Orvieto in 1281. He
amassed a large fortune during his career, and a small library, the inventory
of which is of no little interest (see M., p. 153). Pierre de Vaux (called de
Vent by Buchon in the Index of his edition of the Chronicle) was a respected
courtier of Morea and a close associate of the prince. He is always referred to
in the Chronicle as "the wise man" or "the wisest."

I tell you, but I speak in truth, take it as such from me; if the basileus takes those three castles, he will not hold to the oaths which he has sworn; he will send here against us many armies and troops that will throw us out of here and disinherit us. Therefore, that you may recognize my good faith, I say and affirm I will do this: I will enter prison and the prince, let him come out; or if it is a question of ransoming him for sums of *hyperpyra*, I will pledge my land for *denarii*, and thus let the ransom of my liege lord be paid."

Then the lord of Karytaina arose and said to the princess in front of the great lord: "My lady, all that the great lord says here, we said there in our prison, the risks and dangers that could follow. But because we saw that the obstinacy of the basileus was determined, we spoke thus among ourselves and agreed on it: the castle of Monemvasia, as everyone knows, was won by our lord, the prince, himself; Maine and Mistra were built by him, and it would be a sin and a great rebuke for him and his followers to die in prison for the sake of castles which he himself won and built. Just let him escape the torment of the prison he is in, and afterwards God will help him to capture his castles and to have them as his own. Therefore, I say to you, hold it from me: not for any man in this world, nor for the words and excuses that everyone may speak, will I leave my lord in prison to die. I will fulfill the command he gave me to surrender his castles that he may be released from his torment, and when he has come out of prison may God be his help."

And then the great lord, himself, spoke again to the lord of Karytaina and he answered him thus: "By Christ, good brother, in truth I tell you, if the basileus were to learn and be informed that we are not going to give him the castles he seeks, he is not going to sprinkle the prince with salt and eat him, but will take *hyperpyra* to set him free. And furthermore, I say to you, take it as you will, that if the prince considered what could follow, it were better that he should die by himself, as one man, than that the rest of the Franks of Morea should lose the estates that their parents won with such labor, as did Christ, who tasted death to redeem the souls of the race of men from the eternal damnation whither all were going. Better that one should die, than a thousand for his sake. I am unloading my mind and I am speaking the truth, and you, my brother, do what you have been ordered to do."

Now after, when the parliament was ended,[83] the lord of Karytaina, who held the warrants[84] which the prince had given to him to present to the castellans, set out from Nikli, taking with him the archon of the basileus, who had been sent with him that he might be given the castles in place of the basileus; he went to Mistra, which he gave first, then Monemvasia, and, third, Maine. And as soon as he had surrendered the castles which I have mentioned, he took to give as a hostage to the basileus the daughter of the lord of Passava, who was marshal of all the principality, Sir Jean he was called, de Neuilly, his surname; and with her the sister of that Chauderon who was grand constable of all the principality; these two went to the City as hostages, and the prince and the knights and all the bannerets, small and great, were released, and they went to Morea with great joy.[85]

When the prince went to Morea at that time, small and great received him well.[86] Since he was impatient to see and inspect

---

[83] The chronicler fails to mention the real reason that the terms of the ransom were accepted which was the anxiety of the women for their husbands. L. de F. says that when the women heard that unless the castles were surrendered, the prince and his men would never be released, "the princess and the wives of the barons, who had their husbands in prison, began to shout loudly, saying that they wanted to have their husbands and they would be quite willing that said castles be surrendered to the emperor" (§ 298-304). Sanudo, on the other hand, claims that Guy struggled to convince the ladies that the prince had to be ransomed at all costs (see Z., p. 20, n. 2).

[84] Τὰ σημάδια. L. uses the phrase les commandemens et les seigniaux. Apparently these were some sort of warrant that he was to show to the castellans, which gave him power to surrender the castles for the prince. After this word in H., there occurs a break in the manuscript. A whole page is missing. Ll. 4496-4535 are taken from P. See below, p. 213, n. 12.

[85] Marguerite of Passava was the daughter of Jean II de Neuilly, hereditary marshal and baron of Passava, who had married a daughter of Gautier I de Rosières of Akova. She was involved in the celebrated case described in ll. 7301-7752 below. Jean de Chauderon was also a nephew of Prince Guillaume.

[86] L. de F. adds that he went first to Euripos, where he was received with honor, then to Thebes, where the great lord offered him hospitality and accompanied him to Nikli (§ 309). While he was at Thebes, he signed the Treaty of Thebes with Venice (see M., p. 117).

his castles and towns, of which he was very fond, he did not wish to lose any time there at all; he took the knights whom he had in his company, and they traveled, inspecting the castles and towns, and went straight to Lakedaemonia. So long as he had the desire and inclination to see Morea, he did not travel alone as a poor soldier, but went as a prince and well accompanied, to those places where he was loved and missed. All hurried to travel in his retinue, some held arms and others were without arms. And when the Romans, the representatives of the basileus, saw them from up in the castle of Mistra, they thought and came to the conclusion that the Franks were seeking battle with them, that is, the Romans. They notified the commanders of the *drongos* of the Melings, and they made an agreement and swore oaths to stand for the basileus and to deny the Franks. Messengers were sent to a certain Kantakouzenos,[87] who was their captain; they wrote, affirmed, and informed him that the prince had come with all his armies and had launched a war against the basileus. And he believed it and outfitted a ship; he sent messengers and they went to the City to the basileus and informed him that the prince of Morea, Guillaume, had broken his oath and had begun a war in Lakedaemonia with all his armies; he had begun to plunder the lands of the basileus.[88]

Now when the basileus, the great Palaiologos, heard, he believed these things which I am telling you, which his governor[89] had reported to him from Monemvasia. He was greatly amazed and overwhelmed that Prince Guillaume had so soon broken his oath which he had given him and had begun a hot war in Morea. Thereupon, he went into Turkey and hired the Turks as mer-

[87] This Kantakouzenos was Michael Kantakouzenos (more often spelled Cantacuzene), a member of an old and important Byzantine family that was settled in Messenia at the time of the Frankish conquest, and was most probably the grandfather of the later emperor John Cantacuzene (1347-55). Michael is referred to in this passage as the imperial governor of Mistra, and possibly of Monemvasia in l. 4548, whereas in l. 4635 ff. it is stated that he was sent into Morea with troops after the trouble broke out. See below, l. 4629 and note.

[88] For the motives that led Guillaume to break his treaty with Michael, for the reactions of the basileus, etc., see the excellent discussion in Z., pp. 27 ff., where the war is related to the international situation of that period.

[89] Κεφαλή is the name given to a military commander, or captain, and also to the Byzantine imperial governors in Morea.

cenaries; he hired 1,500 select troops, and around another 2,000 Anatolians went with them. He appointed a cousin of his and placed him as captain over all of these whom you have heard me mention; Makrynos, he was called, thus was he named.[90] He called him and ordered him to take the armies which he was giving him and to go to Morea to carry on war and battle with his relative by baptism, he who was called Prince Guillaume. He gave him his orders and told him to tell him whatever moneys he would need to hire troops and to reward any of his men; he was not to be miserly nor hesitant, nor in any way negligent, but to hurry with eagerness to conquer the land; "for, since the prince has begun the war when we two had sworn to maintain peace, he bears the sin and he, the blame." He sealed with his gold seal some blank papers for him and spoke thus to him: "Makrynos, take these with you and if you should find it necessary to create fief holders or grant favors, do so according to the worth of each man as you will find in him and order that they be written down on these papers."

To the chiefs of the *Drongos*, to those of Gardalevos,[91] and also to those of Tsakonia, he brought a chrysobull, stating that all

[90] L. and the Greek Chronicle state that two expeditions were sent, one under Makrynos and the second under Konstantinos Palaiologos. Pachymeres (I, 205-6) states that the emperor sent immediately an expedition under the command of his brother Konstantinos, accompanied by the *parakoimomenos* Makrynos and Alexios Philes. Miller (p. 122), probably under the influence of the statement in the Chronicle, suggests that reinforcements were sent in a second expedition under the command of Michael Kantakouzenos. Zakythinos follows Pachymeres, whose information he finds "plus probable" and mentions only one expedition, and places Kantakouzenos in Monemvasia as governor at the time the war breaks out (pp. 32-33 and n. 3, p. 33). According to Zakythinos (*ibid.*, n. 2) the Makrynos family held a position of considerable importance under the Palaiologos emperors. Though he was *parakoimomenos* or grand chamberlain, there seems to be no truth in the statement that Makrynos was the emperor's cousin.

[91] *Drongos* with a capital letter may refer either to the *drongos* of Skorta or to that of the Melings. In this case, in my opinion, it refers to the latter. Gardalevos is located by Schmitt (Index, p. 634) "as a place in Laconia, north of Vatika, Monembasia and Helos." Kalonaros (p. 191, n. to l. 4576) states that the name persists in the present Dragalevos, a town "in the neighborhood of Tsakonia and near to Hagios Petros."

would be privileged;[92] they would bear arms, but would not perform *corvées*. They boarded galleys, transports, and tarettes; and they went to Monemvasia by sea.[93] In this way, just as I am telling it to you and as I am relating it to you, did the war begin in Morea, in which these two fought, the basileus and the prince, who were, even so, relatives by baptism.

And when Makrynos arrived in Monemvasia, he and his troops disembarked from the galleys. He went directly to Lakedaemonia with the armies; he asked the names of the chieftains who were in the *drongos* of the Melings and in that of Tsakonia and he sent documents to all of them from the basileus, making some of them *sevastoi* and the leaders even *tzastades*.[94] Vatika submitted, as did Tsakonia; the *drongos* of the Melings and the territory of Gisterna, in fact, revolted in favor of the basileus.[95]

[92] See above, p. 157, n. 11.

[93] The tarette was a kind of cargo or merchant vessel. The word appears in Latin as *tarida* or *tareta* in Du Cange, who derives it from the Arab *taridah*. Eugene Byrne in his *Genoese Shipping in the Twelfth and Thirteenth Centuries* (Cambridge, 1930), p. 5, describes it as "heavier and slower than a galley, equipped with oars and a full set of sails on two masts." The army was transported in Genoese ships and arrived in Monemvasia around the beginning of 1263. At the same time the Byzantine navy under the command of Philanthropenos, after ravaging the Cyclades, occupied the southern coasts of Lakonia. See Z., p. 33 and notes.

[94] $\Sigma\varepsilon\beta\alpha\sigma\tauο\iota$ and $T\zeta\alpha\sigma\tau\bar{\alpha}\delta\varepsilon\varsigma$ were Byzantine court titles. The latter may be derived from the Turkish word *chaush*, a sergeant-at-arms, according to Kalonaros.

[95] L. de F. presents at this point a curious story that does not appear in any of the other versions. It states that the Greeks of Karytaina remained loyal to their Frankish lord and helped him inflict heavy damage on the imperial troops. The Greek commander, in order to force them to desert the Franks, drew up some incriminating letters in the form of answers to previous correspondence from the Greeks of Karytaina. These he had dropped into a room of the Frankish lord's manor, as if they had been dropped by accident. Lord Geoffroy, however, was too shrewd and too confident in his vassal's loyalty to be deceived by this clumsy device. He called in the Greeks and showed them the letters. They "began to cry and took their handkerchiefs, with which they customarily wipe their faces, and placed them around their necks" and swore they were innocent. He believed them and together they laid a trap. The Greek vassals pretended to negotiate with the imperial forces and finally led them into an ambush, where many were killed (§ 312-30). The Chronicle

And when the prince learned the news that Makrynos had arrived and had begun the war and was looting and heavily damaging his towns, he sent messengers to the great lord, to Euripos and to the islands, for the bannerets to come with their armies to help him. And they disobeyed him and did not go there.[96] The prince was enraged at them; he took whatever armies he had in Morea and went to the castle of Nikli with the troops that he had. And when he heard and learned that Tsakonia, Vatika, and the *drongos* of the Slavs had revolted, he was advised not to go against them, for they were many troops, and he had few. But he was advised to garrison the castles, to supply them heavily and fortify them well, and he himself to go in person to Corinth to force the great lord, himself, the three lords of Euripos, the marquis of Boudonitza, I tell you, and the lords of the islands to come quickly. And as soon as he was given this counsel, he went to Corinth; the confident hope of the prince, and his expectation, was to give battle to the captain of the basileus, this Makrynos, should he find him in the field.

Now when this Makrynos saw that at the very first stroke the places which I have listed for you submitted to him, he sat down and wrote letters and sent messengers to the basileus, who was in the City, reporting that he had come into Morea with his armies and that God and the blessing of the basileus had granted that he win a third of Morea without a stroke of the sword. Therefore, if the basileus would send him a great number of armies and more than those he had already given him, he hoped in Christ and with the blessing of the basileus to win the whole land of Morea for him.[97]

then goes on to state that Geoffroy de Bruyères fell in love with the wife of his liege man, Jean de Catavas, and fled with her to Italy (§ 332-34). Undoubtedly, his absence at that critical moment and the resulting revolt of the Slavs in favor of the Greeks was a serious blow to the prince of Morea (see below, ll. 5653 ff. and 5739 ff.).

[96] Sanudo (p. 116) claims that an Athenian contingent did arrive.

[97] As stated above, p. 203 n. 87, in all probability only one expedition was sent, and this under the command of Konstantinos. L. de F. states that the Greeks asked for help and the emperor sent his brother and Kantakouzenos, who was "grandfather of the Emperor Kantakouzenos who is reigning today" (§ 335). Kantakouzenos was emperor from 1347 to 1355.

Hearing this, the basileus was very happy; so he called the grand domestikos, who was his brother, and said to him: "Brother, I want you to go from here into Morea and take with you a thousand men, all mounted on horses you will choose them; pour out the mercenary fee and *hyperpyra* and give them as much as they want. And let Katakonzenos go that he, too, may be with you, for he is an experienced soldier of renown; go as speedily as possible that you may help Makrynos, whom I have already sent, and conquer Morea."

And the grand domestikos, hearing the command which his brother the basileus, himself, had given him, hastened to enlist the flower of Romania. They boarded the galleys and the transports and reached Monemvasia in fifteen days. Now after the grand domestikos, brother of the basileus, landed in Monemvasia, he asked where Makrynos was to be found; and he was told that he was based at Mistra with his armies, from which he was besieging Lakedaemonia, "and he awaits your majesty day by day, my lord." And on hearing this, he hastened to go to Lakedaemonia and joined Makrynos; they took counsel together as to how they might proceed. They learned that the prince was in Corinth, and they suspected that he had his troops with him. Therefore, counsel was given that they go to Morea where they would find the land unprotected, and they would conquer it. They then separated the squadrons of the army; there were found to be 6,000 knights; eighteen squadrons were formed, each three making a thousand men. They had foot soldiers past counting, I tell you, for they had the troops from Gardelevos together with those of Tsakonia, of the *drongos* of the Melings, and those of Great Maine;[98] the Skortinoi had revolted and were with them.

They set out and passed through the region of [Mount] Helmos;[99] they reached Veligosti and set up encampments; they burned the

---

[98] At this point there is a serious break in L. Six pages are missing, corresponding to ll. 4664-5045 of the Greek text.

[99] This is not the Mt. Helmos of Achaia, but a much lower peak in the mountains between Lakedaemonia and Arkadia, located near Veligosti. It is on the upper waters of the Eurotas, about midway on the route between Lakedaemonia and Karytaina.

mart[1] and left only the castle. The next day they entered upon
the plain of Karytaina; and they spent the night beside the tributary;[2] in the morning they set out and went to Liodora, going
straight down the tributary of the Alpheios; a squadron of Turks
went to Isova[3] and burned the monastery—see what an evil deed
took place. From there they went straight down to Prinitsa; they
encamped there and set up tents. Now the Skortinoi, seeing the
great multitude in the army, all quickly submitted—they committed a big mistake—and they served them as guides and accompanied them.

Now, at this point, I here leave off speaking and reciting about
the grand domestikos and his armies, and I am going to tell you,
and with minuteness, of the battle which took place at that time
in Prinitsa.[4] Three hundred Franks defeated those armies, as I
intend to relate further on in my book. When the prince went to
Corinth at that time (in order to arrange that the duke of Athens
and the other lords of the islands would come with their armies

[1] Ἐμπόριον. The Chronicle here distinguishes between the castle and the
surrounding town or bourg. See above, l. 1687 and note.

[2] This is a reference to a tributary of the Alpheios River. Kalonaros in a
very long and detailed footnote (n. to l. 4667, p. 196) states that, owing to
the complicated drainage system of the area, the chronicler and apparently
the inhabitants of the region, as well, were unable to distinguish the main
stream from its numerous tributaries. As a result, the main stream was mistakenly called a tributary, as here in l. 4668, while the largest of the tributaries,
the Ladon, was thought to be the main stream. The name for the Ladon and
that part of the Alpheios below the junction was Rouphias in the vernacular
Greek, a corruption of Alpheios, while its French name was Charbon. In
other words, the Greeks were following the main stream of the Alpheios, whereas
the chronicler states they followed a tributary from Karytaina to Liodora
(l. 4669), the point where the Ladon joins the Alpheios. The name Liodora is
derived from Ladon and indicates a town and the surrounding region, located
near the site of the ancient Heraia.

[3] The ruins of the Latin monastery of Our Lady of Isova still stand, overlooking the Alpheios, near the present town of Mpizmpardi.

[4] That a Byzantine defeat took place at Prinitsa is not open to doubt, for
all the versions of the Chronicle mention it and they are supported by Sanudo
(p. 118). However, the details, as set forth in the Greek Chronicle, are obviously
fiction. The Chronicles themselves are in disagreement as to what happened
exactly, and it remains unexplained to this day how such an overwhelmingly
superior force was defeated by 300 or 312 knights.

to the assistance of the prince that they might fight the grand domestikos with his armies), there was left in Morea as his legal *bailli* Sir Jean de Catavas, one of his knights; he was a wise man, highly experienced, a bold soldier and craftsman in arms. He had a terrible affliction in that he was rheumatic and could hold neither sword nor lance;[5] and when he learned the information that the army of the basileus, which the grand domestikos commanded, was coming, he made great efforts and gathered from the plain of Morea as much of a force as he could and was able. And as soon as he had gathered them, he estimated how many there were; there were found to be only three hundred and twelve. He took them and went up into the neighborhood of Krestena, seeking and inquiring where the armies of the basileus which were invading the plain of Morea were located. And when he learned that they had arrived at Prinitsa, he entered the valley of the tributary of the Alpheios to travel by its side. And when he found the nail marks [of the shoes] of that army, he fell in behind them and began to follow them. And when he came and arrived at a certain narrow gorge nearby, which is called "At the Agridi of Kounoupitsa,"[6] and saw the fields filled with the armies—it was still rather early, the hour of dawn—they suddenly attacked those armies. Sir Jean de Catavas, the dread soldier, did not at all lose heart at the sizable army. He became jubilant and he called his company and with much eagerness he spoke to them in this wise: "Lords, friends and brothers, beloved comrades, all of you must rejoice and praise God when God brings us, in such a favorable spot, so many armies, past counting, that we may defeat them. Take care, good brothers, that no one of you be afraid of them because there is a multitude of troops, for this reason which I am going to tell you: it is better for us to fight these, than that they be fewer, but men of one race. These are total strangers from several lands, with no experience

---

[5] This affliction was undoubtedly the cause of his wife's escapade with the lord of Karytaina. (See above, p. 205, n. 95.)

[6] Leake (*Peloponnesiaca*, pp. 144, 155) identifies this as a narrow pass in the river basin of the Alpheios, between Krestena and Prinitsa. Dragoumis (p. 133, n. 1) adds nothing more definite as to its location. The word ἀγρίδι is probably ἀγρίδιον, dim. of ἄγρος (Lat. *ager*), and signifies here a lonely or isolated countryside or spot.

in fighting with Frankish men; let us not hesitate an instant, lest they discover us; with a sudden swoop let us all lay on with our lances. Their horses are all nags and one of our steeds will knock fifteen of them over at a time. And furthermore, I say this, brothers, I remind you of the labor which our lords our parents expended in order to conquer the lands which we hold. And if we do not set our will on this day, each of us to defend it with his life and to show them in arms that we are soldiers in arms and thus, at the same time, save our patrimonies; and if we do not act in this way that I am telling you,[7] then we ought not to be considered men of arms, nor to hold fiefs, nor honor in the world. And in the second place, lords and comrades, consider that should God and our fortune grant that we here defeat the brother of the basileus and these armies with battle and with sword, as long as the ark remains on Mount Ararat, so long will remain the praise of this day, with which all those who will hear of it will praise us. Now I, as you know and behold in me, am not able to hold sword or lance, nor to stand in battle that I may fight; but that I may show the same zeal as you, I will hold the banner of the prince and you will tie it to my hand that I may hold it steady. I can see the tent of the domestikos from here, and I swear to you by Christ that I will go straight to it. And whoever should see me hesitate or show any fear, I hold him an enemy of Christ if he does not cut me down at once."

The grand domestikos was seated in his tent on a hillock in the village of Prinitsa.[8] And as soon as the Franks suddenly appeared, he spoke this speech—he, himself, said it: "I see that a little light breakfast has come our way." He ordered only three squadrons to ride out, a thousand mounted troops to meet the Franks; they rode quickly and attacked the Franks and with a shock they met them, all with their lances. In their first attack, a good third of the Franks fell from their steeds; for one Frank

---

[7] Kalonaros inserts this line from P. into H. and numbers it 4737b. He gives no explanation—Schmitt does not indicate a lacuna—though he apparently feels it is necessary in order to complete the meaning of the phrase that follows it.

[8] The village of Prinitsa (Fr. La Brenyce) no longer exists. It lay near the present town of Vyliza, near Olympia.

there were ten Roman lances. Listen! By Christ's favor, not one
of the Franks received a lance thrust and not one was wounded;
those who had fallen remounted quickly, drew their swords and
began to kill the Romans. A long time went by, during which
the Franks were lost to view and could not be discerned amongst
the Romans, and with them was Sir Jean de Catavas, I tell you.
When the Franks had arisen, there where they had fallen, where
the great number of Romans had beaten them down, they un-
sheathed their little swords and began to fight and they slaughtered
the Romans as a scythe, the meadow. The Franks were lost in
the great numbers of the Romans, and the grand domestikos
did not see them at all from there where he was sitting in his tent.
But Sir Jean de Catavas of blessed memory[9] did not wait for them
to give battle to the Franks; straightway he strove time and again
to reach the tent which he saw from afar was that of the domestikos.
Some of those who took part in that battle saw and testified that
they saw a knight mounted on a white charger, carrying a naked
sword and always leading the way wherever the Franks were.
And they said and affirmed that it was St. George and that he
guided the Franks and gave them courage to fight. Others said
that the most holy Theotokos, who was in the monastery in Isova,
which the Romans burned on their journey, was angered; and still
others said that the perjury committed by the basileus—who
had given his oath to Prince Guillaume and, without his doing
him any injury, had sent his armies to attack the prince because
of truthless words and groundless reports—because of this, God
and the most holy Theotokos were angered and gave victory to
the Franks and were enraged with the Romans.

The battle began at the first hour, and the Franks arrived at
the hour of noon at the tent wherein sat the grand domestikos.
Now the grand domestikos from his tent kept his eye unceasingly
on the army to see what was becoming of the Franks of Morea;
he did not see a single Frank, only Romans; he raised his hands

---

[9] Μακάριος. Schmitt, I think, is correct in pointing out the significance
of this phrase. It is always used in connection with the name of a relative
or a well-known person who has died within the speaker's lifetime or not too
long before. See S., Introduction, p. xxxviii.

and praised God, thinking and reasoning that the Franks were lost. And thus, as he stood gazing at the armies, suddenly there appeared before him the banners of the Franks; he recognized the banners of the Frankish army. They were advancing on the tent before which they saw the scepter of the brother of the basileus, the grand domestikos. He sent forth a shrill little cry, as loud as he was capable of, to those pages who attended him: " You there, bring my horse, dolt,[10] the Turkoman; look at the banners of the Franks, who have overwhelmed us."

But when they saw the naked, shining swords that were coming upon them—these were held by the Franks and were bloodied with the blood of the Romans—each sought to save himself; they all took to flight, to wherever each was able. A certain one who was prudent and loved his honor ran and brought a horse which was standing already saddled and which was the best one the grand domestikos had; he helped his lord, who mounted with a leap. He found some inhabitant of that land who knew and was familiar with the territory of Prinitsa. He guided him and accompanied him; he went from Levitsa up to Kapele,[11] traveling through wild places so that they would not be discovered, and they made their way with such prudence and with such skill that they arrived in Mistra, which he had been very anxious to do.

When the armies of the Romans who were at Prinitsa saw that the Franks had arrived at the tent of the domestikos and had struck and cast down the scepter of the basileus, all turned to flee and took to flight; no one saw whither the other went. Why should I tell you all the details and who is to write them all for you? The Franks desisted from slaughtering the Romans ; they found a formidable impediment in the forests of Prinitsa, that difficult and heavily wooded area. In these, all those Romans who ran and entered them were saved, for if the difficult places that I am telling you about had not been there, I have come to the

---

[10] The word μωρέ is a Greek epithet of abuse derived from μωρός, a fool. In Matt. 5:22, Christ strictly enjoins his followers not to use it.

[11] Dragoumis, who locates Prinitsa near the present town of Pyri, claims (p. 136) that Levitsa corresponds to the modern town of Vervitsa, near Gortynia in Elis. Kapele is a wooded district in the same area.

conclusion on my information that not even one of them would have escaped from there, and that if the Franks had been able, they would have slaughtered the Roman race. The Franks ceased killing their enemies, and when they saw, furthermore, that they fled and took to the mountains and that they fled into the woods in the direction of the army,[12] they left off pursuing them and returned. The Franks captured a thousand horses on that occasion.

When the men of the villages in those parts learned of this, small and great rushed in that they might make some gain and derive some profit from the goods of the Romans. Now the Franks then remained in Servia,[13] for even had they wished to go to camp farther down, they were not able to go, because they were so loaded down with the great amount of booty they had captured ; the next day they went straight to Vlisiri.

Sir Jean de Catavas, the gouty soldier, ordered letters to be written and he sent messengers to the prince in the castle of Corinth. He described in great detail the deed and affair, how the battle of Prinitsa had taken place, the action he had taken and the victory that had fallen to them. When he heard this, the prince raised his hands and praised God and the all-chaste Theotokos. On the one hand, he rejoiced ; on the other, he grieved; he rejoiced because his troops had been victorious, and, on the

[12] This is a troublesome phrase (πρὸς τὸν στρατέαν). I have interpreted it to mean that they fled towards the camp of that part of the army that had been held in reserve and had not taken part in the battle. This point marks another major lacuna in H. Ll. 4854-74 are taken from P. However, a lacuna follows l. 4874 in P., also. As a result, though the first line of H. after the break is given the number 4875 to keep the sequence of lines, there is something missing between the last line of P. before the lacuna there and the first line in H. after the text resumes. Schmitt in the footnote explainihg these lacunae (p. 320) indicates that two full pages are missing from the manuscript. He suggests that this may indicate that a patriotic Greek, overcome by rage at the uncomplimentary remarks about the Greeks in these passages, tore out the two pages in a fury. However, Kalonaros dryly points out (p. 204, n. to l. 4853) that if this were the case, all of the existing versions of the Chronicle in Greek would be destroyed or mutilated. It is interesting that lacunae appear in the description of the battle of Prinitsa not only in the three texts of the Greek version of the Chronicle, but in the French and Italian ones as well.

[13] A town somewhere between Prinitsa and Andravida (see below, p. 222, n. 24). For Vliziri, see above, p. 138, n. 76.

other hand, he grieved because there did not appear ... the more
he whipped him so much the more he had to be careful of him.[14]
If at that time the prince had taken the great lord and the armies
of the islands and those of Euripos and had gone quickly straight
to Nikli and had entered Tsakonia and had pillaged the whole
area, the grand domestikos would have been a long time in making
his campaign; but as each man will act, so will he find it before
him.[15] Now I leave off speaking about the prince and I am going
to relate to you the deed that the grand domestikos committed
in Mistra where he was.

I have already described to you above in my book the action
that the grand domestikos took at Prinitsa with his armies; when
he was able to get to the castle of Mistra, he sat and grieved, day
and night he cried; first, because of his shame before men's eyes
and second, because of the basileus, of whom he had great fear, lest
he seize and blind him and throw him into prison and he receive
an unjust death and lose his life. The basileus had sent him with
his armies to conquer the whole land of Morea, and if he were
to learn that the Franks had won the battle, a mere 300 against
over 20,000, how would he receive him, how would he greet him,
but to say that he was a traitor and to execute him. A certain
noble Frank, an experienced man, who had come from the City
from the basileus as a messenger to him, comforted him: "My
despot, in the name of Christ, why do you grieve thus? Do you
not know that a campaign depends on luck? He who knows cunning and acts with slyness undoes the brave and takes away their
bravery; cunning and slyness conquer bravery. You saw the
cunning which the sevastokrator used at Pelagonia and won the
field; he did not consider to say that he had many armies, but
he applied cunning and left aside the bravery. All men in all the
universe know that the Franks are brave with the lance and the

[14] This marks the end of the passage taken from P. and the resumption of
H. The meaning of the last phrase is obscure, because the beginning of the
sentence is missing. Apparently what grieved the prince was that the domestikos had escaped and that, now that he had been defeated, he was even more
dangerous than before.

[15] Probably the equivalent of "Whatsoever a man soweth, that shall he
also reap."

sword. For this reason, the sevastokrator, shrewd man that he was, set the Germans to meet the Franks and to counter the fury and lances of the Franks; then he had the Hungarians, the Turks, and the Cumans shoot arrows at all of them, Franks and Germans and they slaughtered their steeds and won the battle. If it had not been for the archers who slaughtered the steeds, they would never have won that battle. You see, despot, my lord, how you erred in this, there where the Franks fought you at Prinitsa. According to what the leaders of the army, who were with you in the battle, have told me, your lordship trusted in the multitude of the army that you saw were with your highness and you despised the Franks, because you saw they were few, and you did not consider at all how you would fight them, a thing which wise soldiers do not do; for no matter how much a soldier a man is, and brave, it behooves him to have cunning and slyness at his side to fight carefully against his enemy, for wise men say—and it is the truth—that skill and slyness conquer bravery. You should, O despot, have had your archers, when they saw that the Franks were coming against you, slay the steeds that they were riding and you would have defeated them right away and you would have conquered them, but you ordered a thousand lances to go against them, intending and expecting that they would beat them; this thing you did by your own will, my lord. What I said before, I say again, and it is indeed the truth, one Frank on horse is worth twenty Romans. You saw, my lord what the Franks accomplished at Prinitsa; wise and experienced in campaigning that they were, seeing the great numbers of troops and armies that you had, they quickly rode into the middle of them, threw their lances and drew their little swords and slaughtered your troops, and your men were not able to scatter. They acted in just the same way that the wolves do, who enter the fold and scatter the sheep. Well, do not grieve over what has happened, for this, you see, is always the way of campaigning, one occasion wins profits and another, again, loses them. Console yourself, my lord, and take another road; order all your armies to gather, and consider how to gain honor and profit and that you may amend the thing that has happened. I have learned that the prince has returned to Andravida and that the armies that he brought have gone home; let us go straight to him there in Andravida; and if he should have such misfortune as to come out to battle, do not set yourself to fight him with arrogance, but fight him only with skill and cunning. Do not do battle against him with lances at all, but order the Turks, who carry bows, to shoot arrows at the steeds so that the knights will fall. And if it happens that by luck you capture the prince, after you have captured him, hold him, and you win the land as well."

The grand domestikos believed the Frank; he called the leading archons that he had with him and he related to them in detail what the Frank had told him; all said in praise of it that he gave him good advice. He ordered that the leading commanders of the army come; he said to them: "Archons, make haste at once that we may go to the town of Andravida, where the prince is." He called Kantakouzenos and also Makrynos and related to them all the words of the Frank and the counsel of the archons and of the commanders as well. And they answered him and said to him: "Why do you hesitate, O despot, grand domestikos? Does it not strike you that the shame which the Franks brought upon us, fell on us as well as on your lordship and that we would do anything for our honor, so that the basileus may not call us faithless traitors? But we are thinking of the season, the most unfavorable of the year, and we need to act like wise soldiers. As yet we do not know which ones have been killed, which ones escaped alive, and which ones have their horses. The summer is ended now and has departed, and winter has taken over, and the armies have brought a halt to their campaigning; let us look forward to this period to inspect our troops and to see which ones have remained to us from all our troops; and if God and our fortune grant that we live until March, in the spring of the year, which is a suitable season for armies to gird themselves with arms and advance into battle, at that time, my lord, let us gird ourselves, and wherever we find the prince, let us go against him and let us die together or be revenged." The grand domestikos thereupon answered: "God knows, my friends, companions and my brothers, it destroys my reason and eats my heart that it was a penniless soldier that routed us. If we had fought or battled with the prince, who is a great man and renowned in all the world, and he had beaten me in battle, I would consider it some consolation. But to have it said that some pauper, some rheumatic, defeated the brother of the basileus in the field and, further, something even worse, worst of the very worst, that with three hundred, he defeated 15,000!" As they decided in counsel, these archons, the grand domestikos together with Makrynos, and with them, Kantakouzenos, the famous soldier, thus did they resolve the affair and determine it. The season passed, winter departed and there came the month of March, the spring of the year, when all men set out in arms and battle and march out on sea and land. The brother of the basileus, the grand domestikos, ordered that all his armies come together. The mustering took place in the fields of Sapikos, on the broad meadows, midst the sweet springs.[16] He gathered many armies from various lands; foot soldiers from Tsakonia and from the *drongos* of the Melings and from as far away as Monemvasia and the *drongos* of Skorta. They separated their squadrons, made ready and set out; they spent the night at Karytaina and went straight down the tributary of the Alpheios; they passed Prinitsa and gazed upon the spot and remembered what they had gone through there on that spot. They continued on their way, thinking to threaten the Franks and that the thing that had ruined them would not happen to them again, should they go into battle, to attack with lances; this time they would kill them all with arrows. Everywhere they asked where they might find Prince Guillaume and learned that he awaited them at Andravida, which town he had encircled completely with ditches, and he was waiting there to receive them with all his armies.

The grand domestikos called his commanders; he asked counsel of them as to how he ought to proceed. And those who were inhabitants of the land and who were familiar with the territory and the mountain passes, gave him this counsel: that he not un-

---

[16] The plain of Sapikos is the ancient plain of Asea. The word $\Sigma a\pi \iota \varkappa \grave{o}\varsigma$ according to Schmitt (Index, p. 639) is derived from $\sigma \acute{a}\pi \iota o\varsigma$ (rotten) and indicates a swampy area. This refers to the swampy area, called Frankovrysis today, that lies in the middle of the plain, which is now called Sapolivado ("rotten meadow"). The Alpheios has its source in this swamp. (See Z., p. 38 and n.; K., p. 209, n. on l. 5022; Dragoumis, p. 68.)

dertake to go to Andravida, because the approaches were too narrow for the balistas and their crews.[17] They brought him straight over to near Sergiana and established him above that place, towards the east. There is a small church there called St. Nicholas at Mesiskli, which is the name of the spot, and there they set up his tent and encamped him.[18] The hillsides and the fields were all filled with the armies; there they camped for the night and they stayed there that night.

And when the next day dawned, at the hour of sunrise, the prince came there with his armies. The knights and foot troops all came with him; he separated his squadrons and formed three regiments. He went out from Sergiana against the Romans and the regiments stood ready for battle.[19]

The forward squadron of the Romans and its regiments were under the command of Kantakouzenos, that praiseworthy soldier. He rode out from his squadron upon his steed; he wore his quivers and held his mace; he rode speedily forward and backward between the Franks and his own squadron, displaying great conceit. And when he had gone up and down three times with this horse, he dismounted and changed horses, mounting another, and began to display himself before the Franks. That is what Kantakouzenos did, riding up and down, giving the spur to his steed, with contempt for the Franks because they were so few and with haughtiness and arrogance because the Romans were a multitude of troops and many more than were the Franks. Well, he went up and down, riding his steed; the horse lost its head and carried the knight into a bramble near the prince; the horse stumbled

---

[17] The word τζάγρα usually signifies an arbalest or crossbow and τζαγρατόρος a crossbowman. However, here the reference seems to be to an engine of war, or a large crossbow. I have therefore translated τζαγρατόρους as balistas and their crews, for the balista was such an engine.

[18] For Sergiana and Mesiskli, see below, p. 222, n. 24.

[19] It must be remembered that words such as squadron and regiment are intended to approximate the Greek terms, which are difficult to translate with exactness. For an interesting discussion of the Byzantine army, see Oman, History of the Art of War, I, 171-228. An authoritative work on the organization of the Byzantine army, especially useful for troublesome terms, is N. Kalomenopoulos, Ἡ στρατιωτικὴ ὀργάνωσις τῆς Ἑλληνικῆς αὐτοκρατορίας τοῦ Βυζαντίου (Athens, 1937).

and both fell. The prince's troops, seeing this, ran to the spot, killed the knight, and seized the horse. When the grand domestikos and Makrynos, as well, saw that their captain over the armies was lost, it seemed to them that they themselves had died, all of them; they ran up and took him away, dead as he was; they blew their trumpets, betook themselves and retired.[20]

The prince wanted to go after the Romans, and they all put the scheme out of his head and together they stopped him, saying that if the Romans should rally and surround the horses with their multitude of archers, they would kill their horses very easily, and when the horses were dead and the knights fallen, they would defeat them like women and children, and the prince would lose, first his own person, and then his land and all his troops. Hearing this, the prince, thereafter, fell in with their views and returned to his house in Andravida.[21]

The grand domestikos with his armies traveled directly to the fields of Nikli and arrived there. He surrounded the castle and besieged it. And there a fate overtook him, a fate he had not hoped would befall him.[22] The Turks, who were under his command

[20] L. de F. explains the death of Kantakouzenos differently, stating (§ 342) that he was in command of the advance guard and rode forward to make a reconnaissance; on his way back, his horse stumbled in a ditch and he was thrown. The Franks leaped upon him and killed him before he could be rescued. This version of the episode is much more in keeping with his character than the tale given in the Greek and French Chronicles. It should also be noted that L. de F. places the accident at Sergiana before the battle of Prinitza. Z. (p. 39, n. 3) points out that the chronology of L. de F. is confused and that undoubtedly the accident took place after the battle of Prinitza, as the other Chronicles state.

[21] L. de F. states that the prince pursued the Greeks until they escaped into the mountains (§ 344). It also states that after this victory the prince built the chapel of St. Nicholas at Mesiskli and the other churches in Andravida (§ 346).

[22] The Chronicles are not in agreement concerning the revolt of the Turks which is described in the following passage. L. de F., placing the encounter at Mesiskli before the battle of Prinitza, states that before the battle of Prinitza Melik with 1,500 of the Turks deserted the Greeks and went over to Guillaume. These 1,500 settled permanently in Morea with their leader, who married the lady of Pavlitsa (§ 359-63 ff.). Sanudo (p. 118) gives this same version of the events, including the statement that they took place before the battle of Prinitza. As before, the information given by L. de F. may be correct, but the chronology

and who were one thousand in number, asked for their pay as mercenaries, claiming six months' [arrears]; and the grand domestikos—because he was distressed at having gone to receive victory and honor over the Franks only to receive disaster and to return with dishonor—made the Turks an arrogant reply and said to them in anger: "Are you men not ashamed and abashed to ask me for pay when you have become rich in the land of the basileus on the goods of the Franks and on those of the basileus? When you came here to Morea, you were naked, bare,[23] all of you destitute; and after you came here to the land of the basileus, by the blessing of the basileus and from his rule and from the many raids we have made against the Franks, you have become rich, and the basileus—what does he have? Tell me his profit and receive your pay, otherwise never in your lives will I, on my part, ever give you a salary."

When the Turks heard this, they let out a loud cry: "What is this that you are saying to us, despot, why are you insulting us? In what battle have you placed us in which we did not commit some exploit? We went to Prinitsa, there where the Franks came and you did not let us fight, but you sent in your archons, the Romans, who fought the Franks with the lance; see what they won for you and what honor they did you. What Roman did you ever hear of who has fought with a Frank and has vanquished him with lance or sword? Everyone knows it, and it is the truth; in the use of the lance and sword the Franks are soldiers. But we

---

is faulty. It is quite certain, in any case, that after the Turks deserted him Konstantinos left his command in the hands of Philes and Makrynos and returned to Constantinople. It is true then that he was not captured in the battle of Makry-Plagi that followed, not because he fled, as L. de F. states. (§ 372) but because he was not present. (See Z., pp. 39-40; M., pp. 123-25.)

[23] Τετράχηλοι, a curious word, which Schmitt translates as "uncovered, without clothes." He states it is a mistake for τετραχηλισμένος (from τραχηλίζω, "to lay open or bare"). He rather shrewdly points out the similarity of this passage with Heb. 4:13 (not 5:13, as he states), suggests that the chronicler had the biblical passage in mind, though incorrectly, and infers that he coined the word as a result. It appears to me that it is more of a pun than anything else, for in the biblical passage (γυμνὰ καὶ τετραχηλισμένα, etc.) the word means laid open, i.e., to view. But laid open or bare can also be used to extend the meaning of γυμνοί, which precedes it.

were shamed on that day because of the Romans and we fled
from the battle through no fault of our own; we did it to keep
you company and we were in no way at fault. And again you
led us to Andravida; you threatened to destroy the prince, and
when we got there and the Franks lined against us a bowshot
away, all ready for battle, because of the death of one man, who
was lost throught his own fault, you gave orders that we turn
and flee like women. Did you ever order us to fight, that we retreated one foot or disobeyed you? Whoever holds back his servant's pay and his salary gives him leave to go at once wherever
he will. And to us, O lord, from this moment, you give us this
leave, since you are holding back our pay, and we salute you and
go to find elsewhere the means to live as soldiers."

They went into the camp and took counsel right away; they
struck their camp and leaped into their saddles. They went out
of Nikli and took up their road and, going back again, they went
to Karytaina; there they camped that evening.

And when the grand domestikos heard of it and when he was
informed that the Turks had set out from there and had left, they
who were the best of all his army, and were going to the prince,
who was his enemy, he cursed the deed mightily and would have
gone after them himself to turn them back. But the most prudent
who were in his company told him and counseled him that it was
not to his honor to go after the Turks, he the brother of the basileus, for the Turks were greatly enraged in anger, "and if it happens that they are diligent and fight you, and if, by chance, they
should happen to give you battle, and perchance defeat you in
that battle, it would be an unseemly and blameworthy thing;
but why not instruct archons, prudent men, to go to catch up
with them and to cajole them with words, to tell them that you
promise them their pay and as much extra largess as is their due
to have." He appointed two archons, who were from the City,
and gave them a company, and they went out thereafter. They
arrived in Karytaina that evening; there they found the Turks,
who were encamped. They made their way to Melik, who was
their captain, and they dismounted and went straight into his
tent; they gave him greetings on behalf of the domestikos, the
brother of the basileus, and from the archons: "The archons are

greatly amazed at this that has happened, that you separated from us because of words alone and abandoned your oath and your military service which you owe to the basileus and went away bacause of that reason. Go back, O archons, upon your oath, and you will be paid immediately all your pay."

Thereupon, Melik, himself, answered them, as did the captains of the Turkish army, and they spoke and answered in these words: "It is not fitting that a brother of the basileus go back on the word which he has given and promised to any mortal man. Therefore, we declare, archons and comrades, that the grand domestikos, himself, told us and affirmed his word that he would never pay us. Go back and tell him for us that we will never return, nor will we ever serve him one single day of his life, for never once in his lifetime have we found any truth in him. Now, the Franks, we have heard, hold to the truth, and we are on our way to find them and to live with them."

The archons were going to return when a certain Turkish friend told them and counseled them to stay there with them that night, lest the Turks change their minds about returning.

But the Turks, very eager to go to the prince to serve him, very early in the morning blew the trumpets, the Turkish *buccinae*, of which they had a great many, took up their tents and set out along the road straight along the tributary of the river Alpheios and went to Perigardi, in the direction of Vlyziri. Now after they had arrived in Servia,[24] Melik called two of his Turks, his wisest,

---

[24] The route followed by the Turks seems fairly clear, but the places named in this passage are difficult to locate with exactness. The Turks left Nikli and crossed over to Karytaina. They then followed the Alpheios, probably as far as the mouth of the Erymanthos. Then they struck north, traveling by way of Vliziri (La Glisière) towards Andravida. Perigardi (Fr. Beau-Regard) apparently lay between the Alpheios and Vliziri. Schmitt (Index, p. 639), however, suggests that Perigardi (Beau-Regard) and Pondikos (Beauvoir) are one and the same, but quotes Buchon as placing Perigardi near the site of the ancient Elis on the Peneios River. I believe that ll. 5204 ff. in the text above make it clear that neither of these identifications is correct. It is also clear that Servia lay between Vliziri and Andravida, though its exact location is difficult to find. Schmitt claims it is near Prinitza and that Sergiana is another name for the same town. This cannot be, because the town lay much less than a day's ride from Andravida. It probably lay near Palaeopolis, the

who knew the spoken language of the Romans, and also gave them a company of twelve more Turks. He sent them to the prince in Andravida to tell him with what purpose they were coming to him. And when they came to Prince Guillaume, he received them with great honor. Thereupon, they told him why they had left the brother of the basileus and that they were coming to him because of his good rule and his good reputation; in the war he was waging with the basileus, they would help him as much as they were able according to their strength, because they had good information and knew with truth that the basileus was fighting him with unlawful design, whereas every man who holds arms should fight his enemy with God's truth. "Therefore, lord prince, if you need our service, we will serve you for one full year. If, on the other hand, you do not require us and have no need, as our prince and lord, we entreat and beseech you to command that we be given a route that we may go to a place from which we may make the crossing to go to the land of Anatolia to return to our own estates."

And the prince, wise and well experienced, called for Ancelin, de Toucy was his surname—he was brother to the caesar called Sir Philip, who was at that time in prison in the City—because Sir Ancelin was an experienced man who knew with accuracy the customs and language of the Romans, and he ordered him to go to meet the Turks.[25] He took knights and sergeants with him

site of ancient Elis, on the Peneios, in the area called Sergiana in the Chronicle. Sergiana, in fact, was the area lying east and southeast of Andravida, drained by the Peneios. The text states (l. 5046) that the Greeks went to Mesiskli which was just east of Sergiana. L. de F. (§ 339) states they went to Palaeopolis, which was on the Peneios, near the site of ancient Elis. There can be no question, then, that Mesiskli and Palaeopolis were both close to Sergiana, the former to the east. Servia, too, must have been close by. It then follows that Sergiana, Serviana, and Servia cannot be the same place, as Schmitt contends, for he claims that Mesiskli was "a place near Serviana (sic) and at no great distance from Andravida," whereas he says Sergiana and Servia were near Prinitza. It is obvious that he has been misled by his insistence that Serviana and Sergiana are the same word. As to Mesiskli, Kalonaros points out (p. 210, n. to l. 5046) that the name should read τοῦ Μεσίσκλη, rather than τὸ Μεσίσκλιν, because it is really a family name, indicating lands of the Mesiskle family.

[25] For de Toucy's entrance into Moreot affairs, see ll. 1308 ff. above and

to the number of 300 and went to Vlyziri; there he found the archons of the Turkish army. Melik was very happy: "I have been very eager to see you, my lord and brother, for you are an experienced man from Romania and know how to speak to us in Turkish." And thereafter he began to speak and to tell him with what purpose and aim they had come there. And the other answered him with great sympathy: "Welcome, my friend, welcome, my brother, I have been very eager to see you here in my company." And when they had celebrated there in Vlyziri, they went that evening to Andravida.

The prince went out to meet the Turks, and all of his knights were all together with him; they met at the Eleiakos River.[26] Now, the Turks dismounted, as is their custom, and bowed before the prince, small and great, with the exception of Melik and Salik, who were their leaders and whom Sir Ancelin held back, and they did not dismount as did the other Turks. The prince, himself, greeted them respectfully; he held them by their hands, and they began to travel. The Turks did not wait until they were encamped, but riding along, they began to speak and to tell the prince their complaints and the aim and purpose why they had come there, how the grand domestikos had held back their pay and earnings, which they had earned, and they had not done anything deceitful towards him, nor had they shown any disrespect for the basileus. "We took leave of him as soldiers; in broad daylight and in the open we went away from him and came here, our lord, to serve you with arms, and truthfully, as is the way of soldiers,[27] and when we have served you at your command, we ask of you as a reward and beneficence that we have leave to go on our way. We, in

note. L. (§ 357) says he was chosen because, having been brought up in Constantinople, he knew the customs and language of the Greeks. The fact that he knew Turkish (see below l. 5242) was probably a more important factor. L. de F. says that Melik had gotten to know de Toucy in Constantinople and that they came to an understanding in a series of letters (§ 360-61).

[26] The Peneios River is called Eleiakos because it flows through Elis. They probably met at Palaeopolis. L. calls the river La Rivière d'Andreville (§ 359).

[27] From this point on, the following passage, ll. 5272-80, is almost illegible in H. Whatever words are not blotted out correspond, however, quite closely to P. I have therefore used P. and have omitted the disconnected words and phrases of this passage in H.

truth, my lord, did not come into these parts to stay for long, our time to slip by. Today, lord, prepare all your armies and on the morrow let us set out to go against the Romans, against the faithless brother of the basileus; we never once found truth in that one; he detained us with words and took our pay from us. This, lord, is what we want and this is what we ask of you; come with us as far as the spot and stand in your safety, and we will fight the Roman people." Hearing these words, the prince was very happy, as were the bannerets and all the knights. He called Sir Ancelin, his first counselor, and requested and ordered him to prepare the armies to start out on the morrow to take to their road to go straight to where the Romans and the grand domestikos were in Lakedaemonia. As the prince ordered, so did it take place, and on the morrow they set out from Andravida. The Turks informed the prince truthfully that they had learned from the sorcery which they knew that in the first battle they would fight with the grand domestikos they would defeat him.[28] Well, as soon as they went out from Andravida, the Turks rode from then on in the advance guard; they had native guides who guided them and they traveled until after four days they arrived in Kopronitza, near Arkadia; the Turks arrived and encamped in the spot called Mountra, which has a very fine spring.[29] And after they had encamped, they took up their sorceries and found, as they revealed, and it was the truth, that on the following day, Saturday, they would fight over by the mountains which they could see from there. They called the Franks whom they had as guides with them and said: "Archons, lead us to where the prince is; we must speak to him about the benefits and honor which he is going to have." And when the guides heard this, they leaped into their saddles, took the archons of the Turkish army, Melik, Salik, and another fifteen,

---

[28] L. de F. states that after they had encamped for the night Melik, the Turkish general, took two arrows and with these performed some magic arts, from which he learned there would be a battle, in which they would be victorious (§ 365).

[29] Kopronitza corresponds to the present town of Kopanitsa, near the ruins of ancient Phigalia. To the west and slightly south lies the town of Mountra or Moundra, which still bears its medieval name. Both towns lie a short distance northeast of Siderocastro.

and went to the prince in Kopronitza. Seeing them, the prince arose in their honor; "Welcome, my Turks; welcome, my brothers." They, in turn, made obeisance before him and said to him: "Know, O lord basileus, have it from me,[30] that on the morrow, Saturday, in the morning, we are going to do battle. Therefore, we have come here to tell you of it." Thereupon, they said goodbye and went back.

When he heard this, the prince spoke to his captains and asked counsel of all of them as to what they would do. Thereupon, Sir Ancelin gave his counsel and said to the prince: "Lord, know that I have learned from one of my men, a spy, that the brother of the basileus, the grand domestikos, has gone to Veligosti with all his armies, because he learned that we are on our way to go there, and he has taken possession of the passes and all the defiles of the high ridge called Makry-Plagi.[31] Therefore, it is my wish, my lord, that the Turks, who are riding in front of our armies, ride in the center, lest they be seized with panic and break into flight and we lose the battle and our expectation. Therefore, I propose, my lord, if it be your command, that I have the first squadron of all the armies, and let the Turks be in the middle and you in the rearguard, and that I go before all the squadrons; I hope in Christ's mercy to perform such an exploit as will please God and on which you will look with favor."

When the prince heard this, he approved of it highly; "It pleases me, Sir Ancelin, that it take place as you have said; separate the squadrons and let the Turks be in the center." Thereupon, Sir Ancelin went to the Turks and spoke to them flatteringly as the shrewd man he was; he said to them: "Friends, brothers, the prince commands, since you are foreigners and do not know this territory, that I have the first squadron and go in the fore, and that you come behind me, and the prince behind you; and

[30] At this point begins a long lacuna in H. A whole page is missing. Ll. 5321-54 are taken, therefore, from P.

[31] As pointed out above, p. 219, n. 22, Konstantinos left Morea before the battle of Makry-Plagi. All that is related in the Chronicle, therefore, about his presence at the battle, etc., must be understood to relate to Philes, Makrynos, or Kavallarios (or Kavallaritses).

wherever there is need, you will give aid." And the Turks, when they heard, took this for a compliment.

Thereupon, they mounted and began to travel. Sir Ancelin moved out with his squadron and he passed up from Kalami and went to Makry-Plagi.[32] He paused there just a bit and said to his men: "Archons, friends and brothers, know in truth that the brother of the basileus here awaits us with his armies, here in these mountains and in these defiles where we are going. For this reason, I beseech you to bear it in your minds, that they may not come upon us unexpectedly and you be at all seized with panic, but that, as the wise men that you are and soldiers, you may stand firm in the battle like brave men and receive the praise of all the army; for—God forbid—if they put us to flight, we have lost the battle and all the principality."

Now when they heard this, they made him a promise that all of them would die together for his honor. They blew their trumpets and began to climb the slope of Makry-Plagi and reached Phonemene.[33] And while they were bent forward, climbing up the ridge, the hidden troops of the Romans leaped out and attacked them with tumult and eagerness; because they were more numerous, they scattered the Franks, who fell back a good bowshot length down the slope; the squadron of Romans was killing and routing them.[34] Sir Ancelin let loose a great cry: "Boys,

[32] Kalami or the Valley of Kalami (Val de Calamy according to L., § 367, 736, 743, 830) was the name for the northern portion of the plain of Messene in the Middle Ages. In this area were the Villages of Lakkos, mentioned in l. 1719 (see above, p. 120 and n. 37). These seem to have centered around the town of Loutro (La Lutra, L., § 736). Kalami definitely does not refer to the town of that name near Kalamata.

[33] Makry-Plagi (broad hillside) is the most important passage between the central Peloponnesos and Messenia. The narrow defile lies about an hour's distance from the town of Kourtaga, near Megalopolis. The pass proper begins at Chani Makryplagiou and ends at Chani Tsakona, about an hour away. Nearby is the Palaiokastro of Kokla or Kokala, near the present town of Derveni. This is considered to be the site of ancient Ampheia and also the medieval castle of Gardiki. Among the many ruins in the vicinity are some Byzantine churches, one of which, τῆς Φανερωμένης, lies close to the Phonemene mentioned in ll. 5373-84. For a discussion of this battle, see Z., pp. 40-43.

[34] L. 5379 is missing in H. I have inserted the corresponding line from P.

comrades, up and at them! Let's not be shamed by them!" And
the Franks rallied and, turning towards the Romans, with lances
and swords they rushed against them; they pushed them up to
the top of the ridge at Phonemene. And from so much tumult
that the Romans raised, their other squadrons heard the uproar
and another division ran up and went to their aid. And because
of the great numbers of the Romans who attacked the Franks,
they were thrown into panic yet a second time, and they turned
down the slope for a good bowshot length, in truth do I tell it to
you, and thus they were crushed as falcons crush the crows. Thereupon, Sir Ancelin roared mightily and said to his comrades:
"Archons, what is this? Aren't you ashamed at all that we play
like little children? It is as though we were playing the game
called prisoner's base;[35] let us die today rather than be shamed;
all of you, with me, let us rush against our enemies." Then, the
Franks were shamed by these words and all together they took
heart and rushed against the Romans; with their swords they
began to cut them down. And seeing this, the Romans fell into
panic and, fleeing, they climbed to the top of the ridge.

And the Turks who were coming in the second squadron, when
they heard the uproar that the Romans were making, quickly
ran up the slope and arrived on the scene; and when they found
that the Romans had panicked, they attacked with alacrity and
killed and routed them. And when they heard the uproar and
the panic of the army, the other squadrons of the Romans, who
were in ambush, all broke into flight, all fleeing to wherever they
reached.

And then Sir Ancelin called his men—for he had a brother,
caesar he was called, who was being held in prison in the City—

[35] Ll. 5390-91 are taken from P.

'Αμπάρα, ἀμπάρες (bar, bars). Schmitt suggests hide-and-seek for this game
(Index, p. 600) and Miller (p. 123) follows him. However, the French equivalent is *jeu de barres*, which is rendered in French dictionaries as "a game
of base" or "a game of prisoner's base." This game is much more in keeping
with the situation described than hide-and-seek. Dragoumis claims that ἀμ-
πάρα is an iron bar used to fasten a door and ἀμπαρώνω means "barricade
or lock in." D. Loukopoulos describes the game in his Ποιά Παιγνίδια παίζουν
τὰ Ἑλληνόπουλα... (Athens, 1926), pp. 29 ff.

and said: "What is this evil deed that befalls me,[36] that one or two of
the archons or of the captains are not taken that the lord my brother may be exchanged, he who is caesar of Romania and who is
being held in the City in prison in the old palaces?"[37]

Thereupon, on hearing this, a certain one of his sergeants called
Perrin Coumain, thus was he named,[38] said: "What shall I have,
lord, from you should I point them out to you?" And Sir Ancelin
said to him: "Whatever you wish to have, except my life, my
honor, or anything reflecting upon it."

Hearing the proposal that Sir Ancelin made to him and promised him, this sergeant said to him: "Come with me and I will
show you where they are." He took him and they went up to
a hollow which is between two mountains, within a gorge, where
today stands the castle of Gardiki.[39] "Behold, lord, down there
in the gorge, the grand domestikos and Kavallaritses and, besides
them, Makrynos on the other side of the hollow.[40] Eight Turks
hold them and are talking to them, insulting and reproaching them
greatly; they held back their pay and made them their enemies."
When Sir Ancelin went up to the hollow and looked in and recognized those archons—he recognized them well from the arms
they were holding—he shouted a great cry and said to the Turks:

---

[36] Ll. 5412-14 are from P.

[37] Philippe de Toucy was *bailli* of the empire on many occasions after 1241.
His title was caesar (see above, p. 105, n. 93). The only source for his captivity
in Constantinople at the time of Makry-Plagi is the Chronicle but, if this is
true, he was apparently exchanged for Makrynos. In 1271 Philippe was made
grand admiral by Charles of Anjou, an office he held until his death in 1277.
(See Lg., pp. 182-83, 185, 234, 253; Z., p. 42.)

[38] I have not been able to find any mention of this man beyond this reference
to him as a sergeant or squire of Ancelin de Toucy.

[39] For the castle of Gardiki (Gardichy, L., § 375, 830, and Gardisco, L. de F.,
§ 714-22) see p. 227, n. 33. Dragoumis (pp. 186-88 and 190-96) discusses at
length the probable site of Gardiki in relation to the hollow and gorge mentioned in the text.

[40] It is interesting that the name of Philes is missing here as well as throughout this passage. This tends to confirm the fact that Konstantinos was not
at the battle, but had returned to Constantinople and had left Philes as grand
domestikos and head of the army. Ll. 5430-82 which relate the capture of
the Greek commanders are missing from P., demonstrating again that it was
copied at some time by a pro-Greek scribe.

"And what is this you are doing, my comrades and brothers? Take care not to commit an act of treachery; bring them here immediately under heavy guard." The Turks, when they recognized him from the arms he bore, said: "It is Sir Ancelin who calls us." Quickly they disarmed them and they led them up to him; holding them, the Turks brought them before him. He raised his hands and praised God, for he had been informed and held it true that he would ransom his brother with them. He ordered that his own trumpet be sounded; he took them and went with great joy to Veligosti where he gave them to the prince, who gave him a large gift and thanked him deeply.

Now when the Frankish army was gathered at Veligosti, they made an enumeration to see and reckon what troops they had captured. Thereupon, they made their enumeration and found the truth: that they held alive in their custody the grand domestikos and Makrynos and likewise they also held Kavallaritses; also, they held 354 archons and *sevastades*, and these were all titled archons; and they found with them lesser archons and other troops to the number of five times one thousand and thirty and more.[41]

Now the prince ordered that all his armies rest in the town of Veligosti. Then, after they had rested that day, on the morrow there came all the archons of Skorta, who had been all in revolt; they asked him for mercy and that he pardon them. Thereupon, all his knights besought him to pardon them and that he show them mercy. And the prince, as the wise and good lord that he was, sweet, calm, affable, such was he in all things, quickly par-

---

[41] The prisoners were: the Grand Domestikos Philes, who later died in the castle of Chloumoutsi, where he was imprisoned (l. 5581); Alexios Kavallarios (also called Kavallaritses in the Chronicle), who was at some point released, for he later commanded the Byzantine army (Pachymeres, I, 324); and the Parakimomenos Makrynos, who was probably exchanged for Philippe de Toucy and who was accused of treason and blinded on his return to Constantinople. All references to Konstantinos in this connection are false, including the story that he bribed his captors, told in L. de F. (§ 372). The actual numbers as given in the Chronicle are, of course, false, but that Byzantine losses were heavy cannot be denied. The complicated problem of the chronology and actual events of the battle of Makry-Plagi is discussed at great length in Z., pp. 40-43.

doned them and ordered that they swear to him to desist in their evil ways and to be faithful to him. On the following morning Prince Guillaume ordered that the Romans, the brother of the basileus and all the captains, be brought before him that he might see them with his own eyes and talk with them. Thereupon, they brought first the grand domestikos, the brother of the basileus, whom he was very eager to see now that he happened to be in his custody. When he came, he rose to meet him and sweetly greeted him, and, holding him by the hand, he seated him by his side. After this, all the captains seated themselves as well, and then he began to speak and said to the domestikos that he had made an oath with the basileus that they would stand together always and that they would maintain peace and never be false to the relationship by baptism they had entered; but he was false to it and abandoned his oath and launched a war and sent armies. He destroyed his land with plundering and warfare, in which he, as a basileus that he was, committed a crime; thereupon, God, the avenger of all things, seeing the evil deed he committed and the murder, was angered and enraged with him. "Look what has happened, the evil deed of the basileus has fallen on you. Look, my lord and brother, how many troops you had, around 18,000, indeed, knights and foot soldiers at Prinitza, where you came with great self-confidence, with assurance and the expectation that you would seize Morea; 300 Franks, who were my supporters, turned up and they won the battle and you, they slaughtered. And then again, brother, at Makry-Plagi, just see what happened to you with your armies. Now I do not boast, nor do I praise myself, but I give thanks to God, the just in all things, for he has avenged me as you yourseves have seen."

After Prince Guillaume finished with all that he had related and said to the domestikos,[42] the grand domestikos began, in his turn, to speak and he made such answer to the prince: "We do not have, brother, prince of Morea, equality that I may speak as is required in this matter, for I, alas, am in custody and you have me in chains.

---

[42] L. 5511 of H. reads: "These things which he related and said to the domestikos." The next line is missing. I have, therefore, used ll. 5511 and 5512 of P. to fill the gap.

However, were you to cut off my head on the spot, yet should I not fail to speak and give answer to all that you have said, for it was an accusation against me. Indeed, it is not seemly for a noble man to boast when his luck gives him the victory in battle and brings into his hands to have in his power him whom he is fighting and has as his enemy; the fortunes of war are common to all. And in this which you have said about my lord, the basileus of the Romans, you are very wrong; for all men know, and it is the truth, that the land of Morea is not yours by rightful inheritance; you hold it by despotic force, but it is the patrimony of the basileus of the Romans; and with rebellious sinfulness your forefathers came and seized the land of the basileus and you hold it. Behold how your murdering and sin brought you into the hands of my holy lord, the basileus; and if he had wished, as basileus, he had the power to do whatever he wished to you at that time. But he is very merciful and Christian to all men; with honor he released you from his prison, with agreements he released you, and you swore him an oath that you would never attack him and his troops with arms; and he made you a relative by baptism that your friendship might be strengthened.[43] And after you were released from there, from his prison, and came here to Morea, you never paused for a minute. Quickly you gathered together armies and took up arms yourself and went to Lakedaemonia that you might show off before the world; you displayed empty glory that your lordship might glitter and you were unfaithful to the basileus and trod upon the oath and did to him the opposite in all that you had promised him and launched a war after you had armed yourself. In this way, you proceeded to commit a crime and trod upon your oath; and if you but recalled what happened to you at Pelagonia, you would never be boastful and belittle another. For the adversities of life and of campaigning as well do not come into being all together, nor ought they to entail any bragging. However, if the spur of the moment and the sorrow of my imprisonment have brought me to say more things than

[43] This ceremony had taken place in 1262 after Guillaume's release from prison. See Geanakoplos, *Michael Pal.*, p. 155 and n. 75.

I ought to have said, then may I have pardon from you and from the captains."

The prince wisely answered him in this way: " You, brother domestikos, I know, have said and spoken many things because of your bitterness and, as a noble man, I endure them from you for you are in my custody. But if this were elsewhere, and you were free and said that I forswore myself in the oath that I had given, even if it had been the basileus himself, I should have fought with him to the death. But because you are in prison, you are forgiven; all men know that I committed no felony. Because of the lies which the perfidious Romans of Monemvasia sent him from here, the basileus, believing their words, sent armies and began to make war and committed a sin. And may God the Pantokrator forgive him, for I have been informed that others deceived him and he believed their words and sent armies here and began our war and the damage to us both came about."

After this, both sides were silent and they threw the blame on the Monemvasiotes. After these events, the prince that evening with counsel assigned his prisons where he would put each one according to his rank. He sent the grand domestikos to Chloumoutsi and in his company Kavallaritses also, the others, he sent to his other castles. And as soon as he had sent them off, as I have told you, he ordered that all his captains be called, as well as the wisest men of his whole army. He took counsel with them as to how they would act, where they would leave from, where they would go, and where they would ride; some said that they should go, each to his own home to rest a while, for they were fatigued; others, the more prudent and those who were wounded, agreed to go to Lakedaemonia, for it was a town well suited for an army's respite, and they had an abundance of goods for their sustenance[44] and to undertake the siege of Mistra. And if by chance they found a way to capture the castle, they would thus be able to conquer the land.

[44] Ll. 5595-5635 are taken from P., as they are not given in H. The original numbering of the folios, however, indicates no lacuna. This leads Schmitt (p. 364) to suggest that H. was "incomplete when paged, or perhaps never contained the full account of the original ms."

Immediately, the prince spoke to Sir Ancelin, who was the commander in chief of all the armies, and to Jean de Catavas,[45] his marshal, and ordered them to prepare the armies to move out to go to Lakedaemonia as had been counseled.

And they most eagerly made ready and set out; on the following morning they arrived there. And when they arrived there, they found the following reports: Most of the Romans of that town had gone with their families to the castle of Mistra. And when the prince found the town empty of the native castle troops, he was very sorry and it seemed very bad to him. He immediately assigned and gave their houses to certain others whom he put to live therein, who were Franks of the land, men of truth, and in whom he had more faith than in those others. Then he ordered his troops to go to plunder the towns and the suburbs which were in revolt. He supplied the town of Lakedaemonia; he placed troops in it and ordered that they build it up and strengthen it in any way needed.

His armies overran Vatika and Helos and plundered the land as far as Monemvasia; then they raided and destroyed Dragaligos and all of Tsakonia, devastating the lands; they supplied the town, and the people whom the prince had placed in the town to live prospered, and so he decided to spend the winter there.

But, as are the chances and fate of men, they expect one thing to happen and quite another overtakes them, and the peril that befalls man impedes not a little; not even one whole month had passed when reports were brought to Prince Guillaume that the Skortinoi had revolted, had gone with the Romans and had laid siege to the castle of Araklovon and had placed troops in Karytaina with the intention of holding it for the basileus. Hearing this and being informed of it, the prince supplied the town of Lakedaemonia with troops and goods for their sustenance and he took his armies and went to Veligosti. He called the captains of his whole army; and they took counsel together as to where

---

[45] L. erroneously states that Jean de St.-Omer was charged with the siege of Mistra (§ 386). This is an anachronism, for he did not enter Moreot affairs until after his marriage with Marguerite de Neuilly (of Passava). See ll. 7370 ff. below and Z., p. 41, n. 1.

they might enter the *drongos* of Skorta,[46] for the terrain was harsh with mountains and passes and with cruel defiles. The prince called the shrewd soldier Sir Ancelin and spoke to him with a candid mind. "You, brother and comrade, have done much for me; with the counsel and wisdom that I have had from you, I have accomplished great achievements and military exploits by which I have benefited, as all men know, in the war which we have with the basileus. For this reason, brother, my friend and kinsman, I again beseech you and pray you will do this for me because of the despite and outrage committed against me by my nephew, the lord of Karytaina, the great traitor—who forsook his land and me, who is his uncle and from whom he holds the suzerainty which he has from me, and went to parade himself in the kingdom of Apulia—[47] and also because of the wickedness and the treachery of the perfidious Skortinoi, those traitors, who have betrayed me more than two times now. Direct the Turks, whom we have newly with us, to enter the *drongos* of Skorta and to burn and destroy the houses and villages and let them slay on the spot whatever men they capture and keep as their own whatever they acquire from them."

Thereupon, Sir Ancelin, as the wise man that he was, recognized that the prince was distressed and he said and promised him that he would fulfill what he ordered and he answered him sweetly; "Lord, do not be angry; and I will do what you wish and what will please you." He called the captains, Melik, first of all, and related to him in detail the command of the prince, that he had commanded them to enter the drongos of Skorta; that whatever booty and spoils they might acquire, he and his Turks might keep as their own. And Melik, when he heard it, was delighted and he gave him the answer that he would do it eagerly; small and great became joyful. He drew them up so that they were divided into three squadrons; Sir Ancelin gave him native guides. The

---

[46] For Skorta, see above, p. 129, n. 39. The principal castle of the area was Karytaina; lesser ones were Akova (Mategrifon) and Araklovon (Bucelet). For the Greeks of Karytaina, see above, p. 205, n. 95.

[47] For this new escapade of the unreformed lord of Karytaina, see below, ll. 5739-5911.

Turks invaded Skorta and covered, burned, and destroyed the land and towns; all whom they captured with arms, all these they cut down, and all who fell at their feet, to them they were merciful and brought them to the prince and surrendered them. And when the archons of Skorta saw this, they fled into the mountains and high peaks; they took counsel together as to how they would proceed. They sent a messenger to the prince and asked him for mercy and that he pardon them, denying that they had revolted; what they had done had been for a different purpose. They had taken counsel together as to what they would do about the war with the Romans and with their basileus, because their lord, he of Karytaina, was absent.

When he heard this, the prince would not receive them; the great men and all the captains, who had compassion and friendship for the lord of Karytaina, besought the prince, on their knees they begged him, to pardon the troops, since they had asked quarter. And the prince, as a shrewd man, did it eagerly. At once he sent a messenger to Melik, to halt his raiding and to come before him. And he, when he heard, went to Veligosti and saluted the prince, who received him well.

Then the prince dismissed his troops and each traveled to his rest. And he went to Morea with his retinue, and all who were from Morea traveled with him.[48] Likewise, the Turks there went with him, and they had arrived there, they asked for their release from the prince, as was in accordance with the agreement which they had made when they first came to Andravida. Their departure seemed to him very grievous; he ordered that they be paid their entire salary and he gave Melik gifts and afforded him hospitality. He requested him and told him to remain with him for just six months more and then to leave; and the other answered him, saying to him humbly: "My lord and basileus, I hope that my service has brought you profit and gain. When I made an agreement with that enemy of God, the domestikos, there in the City, I promised to serve him for a year; and now two years have passed that I am away from my lands. And they who are with me, all my comrades, will not allow me to remain here in this

[48] Morea here means Elis.

land. And I beg of you, my lord, do not press me, for I have an oath to return to my patrimonies."

Seeing this, the prince did not overpress him; he gave him presents and large gifts of friendship and sent him off with guides, and he went to Vlachia. In truth, it did happen that some of them remained with eagerness in Morea; and the prince ordered that they all be baptized. He made two of them knights and gave them fiefs and he even gave them wives and they begot children who are still in Morea, in Vounarvi and Renta.[49]

At this point, I turn from what I have been telling you and I am going to tell you about that soldier, the lord of Karytaina, what he was doing and where he was during the time of the prince's war and was not in Morea during the war with the Romans at the time that I am speaking of, and listen to what I say! During the war which Prince Guillaume had with the basileus and his brother, the lord of Karytaina (who was considered one of the leading knights of the world and was a soldier, famous in all the kingdom) by demonic sinfulness and love of woman—which has befallen many other shrewd men and soldiers!—he fell in love with the wife of a certain one of his knights, Sir Jean de Catavas, thus was he named. He took her from Morea and went to Apulia, saying they would make a pilgrimage there to the monasteries, to the church of St. Nicholas at Bari and that he would go to Rome and also to the church of the Archangel and the great monastery which is on a mountain peak near Manfredonia.[50] At that time,

---

[49] Kalonaros suggests that these towns correspond to the present towns of Vounargon, near Letrina, and Retentou, near Olena, both in Elis. He also suggests that, if L. de F. is correct in stating that Melik remained in Morea (§ 363), the town of Maliki was probably named after him and the Melikes family are his descendents. (See K., p. 236, n. on l. 5738.) Facing p. 209 of K. is a photograph of the cornerstone of a medieval bridge over the Alpheios, near Karytaina. In the inscription there is a reference to Manuel Melikes as its νέος δομήτωρ, or new fief holder, perhaps a reference to the Melik of the Chronicle or to one of his descendants.

[50] The churches of St. Nicholas at Bari, which contained the body of that saint after 1087, and of the Archangel Michael on Mt. Gargano were, after those of Rome, the most important goals of pilgrimage in medieval Italy. Manfredonia, founded by Manfred in 1263, lies to the south of Mt. Gargano, on the bay which bears the same name.

King Manfred was king in Apulia and lord of Sicily and of all the kingdom;[51] and when he heard from certain men who came and told him that the lord of Karytaina had come into Apulia, the man famous in arms throughout Romania, he was greatly amazed and inquired to learn his aim and purpose and what he wanted there. Some, who heard it from his retinue, told him that it was to make a pilgrimage to the holy monasteries which were in his kingdom and to go to Rome; and someone else, a shrewd man (who was experienced and who had asked a certain relative of his who was in the retinue of the lord of Karytaina and who had told him the true reason and purpose) spoke to the king in private and informed him of the real reason and purpose and all the truth; the lord of Karytaina, the famous soldier, had fallen in love with the wife of a certain one of his knights and had brought her from Morea and they had come here into Apulia [for him] to have her as a mistress and to enjoy himself with her.

On hearing this, King Manfred was greatly disturbed and sorrowed for the shame of the noble soldier; he sent out a knight well accompanied, and he went to Sir Geoffroy, the lord of Karytaina. He spoke to him on behalf of the king and requested him to go there to see him, for he needed to speak with him. And he, on hearing it, leaped upon his horse and went with all his retinue to the king.

On seeing him, King Manfred rose to greet him, took him by the hand, seated him by his side, and began to ask him why he had come there. And the other answered; he had come to make a pilgrimage to the monasteries, which he had vowed that time in the City, in the prison of the basileus of the city of Constantine. And the king answered him and spoke such words : "I am amazed, in your good sense and in the praise which you have, that you, a soldier famous in arms, deserted your lord Prince Guillaume

---

[51] Manfred (1232 or 3 ?-66) was the natural son of the Emperor Frederick II. By the terms of his father's will he was the representative in Italy of his half brother, Conrad IV. After 1254 he was regent for Conradin, Conrad's infant son. On August 10, 1258, on false rumor that Conradin was dead, he was crowned king of the two Sicilies. He later refused to abdicate and remained king until his death in the battle of Benevento on February 26, 1266. See above, p. 162, n. 23, and p. 175, n. 51, for his earlier connections with Moreot affairs.

during such a violent war and need for an army, as he is carrying on with the basileus of Constantinople. A noble should not be a liar, nor should a soldier like you, who are celebrated, and every noble man ought to be disturbed and be very grieved when he hears that he is in error. Lord of Karytaina, I want you to understand and be informed that I know the truth, the reason and purpose for which you have come here and I am grieved by it, by God, because of the renown that you have. The affair is ugly and I am loath to speak of it. However, for love of you I am going to denounce it, so that you will understand clearly the wrong you have done. You deserted the prince, your liege lord, who is carrying on a violent war with the basileus, and you trod upon your oath which you have to him and you are forsworn and unfaithful to your liege lord. And, furthermore, another ugly thing and a great treachery, you took the wedded wife of the knight, your liege man, and you are wandering around with her, when you have an oath with him and he with you. Therefore, since your praise is renowned, I give you a long term, fifteen days, to be gone from my land and to go to Morea to aid your lord the prince in the war he is waging with the basileus of the Romans. Should you be found in my land after the two weeks have passed, I swear to you on my crown and upon my soul, I will order that your head be cut off at once."

And when Sir Geoffroy, the lord of Karytaina, heard that the king had found him out by himself and had told him the felony and error he had committed, from the shame and disgrace which he felt before the king, his speech faltered and he had nothing to say. But, as well as he could, he answered the king: "Lord king, I entreat you, I fall before you and worship you; in all that you said to me and have spoken, you speak like God, for I know by myself the felony I have committed; and I worship and thank Your Majesty for this and hereafter I will leave and set out from here and will go to my lord Prince Guillaume."

He asked leave to depart and the king gave it to him. He returned to his camp, took his retinue, and hastily departed from there, he set out and went away. He arrived in Brindisi within six days; he found a galley ready and he boarded it and arrived at Klarentsa within three days. He asked where he might find the prince, and he who knew informed him; Prince Guillaume was in Andravida. He was holding a high assembly with all the captains, the bishops and burgesses and the knights, and they were taking counsel together about messages which they had received; messages had been brought them that were not too good.[52] A large body of troops had disembarked at Monemvasia; the basileus had sent them to reinforce his land and troops, which had fallen into danger.

And when the lord of Karytaina heard what I am telling you, that the prince was in Andravida with all his captains and knights, he rejoiced greatly in this hope, that because they loved him, all would put pressure on the prince of Achaia to pardon him. His friends there loaned him horses; he rode quickly and went to Andravida; all met him and had great joy. He made a request of all of them, as brothers and friends; he said: "Now may I see who of you, my relatives, friends and brothers, really love me, let me have your help in the felony I have committed, for you know well that I have gravely wronged my liege lord Prince Guillaume."

All promised him, small and great, to help him with all their power. They took him and went straight to the prince, there where he was lodged in the church of Saint Sophia. Thereupon, he bowed before Prince Guillaume; the prince was angry with him and he showed him deep rage, and he had great right, for he had hope in him and, more, he had had confidence that he would have help from him in all his needs, and he had deserted him in the midst of his great effort. The lord of Karytaina, the laudable soldier, was wise and knew the felony he had committed, and he took off his girdle and placed it around his neck; he fell quickly to the floor and called for mercy and said to the prince in the presence of all: "I, lord, have committed a felony and have come that you may judge me." On his knees he said to him these words which I am telling you. The bishops and all the other captains and knights quickly fell to their knees with him, saying to the prince in entreaty: "In the name of Christ, forgive him, our lord, do, and if he should fall again into felony, cut off his head.

---

[52] Ll. 5851-5934 are missing from P.

You know, our lord, the war you are now waging; we ought to have others to help us." And the prince, prudent and merciful as he always was, answered them thus and spoke these words: "Archons, know this and understand it well; the lord of Karytaina happens to be my nephew and is my liege man and the foremost, and the more he has erred, so much the more do I grieve for it. However, because of your love and your entreaty, let him be forgiven again this time." Everyone bowed before him and thanked him, and he returned to him his land and castles. The prince then spoke in the presence of his troops: "Archons, all of you know the felony he committed during the time he was going around with the great lord; he fought with arms in the field against me. I forgave him, as all of you know; I returned his land to him, giving it to him as a new grant to hold in perpetuity, he and his children, for he had disinherited himself with his own felony; now again, I want him to hold it from now on in the same manner."[53]

Since he had been pardoned, the lord of Karytaina sat down in the council, he and the captains, the prince of whom I speak and all the knights. The prince asked them to advise him about the troops of the basileus that he had learned had come. "Since it was the will of God and the most holy Theotokos, and the lord of Karytaina has returned to us, give him armies and troops so that he may go to Nikli to take a stand there to fight, and defend the land, and later when there will be need, we shall all help him."

---

[53] For the earlier felony of the lord of Karytaina, see above, ll. 3220 ff. and 3348 ff. For "new grant," see above, p. 171, n. 40. On the occasion of his earlier trial, he wore a halter around his neck; here, it is his girdle. Likewise, see above, p. 205, n. 95, where the Greeks of Karytaina are described as hanging their handkerchiefs around their necks. Hanging a rope or yoke around the neck was undoubtedly a sign of submission or humility. It is interesting to note that in Mane, a region of Greece that has a reputation somewhat similar to that of the Kentucky hills, this sign of submission was used until fairly recently by defeated enemies in the blood feuds, for which the area is notorious, when they came to ask quarter. (See K., p. 242, n. on l. 5892, and Adamantios, Τὰ Χρονικά, pp. 630, 656-57.) Another archaic vestige in Maneote custom is the use of the word ἀγάπη for a truce or cessation in the blood feuds. Throughout the Chronicle, this word is used with the same meaning, as in l. 6882, where it is in apposition to τρέβα. (See M., p. 127, n. 2.)

At this point, I now leave off speaking and reciting about Prince Guillaume and his troops and I am going to tell you, so that you will know about it, how the brother of the king of France, Sir Charles he was called, the lord of Provence (the pope, indeed, crowned him king of Sicily), came and how he became an in-law and entered an agreement with the prince of Morea, that Guillaume, and the son of the king took as his lawful wife the daughter of the prince, the Lady Isabeau, with treaties and agreements, which they made with one another, to the effect that the son of the king would inherit the principality and the prince would hold his land from the king.

At the time of which I speak, and tell and relate, the count, who was called d'Anjou, the lord of Provence,[54] had with his wife the countess three beautiful daughters, who were their children. Now the eldest (who was the heir) married the younger brother of the king of France, Sir Charles, he was called, the famous soldier. He inherited with his wife the dominion of the Count d'Anjou and all his county. Now the king of France took the second sister, daughter of the count, as lawful wife. A short time later, the king of England took the third sister of the two whom I have mentioned to you as his crowned wife and he made her a queen. And, after the count of Provence had married off his three daughters, as I have been telling you, a short time later, the count died and there remained in his land as lord heir Sir Charles, brother of the king of France, for he had the eldest sister of these three.

Well, at that time and in those years, Emperor Frederick of Germany ruled the kingdom of Sicily, in addition to which, he held the suzerainty, I say, of Apulia. He offered violence to the pope and took Campania away from him, as well as Romagna and the suzerainty of Rome; he banished the pope, who set out from Rome

---

[54] Raymond-Berengar IV (1198-1245) was count of Provence and Forcalquier, not Anjou, as the Chronicle erroneously states. He had four daughters by his wife Beatrice of Savoy: Marguerite, who married Louis IX of France in 1224; Eleanor, who married Henry III of England in 1236; Sancha, who married Richard, earl of Cornwall, in 1244; and Beatrice, the youngest. This last was designated his heir by her father and inherited Provence and the title of countess. In January, 1246, she married the brother of Louis IX, Charles d'Anjou, thus making him count of Provence.

and fled to Venice, lest he kill him. From there, the pope and the churches excommunicated him and his lands and his followers. In no church were hymns sung nor even mass celebrated, children were not baptized, the dead were not hymned, nor was a couple ever married. He was excommunicated forever in all the churches in all the kingdoms throughout Christendom, and in the monasteries and by the bishops of the whole world.[55]

The Emperor Frederick had a son, an illegitimate one; Manfred, he was named, prince of Salerno; he held suzerainty over Capua and all within it.[56] The Emperor Frederick died, and King Manfred was crowned king of Sicily, and he was sovereign over all that his father had held; he, too, held the lands and the suzerainty;[57] he profaned the Church like the tyrant he was. And when some time had passed, as I presume, the pope's cause was supported, and he returned to Rome. Now, he knew and recognized that Sir Charles (he was called the count d'Anjou, lord of Provence, and was the brother of the king of France) was an awesome soldier, famed throughout the world. With the counsel of the bishops and cardinals, he sent a message to him and likewise to his brother, blessing and entreaty and great promises, that if he would go on his behalf to take up the war against King Manfred (that tyrant who held the lands and property of the Church) to give him battle and destroy him, he would have the treasury of St. Peter and all his money at his disposal to hire armies. And all those who believed in Christ and all who were baptized would take the cross to go with him; he would surrender to him the scepter of the Church, he and his children to hold it in inheritance, and he would be hailed

---

[55] There is an extensive bibliography for the reign of Frederick II. (See *Cambridge Medieval History*, VI, 869-74). The details as given in the Chronicle are, as usual, incorrect, but contain some truth. Frederick was excommunicated by Gregory IX on September 29, 1227, for breaking his vow to go on a crusade. This excommunication was reviewed on Holy Thursday, March 23, 1228. On Easter Monday, Gregory preached against Frederick, but the enraged Romans drove him from St. Peter's, and he had to quit Rome for two years.

[56] For Manfred, see above, p. 238, n. 51.

[57] Ll. 5977, 5979, 5980, and 5995 are missing in H., and I have inserted the corresponding lines of P.

as king, and the crown would be placed upon him, and he would be king of Sicily and of the kingdom of Apulia.[58]

And when that wonderful, brave Sir Charles, I tell you, the count of Provence, heard what the most holy pope promised and wrote to him, he would by no means undertake it, saying and reasoning that, should he undertake it, he would force the king of France, who was his brother, into discord and a great war with the Germans and also with the Ghibellines;[59] and he would bear the sin for the massacres of the war and for the obliteration of the Christian people. At this point, there occurred this affair which I now record for you.[60]

The king of France wished to hold a celebration and a brilliant reception with his kinsmen; he notified his brother-in-law, the king of England, writing to him of it in a friendly way and requesting him to come with the queen, his sister, that they might join together in Paris to hold their celebration. And he accepted in sincere love; it seemed to him most agreeable that they meet and make merry. So, he took the queen, well attended, and they went to Paris, and the two queens had great joy in their meeting when they came together. And one day, a Sunday, they were holding great celebrations and, the two sisters, the queens, met together;

---

[58] Repeated attempts were made by the popes to bring Charles into Italian affairs. Those made in 1240-41 by Gregory IX and in 1253 by Innocent IV were unsuccessful because of the opposition of Louis IX. In 1263-64, the French pope Urban IV gained the support of Louis IX and an agreement with Charles was all but completed when the pope died. His successor, another Frenchman, Clement IV, finally concluded the treaty with Charles in April. The terms of the treaty can be found in the *Cambridge Medieval History*, VI, 183-84.

[59] By the middle of the thirteenth century, the Tuscan names of Guelf and Ghibelline had come into general use to designate papalist and imperialist in Italy.

[60] This incident is to be found in other chronicles covering the same period. For example, in ch. 32 of Muntaner's *Cronica* (English trans. by Lady Henrietta Margaret Goodenough, 2 vols., London, 1920-21) and in Bk. 6, ch. 90 of Villani's *Historie Florentine* (ed. Muratori, *Rerum Italicarum Scriptores*, XIII, Milan, 1728) the details are quite similar. There may be a modicum of truth in the tale, therefore, even though Charles's personality was such that one does not expect to find him particularly influenced by his wife, especially in this matter.

the second was of France and the third of England.[61] And while they were seated in the queen's chamber, there also arrived the first sister, the countess of Provence, who held her father's patrimony. Seeing that she was coming, they rose to greet her; and so they sat down together, as is the way of women. And as soon as they were seated together, the queen of France, who was the middle one, said to the first sister, who was the countess: "It is not fitting for you, good sister, to sit with us as if you were the same as we two who are queens; we are in a different class and rank from you."

And when the noble countess heard this, from bitterness and shame, she arose from there; she left there immediately and went to her home and entered her chamber with many tears. And thereafter, the count of Provence appeared; he asked from outside where the countess was and some one answered him and said to him: "Lord, there within her chamber, I believe she sleeps." So the count went in lightly; now, the noble lady realized that the count was coming and she wiped her eyes with her handkerchief.[62] Now the count recognized that the eyes of the countess were swollen from many tears and he said to her with anger, "What are you crying about, countess?" And she wanted to deny it and not disclose it. Immediately, he swore a dreadful oath and said, "If you do not tell me truthfully, at once, why you are crying, I will give you such a beating that you will really cry."

And she, frightened, told him the truth; that she had gone to see her two sisters and had sat with them to chat; "and because I sat with them as if of equal rank and did not show them deference because they were queens, my sister the queen of France began to speak to me and said to me: 'It is not right that you, my good sister, sit with us as an equal in the same rank nor of the same worth, for it is fitting that we have higher glory and worth, than a countess or a duchess or any other lady.' And I, on hearing it, was immediately so sorely grieved that from grief and shame I left there and came here to my chamber and wept many tears."

[61] See above, p. 242, n. 54.
[62] Ἀναπετάριν (something that floats or has wings). Handkerchief, or long sleeve?

Now when the count heard this, he made a dreadful vow and said to his wife, the countess: "I swear this to you by Christ and his mother, that I shall never rest nor be content until I bring it about that you become a queen with a crown."

He left there at once and went to the king, to his brother, I tell you, the king of France, there where he was conversing with his brother-in-law, the king who is called king of England. He took him aside and began to speak to him: "Lord king and brother, you must know well that our holy father, the pope of Rome, many, many times has sent me blessing and a request that I go to Rome, and that if I will come to grips with King Manfred in war and fight with him in the field with armies, he will crown me king of Sicily and give me the scepter and I shall be the Defender of the Church of Rome. And I have never wished to undertake this, God knows, because of you, lest I should force you into war and trouble, to fight with the king of Germany and also his party, with all the Ghibellines. Well, lord, the will to do it has just come to me; therefore, I beg of you, I bow before you as my lord and brother, that I have, first, a command from your lordship and then help, money and armies, that I may go honorably as befits your honor."

Now when the king heard this, he approved highly, and spoke thus to his brother: "I give thanks to the Basileus who created the world that he gave you the desire to do this, for it is a thing of honor and the salvation of the world. And in this matter, I bring forth as witness the Lord of Glory that I wanted to advise you to do it with a will and that you undertake it. But, again, I feared that you might chance to think that I wanted you to be away from my company. Well, since God has given you the will, and you wish, by your own statement, to undertake it, take of our monies and likewise of our troops, and hire good armies to have behind you, and may God and the blessing of our most holy father and also the blessing of me who am your brother be your aid wherever you may go; for I have hope in God and in the holy Theotokos and in the wisdom and in the military prowess which are in you that you will perform a deed for the honor, first of the Church, and then of me, and of you and of all our kinsmen."

Now, the count, wise that he was and skillful, thanked the king, as his lord and brother, and then he made ready; he took money and hired many armies, experienced men, knights and infantry, all brave soldiers. He said goodbye to the king and went to Provence, equipped his ships, boarded them and arrived in Rome within a month.[63]

The sea lies twelve miles distant from Rome; and after he landed and his troops had disembarked, he ordered that the horses and the steeds and the armor and the foodstuffs and the supplies be loaded on to wagon carts and pack mules, and he set out and went straightway to Rome.

When the most holy pope of Rome[64] heard that Sir Charles, the count of Provence, was coming with splendid armies, the flower of France, he raised his hands and praised God, Saint Peter, and likewise Saint Paul, who had enheartened him to go to the aid of the most holy Church against the tyrants; for he had just been informed[65] and had hope in God that the tyrants and enemies of the Church would disappear, and he would remain upon the throne of Rome. Thereupon, the pope from the happiness he felt because of the count and to encourage the count, as was fitting, he himself rode out with his cardinals and also with the noblemen of Rome and went to meet the count of Provence;[66] he did him great honor in that meeting.

And after they had arrived and had gone to Rome, each dismounted at his quarters. And as soon as they were lodged, just as I am telling you, the pope sent five cardinals, four metropolitans, and twelve bishops, to the count, he sent them, requesting him to come to see him and to speak with him; thereupon, they escorted him with great honor. Now the most holy pope rose to greet him, took him by the hand, and seated him beside him. "Welcome is the nobleman, the blood of France, the defender of Christians, the son of the Church." He began to ask him for

[63] Charles set sail on May 15, 1265, landed on the 21st, and entered Rome on the 24th.

[64] Clement IV, who was pope 1265-68.

[65] In a dream?

[66] Ll. 6143-45 are not to be found in K. and Schmitt (p. 398, n.) suggests they are an interpolation in P.

messages from the king, his brother, I tell you, the king of France; and after he had related the messages of the king, he thanked him and praised him a thousand times because he had come there and labored in the need of the Church, which thing would be a source of honor and gain for him and of comfort for Christians snd the whole Church. And after they had conversed and had spoken all that they wished, the count returned to his lodging. And then the most holy pope ordered that all, small and great, be summoned; he held an awesome summons and high court and invited those who had come at that time with the count and likewise the noblemen of Rome. The pope celebrated mass in the church of St. Peter and after he had said the mass and had come out of the altar-sanctuary, the pope, himself, crowned Sir Charles king of Sicily with his golden crown; all present, small and great, acclaimed him.[67]

And after the count d'Anjou was crowned king of Sicily, he did not want in any way to waste his time; he went to the pope and said to him: "Lord, holy father, I did not come here to sit like a woman, now that I have undertaken the war with King Manfred and his Ghibellines, who are enemies of the Church and are excommunicated. I do not vaunt myself and I am not able by myself to fight the tyrants and enemies of the whole Church. But since you sit upon the throne of Rome and have made me the Defender of the Church, order and send everywhere to all the kingdoms that all who believe in Christ and are at your command, that all these help you with their armies that you may battle those who are the enemies of the Church." When the most holy pope of Rome heard this, what the king had said seemed attractive to him. Immediately, he ordered that letters be written and he sent messengers to the kingdoms and also to all of Italy, [bearing] blessing and invitation that they come to help him to expel from the dominions and lands of the Church the tyrants and impious who were profaning her. Splendid armies came from all the kingdoms, and in Italy all came who were Guelphs. And after they

---

[67] Charles was first crowned in the Lateran on July 28, 1265, by two cardinals. Later, he was crowned a second time with his wife on January 6, 1266, a few days before the battle of Benevento.

all gathered in Rome, the king divided each man's squadron and ordered that they go out of the city of Rome. And he armed himself as befitted him as king; armed in his arms, he went to the pope and on his knees he asked him to give his blessing. And the pope blessed him and made the cross over him; he ordered that the imprint of the holy cross be placed upon the left side of his breast that he might keep it with him; likewise he blessed his armies, small and great, everyone, and he prayed for them and said: "All those who die by the sword on this expedition will have pardon from Christ and also from the pope for whatever sins they have committed in their lifetime, just as though they had died in the places of Syria to wrest that holy tomb of Christ from the hands of the non-Christians, the race of barbarians." And after the king had received the blessing from the pope—as he had likewise given it to all the armies—they set out and went straightway to Apulia.

When King Manfred heard the reports that King Charles, himself, was coming against him, he sent for and there came from Germany many good armies, all were brave men, and likewise from Lombardy and also from Tuscany there came those of his party, all who were Ghibellines; they came from Sicily, and also the men of Calabria, and he gathered so many armies that they were past counting. He took up a position at Benevento and awaited the king; and he awaited until he arrived. There they fought with all their armies; and as it is God's will that he who has the right, God gives him good fortune, and he takes the victory, the great King Charles won the battle.[68] There King Manfred was killed and lost the battle, and those who remained after him, I speak of his troops, all did homage to great King Charles, and thus he was left, with comfort and peace, lord king of Sicily and of the kingdom of Apulia.

---

[68] The battle of Benevento took place on Friday, February 26, 1266. As a result of his overwhelming victory, Charles remained undisputed lord in Italy and established himself in Naples as king. The name Benevento in the Chronicle is given as *Μπονιβάντ*, a faithful rendition of the name as it would sound in French — another indication that the Greek Chronicle was written by a Frenchman.

At this point I shall leave off speaking of what I was telling you about, and I am going to return to Prince Guillaume again, to tell and recite the deeds that he performed. Here I shall begin to speak and to tell you about the prince of Morea, Guillaume, and what he did and how he acted at that time when the noble lord of Karytaina returned from the kingdom of Sicily, there from Apulia. As I told you above in my book, Prince Guillaume, himself, pardoned him;[69] he returned to him his land, which he held from him, in such manner and agreement, as they had established, that he was to hold it in inheritance only to his child, just as he had returned it to him before at Nikli, when the prince was fighting with the great lord. As is the custom of warfare wherever it may be, sometimes battles are won, other times they bring disasters, which fact would have given me great trouble, if I were to write all of them for you in this book.

But to make it lighter for me, who writes it. and you, who are listening to it and reading it, I have made great efforts to select the best and I have written and recited the deeds and undertakings which bore fruit.

Therefore, I shall begin at this point; listen that you may learn ![70] When the prince heard and was informed that at that time King

---

[69] L. 6250 is from P.

[70] The account which follows of the entrance of the Angevins into Moreot affairs, of the battle of Tagliacozzo, of the marriage of Charles's son to Guillaume's daughter, and of the treaty of Viterbo is quite confused and inaccurate, especially in its chronology. When Charles defeated Manfred at Benevento, he became heir not only to the Hohenstaufen lands in Italy, but also to Manfred's interest in the East. His first step was to lay claim to the Ionian islands which Helene of Epirus had brought as her dowry. By early in 1267 these were in his possession. Apparently his scheme was to use these as a stepping stone to all of Greece and then to a grandiose Angevin empire of the East. Accordingly, late in 1266, he began a long involved negotiation with the deposed Emperor Baldwin II of Constantinople and Guillaume de Villehardouin. On February 17, 1267, he issued a safe-conduct to Guillaume, who set out for Rome soon after that date. When he arrived, he found the Roman curia in turmoil over the Eastern question. The bishop of Negroponte and the bishop-elect of Lakedaemonia had just been to Rome *ad limina* and had brought their problems with them. Envoys of Michael Palaiologos were negotiating for the union of the two churches. Baldwin II had arrived to meet with Charles,

Charles had defeated King Manfred in battle and had cut off his
head and had seized the suzerainty of all his kingdom, he was very

after an unsucessful attempt to enlist western support for a reconquest of
Constantinople.

Zakythinos (p. 46) believes that Guillaume did not participate in these
discussions and that he was not present when the Treaty of Viterbo was signed.
He points out that if he were, he would have signed it himself and would not
have had Leonardo de Veroli sign as his representative. On the other hand,
one wonders how he could have left in the midst of such important negotiations,
which indeed were vital to the future of Morea. Buchon (*Rech. et Mater.*,
I, 193, and *Nouvelles recherches*, I, 201) states that he did remain and that
he was present when the treaty was signed, though he does not explain why
he did not sign himself. Longnon has given the best explanation of the events
(see "Le rattachement de la principauté de Morée au royaume de Sicile en
1267," *Journal des Savants* [1942], and Lg., pp. 236 ff.).

According to him, Guillaume arrived in Rome around the end of February.
Charles arrived around the end of April. The negotiations were long and bitter.
Charles was quite aware that both Baldwin and Guillaume needed his help and
he was determined to get as much as he could in return. The first result was
achieved on May 18. On that day, a treaty was concluded whereby Philippe
de Courtenay, eldest son of Baldwin, was to marry Beatrice, daughter of Charles.
Then on May 24, a treaty was concluded between Charles and Guillaume.
Its terms were extraordinary. In return for a promise of help from Charles,
Guillaume, with the consent of his overlord Baldwin, ceded the principality
of Morea and its dependencies to Charles on these conditions: one of the king's
sons would marry Guillaume's daughter Isabeau; Guillaume would remain
prince during his lifetime; on his death Morea would fall to Isabeau's husband,
or, if he should die before Guillaume, to Charles, himself; if a son should be
born to Guillaume — he was about fifty-five at the time the treaty was signed —
the son would inherit a fief amounting to only one fifth of his father's possessions; should Isabeau die without issue, the Villehardouin were to be disinherited completely in favor of Charles or his heir.

Three days later, on May 27, 1267, a second treaty was concluded between
Baldwin and Charles, whereby Baldwin surrendered almost all his holdings,
including Morea, to Charles, who was to undertake the reconquest of the Latin
Empire within six or seven years and to grant to Baldwin a third of whatever
was conquered. The marriage of their children was to make the treaty binding.

Zakythinos and Miller were unaware of the treaty concluded in 1267 between
Charles and Guillaume. They do speak of the marriage treaty, and state that
it was concluded right after the battle of Tagliacozzo (Z., p. 47; M., p. 129).
The Chronicle places the marriage itself *before* the battle, which is completely
inaccurate.

After the treaties were signed Guillaume returned to Morea. Zakythinos

happy and approved of it highly, because the Frankish race, to which he, too, belonged, had come closer to Morea, to his own land. As a result, he pondered well within his mind and spoke and analyzed in just this way as I am stating it: since the basileus of the city of Constantine was rooted in Morea and his dominion was spreading, he would never be able to expel him from the land alone, all by himself, with the troops that he had, if he did not have strength from some other dominion. Well, now that God had given his command, and the dominion of King Charles had come to nearby Apulia (and God had not given him a son as his heir to leave as lord in his land, and when death was to overtake him, at the hour of his death, he was to have only female children as heirs), if he should be able to make an in-lawship with that most exhalted King Charles, King Charles to take the daughter, I tell you, of Prince Guillaume as his daughter-in-law,[71] he would have power and brave armies, to expel the basileus from the principality.

And after the prince had pondered well by himself, he ordered that all the captains be called, those who were the wisest and foremost of his council, and he spoke to them and told them of his desire. And as soon as they had heard him out, they debated together; they pointed out and suggested many ways and means by which the thing might be realized and accomplished, for he was a noble and powerful beyond nature, while the prince was small of means; and perhaps he would not accept it and would

states that envoys came to him in early 1268 from Charles to deal with the prince and to get the acceptance of the princess and the barons to what was agreed (pp. 46-47). He is mistaken in that date, however, for Longnon places this mission in June, 1270 (Lg. p. 240). In March, 1268, Guillaume was back in Italy, took part in the battle of Tagliacozzo (August 23, 1268), and apparently stayed in Charles's service at least until March, 1269. During the rest of 1269 Charles was occupied with a revolt in southern Italy, but managed to send some help to Morea. In June, 1270, the mission spoken of above arrived in Morea. The envoys also put pressure on Guillaume in the matter of Isabeau's marriage. By the terms of the treaty concluded three years before, she was to have been sent to the Neapolitan court immediately, but three years latei she was still in Morea. The wedding was finally concluded on May 28, 1271.

[71] Ll. 6287-88 are from P.

not condescend to it. Well, at that point, there spoke the most
prudent of them who was to be found in the prince's council at
that time, and who was called and named Nicolas de St.-Omer.
He was lord of Thebes and had wide knowledge and he spoke to
the prince, giving him this counsel: "If you wish, my lord, to accomplish this, I take it upon myself, if you carry out my advice,
that the in-lawship with King Charles be effected. It is the truth,
as all men know and recognize, that the lord your father together
with our parents, who conquered Morea, which is called a principality, and won with the sword whatever we hold in fief. And
your lord and father did not hold the land of Morea from anyone,
to hold it from him; he held suzerainty from God alone and by
the sword. And as soon as his lord and father died, Sir Geoffroy,
your lord and brother, became lord, and he held the daughter of
the Emperor Robert, whom he was sending to the king of Aragon
to be his wife, and thereafter he married her, as all men know.
As a reparation to the basileus because he had committed a felony
against him, and to have peace with him and the affair be quieted,
he made a treaty and became his man, to hold his land from the
the emperor. Well, according to the manner in which your brother
settled it at that time and became the liege man of the emperor,
he could not serve any one else and only to him could he give his
entire services. Well, just as he did this for his own gain, to
satisfy a desire and to profit, do the same thing yourself, and right
away, with King Charles, to satisfy a desire and to profit. And
if you do as I say, I take it upon myself that the king will become
your relative with eagerness."

When the prince and those of his council heard this, all were
pleased with it and praised it highly. And after the counsel was
given, as I am telling you, the matter was decided and they took
a stand on it. The bishop of Olena with Sir Pierre (his surname
was de Vaux, thus was he named, and throughout the principality
he was considered a wise man),[72] these were chosen to go to the
king as envoys. They made ready and crossed straight over to
Brindisi; and after they had landed, they purchased horses, took
to the road and went to where the king was. They found him in

[72] See above, p. 200, n. 82.

Naples and bowed before him; they held letters for him and they presented these, which wrote and declared that he was to believe these men in everything they would recount and say by word of mouth.

And after the king had received the letters and had understood the declarations that he was to believe these men, the king ordered that they be called to a place aside and began to question them as to what they wanted to say. And they, as they were prudent, began to speak to him: they told him in detail what they wanted there, the prince's desire that, God and the king willing, they enter in-lawship and become as one. And after the king had listened well to what they had told him, he answered them that he would take counsel and then would make an answer, as was right and seemly.

Thereupon, the king ordered that the captains be called, the first and best that were in his council; in detail he told them about the prince of Morea and what he proposed and wrote that he effect with him. And then they began to speak and to take their counsel; and after they had debated, they said this also: that they call and question the envoys to learn and hear all their particulars. Thereupon, they called them and began to question them: how does the prince of Morea, Guillaume, hold his land and whom does he have as overlord and what kind of land is Morea and what might its worth be? Thereupon, Sir Pierre, who knew and understood everything about Morea, made answer and related all from beginning to end.[73]

And after the king and his council, as well, heard what the principality of Morea included and what it was worth, all counseled him that the affair be accomplished, for they saw and realized that it was to his advantage. And the king determined that their counsel be carried out; and after the king determined to effect an in-lawship with the prince of Morea, Guillaume, he directed a bishop, two bannerets, and another two knights, who were with him, to go as envoys to Prince Guillaume to carry back an answer to him with his men, the will and answer that the king announced to him.

[73] L. 6375 is from P.

Thereupon they set out and went to Brindisi; they found the ships, which were ready for sailing, and they went aboard together, and they went to Klarentsa and found Prince Guillaume in Andravida. The bishop of Olena with Sir Pierre spoke to the prince and told him in private all that they had accomplished and effected with the king. And after this, they also called the messengers who had come with them from King Charles. And then they reported what they had to say from King Charles to the prince of Morea: that it was pleasing to the king, he desired and wished that the in-lawship be accomplished in accordance with the agreements which had been declared to the king by those envoys which the prince had sent to the king, which stipulated that the prince take his daughter, who was his heir and who was called Isabeau, and that they go to Naples to join the king, and that the children be married, the son of the king to take the daughter, I say, of Prince Guillaume; and after this, that the prince do homage to hold his land from King Charles.

And when the prince heard this, he approved of it highly and he bestowed high honors and gifts on those who had come to him as envoys. And he directed them to go back to the king to carry back his answer and to inform him that the prince of Morea was pleased with the agreements and was preparing to come to consummate the affair. And the prince sent immediately to Euripos, and a well-equipped galley was brought to him, and in Klarentsa he directed another to be equipped for him. He made ready as befitted such a great man; he boarded the galleys with his daughter, who was named Isabeau, and with his retinue, and he took as many knights as he needed, and they set out from Klarentsa and arrived in Brindisi. And after they had landed in Brindisi, they quickly brought horses and took to the road. And thus, riding to Naples, which was his residence, they arrived before the king.[74]

Now, when the king heard and was informed that the prince was approaching the town, he himself rode out and went to meet him. There where he met him, he greeted him sweetly and, holding him by the hand, the two rode side by side; he did him great

---

[74] L. 6424 is missing from H. To maintain continuity, I have used ll. 6424-27 from P.

honor and everyone was amazed at it. And afterwards they dismounted at the king's house; he ordered that he be settled honorably in the town. He invited him to dine with him the next day; and in honor of the prince he invited all the nobles who were in the town. He held high court and there was much celebrating; and after they had celebrated well that day, each went to his quarters.

On the following morning, the prince went over and came before the king that he might converse with him. The king ordered all his counts to come; they sat in council and began to converse. Then the envoys who had gone to the prince in Morea came and began to speak, wishing to relate how they had gone to Morea, to Prince Guillaume, with the command of the king concerning the in-lawship and what they had established and to what point they had advanced the matter, the affair about which they had been sent. "So, now that the Basileus of Glory has commanded, and the prince has come here to your majesty, the affair has been left to you two lords to execute and consummate the matter in such wise as will be to the honor of both you lords and to the glory and well-being of you and of your troops."

And as soon as the envoys finished what they had to say about the in-lawship, the prince then began to speak and to tell about the affair and its beginning, the way the affair began, and that at the behest and will of the king, he had come there and had brought with him his daughter and that he was ready do to all that the king's envoys had established with him in Morea, in the agreements they had drawn up and in all particulars.[75]

Then the king answered by himself that all that the prince said was the truth and he wished and desired that the affair be consummated, as they had agreed and had established. And after they had finished and had declared the particulars, they ordered that their children be brought there. The archbishop of Naples, who was a metropolitan, then betrothed the children; and after he had betrothed them and had performed the marriage ceremony, the prince did homage to the king to hold his land from King Charles. He divested himself of his land and gave it to the king and

---

[75] Κεφάλαια ("chapters," "main points," "particulars").

the king thereupon invested his son, Sir Louis, with the principality; and he returned it to his father-in-law again, to hold and administer for as long as he lived in this world.

And after they had concluded these things which I am telling you, the prince remained there fifteen days with King Charles; they held big celebrations. Then, reports from Morea came to the prince that a certain nephew of his had come from the basileus to Monemvasia and had brought armies, Cumans, Turks, and Romans from the region of Nicaea, and that in Morea, the men of the land were afraid and asked the prince to return there. On hearing this, the prince went to the king and told him these reports in detail and asked his leave to go to Morea to succor and strengthen his land and troops; to go to his castles to provision them. And the king, when he heard this, said that it was good that he go to his land to succor it and to protect it from his enemies. Thereupon, the prince took leave of the king; he rode swiftly, arrived in Brindisi, found the galleys ready, boarded them, and in two days arrived in Klarentsa and from there he rode out and went to Andravida.

When all the people of the land of Morea heard that the prince had come, they were very happy; they became strongly confident against their enemies. He sent written orders everywhere to the *chevetains* that all of them keep heavy guard with their troops, for he was on his way to help them, and that they should provision the castles and muster the troops, to stand fast and guard the land and the frontiers. And when he had rested for about four days, he wrote to the captains and the knights, and they came there to him, and they rode out at once. He took them, and they toured all the castles, and he ordered that guards be set throughout the land, so that they might be protected from their enemies.[76]

At this point, I shall pause here for a moment in writing and speaking about Prince Guillaume of Morea, and I am going to tell you about King Charles, the deed he committed, and the compassion he showed at that time to the prince of Morea.

The all-wise king, this King Charles, from the great compassion and emotion which he felt toward his in-law Prince Guillaume,

[76] L. 6519 is from P.

and because he was also experienced in the warfare of armies,[77] after the prince had left and had gone away from him, he pondered and reasoned that, since the basileus had sent armies of his own into Morea to fight the prince, who was his in-law, the prince would have need of aid of armies and troops to protect his land. Thereupon, he ordered that there be called a knight of his, who was a soldier experienced in warfare; Sir Galeran, he was called, d'Ivry was his surname.[78] He said to him: "I want you to go to Morea to the assistance of the prince, who is my in-law, with one hundred mercenaries on their steeds and also two hundred foot soldiers, all select men, these, too, one hundred of them to be arbalesters and the others, shield-bearers.[79] And I order that all be paid for six months and that you be over them as *bailli* and captain; make ready immediately and go quickly. The ships are

[77] Ll. 6525-28 are from P.

[78] Zakythinos seems to have confused the chronology for all these events. He accepts the statement of the Chronicle that Galeran d'Ivry was sent, but claims he was sent as *bailli*, and that this occurred in 1268 (pp. 48-49). He goes on to say that he was replaced by Philip de Lagonesse the same year. Then he states (p. 51) that in 1272 Drogone di Belmonte (Dreux de Beaumont) came to Morea as *bailli* at the head of troops, etc. Kalonaros, of course, follows this interpretation (p. 267). Longnon, however, is more reliable. According to him, the first *bailli* sent to Morea by Charles was Galeran d'Ivry, seneschal of Sicily, and the appointment took place on August 26, 1278, after the death of Guillaume de Villehardouin (p. 254). This is the only possible interpretation for he would have had no right to send a *bailli* until after he became prince of Morea. However, in 1271 and the following years Charles did send captains-general to Morea. The first of these was Drogone di Belmonte (see above), who came with troops in 1271, but he was not *bailli*. The Chronicle has confused Drogone with the first *bailli*. Ll. 6535 ff., then, deal with Drogone di, Belmonte and not Galeran d'Ivry. (See also M., p. 130, n 2; Hopf, *Geschichte Griechenlands* [Leipzig, 1867-68], I, 292.) The Greek spelling of the name Galeran d'Ivry is Γγαλεράν ντὲ Βρή. In L. it is given as Galerans de Vry. Schmitt (p. 624) claims that this is proof that the French Chronicle is dependent on the Greek one, for "an aphaeresis of this kind [i.e., Ivry to Vry] is common in Greek, but hardly possible in French, where in this case only the *e* in *de* is subject to elision." It is equally possible that in the original Chronicle the name was given as de Vry rather than d'Ivry, simply because the chronicler made a mistake in the name.

[79] There is a page missing in L. at this point, the lacuna corresponding to ll. 6543-6604 of the Chronicle.

ready in Brindisi, so board them and go quickly to Morea, to the assistance of the prince, and give him many greetings from me and tell him on my behalf that if he needs more armies, let me have a short notice, and I shall send them to him at once."

The knight, like the wise man he was, most quickly made himself ready, as the king had ordered. He left Naples and went to Brindisi; there he found the ships ready, and he went aboard them and within three days he arrived in Klarentsa. The prince happened to be at that time at Vlisiri. Sir Galeran sent him six messengers; four were sergeants and two were knights; and he informed him in detail that he had come from Apulia at the behest of the king with the army that he had to the assistance of the prince and to do his bidding.

And when the prince learned of the arrival of that *bailli*, Sir Galeran, who was come from the king and had brought with him the splendid army, knights and infantry, as I have told you, it seemed to him most agreeable and he rejoiced at it; and to do honor to the *bailli* for the king, he rode out at once with the troops he had and went straight to him in Klarentsa. And, on the other hand, when Sir Galeran, wise man that he was, heard and learned that the prince was coming to him, he quickly rode out with his company, in armor on their horses, infantry and knights, and they met Prince Guillaume on the Eleiakos River, at a spot called Kriveska.[80] There they met and rejoiced together; Sir Galeran greeted the prince on behalf of the king and said to him: "The king has sent me here and sends you many greetings and he sends you with me all these troops to the assistance of your land, and as an aid in the war you have with the basileus of those Romans. And, again, if you should need more, let him know that he may send them to you."[81] And the prince wisely thanked the king for the assistance which he had sent and also for the aid.

Now after the two had arrived in Klarentsa, the prince ordered that horses be found, [the kind] that are called pack horses, to

---

[80] Kriveska (or Kresaiva, as it appears in P.) is no longer in existence. It probably lay south of Andravida, on the Peneios River, somewhere between Kavasila and Palaeopolis.

[81] Ll. 6583 and 6585 are from P.

be given to the mercenaries, one to each man, to give them a respite by bearing their clothes and armor. And after the prince
had outfitted the Franks who had come to his aid, whom the king
sent, he took counsel with those who were in his council as to what
road they should take and in what place they should attack their
enemies, the Roman race. And when they had taken counsel, they
set out from there and arrived at the tributary of the Alpheios,
at a place called Isova;[82] the *chevetains* came with their troops,
as did the bannerets; they had been given orders to have a two
months' supply of bread, and there they took counsel as to where
they should campaign. Thereupon, they were advised to go to
Nikli, being of such thought and purpose because that place was
spread out enough so that their armies might have rest and lodging and might approach the armies of the Romans, should they
perhaps wish to campaign; and should they come to a decision to
fight, the prince was confident in the armies he had and in the
hope that God would give him aid that he would be victorious
over the Romans. And if Christ was pleased to give him the victory, he would conquer very easily all of the principality.

Then, they mounted and separated the squadrons, left Isova,
and arrived in the evening at Karytaina at the splendid castle.
When the lord of Karytaina learned that the prince was coming
with his armies and that he was coming up the tributary towards
him,[83] he quickly rode out with his men and went to meet the
prince of Morea. And on the other hand, from Akova came Sir
Gautier, lord of that castle, with the armies that he had;[84] they
joined together in Karytaina; they reckoned what armies each
one had and found that those two bannerets, the lord of Karytaina and he of Akova, had a good one hundred and fifty mounted
men, who were all select and experienced soldiers; they had two
hundred foot soldiers, all armed.

And after they had encamped in the plain of Karytaina on the
banks of the tributary, in those most beautiful meadows, the
prince ordered that the captains be called, the lord of Karytaina,

[82] For Isova, see above, p. 203, n. 3.
[83] For "tributary," see above, p. 203, n. 2.
[84] Gautier II de Rosières.

the lord of Akova, and also the others, the leaders of the army. He asked counsel of all of them as to where they advised his armies to attack his enemies. Thereupon, the lord of Karytaina spoke first and next after him the lord of Akova, and they said and advised that they go to Nikli, just as they had been advised in the first place. The lord of Karytaina told the captains that he knew and recognized the captain that the basileus had over his troops and that he was a braggart and had great glory and pride in his troops, the ones which he had with him:[85] "He will want to come quite promptly to fight wherever we invite him, on the plains or in the mountains. And if God and fate grant and decree that we fight together and that we receive the victory, we shall take all Morea out of the hands of the Romans."

Thereupon, they made ready, separated the squadrons, and gave directions to their armies, first of all, to the marauders, who penetrated into Gardalevos and raided Tsakonia, for these were in revolt on the side of the basileus; they gathered much booty, it was past counting. For five days those armies raided and then they returned to Nikli. And the captain of the basileus with his armies was in Lakedaemonia; and he did not once go out of there. And if someone were to ask me with what purpose he acted in this way, I should answer him that it was because of the command he had received, for the basileus, himself, Sir Michael, gave him orders that after the battle of Prinitsa had taken place, and again, after the second battle, that of Makry-plagi, Romans were never to meet in the field to fight with the Franks in Morea for any reason in the world. The basileus swore and thus commanded: that in the area of Morea, in the field and with lances, Romans would never meet with Franks to give battle, for three hundred Franks alone had defeated the brother of the basileus, who had six thou-

---

[85] Zakythinos suggests (p. 52) that this nephew of Michael VIII was Alexios Philanthropenos. The imperial troops arrived in Morea some time in 1270, but they had learned their lesson in earlier battles with the Franks and refused to give battle. The Frankish forces, on the other hand, were not strong enough to maintain the siege of Mistra. This stalemate lasted until the winter of 1271, when Drogone arrived. This section is one of the most confused and least comprehensible passages of the Chronicle, as is pointed out in a long footnote by Zakythinos (p. 53, n. 4).

sand troops on horse, besides his infantry. If other, more numerous Franks were to find Romans in the field, the basileus would no longer have Morea. He ordered the Romans to take a stand in the mountains and to guard the land, all armed with their bows; and whenever they found the opportunity and had the advantage, with guile and strategy, they were to fight the Franks.

And after the prince had heard of this command, he called his captains to advise him. And of some these spoke and gave him this advice: that he take his armies and go straight to where the captain of the basileus was in Lakedaemonia, fight with him, and utterly defeat him.

But others, the wiser ones, who understand strategy, did not approve of their acting in this way, saying that the stretch of land from Nikli to Lakedaemonia was a wooded area, with mountains and narrow gorges, favorable for archers to take up positions and shoot at us and our horses, while we should not be able to injure them.

Thereupon, the prince called that Sir Galeran, the lord of Karytaina, and the lord of Akova, as well as all the other captains; he asked them to give him counsel as to how they should act. To this, some said they should remain in Nikli and blockade the Romans in the territory around Mistra, so that they would have no means to get out to damage the lands, and that they should hold the passes and guard the land so that the captain of the basileus should not pass to do any damage to the territory of Skorta nor to Argos, nor to Mesarea; for if they were to set out from there and leave the land exposed and unguarded, the Romans would come and attack and, plundering, they would devastate the land. Now, in the end, the prince and the wiser of them did not agree to act in this way, saying with respect to Sir Galeran and the mercenaries that, because they had not found food for them and their horses, they should find some and buy it, as is the way of armies.

Thereupon, the prince ordered that Nikli be provisioned with all the things that the castle needed; he left Sir Jean de Nivelet as *chevetain* with one hundred mounted men to remain with him, and one hundred arbalesters, one hundred shield-bearers, and three hundred archers were to stay with him also to patrol the villages and fields of Nikli and as far as Veligosti and the places of Helmos, so that no Romans might pass to raid nor give battle nor do any damage to the lands of the Franks.

And after Prince Guillaume had provided for the garrisoning and guarding of the territory of Nikli, he took his armies and went to Karytaina and there he dismissed all his armies. The Kalamatianoi, those of Argos, the lord of Mesarea, and he of Akova departed, as did the Skortinoi, foot soldiers and knights; the lord of Karytaina with his retinue went with the prince together with Sir Galeran, who was *bailli* for the king; they went into Morea straight to Klarentsa.[86] And after they had arrived and had encamped, the prince ordered that the logothete,[87] Sir Leonard, who was from Apulia, and the lord of Karytaina be called and he said to them: "You have seen the compassion and honor which the king showed me and sent Sir Galeran and with him mercenaries, to the assistance of all the principality. Therefore, I say to you: give me your counsel as to what honor and benefice we should bestow upon him, for you have seen with your own eyes that only by means of his troops did we go seeking to fight with the troops of the basileus and with his captain."

And after Prince Guillaume had been counseled as to what honor and benefice he should bestow upon him (he was thinking mostly of the honor of the king), he then called before him Sir Galeran and said to him aloud in the presence of all: "You, my lord, the king sent here with the troops you brought to the assistance of the land, which thing I deemed a great glory to me and a benefice and aid to me and to my troops. Therefore, I desire, my friend, I beseech you, as a reciprocation for the honor which the king did me, that you receive from me the office of the bailliage and that you be *bailli*-governor of all the principality on behalf, first of the king, and, secondly, of me, to govern our land of all the principality for the increase and honor of us and you as well."

On hearing these words, Sir Galeran's inclination was to give this sort of answer to the prince: that he was not able to do this,

---

[86] Morea here means Elis.

[87] The λογοθέτης (*locum tenens*, lieutenant) was one of the four higher ministers in the Byzantine bureaucracy. In the Chronicle the word is always used to indicate the chancellor. For Leonardo, see above, p. 200, n. 82.

since he was planning and expecting to return to Apulia. But on the other hand, he pondered a bit and said to himself that, since the prince was appointing him *bailli* in his land because of the king, it was a high honor to him, and he said to the prince: "At your command, lord, I shall do whatever you tell me with all my power." Thereupon, the prince immediately took his glove and invested Sir Galeran as *bailli* of all the principality, and he was *bailli* throughout the rest of Prince Guillaume's lifetime.

At this point, I here bring a halt to what I have been telling you and I am going to speak to you about King Charles and the war he waged with Conradin, the nephew, I tell you, of Emperor Frederick and also cousin of that King Manfred.[88] Now after the great King Charles had conquered the kingdoms of Apulia and Sicily and had killed King Manfred in battle, he held his kingdoms in tranquility and peace. A certain great noble from Germany, who was named Conradin, since he was the nephew of Emperor Frederick and also the cousin of King Manfred, about whom I am telling you, when he heard and learned and was informed that King Charles with his armies had fought in the field with his cousin, had defeated King Manfred and seized his dominions, he desired and urgently requested of his kinsmen that he might go on a campaign into Apulia to fight with King Charles; should God grant it to him, he might perhaps avenge that King Manfred, who was his cousin. He, therefore, journeyed throughout Germany and requested all the generals and lords who were then ruling Germany to help him and to go with him to Apulia to fight with King Charles and together to avenge King Manfred. Now, all promised him that they would help him; some gave him troops and others went with him. He gathered many troops, foot soldiers and knights, went out from his land, there in Germany, and went to Lombardy where he found the Ghibellines, the tyrannizers of the Church,

---

[88] Ll. 6774-76 are from P. There is a lacuna in L. corresponding to ll. 6783-6904 of the Chronicle (§ 475). Conradin was son of Conrad, heir of Frederick II, and nephew of Manfred. When Conradin came into Italy, he was about sixteen years old, but he had the enthusiastic support of the Ghibelline party. His forces met those of Charles d'Anjou at Tagliacozzo on August 23, 1268. Conradin was captured after the battle and beheaded.

who were enemies of the pope, and he invited all of them and they went with him, eager and willing to die with him; they preferred the Germans to the Franks. He gathered so many armies that they were past counting. And after all his armies had gathered, he separated his squadrons, quite apart from his infantry, and went out of Lombardy and went to Apulia.

Here at this point, I am going to stop writing and reciting about that German, the renowned soldier Conradin, I tell you, who was a nephew of Emperor Frederick, the enemy of the Church, and instead I am going to turn back and tell you of the deed that the great King Charles did when he heard and learned the reports that Conradin was coming to fight him.

When the renowned great King Charles heard that Conradin was mustering armies to come against him to do battle with him, since he was an all-shrewd soldier in all things, he was not so negligent as to underrate him. Quickly, he hastily sent to his brother, who was king of France, to help him with armies from his land, experienced soldiers, who might help him in his war need. And the king, when he heard of it, called his brother the count of Artois[89] and told him those messages and ordered him to take at once two thousand mounted knights from the flower of France and go to Apulia to the assistance of their brother the renowned King Charles.

Along with this, King Charles sent into his own land, which was Provence; sixty galleys [full] came, and merchantmen and tarettes, which carried the troops with their horses and the supplies and food for that army.

Next, furthermore, the most holy pope of Rome, when he heard and learned the reports that Conradin was coming with a multitude of armies against the lands and towns of the Church, he called King Charles and said to him: "My son, now that we have learned and know in truth that Conradin is coming against the Church, I give you authority to take from the treasury of St. Peter, Apostle of the Church of Rome, as much as you order and desire, it is all at your command; and hire armies for yourself, as many as you can find, and protect the property and land of the Church."

[89] Robert II, count of Artois, who was really the nephew of Louis IX and Charles and not their brother.

And the king, most discreet, thanked the pope; he bowed low before him and the pope blessed him.

And after this, the most holy pope of Rome ordered that letters be written to all the kingdoms and he sent out cardinals and bishops, together with his blessing and request that all give him aid and that they send him armies and troops to go in the company of King Charles, who held the banner and scepter of the Church, and to help him, and, together, to protect the land and property of the Church of Rome. Blessing they would have, and pardon for whatever sins they had committed from the day of their birth, just as if, in fact, they were to go to the tomb of Christ to fight the enemies, the race of barbarians. All sent him from all the kingdoms armies, numerous and goodly, infantry and those on horse.

The king, furthermore, the great Charles, sent word to the principality of Morea, to Prince Guillaume asking in a friendly way that he come to help him with the troops of his land and with the armies that he had.[90] When the prince heard this, he was disturbed at the message, for he was very much afraid of Conradin, because he had heard of his strength and that he had many armies; it might perhaps befall, by misfortune, that the victory fall to him, and King Charles lose the lordship of Apulia. However, on hearing this message, the prince sent [word] to the captain that the basileus had in Morea, and who was his representative. He made a truce with him, an armistice for one year, that his land might remain in tranquility and peace. Then, after this, he made ready to take with him the foremost and best, the flower of Morea. First of all, he took with him the lord of Karytaina; likewise, he took with him the lord of Akova, the grand constable Chauderon, Sir Geoffroy de Tournay, and other knights to the number of 400,

---

[90] Guillaume was summoned not so much because he was a friend as because it was his feudal duty to go, since he had become liege to Charles by the terms of the Treaty of Viterbo. He was accompanied by Geoffroy de Bruyères, lord of Karytaina; Gautier de Rosières, lord of Akova; Jean Chauderon, his nephew and grand constable; and Geoffroy de Tournay, lord of Kalavryta. He was in Apulia by March, 1268, for a letter of Clement IV to his legate, written in that month, recommends that Guillaume be placed in charge of the troops gathered in Foggia (E. Jordan, *Régistres de Clément IV*, no. 1336, p. 427).

all on their steeds. They did not delay; they crossed over from the Despotate, and went straight to Brindisi; whatever horses they were lacking, they found and bought; and then they rode out and traveled until they reached Benevento, and there he found the king.[91]

And the king, when he heard and was informed that the prince was coming, went out to meet him; he greeted him sweetly, and they embraced each other, and the king held the prince by the hand. When he saw the handsome troops which he brought with him, he thanked him warmly, and they rejoiced in each other. Then he talked with him and informed him that Conradin had come and had entered Apulia with a force of many troops, which he he had in his support. Asking everywhere, he came looking for the king, and he sought him until he came close upon him. And after the two armies had come close to one another, the prince (who knew the warfare of Romania, the machinations and slyness which the Romans and Turks practice and which taught them to know all about warfare) called after him those whom he wanted and thought well of; they all mounted and went with him, and they traveled and made their way up on to a hill to reckon and observe and reconnoitre Conradin's troops and what armies he had. And after he had reckoned their number, he was greatly amazed; and he called the knights who were with him and he said to them: "My comrades, come here to take a look; I see awesome armies, numerous and brave; I reckon them to have twice as many as the king."

Thereupon, he took them and returned to the army. And after they arrived, Prince Guillaume called the king aside and said to him: "Know, my good lord, I inform you, that I went to a place from which I observed the armies, the strength and troops which

---

[91] The two met at Tagliacozzo, not Benevento. The description that follows of Guillaume's part in the battle is highly biased. What the Chronicle attributes to him is attributed to Erard de Valeri by Dante (*E la da Tagliacozzo, ove sens' arme vinse il vecchio Alardo*, Inferno, canto 28, ll. 17-18) and by Villani (*Historie Florentine* in *Rerum Italicarum Scriptores*, vol. XIII, pp. 249-252). However, Villani makes special mention of him, saying that "Guillaume de Villehardouin, a knight of great importance" was with them that day (*ibid.*, p. 249).

Conradin has, in order to reckon them and see what armies he has. I did not go alone for you to rebuke me; I had soldiers with me, experienced men. And from the evidence that we saw and according to the reckoning we made, I estimate that Conradin has in the armies that I saw twice as many armies as we; they seemed splendid troops to me. Now, I say, my lord, and it is no secret to you, that the Germans today throughout the world are witless troops, untrustworthy,[92] all of them; and when they go into battle to fight, they do not have any of the enthusiasm nor the behavior of good soldiers; thus they go into battle like madmen. Well, I say to you, my lord, if your majesty be willing, that we should not fight them the way the Franks fight and lose the battle, for they are more than we; but let us fight them with cunning and prudence as the Turks and Romans fight in Romania. And if we do as I say, I hope in God and in the right which is on our side that the victory will fall to us."

And the king, as the all-prudent soldier that he was, spoke to the prince and answered him thus: "Know, brother prince, my friend and relative, that there is not a thing today in the existing world, either slyness or cunning or any cleverness, that I would not commit against my enemy, so long as I defeated him and seized his dominions. Therefore, good my relative, shrewd man that you are, since you have gained experience in the wars of Romans, and also know the cunning which the Turks use, here you have our armies, direct them as you will."

Thereupon, Prince Guillaume answered him: "Lord, since you wish and command that I do this, and that we act with slyness and with cunning, listen first while I tell you the plan that I suggest, and if it seems agreeable to you, thus shall I arrange the matter."

Thereupon, he began to speak and to tell him that the Turks and Romans are not soldiers to fight face to face as we Franks do, for they are sly and fight with strategems; "and since you

---

[92] Θεληματάροι (willful). Schmit (p. 608) gives the singular as Θεληματάρος, but Kalonaros (p. 282) corrects this to θεληματάριος and θεληματάρις in κοινή. A people called Θεληματάροι or "Voluntaries" lived at this time in the vicinity of Constantinople. Apparently, they were called by this name because they were prone to change allegiance to Greeks and Latins at will. (See Geanakoplos, *Emp. Mich.*, p. 95 and n. 11.)

command that it happen that we act as I suggest, let me instruct you and tell you how we shall act. This country where we are is uneven terrain and is not a wide, even plain for warfare as it is fought in France and all the kingdoms. For this reason, let us separate from all our squadrons some light troops, shrewd experienced soldiers, and let them have light horses so that they may hit and run; and let us separate them into three or four squadrons and direct them to attack the Germans and give the impression that they would give battle; and they, as they are very eager in their warfare, I know, will come against them with eagerness. And they, if they be prudent, let them allow them to come on and when they get very close to them, let them give the impression they are fleeing; then let them go straight towards the camp, and when they get close to it, they will not go into it, but at a run, let them pass by on the other side and let them always be in closed ranks, lest they be scattered. And I know so clearly the Germans and the Lombards, as well, and likewise mercenaries, that as soon as they see our tents, the vestments, the clothes, and the splendid things our camps contain, they will stop pursuing our troops and will enter the camps to seize our clothes. And we two, my lord, let us separate into two divisions with our armies and let the squadrons be separated, and let us place ambuscades in suitable places. I need to have with me only my troops, which I brought from Morea, for I know them. And when our lookouts see from the hilltops that the Germans have entered the camps, and their squadrons have dispersed and have set themselves to plundering, let them them sound the *buccinae* so that our troops may understand, and we shall come out of our hiding places and attack them. You come from the one side and I, again, from the other with the armies and troops that we have with us; and those four light squadrons of ours, on hearing the *buccinae*, will come back and all of us will surround them with alacrity. And when we have driven them out, and the squadrons are dispersed, very easily and quickly they will be in grave peril."[93]

[93] The Battle of Tagliacozzo is described by Oman, *History of the Art of War*, I, 488-98. See also remarks in H. Delpech, *La Tactique au XIIIe siècle*, I, 454-56.

And when Prince Guillaume had finished with what he was explaining and telling to the king, the king had heard him out, then praised him highly, for all he outlined for him seemed pleasing to him; and, turning to the prince, he said to him: "I beseech you, brother, that you direct that it be done just as you have outlined it to me, for it pleases me very much."

And the prince, when he heard this, called the captains and *chevetains* of the troops, who were in command of the squadrons. Together, he and the king, they directed that the four squadrons I told you about be separated; they called the captains and generals aside and they explained how they were going to act. And these took the troops, the remaining squadrons, and concealed the troops in ambush and those in hiding in the spots where it was necessary and seemly, and where it was skillful. And then the four squadrons set out and went straight against Conradin.

And Conradin, when he learned the king was coming towards his camp to give him battle, ordered that his own squadrons be separated, each nationality to fight by itself, and they set out and went to meet the king. Well, if I were to write you in detail all the deeds that took place in that battle, perhaps you would be bored with the much writing, as I should be bored with writing it twice for you. But, just as you heard me describe it minutely, just as Prince Guillaume explained it, so did he carry it out and accomplish it. Now, this battle took place at Benevento, where the terrain is uneven, with slopes and ravines; and because of these the Germans were confounded, for they did not see Charles's armies clearly; all of a sudden, those four squadrons who went out to decoy them fell upon them. And they thought that the others were coming also; for this reason they immediately set out to attack them eagerly and swiftly, as is the way of armies. And as soon as they were about to meet and exchange spear thrusts, the four squadrons turned to flight and set themselves to going straight to the camp. And the Germans, when they saw that the Franks were fleeing, bethought themselves of the battle and began to pursue them, and they pursued them until they reached the the camp. The Franks looped around[94] and avoided the lodgings,

---

[94] Ἀναγαμήσασιν. This word is derived from ἀναγαμμίζω (from γάμμα:

passed along the side and went beyond. And the Germans, when they saw the tents which stood with the splendid arms, the clothes, and the money, left off pursuing the Franks who were fleeing and set upon the lodgings and they entered them and began to scatter and to seize the clothes and the chests which contained the money and, breaking these open, to take whatever they found within; they started to quarrel among themselves and to strike out with their swords.

The lookouts of the Franks, seeing what the Tedeschi[95] were doing, sounded the *buccinae*, and those who were hiding understood the signal and came out of their hiding places, the prince from the one side and the king from the other. And those who were fleeing, the four squadrons, made a return run towards the camps and surrounded all the Germans on all sides; the foot soldiers arrived with arbalests and bows; they butchered them as if they were wild boars, and few, indeed, of the Germans were saved. But of the Tuscans, and also of the Lombards, many escaped, because they were familiar with the country, and others had friends who guided them. Conradin was captured, and his head was cut off by some men from Naples, who were hostile to him, because they were pleased to have the king's rule. They bore his head on the tip of a lance and brought it to the king and presented it to him.[96] And the king, noble and wise that he was, cursed roundly and was deeply sorrowed and he was enraged at them who had committed the deed and declared openly, and all heard him, that he would

---

to execute a maneuver in the shape of γάμμα, a loop). Schmitt (p. 600), rather embarrassed, derives it from ἀναγαμῶ, which, as he says, would be rather vulgar. See K., p. 286, note on l. 7053, which cites a long discussion on this word by G. N. Hatzidakis in 'Aθηνᾶ, XL (1928), 14-15.

[95] Ντουδέσκοι. This is the only occurrence of this word in the Chronicle to indicate Germans, who are usually referred to as 'Aλαμᾶνοι. It is obviously derived from the Italian *Tedeschi*.

[96] Conradin attempted from the very beginning of the battle to flee with his friend Frederick of Austria. The two were recognized and captured a short time later and were turned over to Charles in return for a reward (L. de F. § 406-9). Charles brought them to trial in Naples and they were condemned to death. They were both beheaded on October 29, 1268, an execution which (because of their youth and lineage) shocked all Europe.

have wished and preferred to have lost one of his towns, one of his very best, than that they should have killed Conradin. For, if they had taken him alive while he was fighting, he would have done him great honor, for he was, after all, a nobleman and soldier and had come as a soldier to avenge the death of King Manfred, who was his cousin, and did not deserve to have his head cut off.

Now, after that battle was over, the king ordered that all those captured alive be divided and sent to the castles. And of the spoils which had been won, the king, again, ordered that each was to have as his own whatever he had won. Conradin's tent, which had ten poles, and the splendid arms, the clothes, and the money which he had in his camp, these the king kept for himself as his share and he had need of nothing more. And the lodging of the duke of Carinthia[97] and all that he had in his tents of arms and money, these he ordered given to Prince Guillaume as a benefice and as his own share of the battle.

And after he had bestowed benefices on all his soldiers and had divided his booty and the spoils he had won, he ordered that all his armies be dismissed, and each man journeyed whence he had come. He kept the prince and took him with him, and the two went straight to Naples, Prince Guillaume saying that he would see the queen, as well as his daughter Isabeau, whom the king's son had as wedded wife. And after the prince and the king had arrived at Naples, the two of them, the king began to speak to the queen and told her to praise the prince and exalt him, for by all his wisdom and strategy he had won the battle and had been victorious over his enemies the Germans. And the queen, as a noblewoman, thanked the prince, did him great honor, and gave him gifts. And the king, in his turn, did such great honor to the prince and gave him such largess that all were amazed; he kept him with him with great celebrations for around eighteen days, twenty-two, if you wish, and he had a goodly desire to keep him for around a month, two, if you wish, that they might rejoice with one another.

[97] This undoubtedly refers to Frederick of Austria (Frederick of Zähringen), Conrad's friend and ally. This is not the duke of Carinthia mentioned in ll. 4021 ff.

Thereupon, messages came to the prince from Morea that his opponents, the lawless Romans, had broken their oath, resumed the war, and had abandoned the term [of truce] they had with him. On hearing this, the prince went to the king and asked leave to go to Morea, that his land might not be imperiled and suffer damage. And when the king heard this, he cursed it most soundly; and because he knew and recognized, as was the very truth, that it was due to the direction of the prince of Morea that he had won the battle with Conradin, and the suzerainty of the kingdom of Apulia had remained his (which those Germans, the Ghibellines, and with them the Tuscans and Lombards had wished to seize), and because he realized that the prince had spent so much for the troops he had brought at that time from Morea to the assistance, service, and aid of him, he ordered that he be given from the treasury a great deal of wealth, money of gold and silver, and he gave him one hundred of his very best steeds. With these he further gave him fifty men-at-arms on steeds, all choice soldiers, and two hundred arbalesters, all of whom were paid for six months, foot soldiers and knights, to take to Morea, to stand by him to help him fight the lawless Romans, who never in their lives hold either to truth or to oath. So, after the prince of Morea had organized all the things which the king had given him, the troops, arms, steeds, tents, and money, he left Naples and went to Brindisi and found the ships ready, as the king had ordered; he went aboard these with his troops and arrived at Klarentsa on the second day.

When all the Moreots heard that the prince had arrived and had come to Klarentsa with the armies and troops he had with him, healthy, uninjured, not one of them missing, with the spoils, awesome wealth, which they had won in the battle they had fought with Conradin, they all praised the Lord and the holy Theotokos. All the people of Morea held high celebration and they showed devotion to the prince and the bannerets; whoever had a friend or a relative rejoiced with him, and all praised God when they saw that they had come.

The prince asked to learn the truth about how the pretext for breaking the peace had arisen. And those who knew informed him that they had begun the war and had become perjurers because some people had told them, and they hoped it was the truth, that the prince had been killed in the battle which the king and the Germans had fought. Thereupon, the prince answered and said: "Pretexts are never lacking to the faithless Romans; as they are guilty of perjury so are they guilty of other evil intentions." Thereafter, the prince called the lord of Karytaina and said to him: "Good nephew, take with you the Franks whom we have brought with us from Apulia and with whom the king has rewarded and helped us, so that they might help us and fight the Romans with us; and let them be with you in Skorta, along the frontier, to guard our land and to confound the Romans."

On hearing this, Sir Geoffroy, the lord of Karytaina, approved it highly, and it seemed attractive to him, for he reasoned and hoped that with these troops he would inflict damage on the Romans and protect his land.[98] He took them and they went to the territory of Skorta; there he directed them to settle and take up positions at the village called Great Arachova,[99] through which runs the frontier of Skorta against the Romans, and to fight them and protect the land. Thereupon, it came about, perhaps from sin, that before a month or two had gone by, apparently from the cold waters of that spot, the stomach disorder struck them and most of those Franks who were in the town of Arachova died. The lord of Karytaina had no rest; as many of those who were left who were healthy enough to hold arms and ride, these he took with him and they went into battle, time after time, meeting the Romans and damaging them a great deal.

Thereupon, from the sin of the land, there befell the Franks of Morea of that time a misfortune, and the lord of Karytaina, that renowned man, fell into a dreadful illness, a grievous sickness, and the nature which is man's was victorious, and death took

[98] Following the inconclusive campaign of 1271 (see above, p. 258, n. 78), the war with the Greeks continued in a desultory way. Michael's forces slowly infiltrated Frankish lands, taking over fief after fief. This incident, described above in ll. 7195 ff., took place in 1275. After the loss of the redoubtable lord of Karytaina, the fief was helpless and fell to the Greeks in 1277.

[99] Great Arachova (Grant Aracove, L., § 495) is the town of Arachova which lies approximately on the border between Arkadia and Lakonia, on the Tripolis-Sparta road. It was called Great to distinguish it from at least five other Arachovas in Morea at that time.

him; behold the great harm that befell Morea at that time, and great sorrow ensued. The prince, who was also his uncle, grieved for him, and all wept for him, small and great, and even the speechless birds, these, too, wept for him; alas, for the great harm that occurred in Morea that day! And who did not grieve? The orphans had had a father; the widows, a husband, the multitude of the poor, a lord and protector. He had protected all men from injustice; he had never allowed a poor man to suffer the hardships of misfortune, nor a man of worth to fall into poverty. Behold the misfortune death wrought that day; to take such a man, such a renowned soldier, and leave orphaned all those who loved him. Well, as it happened, unfortunately, that he had no heir, no son of his body to leave to inherit the castles and dominions which he held in Morea, in the defile of Skorta and in other places, his land was divided into two parts; the one the prince took, for he held the suzerainty, and the other, his wife took as dower, which was her due.[1] Now, this archontess was the sister of Sir Guillaume, the duke of Athens, great lord, he was called, a name from the Hellenes.[2] Now after some time had passed, months and days, the great lord sent to the kingdom of Apulia prudent messengers to the count of Brienne, Sir Hugues, he was called, and he was count of Lecce. They made an agreement that he take [the the great lord's] sister, the lady of Karytaina, as his wedded wife. And after they had come to an agreement, the count made the crossing and went to Morea, to the town of Andravida; and the great lord likewise went there from the town of Thebes. And when they came together, they came to an understanding with

[1] It will be remembered that after Geoffroy de Bruyères's betrayal of Guillaume during the war in Euboea, his fief was returned to him as a "new grant," restricted to heirs of his body. (See above, ll. 3363 ff., 5904 ff.) On his death, since he had no direct heirs, the fief escheated to the prince of Morea, who kept half of it for himself and gave the other half to the widow, Isabelle de la Roche, daughter of Guy I, lord of Athens. For the feudal dower in Morea, see Topping, *Feudal Institutions*, pp. 150-52. The last phrase in l. 7239 above, "which was her due," may perhaps be better read as "which was hers."

[2] At the time of Geoffroy's death, Jean I was duke of Athens (1263-80). His brother Guillaume succeeded him (1280-87). Isabelle was their sister and was aunt to Guy II (1287-1308), son of Guillaume.

one another and they sent for the lady of Karytaina, and she came, and there Count Hugues of Brienne married her. And after he had tended to the castles and towns which he had in Morea from the archontess, he took her, made the crossing, and they went to Apulia. And not much time passed, as the Lord willed, before the archontess conceived by Count Hugues and gave birth to an outstanding son, who was called Gautier, and who turned out to be eager in arms and campaigning and renowned and praised throughout the kingdoms of the West.[3] And after some time had passed, even years went by, Sir Guy, de la Roche, his surname, the great lord, I tell you, and duke of Athens, died, and his land and the suzerainty he held fell to Count Gautier, the son of that Count Hugues, that praiseworthy soldier that I am telling you about, who was the cousin of that Sir Guy. And so, he came and received the Megalokyrate and became duke of Athens, lord by inheritance. And so, he found that at that time the Catalans, who were called and named the [Grand] Company,[4] had come to Halmyros, where the duke of Athens, that Sir Guy, had brought them in the expectation and with the agreements that they would go to Morea, conquer the land, and seize the lordship for his spouse, who was the heir, she who was named and called Mahaut—the prince of Taranto held her patrimony, the principality of Achaia, in an illegal manner.[5] Well, when the duke, Sir Gautier, found that the company had come there and had a thousand and more Turks

[3] Isabelle married Hugues de Brienne, count of Lecce, in 1277. Their son, Gautier de Brienne, was destined to succeed his cousin Guy II and become the last French duke of Athens (1308-11). Isabelle died soon after his birth.

[4] Miller (p. 218) accepts in part the explanation as given in the Chronicle in ll. 7270 ff. for the entrance of the Catalan Grand Company into the affairs of Frankish Greece. For the Catalan period, see K. M. Setton, *Catalan Domination of Athens 1311-1388*, the many works of Rubio y Lluch, which are fundamental on this phase of Greek history, and R. I. Burns, "The Catalan Company and the European Powers, 1305-1311," *Speculum*, XXIX (1954), 751-71.

[5] Mahaut de Hainaut (1293-1325) was the daughter of Isabeau de Villehardouin by her second husband, Florent de Hainaut. Mahaut claimed the principality on her mother's death, but it had escheated to Philippe of Taranto, son of Charles II of Anjou. (See below, ll. 8500 ff.) Mahaut was married first to Guy II de la Roche, then to Louis de Bourgogne, then to Hugues de la Palisse, and finally to John of Gravina.

with them, he came to an agreement with them with great treaties to make war on Romania and seize Vlachia. And as soon as they captured the castle of Domokos, they fell into discord and heavy fighting. The Catalans apologized submissively to the duke; but he, from arrogance, which is a trait of the Franks, and from bad advice, which others gave him, undertook to give battle; he lost the battle, was captured during the battle, and they cut off his head and took his land, the Megalokyrate, and today the company are still lords therein. The battle took place on Monday, the fifteenth day of the month called March, in the current year of the 6817 years since the creation of the world and in the eighth indiction.[6]

Here, at this point, I shall stop talking and writing about the count of Brienne, who was duke of Athens, and I am going to tell you another tale, about what happened during the time that Prince Guillaume was in prison in Constantinople and was released with the agreements which he made at that time, and which, indeed, you have heard about in this book. Now, at that time, he gave as hostages to the basileus the sister of Chauderon, the grand

[6] After the initial entrance of the Catalans into Greece they soon found themselves in a precarious position. Almost entirely surrounded by hostile Greeks, they made their way towards the duchy of Athens. In 1308-09 they fought some skirmishes and at least one pitched battle. Meanwhile, Gautier had become lord of Athens and had begun a vigorous campaign against the Greeks. In 1310 he hired the Catalans as mercenaries for a period of six months. They immediately began to ravage Thessaly and captured more than thirty castles, including Domokos. At the end of the six months, Gautier decided to get rid of them. He rather haughtily demanded the castles and tried to send most of them away. When they refused to go, he decided to use force. He called on all his allies, gathered a sizable army, and in March, 1311, advanced on the Catalans. They met in the neighborhood of Skripou (Orchomenos) near where the Kephissos enters Lake Kopais. The battle which ensued in the marshes was a disaster for the Franks. The exact date of the battle has been questioned. The Chronicle (ll. 7296-7300) gives it as Monday, March 15, 1309, ind. VIII. L. (§ 500) gives the year as 1310. However, the will that Gautier drew up just before the battle is dated March 15, 1311, and since the fifteenth was a Monday in 1311, this seems to be the date. (See M., p. 229, n. 3.) All the Chronicles give the place as Halmyros, but this must simply indicate a salt marsh near Kopais and not the city of that name in Thessaly.

constable, and the daughter of the lord of Passava, who was marshal of the whole principality.[7] Well, while these archontesses were hostages for the prince there in Constantinople, it happened that the lord of Akova died,[8] Sir Gautier, he was called, his surname de Rosières, and he had no heir of his body but the daughter of the marshal Jean de Passava, who had had his sister as wedded wife, and they had a daughter, who was named and called Madame Marguerite.[9] And because she was a hostage at that time in the City (the prince had put her there in place of himself), and did not chance to be in Morea within the terms to go to the prince to be invested by him with the seigneury of Akova, to which she was heiress, the prince held the seigneury for himself. And when

---

[7] See above, ll. 4502-12.

[8] There seems to be something confusing about the dating of his death and of the legal battle which followed. In ll. 6621 ff. above, he is mentioned as taking part in events that occurred in 1270 or after. Longnon (p. 247) places his death "peu après" the death of Geoffroy de Bruyères (1275). Guillaume himself died in 1278, so the hearing must have taken place some time between these dates, probably in 1276. This would mean that Marguerite was a hostage from 1262 to 1276, certainly a long time. Furthermore, it is known that her first husband, Guibert de Cors, died in 1258 at the Battle of Karydi (see l. 3271 above). She also is known to have then married Guglielmo II dalle Carceri da Verona, triarch of Negroponte, who was killed in the sea battle of Demetrias in 1275. Apparently, then, she married Guglielmo some time between 1258 and 1262, went off as a hostage, and saw her husband no more. A further complication is that we must assume from the dating that Guillaume procured her release almost immediately after her uncle's death, which hardly seems reasonable in view of the fact that after he had had fourteen years in which to do it, he finally did it just when he was able to take her patrimony over for himself. In short, the whole chronology seems faulty. L. de F. (§ 284-396) places the entire episode after the elopement of the lord of Karytaina and before the advent of Charles d'Anjou into Italian affairs. But this is at variance with the indication in the Chronicle that Gautier de Rosières was alive after 1270. It seems almost mandatory to assume more time between his death and the final hearing, but none of the sources and authorities I have consulted shed any further light on the matter.

[9] Marguerite of Passava was the daughter of Jean II de Neuilly, hereditary marshal and baron of Passava, who had married a sister of Gautier II de Rosières, baron of Akova. Since Salic law did not prevail, and since the fief was transmittable to all heirs, in the absence of any direct heirs, Marguerite was heir to the fief as niece.

the archontess Madame Marguerite returned from there where she had been a hostage for Prince Guillaume and went to claim the seigneury of Akova, the prince returned to her such answer: that after the year and a day had passed from the time that that patrimony had fallen to her and she had not come to his court to claim it, as the customs of the land stipulate the terms, whatever she had had, she had lost it, and he would give her nothing.[10]

And when the archontess heard this, she was greatly amazed, for she had never expected to find in the prince such answer as he had given her, for she had been in prison as a hostage for him, and indeed he, himself, had placed her there, and she had committed no misdemeanor, for, if she had been in Morea at her ease, she would never have fallen into committing a breach of the customs. But since the prince had placed her as a hostage and prisoner for himself, she did not expect that he would offer such deceits, such pretexts, and such answer. However, when the Lady Marguerite and those who were her supporters and her counselors realized that the prince of Morea would not return right to her, she left and went in grief to her house. Now, when a short time had passed, a month and more, the archontess returned and went to the prince with the council and company she had with her and claimed and asked for the castle of Akova with its environs and all the barony. She made, indeed, the second and third act of claiming, and the prince gave her the same answer and followed the same line of conduct as on the first occasion.

When the Lady Marguerite had heard well that she would never find right from the prince, she asked all her friends and relatives to counsel her as to how she should act so as not to lose her right and fall into disinheritance. And these, the wisest, who loved

[10] In Article 36 of the Assizes of Romania (Recoura, p. 184) it is stated that an heir must claim a fief within forty days or lose the usufruct of one year. He must claim the fief within one year and a day or "he loses it, even if some hindrance legitimately prevented him." If the heir is outside the principality, he has two years and two days to claim the fief. The Passava case is specifically mentioned in this article. As Topping points out (p. 38, n.), the term of two years and two days may have been added to this article as a result of this very case. Also, the phrase quoted above sounds as though it refers specifically to what had happened to Marguerite.

her, all counseled her to take a husband, a great man, shrewd and of high lineage, "and he with his prudence and with his relatives will place you in the usufruct of your patrimony." To this, indeed, the archontess, prudent woman that she was, agreed and consented to take a husband. Thereupon, the leaders of her family worked together, and she took a noble husband of high lineage, brother of the noble Sir Nicolas, who was called de St.-Omer and lord of Thebes, Sir Jean, also of the name de St.-Omer; they also had a third brother called Sir Othon. And when sir Jean married her, he received the office of hereditary marshal, which was, indeed, the patrimony of that woman. The de St.-Omers had high nobility; their mother happened to be the legitimate sister of the king of Hungary, and their father Sir Bela had her as lawful wife; and these two together produced those three lords. And the duke of Athens, the great lord, had three other brothers, and they were first cousins to the de St.-Omers, in the first degree, I tell you.[11]

And after Sir Jean married the noble Lady Marguerite, he did not wish in any way that the affair of Akova be delayed and that he not claim it in the court of the prince of Morea. He bade his brothers, and they went together with him; they arrived in Morea and went straight to Klarentsa; there they found the prince with his captains, holding a parliament to deal with certain cases he had. They spent two days, making no claim; they played and celebrated with the Moreots.[12] Well, two days having passed, Sir Jean came with his two brothers, the de St.-Omers, and with his wife, who was the heir; and they went before the prince, and she presented herself as heir that she was of all her patrimony. And then she presented her husband as *avoué* and husband, as is stipulated by the customs.[13] And immediately at that moment Sir Jean said to him: "Lord prince of Morea, I beseech and request you, you who are my lord and I, an heir, to order that all your captains, the bannerets of Morea, and the liege knights gather

[11] For details about the de St.-Omers, see above, p. 169, n. 35.

[12] L. 7397 is from P. Was it dropped intentionally from H.?

[13] In Article 75 of the Assizes of Romania (Recoura, p. 212) it is stated that a woman who has a fief must at once present her husband to her lord as a guardian. Article 129 (*ibid.*, p. 242) states that the husband who marries a woman of liege homage becomes liege by virtue of her land.

that you may hear with them what things I have to make claim for, and that you judge me by right, that I may receive a verdict, for I wish to receive right according to the customs of Morea; I ask for no favor, but the right which is mine."

Thereupon, the prince, himself, answered him and said to him: "With pleasure, since you seek right, I am ready with my court to oblige you."

The prince immediately ordered the bannerets, the knights, as well as the lieges of the principality to come; they all sat together in St. Sophia, where the prince was staying in Andravida. Thereupon, arose the aged Sir Nicolas, de St.-Omer he was called, the lord of Thebes. With his right hand he held his sister, the wife of his brother, the Lady Marguerite, and he said to the prince: "Lord of Morea, it is the truth, which everyone in the principality knows, that my sister, who stands here in the presence of your lordship, happens to be the niece of the lord of Akova, Sir Gautier, he was called, his surname de Rosières; this my sister is the child of his sister. And since he died without a child to leave as heir, his land and the castle of Akova have fallen to this my sister, who is the heir. And as you know, my lord, she was hostage for you in Constantinople—you put her there yourself; and she did not happen to be here during the year's term after the lord of Akova died, to come and present herself before your lordship, as is stipulated by our customs of the whole principality, within the forty days and within the year, in which fact she did not wrong you, nor was she in any way at fault, since she was in prison, where you had placed her, as a hostage you placed her and you emerged from there.

"And when you released her and she came here into the land, she understood, indeed, at once and came before you;[14] as the legal heir to Akova which she was, she presented herself to you and asked right of you. And you answered her that she had not right; and she kept on coming back many times, and asked right of you, and you would never hold court for her, but all by yourself you said that she had not right. And she, a woman without coun-

---

[14] This passage may mean: "and, indeed, immediately on arriving, she came before you."

selors, without friends, returned to her home desperate and waited for help to come to her from God. Today, by God's pleasure, she is married to a noble man of great lineage, who can thus safeguard the right that is due her, as is proper for any noble man to do. For this reason they have come before your lordship, and together with them, I, who am their brother, and I present both of them, the one as heir and the other as her *avoué*, and they seek their right. I request of you, I beseech, that you grant them the right which is due them and place them in the usufruct of the castles and dominions of the territory of Akova. And they are ready to perform for you whatever they owe of service, homage, and allegiance.[15]"

Thereupon, the prince, himself, answered and said to Sir Nicolas de St.-Omer: "We have listened closely, as has our court, to the words which you have spoken and to your case and we bear witness and declare that what you have said is true, that in my pursuit and in my cause, the archontess your sister lost and was disinherited of her patrimony and seigneury, the land of Akova. Therefore, I answer you, I say and ask you whether you ask of us that we give right according to law or whether you ask us for a lord's grace and discretion, for she was hindered even in our cause and did not find herself here in our principality and at her ease during the terms stipulated by our customs to make her claim as was proper and to seek right."

Thereupon, Sir Nicolas answered and spoke to the prince such answer: "Lord prince of Morea, I address your lordship; if I saw and had reason to know that my sister, who is here, did not ask with right for the castle and the dominions, the territory of Akova, then it would be appropriate for us to ask for grace. But, in this instance to seek right is correct, as you yourself know, for my sister was held in prison in your stead and was not able by any means to get out of there to come to make her claim for the patrimony of Akova. Therefore, I ask no grace of you, only right as the law requires and commands."

[15] Their case is based strictly on Articles 75 and 129 of the Assizes and also Article 39, on the basis of a legitimate hindrance.

Thereupon, the prince of Morea answered him and said to Sir Nicolas de St.-Omer: "Since you have no need to receive grace from me, and wish to make claim with the right of my court, I declare and bear witness to you, in truth do I affirm it, that I would have evil fall upon me from God and the reproach of all men, if I were to deprive you of this. Therefore, I want the matter to be settled with attention and discrimination and according to the customs of the land, so that I will commit no wrong and be reproached by God, by the saints, and by all men. And I want the bannerets and bishops and the liege knights of all the principality to gather, so that I may present to them the case, that they may judge it with fear of God, in accordance with the Customs of Morea, which Emperor Robert gave to my blessed brother Prince Geoffroy when they contracted a treaty and he took him for his brother-in-law."

Thereupon, the prince ordered that letters be written to all the bannerets of the whole principality, as well as to the bishops and the knights, and they came and gathered in Klarentsa. They entered the Church of St. Francis at [the monastery of] the Minorites and sat in judgment, as is the custom. Then the prince said to Sir Nicolas: "I wish to learn from you who is the *avocat* that of necessity must speak for your sister, to make her plea and to address the court."[16] And he answered him that he himself would be the one to speak and answer whatever appertained to the hearing about the affair of the castle of Akova. And to this the prince answered and said: "Since you undertake to be the *avocat* in this affair of the Lady Marguerite, for love of you and for your company, I shall keep you company and shall appoint myself *avocat* to defend and maintain the rights of the court."[17]

---

[16] He assumes that Marguerite is unable to meet the exacting requirements of court procedure and that she will be represented by counsel, the *avocat*. Articles 145 and 146 of the Assizes (Recoura, pp. 251-52) deal with the *avocat* (advocate).

[17] Article 8 of the Assizes (Recoura, p. 163; Topping, pp. 26-27) expressly states that a lord is required to delegate one of his liege men in his place whenever he is involved in court action with one of his vassals. "And the lord is required to rise, to give the delegate his baton and to leave the council, in accordance with the custom."

Thereupon, the prince called the logothete, his name was Sir Leonard and he was from Apulia;[18] he was a wise man and well educated; he had him as a confidant and leader in his council. The scepter and the rod which he held in his hand, as is customary among generals and lords throughout the world, he gave to him and said to him, "I surrender to you the authority which I hold, that you may stand for the court, to judge and maintain the right with the law and with the council and company which is here in this court; and I put you on your oath by Christ and on your soul, that you and all those who sit with you here in the court will maintain well the right of the archontess the Lady Marguerite, as well as that of the court. Stir not for envy or friendship; take care that you commit no crime upon your souls, for I in company and love of my brother Sir Nicolas de St.-Omer am going to advocate on the other side, to maintain the right of the court."

Then, Sir Nicolas undertook to describe and to outline the affair of Akova, how the suzerainty of this patrimony fell to the marshaless, the Lady Marguerite, as you have heard here above in my book, the causes and the reasons and the whole sequence of events, which I am not inclined to write you a second time, for it would be indeed troublesome and all would tire of it.

And when he had finished what he had to say, then the prince, in turn, began to speak and to set reasons and excuses and rebuttals against what Sir Nicolas had declared and stated, as is customary in lawsuits and in all tribunals, where each man declares what he knows to be to his advantage. And when they had said much and the words had multiplied, the prince ordered that there be brought forward the book in which are written and declared the customs of the land. Then, they found written therein the chapter which writes in detail, declares and interprets that a liege man is obliged to do the following: if it should happen that his lord is captured by his enemy and he holds him in prison, in durance of irons, his lord may demand of him and make claim on him to enter the prison as a hostage for him and release his lord from captivity. It is required according to the customs and according to what the law commands that he himself go into the prison in

[18] For Leonardo de Veroli, see above, p. 200, n. 82, and p. 250, n. 70.

person.   Thereafter, his lord is obliged, in turn, to gain the release of the liege man from there where he entered for him.[19]

All those who were in the court at that time had all been inclined to the opinion and had stated with great discretion that the marshaless was entitled to have the patrimony, the territory of the castle of Akova, since the prince, himself, sent her, and she was a hostage and in prison in the City in his stead. The prince, having brought forth the book of law, stood and held strictly to that chapter; and he pointed out with the book and the customs of the land that by binding right she had been obliged to do it. He had in no way wronged her, for, indeed, she had not appeared to claim her right to the patrimony within the terms stipulated by the customs.

They all set to again and returned and said that, since it befell her and she was obliged to do this (to enter, that is, the prison because her liege lord had made claim on her, which the customs ordain, and she did not chance to be in Morea within the terms, to appear before the prince to demand right from him) and the terms had lapsed, she had lost her right; they gave the decision that she sought in vain.

They called the prince and Sir Nicolas, and they both came before the court. And the logothete, who was the prince's man, he spoke to them and held forth the discourse, how the court had decided and had found according to the law; in detail he pointed out to them the right and reasons by which the court won the castle of Akova with its homages and dominions and its surroundings, according to the customs of Morea and as the law commands.

On hearing this, the prince, as is customary in courts, thanked the court that he had won the verdict; but the marshal Sir Jean would in no wise give his thanks. Thereafter, all the archons and and the liege bannerets asked leave to depart, and the prince gave it to them, and they departed, each to where he pleased and desired. So the court dispersed, and each went to where each of them needed to go.

And after this, the prince called the logothete and said to him in private with great discretion: "I swear to you, my logothete,

[19] Articles 3 and 15 of the Assizes (Recoura, pp. 155-59, 167-68).

in the presence of my Lord, it seems grievous to me, this judgment that was handed down, and that the archontess, the Lady Marguerite, has been disinherited of the castle and domain and the environs of Akova, for I do positively comprehend and know that it is true that I placed her in the prison where she was. And for this reason she did not chance to be here during the terms and period within which she was supposed to come to appear in my court to claim the seigneury of Akova, which was her patrimony. And I am going to tell you how this sin came about. At the time when they brought and told me the message that the lord of Akova was dying (because the Lady Marguerite was imprisoned, she to whom the patrimony was coming because she was his heir, his sister's child), a whim led me to take up the book, the one in which are written the customs of the land. And I chanced to find that chapter which writes and avers, states and explains that a liege man, whoever he may be, is obliged to enter prison, should his legal lord make this claim upon him in order to be released from there himself; and thereafter this lord is obliged to release him from his captivity in that prison. Well, as I supposed, and as we found the law, since the marshaless was in the City in prison, hostage that she was for me, and was not able to appear in my court, to come within the terms which are stipulated by the law, it was right that she be disinherited and lose her patrimony. Then I realized and said in my mind that since she was in prison in my stead and was losing the patrimony which had fallen to her, the sin and blame still fell on me. And for this reason I had come to the decision and had taken as my intention to leave half of the barony to her and to give, in turn, the other half to Marguerite, my younger daughter, to have as her patrimony. And you saw that the de St.-Omers came here with swagger and haughtiness and great arrogance; it seemed very grievous to me, and my heart was angered, and for that reason I asked Sir Nicolas at that time what he was seeking in my court, whether grace or right; and he answered me with great arrogance that from me he did not need to receive any grace, only the right that was coming to the Lady Marguerite. And for this reason I ordered that there be brought forward the book which is the law of Morea and in which are written the customs, that we might be judged by it and that their arrogance might disappear, and I committed the affair to the judgment of the court.

"Well, now that the lieges have judged with the law that the Lady Marguerite has been disinherited, I wish to grant her grace, which will be recognized by all who hear of it and who have wisdom and knowledge within them. In this connection, I have knowledge of what is written in the register;[20] the barony of Akova with its homages is worth twenty-four knights' fees. Therefore, I want you, if you love me, to call Colinet, who is the protovestiarios of all the principality, and let the elders of the barony of Akova come and let them bring with them the minutes which they have.[21] And make this division of all the barony: separate a third part aud select the best for it; whereas the fees come to eight, I want five of them to be all from the best fees *en demaine* of the land, and separate the other three from the first fees *en hommage*, and have a Frankish privilege be written up for me, to the effect that I grant these eight fees of Akova, a third, indeed, of the barony, to the Lady Marguerite as a grace and a new gift to her and to her children."[22]

And the logothete immediately and with great eagerness carried out and fulfilled the command of the prince; the logothete, himself, placed his seal upon the privilege, brought it to the prince and presented it to him. And the prince read it; it seemed all in order to him; he lifted the quilt of his bed and placed it underneath and he said to the logothete: "Go in person and bring the Lady Marguerite here and tell her I have need of her and would talk to her." And the logothete went immediately and brought her; when the marshaless had come, the prince said to her; "I bring God as

---

[20] See above, pp. 125 ff. and nn. 48-59.

[21] The lord chamberlain Colinet (Gr. Κολινέτος) is referred to in L. (§ 526) as *le prothoficier Colinet*, but I have been unable to identify him further. He asks for the elders of Akova to come because they would know the barony's history and boundaries. The "minutes" mentioned are those of the baronial court which would be needed to establish the true condition of the fiefs.

[22] These details are also given in L. (§ 525-27). The terms for fiefs *en demaine* and fiefs *en hommage* in Greek are δεμοσικά and ὁμάτζια. For the location of the eight fees, see Dragoumis, Χρ. Μορ. pp. 233-43. For "new gift," see above, p. 171, n. 40.

my witness, my good daughter, to the desire and wish that I felt toward you, to do you an act of courtesy and grace in the patrimony which was coming to you, the barony of Akova, and that is why I asked the aged Sir Nicolas that time when you came before me in the court what he preferred and desired of me, right or grace, and which of the two he wanted. And he in his arrogance and haughtiness needed to receive no grace from me, but wanted to receive right from the court. And for this reason I brought forth the book of the law; I submitted it to the court, and thereafter they judged us; and since the court has given its judgment, I really do not have to do anything for you. But I, as an act of grace, knowing in truth that it was for me that you found yourself a hostage in the City when the barony of Akova fell to you, and having a deep feeling and compassion toward you, I have separated a third of the barony and give it to you as a new gift and inheritance to you and to your children; lift the bed covers and that quilt and you will find your privilege, and take it with my blessing."

And the logothete reached out and brought forth the privilege, and gave it to the prince, and placed it in his hands; and the prince spoke to the Lady Marguerite: "Come here, my daughter, that I may invest you." And she approched him, and he gave her the document; he took off his glove, and with it he invested her. And she, wise woman, took it with joy, with a low bow and deep thanks. Then she bade him goodbye and went to her house; there she found Sir Jean, her husband. She showed him great joy and in detail she told him of what she had done there where she had come from and of the gift which she had received, the grace she had taken from the prince of Morea, a third of Akova. On hearing this, Sir Jean raised his hands; he was very happy and thanked God, for he had never hoped, never expected to have a portion or lordship in the barony of Akova.

Now, after the prince had done these things that I am writing for you, he called the logothete and told him to draw up another privilege out of the two remaining parts of the castle and territory of the barony of Akova, stating that he gave it as a patrimony to his daughter, Marguerite, I tell you, so was she named.[23] They

---

[23] Marguerite de Villehardouin (1265-1315) and her elder sister Isabeau

were written and sealed, and he called her and gave them to her and invested her at once and installed her in its usufruct and gave her his prayers that she hold it and that she inherit it.

With these things, all these that I am telling you, writing and describing, others also, numerous and many, that I cannot write for you, did Prince Guillaume accomplish, arrange, and establish. As is the natural fact within the race of men, that all who are born taste death and die, the time came to the prince when he had to die, to go to paradise and depart from this world. He journeyed to Kalamata, for which he felt a great yearning, for there he had been born and it was his patrimony, his very own and his by right, which the Champenois had given as a hereditary patrimony to his father, the aged Sir Geoffroy, Villehardouin, his surname. He sent word everywhere for the bannerets, the bishops, and the wise men of the whole principality to come before him; then he fell into the throes of approaching death; he besought all of them to advise him as to what seemly thing he could do at the very end of his life.

He drew up his will with great care; he appointed the grand constable Chauderon and left him *bailli* in the principality.[24] He wrote to King Charles and implored him that first his daughters, and everyone of the principality, small and great, be transferred to his keeping, and that he protect them and govern them all with justice. As to the monasteries of the Franks, as well as those of the Romans, which he had founded and erected that they might intercede with the Basileus of the Heavens for all Christendom,

were Guillaume's daughters by Anna Angela Komnena, daughter of the Despot of Epiros. (See above, p. 162, n. 23, and p. 164, n. 29.) Marguerite married in September, 1294, Isnard de Sabran, and, in 1299 Richard of Cephalonia. By her first husband, she had a daughter, Isabeau, who married Ferdinand, the Infant of Majorca. Kalonaros inexplicably states (p. 313, n. to l. 7749) that Marguerite's first husband was Bertrand de Baux.

[24] This refers to Jean de Chauderon, son of the former grand constable Geoffroy de Chauderon and brother to the lady that went as the second hostage with Marguerite of Passava. In actual fact, he was not *bailli*, but was simply to supervise the affairs of the principality until the *bailli* of King Charles of Naples arrived. L. de F. (§ 418) states it was Geoffroy, the father, but L. (§ 533) states it was Jean, the son.

the gifts for their prayers which they held by his privilege and which he had granted to each one, no one was to interfere with these, nor disturb any part of what he had given them. Likewise was no living man ever to disturb the gifts he had given to men who had served him with eagerness and travail. He commanded and ordered that after he had died, and not before a full year had passed, his bones alone were to be placed in a coffin in the church of St. Jacob of Morea in Andravida, in this church which he had built and which he had given to the Temple, in the tomb he had built and in which lay his father; his brother to lie to the right of him, he to be on the left, and his father in between.[25] He instructed and endowed four chaplains, whom all the Romans call *hiereis*,[26] to continue without cease unto eons of eons to chant and celebrate masses everlastingly for their souls; he ordered as a commandment and excommunicable offense, and it was put in writing, that never should they have interference from any man in the world.

And when he arranged all these things I am telling you about, and many others as well (which I am not able to list for you, for I weary of writing them because of the excessive writing it would take), he surrendered his soul, and the angels took it and bore it to where all the righteous are found; commemorate him, all of you; he was a good prince. Behold the evil that befell, for which the small and great of Morea must grieve, for he did not leave a male, son of his body, to inherit the land which his father had won with such travail.[27] But, on the contrary, he produced daugh-

[25] See above, ll. 2461 ff. and 2755, for the church of St. Jacob and the tomb.

[26] Ἱερός is a Greek word for holy. Ἱερεύς, then, is a holy man. It is the word generally used to indicate a priest, but it can also mean chaplain.

[27] A break occurs at this point in H. and ll. 7811-18 are taken from P. After l. 7810 in H., there is a marginal note written in the same red ink as the initial letters. It reads: "Ἕως ἐδῶ ὁ βίος τοῦ πρίγκιπα Γυλιάμου · ὅταν δὲ ἀπέθανεν ἦτον ἔτους, ζψπέ (To this point, the life of Prince Guillaume; when he died the year was 6785). There follows the calculation of a modern reader:

       6785 (the year given — Byzantine Era)
       <u>5508</u> (the year of Christ's birth — Byzantine Era)
       1277 (the year A.D.)

L. (§ 534) states: *si rendy son ame a Nostre Seignor Dieu Jhesus Crist le premier jour dou moys de may a mil .ij^e lxxvij. ans* (May 1, 1278). See S., p. 506.

ters and his labor went wasted; for it is never found established that a female child may inherit a lord's inheritance, for at the very beginning a curse was laid upon woman; and never in his life should a lord who has produced daughters as heirs rejoice, for, all his power and glory, should God give him a son-in-law, these will he take.[28]

Now after Prince Guillaume died, Sir Jean Chauderon, the grand constable (thus was he called throughout the principality, and he was left, indeed, as *bailli* in Morea), immediately wrote letters and sent messengers to Naples, where King Charles was. In minute detail he announced to him and informed him of the death of the prince and his situation.[29] And when the king heard this, he was sorely grieved; he ordered that the leaders of his council come to him. He asked counsel of them and that they counsel him about the land of Morea and how he should govern it. And his council told him to send a most wise man, an experienced soldier to be *bailli* and governor throughout the principality and to have permission and power to govern everyone in accordance with the desires and well-being of the men of the land.

So, he thereupon appointed a certain knight; Rousseau was he named and de Sully was his surname; he was a noble man and an experienced soldier.[30] And he gave him fifty mercenaries on

---

[28] The sentiment of these lines is in direct contradiction to all we know of Moreot law. They obviously reflect the opinion of the Greek scribe who wrote P.

[29] It will be remembered that by the agreement of May 24, 1267, Morea was to pass to Isabeau and her husband, then to her heir, and if she had no heir, or if her husband were to die before Guillaume, then Morea would go to Charles of Anjou. Philippe d'Anjou, Isabeau's husband, did, in fact, die before Guillaume, in 1277 at Naples. (See above p. 000, n. 00.)

[30] Hugues de Roux de Sully in August 1279 was appointed vicar-general of Albania. He was never *bailli* of Morea. The *baillis* of Morea during the period 1278-89 were:

Galeran d'Ivry	appointed	August 26, 1278
Philippe de Lagonesse	"	August, 1280
Narjot de Toucy	"	October, 1282
Guy de Tremolay	"	October, 1282
Guillaume de la Roche	"	1285
Nicholas II de St.-Omer	"	1287

K. (p. 317, n.) and Z. (p. 49, n. 1) are both mistaken as to Galeran d'Ivry,

their steeds and 200 arbalesters, all excellent in the highest degree, whom the king ordered him to set to the protection on his behalf of the castles of Morea; he issued him orders, which he took with him. To the bishops, bannerets, and to the knights, to the leading men who were then in Morea, to all of these he bore letters on the part of the king. He left Naples with these troops and arrived in Klarentsa in the beginning of May. Now, when he arrived, he sent missives to the bishops of the land, to all the bannerets and to the knights, including letters from the king, which he carried with him. At the same time, he wrote to them on his own behalf that they should gather in Klarentsa to see the commands which he had brought from the king. And they came in on receiving the letters; and as soon as they were gathered, small and great, they opened the orders and read them; the king ordered all men of Morea to accept Rousseau de Sully as *bailli* and all who were liege men and owed homages to perform them to Rousseau for their estates, altogether as if he were the king himself.

And as soon as they had read those commands, the bannerets, the bishops, and the knights as well took counsel as to how they might release themselves. They chose the metropolitan of Patras, Sir Benoit, his name, to speak for all. Thereupon, he undertook to tell the *bailli* that all the men of Morea, small and great, all respected the orders and commands which he had brought from the king and accepted him, to hold and respect him as though he were the king himself. But, the homage and act of allegiance that he ordered them to perform to the *bailli* de Sully, they would never do, for by so doing, they would, in fact, be straying from the customs, which are stipulated by the law of Morea and which they had from the time of the conquest and which were sworn to and written by those who conquered the principality of Morea and seized it by the sword.[31] For the law of Morea and

placing the beginning of his *bailliage* in 1268. For the list above, see Lg., pp. 254-63, *passim*.

[31] This clear statement of the rights which the Moreot barons claimed appears in all the Chronicles (L., § 540, 861-62; L. de F., § 511; and also below, in ll. 8639 ff. of the Chronicle). See Articles 1, 3, 136, etc., of the Assizes and Topping, *Feudal Institutions*, pp. 105 ff.

the customs of the land stipulate that the prince, the lord, indeed, of the land, whoever he may be, when he comes to take up the suzerainty, must come in person into the principality to swear first of all to the troops who are in Morea, and he is to place his hand upon Christ's Gospel, that he will protect and justify them in the customs which they have and not disturb them in the franchise that they have. And when the prince has sworn in the way I have been telling you, then all the lieges of the principality begin to pay homage to the prince. For the liege act that takes place when they kiss upon the mouth is a mutual affair between the two of them; thus the prince owes good faith to the liege, just as the liege to him, and there is no difference, apart from the glory and honor which every lord receives. But should the prince happen to be in another land and should wish to appoint some other representative to receive the homage which the lieges owe, the liege men of Morea are not obliged to perform the act of homage and lealty to any other but to the prince, himself, and within the confines of the principality. "Therefore, the lieges of Morea ask you not to take this as a reflection upon you, for they would rather die and be disinherited than be removed from their customs. However, let the following take place for the glory of the king; and let him not in any way believe that they do this in defiance. Rather, since the sovereign authority of the prince has changed hands, we should come under the authority of our lord the king, if we had the power to do homage. We who are here in the presence of your highness do not have this power unless the others be here: the great lord, first of all, the duke of Athens; the three lords of Euripos and the duke of Naxos, and also the marquis of Boudonitza. However, to avoid a lengthy discussion, if it is your wish, whereas you are *bailli* today and have that power, and you are not rightful lord for them to do you homage, so that you may have confidence in the men of the land, and they, in turn, in you, that you will govern them with justice, let there be made a compromise in fear of God; you, first, to swear on the Gospels of Christ to rule and govern us according to the customs of the land, and then, after you, these to swear to you to be true to the king and to you as the king's official and and his representative that you are."

When Rousseau de Sully heard that an oath was to take place, he immediately fell in with the suggestion and agreed to it. Thereupon, he ordered that the Holy Gospel be brought, and the *bailli* swore first, and then the liege men, to be vassals and faithful, first to King Charles, and after him to his heirs, as is the custom.

With this, Rousseau received the *bailliage* and he began to put his office into operation and to change the officials and put in others who were new. He changed the protovestiarios and also the treasurer, the purveyor of the castles and all the castellans; he distributed the arbalesters among the castles and then assigned the *corvées* of the land.[32]

And so, after the dominion of the king was begun to spread in the name of the prince Sir Louis, who was the son of the king and husband of Isabeau, the daughter of Prince Guillaume, there had hardly passed a short, brief time when, from the many sins that Morea has, and, thus, they do not have the luck to keep a good lord, Sir Louis, prince of Morea, died.[33] Behold the evil that befell with this death, for he promised and he seemed to be a good lord. He was the younger brother of King Charles, the one who was lame, the father of King Robert. And after Sir Louis died, the suzerainty of sinful Morea fell into the hands and power of King Charles.[34]

At this point, I am here going to stop talking and relating about King Charles and his brother, who was called Sir Louis, prince of Morea. And I am going to tell about the great lord, Sir Guillaume, the name, de la Roche, the surname, who was duke of

---

[32] L. states (§ 543): *si clama les officiaux, le prothoficiaires, le thesaurier, le pourveur des chastiaux, chastellains et connestables, sergans et toute autre gent qui office avoient.* For the functions of these officers, see Adamantios, pp. 461, 580, 595, 609, 629; Topping, *Feudal Institutions*, pp. 119-26; Lg., pp. 194-208.

[33] By Louis the Chronicle means Philippe d'Anjou, who had died a year before Guillaume and not later. It is ironic that Philippe was buried in the same church, the cathedral of Trani, where his wedding had taken place, just six years earlier. Isabeau was left a young widow of fourteen (M., p. 147), sixteen (K., p. 321, n. on l. 2947), or eighteen (Lg., p. 249) years of age.

[34] The Angevins were: Charles I, king of Naples (1266-85), prince of Morea (1278-85), and his sons, Charles II, king of Naples (1285-1309), prince of Morea (1285-89), and Philippe (d. 1277). The sons of Charles II were Robert, king of Naples (1309-43), and Philippe II of Taranto, prince of Morea (1307-13).

Athens and was a good lord; likewise, I am going to tell also about Count Brienne, Sir Hugues, his name, count, he was, of Lecce, which he held in Apulia from Charles, the king.[35] In that year and time, of which I have told you here above in this book which you are reading, when the duke of Athens returned from France, he found that Prince Guillaume had been captured at Pelagonia and was in the City, where the basileus was holding him in his prison.

Now, the duke of Athens at that time did not have a wife; and thereafter he came to an agreement with the sevastokrator Sir Theodoros, lord of Vlachia, and took his daughter as wedded wife. And this couple together produced a son, who was named Sir Guy de la Roche, and who lived on, in fact, after the death of his father and became duke of Athens. Great lord, he was called, the surname, of Romania. And when he matured and became a knight, he made an agreement with the princess the Lady Isabeau, since he held his land from her and she was his lady, and took her daughter to wedded wife; Mahaut was she called, this was her name, and she was, indeed, the daughter of Prince Florent. Now, Guillaume, the duke of Athens, his father, lived many years after Guillaume, prince of Morea, died. And when Morea fell to King Charles, the first *bailli* that the king sent to Morea was Rousseau de Sully, and after him, the duke of Athens Guillaume became *bailli* and vicar-general of the whole principality.[36] The king sent him his command from Apulia, his *commission*, as the Franks call it, thus do they name it. And then, he received the office of the

[35] For the dukes of Athens and Hugues de Brienne, see above, p. 275, n. 2, and p. 276, n. 3. The lord of Athens who went to France in 1260 was Guy I de la Roche (1225-63). (See above ll. 1553 ff., 1555, 3302 ff., 3375 ff., 3392 ff., and 3455 ff.) He left two sons, who in turn became dukes of Athens: Jean I (1263-80) and Guillaume (1280-87). The Chronicle confuses Guy I with his son Guillaume (ll. 7964 ff.). Guillaume married Helene, daughter of John, the lord of Vlachia (Neopatras), who is confused in the Chronicle with Theodoros, illegitimate son of Michael II, despot of Arta. (See ll. 3469 and 3504 and notes.) Guillaume's son by Helene was Guy II de la Roche (called Γγί in l. 7975 and Γιωτής in l. 8047), who married Mahaut de Hainaut, daughter of Isabeau de Villehardouin and Prince Florent de Hainaut.

[36] See above, p. 291, n. 30, for the *baillis*. L. de F. (§ 420-23) correctly names Guillaume as first *bailli* of Morea and substitute for Geoffroy Chauderon.

bailliage and was the king's *bailli* for the rest of his life. And at
that time, in his day, he built Dematra, the castle which was in
Skorta and which the Romans destroyed;[37] the great lord, himself,
took his stand there until the castle of Dematra was finished.
Now, a short time later the countess died, the wife of the count
of Brienne, who was sister of the duke of Athens, Sir Guillaume,
whereas she had first been spouse of that awesome soldier the lord
of Karytaina, as I have told you. Now, this countess produced
by the count a son, an outstanding child, whom they named Gautier; he lived and became a worthy knight, a soldier, indeed, renowned in all the kingdoms and was killed at Halmyros by the
Company.[38]

Now, after this countess died, a short time went by, and the
duke died also, he, indeed, of Athens, Guillaume by name. Great
havoc ensued from his death, for he was a wise lord, philanthropic
to all; great sorrow arose throughout the principality.

Thereafter occurred the following: listen to what happened![39]
Count Hugues, that de Brienne, was pleased to cross over from
Apulia and went to Morea, and from there, in turn, he traveled
straightway to Thebes, saying he would see the duchess to console
her, for she had been recently left a widow by Sir Guillaume, the
duke of Athens, his wife's brother. And after he had arrived there
and saw her and talked with her, he stayed many days saying
he would console her. And they were closeted so much together
that each grew to desire the other, and with good agreement, the
count then married his in-law the duchess, he took to wife the
wife of his wife's brother. After the two were joined, as chance
would have it, the archontess became pregnant and bore a daughter; Jeannette, they named her, and as soon as she matured and
became of legal age and became a woman, they gave her for hus-

---

[37] K. (p. 324, n. to l. 7997) condenses a long discussion of Dragoumis and
identifies Dematra (La Dimatre, L. § 547) as the present town of Demantra in
the district of Dorion, province of Trifylia.

[38] See above, p. 276, n. 3; p. 277, n. 6.

[39] Hugues de Brienne, having lost his first wife, Isabeau de la Roche, married
the widow of Guillaume de la Roche (d. 1287), Helene, daughter of John, lord
of Vlachia (Neopatras). Their daughter Jeanne (Madame Jehanne, L. § 550)
later married Nicolas I Sanudo, duke of Naxos.

band Sir Nicolas; his surname was de Sanudo, and he was duke of Naxos; these two never did have good agreement. Unfortunately, it happened that they did not have a child to leave as his heir to inherit all the castles and his lands which Sir Nicolas held.

Count Hugues de Brienne after he married the duchess of Athens took over the dominion and held sovereignty over the whole territory of the great lordship and had in his wardship Guy de la Roche as long as his mother the duchess lived. Now, when two years or so had passed, the countess died and Count Hugues went to his land in Apulia. And after Guyot came of age, he received the dominions, the great lordship. He became a knight and was a good lord and he was called great lord, the surname of the Hellenes, and he was duke of Athens and had a great name; but, from sin, since he passed his life in wickedness, God did not grant that he should produce an heir to leave a child of his body to have sovereignty over the land and domain which his parents had held.[40]

At this point, I shall here stop talking about Sir Guy de la Roche, the great lord, and I am going to tell you about Sir Nicolas, his surname de St.-Omer, and how he married and took as his wife the princess of Morea, she who had been the spouse of Prince Guillaume. Now after Prince Guillaume died, the princess, his wife (she who was the sister of the despot Kyr Nikephoros, the lord of Arta), remained a widow and was in Morea and held a great many towns which she held and administered in the Plain of Morea; likewise in the castellany of Kalamata she held the towns of Maniatochori, Platanos, and Glyky, and other towns with these, over which she had sovereignty.[41] Thereafter, old Sir Nicolas de St.-Omer, because he was a great and noble man and had a lot of money, and his first wife had died (she who was, indeed, the prin-

[40] This information also appears in L. de F. (§ 452) but is related after the account of the wedding of Isabeau de Villehardouin and Florent de Hainaut.

[41] For Guillaume's marriage to Anna, daughter of Michael II, despot of Arta, and sister of Kyr Nikephoros, see above, ll. 3111 ff. and notes. The towns mentioned, which were part of her dower, lay in the peninsula of Pylos, southwest of Kalamata. The only one of the three still in existence, Platanon, lies near the town of Pyla, slightly northeast of Pylos (Navarino). Maniatochori is mentioned in later Venetian documents as being the outstanding town of the neighborhood.

cess of the city of Antioch, and from whom he had received celebrated wealth and money), as a noble and shrewd man, he came
to an understanding with her and took the princess of Morea as
his wedded wife, thus did he marry her, and for that reason he
went to Morea and was with her.[42] With his great wealth and
dominions which he held, he consstructed the castle of St.-Omer
which was in Thebes and he built this castle to be an extremely strong one; he made dwellings within it fit for a basileus.
Indeed, he built it and constructed it and inside he covered its
walls with murals depicting how the Franks conquered Syria.
This castle the Company afterwards destroyed because of their
fear of the great lord, the duke of Athens, who was called Gautier [II], lest he were to capture it and entrench himself there
and with it conquer the Megalokyrate. Behold the evil the deceitful Catalans committed, to destroy such a castle and such
a stronghold !

Likewise, Sir Nicolas also built in the town of Maniatochori
a castelet to guard his land against the Venetians. And afterwards
he built the castle of Avarino, with the expectation and intention
of prevailing upon the king to give it as a hereditary fief to him
and to his nephew, the grand marshal, Sir Nicolas, his name.

Thereafter, time ran on and the great lord died, he who was *bailli*
in Morea, and after him, Sir Guy, who was called Tremolay, lord
of Chalandritsa, was appointed *bailli* and vicar-general. And after
this Tremolay, too, had died, the king sent orders from Apulia
to Sir Nicolas de St.-Omer to be the *bailli*. And thereafter, he
received the office of *bailliage* and he began to act and to set the

[42] With the wealth he acquired from his marriage to Marie of Antioch, Nicolas II de St.-Omer constructed on the Kadmeia in Thebes the celebrated
castle of St.-Omer, which was later destroyed by the Catalans. When Nicolas II
married Anna de Villehardouin in 1280, he acquired her dower of Clermont
and Kalamata, which Charles d'Anjou exchanged for some of the fiefs in
Morea and Sicily of Leonardo de Veroli, who died in 1281. On becoming *bailli*
of Morea, Nicolas continued the work of fortification begun by his predecessor
and built a small castle in Maniatochori and the famous castle in Old Navarino.
His nephew, Nicolas III, also built a castle whose remains are still to be seen
in the town of Santameri, northeast of Andravida. After the establishment of
the Catalans in central Greece, the St.-Omers moved to their lands in the
Peloponnesos.

land to rights in peace, as a noble and wise man that he was toward all men.[43] During the time of the rule of old Sir Nicolas de St.-Omer, lord of Thebes, who was *bailli* in Morea during those days, there was a certain noble Frank who was from Champagne, Sir Geoffroy, he was called, his surname, de Bruyères, and he was the cousin of the lord of Karytaina. And when he heard and learned that the lord of Karytaina, who was his cousin, had died and there had not remained after him a child of his as heir, a fine appetite came upon him, and he got the idea to go to Morea, indeed, as the nearest relative that he was of the lord of Karytaina, to have his patrimony.[44] He pawned his lands and borrowed *hyperpyra* and hired eight sergeants, who went with him. He procured from bishops and knights sealed written affidavits, which testified that he was the legitimate cousin-german of the lord of Karytaina, Sir Geoffroy de Bruyères. He made noble preparations, took the eight sergeants, left his land, and began his journey. And he came to Naples and found King Charles; he showed him the affidavits which he carried that he was the cousin of the lord of Karytaina and that he had come, according to the customs of the Franks, as heir to a patrimonial estate and relative, to claim his patrimony.

He presented his homage, as is the custom. And the king, when he heard and saw his affidavits, ordered that the *bailli* in Morea, de St.-Omer, indeed, the old Sir Nicolas, be written to have all the liege men of Morea, the bishops and the wise men of the whole principality come to hold a high court to examine the affidavits which this Sir Geoffroy had brought from France, and if they should find that he sought with justice the castle of Karytaina and its surroundings, he was to give him its usufruct and to invest him with it.

[43] The passage including ll. 8110-8473 in P. was at some time taken out of its proper place in the Chronicle and placed at the end following l. 9130. There seems to be no explanation of this, and Schmitt returns it to its proper place in his edition. (See S., pp. 527 ff.)

[44] This incident occurred early in 1279, during the *bailliage* of Galeran d'Ivry. Karytaina had escheated to the prince because the lord of Karytaina, holding his fief as a "new grant," had died without direct heirs. See Lg., p. 255 and n. 3, where Longnon quotes a document, now destroyed, from the Neapolitan Archives.

Now, the court, which met in Klarentsa, beheld the command which the king had sent and read the affidavits which he had brought with him. And after they had argued at length and had spoken and had cited, they came to cite the act which the lord of Karytaina committed at the time when he revolted and went to Thebes and went and fought, armed and mounted, by the side of the great lord against Prince Guillaume, who was his rightful lord, and from whom he held the castle of Karytaina and all his lands. He broke faith with his lord and became a rebel, and as a result, he and his descendants were disinherited; and then all the men of the principality pleaded with the prince and besought him, and he returned his land with a stipulation and condition, he gave it to him as a new grant which might be inherited only by children of his body, should he have any. Thereupon, they called this knight, this Sir Geoffroy, and he went before the court. The bishop of Olena held discourse and told him in great detail the decision of the court, about the act which the lord of Karytaina had committed and how he and all his descendants had been disinherited in accordance with the customs which prevail in all the kingdoms: whoever is found to be faithless and a traitor, first, he, himself, is entirely disinherited, and, after him, his descendants, of whatever land and dominions he holds and rules. "Therefore, our good friend, we speak the truth; right does not fall to you in this that you claim."

On hearing that he had received a verdict contrary to his expectation, this Sir Geoffroy de Bruyères went to his camp and sat all by himself; he wept and lamented as though he had lost the kingdom of France, if it had been his. Now, two days later, he set himself to pondering and giving rise to ideas as to what he was able to do, for, if he returned to France and did not manage in some way to stay in Romania to make his fortune, everyone would laugh at him, revile and berate him, because he returned having accomplished nothing and having made no gain. For this reason, he said to himself it were better to die than to remain with nothing accomplished and without having made some gain.

He found a certain man of the land and made friends with him: he asked him to inform him minutely about the castles that were in Skorta, about Araklovon[45] and how it stood, and also about Karytaina and how it was built, and which of the two was the stronger and how many troops it held. And the other, who knew the condition of the two castles. described them to him in detail and instructed him as to the sites on which they stood and what troops they held. And when he heard these things, he made his plan and he set out from Morea and went to Xenochori;[46] and as soon as he arrived there, he said he was dizzy and that the stomach ailment had seized him, and he spoke to the people and asked where he might find well water, for such water was astringent and would stop the dysentery. And someone who was there, a native of that place, told him that there were good wells in Araklovon and let him send to them to give him some of this water and he would be cured thereby of his dizziness. Thereupon, he called one of his sergeants, whom he thought well of and who had a lot of confidence in his secret plan, and said to him: "Take flasks and go to the castle which is close to Araklovon and tell the castellan that I request him to direct that you be given water from the well, which I need for my medication, for the doctor has prescribed it for me and has said that it is good for me. And take careful note, when you enter the castle, of how it is laid out and its entrances and how many men are guarding them, so that you can tell me about it on your return and explain it all to me, and do not dare tell a single living person about it."

Thereupon, his sergeant went to the castle; he found the castellan, greeted him sweetly, and on behalf of his lord, he asked him to order that water from the well be given him. And the castellan immediately gave the order and it was given to him; he himself went into the citadel and reconnoitered it and returned to Sir Geoffroy and told him all he had seen. For around ten days he continued to say that he felt a dizziness and his sergeant repeatedly went to the castle and repeatedly brought him the

[45] See above, p. 121, n. 39, for Araklovon. Dragoumis discusses the site of this castle at length and locates it northwest of the present town of Platiana, Alipheira, Olympia.

[46] Xenochori (Salicore, L. § 563) is located near the present town of Xerochori, near Andritsaina.

water to drink. And then he asked the castellan to come, pleading with him and urging that he might talk to him. And the castellan came to the knight at once. On seeing him, Sir Geoffroy received him sweetly; he told him of his illness and asked him to receive him in his castle with one chamberlain and to give him one room to lie in, so that he might drink the salutary water of the well; and the rest of his retinue would be in the bourg.

And the castellan, not expecting any deceit, immediately spoke and assured him he would receive him in the castle; and afterwards, Sir Geoffroy, on the second day, took his camp and went to the castle. He went into the citadel and was given the chamber; his bed was made up, and he lay upon it. He had only one sergeant there with him, and the rest of his retinue was in the bourg. He ordered that his clothes be brought into the castle, and amidst his clothes were also their arms. Now, he lay on the bed all the time; he called the castellan and supped with him; he was displaying such respect and affability toward him so that he would trust him, and he could deceive him. And as soon as he had his confidence and saw his opportunity, he called his sergeants, whom he had as retainers, and said he would make his will, for he feared he would die from the sickness that he had; he had them swear to him secretly in his cell to keep secret what he would tell them and to cooperate with him if he should do what he planned and wished to bring about. And when they had sworn, he began to speak to them: "Comrades, friends and brothers, who have come with me to the lands of Romania, you know the reason that I hastened to put my land in pawn, to come honorably, in the hope and expectation of obtaining Karytaina with its surrounding lands, which my relatives raised and built and which land my kinsmen conquered by the sword; and you saw and heard how the Moreot hangmen disinherited me and removed me from it, and I grieve and am ashamed, I feel great bitterness. Therefore, I have made a plan in confidence of you, if only you will help, as I have hopes you will, to do a wondrous thing, which we are going to hear. You see this castle, the strength that it has; few men are needed to protect it, since it has provisions and is fortified; it lies within the land of Skorta and it commands it. Let us hold it for ourselves to command it and let us say that we are going to sell it to the

captain of the basileus of the Romans. I expect that when the
bailli of Morea hears this, he will be very happy to come to terms
with us and will give me the castle of Karytaina with the territory of Skorta and will prefer that I hold it from the king than
that I give the castle of Araklovon to the Romans. For if the
Romans had this castelet, they would win both Skorta and all
the principality."

When his sergeants heard this, they came to terms with one
another and they began to consider how it would take place and
how it would be accomplished. And then, Sir Geoffroy arranged
the matter and said to them: "I have heard that out there is a
tavern where wine is sold and that the castellan goes out and sits
there many times and drinks with the others. Well, it seems to
me we should do as I tell you: since we have bread and biscuit,
wine, water, and arms here, as much as we need, you go out for
a chat with him out there in the tavern, two or three of you, as
you prefer, the most clever of you; call the castellan and also the
constable and the sergeants with them, all the leading ones. You
have many *denaria*, so give them to the tavern keeper and buy
a lot of wine and drink with them, and give them so much to drink
that they will get drunk. But, you be careful that you do not
chance to drink so much wine with them that it befuddles you,
and we lose what we hope to prepare. And after you are sure
that they are drunk, let one of you, your leader, slip out of there
quickly and come here to the castle, and afterwards let another
come as well; and seize the porter and throw him out, and take
his keys and lock the door. And quickly climb onto the walls of
the gate to guard the door, lest they set fire to it and burn it and
break in and capture us and we lose what we hope and plan to
carry out."

Just as Sir Geoffroy ordered it and as he outlined it, just so
did the Franks, his retinue, do it. The Franks rose up and captured the castle. Then, Sir Geoffroy had the prisoners released
[from the keep]; there were twelve men therein, peasants and
Romans. He called two of the Romans and had letters written
for them; one of the two who knew how to write wrote it; he sent
it with them to the captain of the basileus writing and declaring
that he should come quickly to the castle he had captured which

is called Araklovon, that he might sell it for *hyperpyra* and surrender it to him. And he, when he heard it, was jubilant; quickly,
hastily he gathered all his armies and set out and, going as quickly
as he was able, he traveled and arrived at the ford in the Alpheios
in the valley of the Alpheios at a spot called Omplos;[47] there they
set up the tents, and the army went to bed.

Now after the capture of Araklovon took place, the castellan,
Philokalos,[48] his name, immediately sent two messengers to the
chevetain, Sir Simon, he was called, his surname de Vidoigne;[49]
he was in Arachova, called the great, with the troops of Skorta
who were on garrison duty at that time. They explained the
affair to him and the treachery which Sir Geoffroy de Bruyères
had committed, and had indeed seized Araklovon and was going
to sell it to the captain of the basileus, to whom he had sent word
to come to give him *hyperpyra* and to take the castle.

On hearing this, Sir Simon rode out with all the men who happened
to be with him there at that time. He sent word everywhere for
his troops to come in; quickly he arrived at the castle of Araklovon.
He surrounded it all around with the troops that he had and he
seized all the passes, roads, and defiles, so that no one could go
in or out of the castle to carry any message to or from the Romans.
Now, when Sir Simon arrived in Araklovon with the troops that
he had, he sent messengers at once to the *bailli*, to Sir Nicolas
de St.-Omer, who was in Klarentsa; he announced and informed
him of the event, that Sir Geoffroy, the surname de Bruyères,
had seized the castle of Araklovon and had sent word to the captain of the basileus of the Romans to bring him *hyperpyra*, and
he would give him the castle, and that he come quickly with all
his armies to give aid immediately lest they lose the castle, and
before the Romans should come and occupy it.

---

[47] Omplos was on the Alpheios near the present town of Ompra, in the
neighborhood of Krestaina.

[48] Philokalos, Greek castellan of Araklovon (Fylocalo, L., § 564), his family,
and his connections with the Voutsarades family are discussed by Dragoumis,
p. 26, 27; and see above, p. 121, n. 40.

[49] L. (§ 576) calls him *Simon de Vidoigne, qui lors estoit chapitaine de l'Es-
corta, a la grant Aracove ou il estoit.*

Now, when the *bailli* heard this, he set out at once with what-ever troops he happened to have with him and he sent word every-where that the armies come in. And when he had come to Ara-klovon and had found the *chevetain*, Sir Simon, with the troops that he had (he was besieging the castle and had captured the roads, lest someone come from the Romans and enter Araklovon and bring it a message), the *bailli* thanked the *chevetain* warmly.

The Frankish armies began to come in from all sides; they seized the whole *drongos* of Skorta and were guarding it. Trustworthy messages were then brought to the *bailli* that the armies of the Romans had arrived at the tributary of the Alpheios, at a place called Omplos. Thereupon, he ordered that Sir Simon, the *cheve-tain* of Skorta, be called and he ordered him to take his own troops and those of the *drongos* of Skorta and the troops of Kalamata and of Perigardi, of Chalandritza and also those of Vostitza, and to go to Isova, to the ford of Ptere, on the tributary of the Al-pheios, to take up a stand and guard it, so that the Romans might not pass into the *drongos* of Skorta.[50]

Then Sir Simon, as the *bailli* commanded, took his armies and went there and stood face to face with the Romans. Now, the *bailli*, a prudent man, with the counsel he received, called two knights and ordered them to go there to Araklovon, to ask for the castle from Sir Geoffroy and that he return it to the suzerainty of the king as he had found it; and he would be forgiven for this that he had done. "But, if he plans in any way to hold the castle, to hold it for himself or to give it to someone else, tell him as in-formation that he may hold to be true that I will first receive death, and all of you with me, rather than leave here with the armies that I have before I shall have destroyed the walls of the castle of Araklovon, shall have stoned him inside of it and have killed him."

Thereupon, those knights went there and approached the castle and asked for a truce; they called out from afar lest they be shot

[50] For Perigardi, see above, p. 222 and n. 24. For Chalandritsa, see above, p. 127 and n. 56; see also Dragoumis, p. 88, and Adamantios, p. 588. Vostitsa is the present port of Aigion, east of Patras, on the Gulf of Corinth. Ptere Ford was a ford across the Alpheios, somewhere close to Isova.

at, that the *bailli* sent them there as messengers to discuss something with Sir Geoffroy for his well-being and honor, if he would
do it. On hearing this, Sir Geoffroy became exceedingly glad and
stood on the walls and asked them what they wanted; and they
said to him:"The *bailli* declares to you, as a friend he greets you,
that he is wonderstruck that in the face of the courtesy and solic-
itude you received, the honor you found in the castle of the king,
you seized it and hold it and would sell it to the captain of the
Romans, as he has been informed. Therefore, he beseeches you,
and all of us join with him, not to be deluded by the expectation
of world-wide fame. For everyone is wonderstruck at this that
you have done; it did not behoove you, as a nobleman, for treach-
erous purpose, to have ever thought of it, nor to have put it into
effect; for the Frankish people, who we are, after all, have been
shamed because of you, and we are grieved. However, we know
that you did it out of bitterness, because you expected and hoped
to have the barony of Karytaina of Skorta and found yourself
disappointed; we know, indeed, that you have repented of what
you have done. Therefore, we say to you and counsel you: with
goodness and eagerness, return the castle and you will have benefaction and honor with forgiveness. But if you are planning anything defiant, take care, for you cannot stand against so many;
for the *bailli* has sent for carpenters to come, Venetian craftsmen,
indeed, to construct trebuchets; those walls which you see will
all be destroyed and you will all be stoned and killed."

Thereupon, Sir Geoffroy began to speak to them: "Archons,
you wrong me and are withholding my patrimony with pretexts
and hollow excuses, you Moreots; and I, from the grievance and
sorrow which I feel, have done this which you have seen, and from
the bitterness that I have; and I know and recognize that I have
it to my dishonor. However, since you tell me to and advise me,
I shall return the castle with the understanding and condition
that we place my case before the king's court, and however it
decides it, I consent to accept its authority. Now, since I came
to the land of Morea, I have come to love it and wish to stay here
with you; give me land to hold, to have my livelihood, for I feel
disgrace and shame to go to France, for my relatives, friends, and

neighbors to laugh at me because I went to Romania and acted like a boy."

Well, if I were to write what those knights there talked over with Sir Geoffroy, and he with them,[51] who would read it? But I will make it clear to you, will write it and recite it in brief; Sir Geoffroy came to terms and surrendered the castle, and they gave him as an inheritable estate the fief of Moraina—it is to be found in Skorta with other towns—and as wedded wife the Lady Marguerite, who was the cousin of the lord of Akova and had as an inherited estate the fief of Lissarea.[52] And after they were wed and the two had joined together, God gave them a child that was a daughter; they named her Helene, and afterwards she married Sir Vilain d'Aunoy, lord of Arkadia. [53] And they, in turn, had a son and daughter; Erard was the son's name, Agnes, that of the daughter, whom Sir Etienne, his name, and Maure, his surname, married as wedded wife. And she, in turn, gave birth to sons and daughters; and of all of them one remained as heir, Erard, he was named, the lord of Arkadia.[54] The orphans became rich, the widows

---

[51] L. 8450 is from P.

[52] Geoffroy married Marguerite de Cors, heiress of her father's fief of Lissarea, near Chalandritsa, and widow of Payen de Stenay, whose fief Moraina, near Andritsena, she brought to her new husband. L. de F. (§ 428-46) gives the details of this story quite differently.

[53] Vilain II d'Aunoy, lord of Arkadia (Kyparissia) married Helene de Bruyères, Lady of Moraina. Their children were Erard II, who was lord of Arkadia and who died before 1388; and Agnes, who married Etienne le Maure, lord of Saint-Sauveur (L., § 585).

[54] This last statement and the lacuna that follows have given rise to much dispute and discussion as to the date when the Chronicle was written. It would appear that the genealogical remarks about Erard III were added when H. was copied, translated, or at least derived from an earlier text. His family was not of such importance as to warrant such details, unless the author had some special reason for paying tribute to him. This would tend to indicate that Erard was alive when H. was written. In l. 8469, there is a slight (in my opinion, very slight) indication that this is so. It is known that Erard III died in 1388, which would then mean that H. dates from before that year. Following l. 8469, there is a lacuna of four lines in H. which I have filled with the corresponding lines of P. These lines indicate most certainly that Erard was dead when they were written, which proves that P. was written after 1388. See K., p. 342, n. to l. 8468; Adamantios, p. 521; Longnon's edition of L., Introduction, pp. liii-lvi; S., p. 624, under Erard III.

became glad, the impoverished and the poor made much money in the time of which I speak, that of the lord of Arkadia. Commemorate him, all of you, a good lord was he. At this point, I shall stop speaking hereafter and relating about that Sir Geoffroy and his inheritance and I am going to tell you, to write and speak about the blessed Isabeau (who was the daughter of Prince Guillaume and who was addressed, called and named in those days the lady of Morea), how God brought her and she returned to her patrimony and became princess of all Achaia.

At that time that I am telling you about, the Princess Isabeau was then in Naples with King Charles. And the king, in fact, held suzerainty at that time over Morea by reason and virtue of those agreements which Prince Guillaume had made with King Charles, the elder, his father, and also through the prince his brother, Sir Louis, his name, the husband of Isabeau. Well, while the king held suzerainty over Morea, there were at that time two certain knights, who were bannerets. The one was called Chauderon, grand constable of the principality of Morea he was at that time; and the other was Sir Geoffroy, de Tournay the surname.[55] The king liked them and esteemed them highly; the grand constable, indeed, Chauderon, he made grand admiral of all his kingdom. And while these knights were going and coming in the court of the king in Naples, the brother of the count de Hainaut was there, Sir Florent he was called, de Hainaut the surname. He was grand constable over all the principality.[56] And as is the universal custom within the race of men, and they come to agreements with one

[55] These were Jean de Chauderon, grand constable, and Geoffroy de Tournay, son of Othon I de Tournay, lord of Gritsaina. The story that follows is given quite differently in L. de F. (§ 447-49). According to this version, when Charles II was released from captivity in 1289, on his return he wished to reward his regent Robert d'Artois for his services. The latter refused any personal reward, but put forward his distant kinsman by marriage Florent de Hainaut as a landless and penniless, but deserving, knight, and asked Charles to give him Isabeau's hand. Actually, the two accounts are not necessarily contradictory and both together may tell the whole story.

[56] Florent was the younger brother of Jean d'Avesnes, count of Hainaut 1280-1304. Florent, dissatisfied with his small holdings, had gone to the Neapolitan court to seek his fortune. His first reward was to be made grand constable of the kingdom of Sicily.

another and make friendships, Sir Florent was pleased with those knights, the two Moreots, Sir Jean de Chauderon and Sir Geoffroy, And in this friendship which they had with one another, Sir Florent, as a prudent man, said to the two of them: "Archons, friends and brothers, if you two would have me there in Morea as your friend and comrade, I shall make an oath to you that we will never be parted, that we will be as brothers and live together. I see with my own eyes the king likes you, and he has you as informants and leaders in his council. Well, if you have love for me, as I hope, speak to him about my taking your lady, the Lady Isabeau, to wedded wife, and point out to him as true reasons and causes that the land of Morea finds itself in a war and is in danger of being lost with his officials; the *baillis* that he sends there, they are mercenaries and are always seeking their own gain, and the land is always melting away, is being lost, is in danger, and the king has all the expense, and others are taking the profit. And it is, indeed, an evil thing for him to hold the heir here—she passes almost for a prisoner and the world is astonished at it. And he would do a thing for the salvation of his soul and to his high praise to marry the Lady Isabeau to a knight, to a nobleman, who would be of her rank, who would feel for and guard the land of Morea, before it slips away completely and the Franks lose it. And why should I state all the details and explain it to you point by point? So urge, as prudent men, and speak of this to the king that you will prevail upon him to fall in with your desire; for my thought tells me and my mind informs me that, if you desire it, as the prudent men you are, the thing will be accomplished, and you will win the principality for yourselves and I will be your man; I will be called prince and you will be lords." On hearing these things, Chauderon and Sir Geoffroy were very pleased and they made him a promise that they would apply their will to accomplish the affair and hoped in God to have good success. Thereupon, they sought an occasion to find the king in a moment of good humor to speak to him. And when they found the moment, the two spoke to him; they found him in good humor in his chamber; they stated many reasons to him and pointed out to him the excuse that the land of Morea, the principality of Achaia, was melting away and in danger and was being lost because the prince, who had been always over it, was missing. "You send to Morea a *bailli* and mercenaries, and they tyrannize the poor, injure the rich, and only seek their own gain, and the land is slipping away. If you do not appoint a man to be heir, to remain constantly, to govern everyone, to have as his thought and purpose to advance the interests of the land, be informed that you will lose the principality. Well, lord emperor,[57] you hold the heir, the Lady Isabeau, daughter of the prince, and give her a husband, a noble man and great, to hold the principality from your majesty, and you will be doing something for the salvation of your soul and greatly to your profit, and all who hear of it will always praise you."

Why should I tell you all the details and why should I write them? They said so many things to the king, those knights, so long did they talk with him, so much did they urge him that he arranged that the marriage take place, that Sir Florent take the Lady Isabeau as wedded wife, to have the principality as his own patrimony and that he inherit it. The agreements were written in detail and the articles, what the prince was obliged to do for the king and the king for the prince, each for the other. One article was written in this privilege, whereas it was sinful and a great wrong: that should it befall that the principality come to a female heir, to a woman to hold the suzerainty, she may not dare to marry any man in the world without the knowledge and command of whoever is king; but if she should happen to do it, she will be disinherited of the suzerainty of Morea and all the principality. Behold the evil that took place because of this chapter; afterwards, the Princess Isabeau was disinherited because, indeed, she married Philippe de Savoie when she went to the Jubilee, in fact, that time in Rome.[58]

Now, after these agreements had been written, the king immediately ordered that the wedding be held; and thereupon, Sir Florent married the Lady Isabeau, the daughter of the prince,

[57] Ἀφέντη βασιλέα. An unconscious use of a Byzantine term of address.

[58] Florent died, probably, on January 23, 1297. Isabeau, by then over forty, took as her third husband Philippe de Savoie, who was twenty-two at the time. The marriage took place on Ash Wednesday, February 12, 1301, in Rome.

the blessed Prince Guillaume. Now, the wedding took place with great pomp, with gladness and celebrations, and at great expense. And there where they were in the temple, in the church, where the Metropolitan, himself, of Naples married them, the king invested the Lady Margaret with the principality, as rightful heir; and then, after this, he called Sir Florent, in turn, and invested him as *avoué* and he made him also an heir; he enthroned him as prince to be called [prince] of Achaia.

And after the wedding was over, the prince's nuptials, he arranged his departure from Apulia, to go to Morea honorably and with pomp. He bowed before the king, took leave and said good-bye to the counts and knights, and he increased his retinue and hired others, as well; he had of mounted knights and sergeants, more, indeed, than a hundred, and three hundred arbalesters. He arrived in Brindisi, found his ships, boarded these, and went to Klarentsa.

The *bailli* of Morea at that time, old Sir Nicolas, happened to be in Andravida; on learning the report, he immediately rode out and went to Klarentsa; he did homage to the prince, as did all who were with him, and the prince gave him a great reception. And as soon as he had arrayed his troops in the church where the Minorites are, he ordered that small and great gather. He displayed the orders and the documents which he held and he presented to the *bailli* the king's command: the king commanded him, in writing he charged him, to surrender to him the principality of Morea, the castles and dominion over all the principality. After this, he pulled out a command by which the king charged in a written declaration all the Moreots, the bishops, bannerets, knights, sergeants, burghers, and everyone, great and small, to accept Sir Florent as prince and lord; the homage, indeed, and the lealty, which each owed for the fiefs and patrimonies they held from him, let them perform it to the prince, excepting the oath, the faith and lealty which they owed to the king. Thereupon, they ordered that the Holy Gospel be brought and then said to the prince: "You swear to us first to hold us and judge us by the customs of the land and not to disturb us in the franchise which we have; and, afterwards, we, in turn, will do homage, for such is the custom we have from our parents."

And the prince swore on the Holy Gospel to hold all the people
of Morea by the customs which they have, and also by the fran-
chises. And afterwards, the bannerets first, the knights and the
others did the homage and the lealty which each owed for the
fief that he held, excepting, of course, the king's own oath.[59] Thereupon, the *bailli* surrendered to him the principality, the castles, and
the suzerainty, to hold them from the king.

And after the prince had received the homages, he changed
all the offices, first the castellans and the sergeants of the castles,
and appointed his own. He appointed a protovestiarios, as well as
a treasurer. and a purveyor of the castles and all the authorities.
So, he began with the counsel of old Sir Nicolas, of Sir Jean de
Chauderon, the grand constable, as well as of Sir Geoffroy de
Tournay and of the other lieges, small and great, to arrange the
affairs and problems of the land. Now, the prince found the land
en demaine completely devastated by the mercenaries and the
king's authorities, who had laid it waste. He asked counsel of
all as to how he should act, and all the wisest said and counseled
that if he were to maintain a war with the Romans, the land would
melt away even worse; but if he would wish to resurrect the land,
then let him effect a reconciliation with them, peaceful and strong,
and swear with the basileus that the peace would last for all time.

In this wise was the counsel given, and all supported it, and the
prince sent two messengers to the supreme captain of the basileus
who was then in Morea in those days, declaring and announcing
that he had come there as lord prince of Morea, of all that the
Franks held, and had found the land laid waste, completely devastated. And he had asked and had been told that this was so
because of the war which the basileus was carrying on with the
principality; for the deeds of war produce such results; even the
very best lands that are in the world, war, indeed, destroys and
completely devastates. Well, if he wished and was pleased that
a truce be effected, let him send him answer, so that he might
learn his will.

When the captain heard this, it seemed desirable to him, and
he praised the prince for a prudent lord. So, noble and prudent

---

[59] L. says: *sauve la fealté du roy que il reservoit a soy* (§ 595).

that he was, he then sent such answer to the prince: that the term
was short before he would be replaced, another captain to come,
and he to go, as is the custom of the basileus, who each year changes
the captain in Morea. But since the prince was pleased to make
a truce, one that would be firm and sincere, for as many years
as needed, he, for love of him and for the well-being of the land,
would announce it to his lord the basileus, for he had hope in God
that it would please him very much. So, the captain then sent
an envoy to Constantinople to the basileus. In great detail he
declared to him by word of mouth and in writing that Prince
Florent, who had come to Morea, sought to make a peace, ε truce
with him so that their men, Franks and Romans, might have
peaceful repose and live in peace.

And the basileus, on hearing it, approved it highly; to the captain
that he then sent to Morea[60] (a certain great man of the palace, who
was called Philanthropinos and who was of the twelve houses),[61]
to him, indeed, he gave orders to make answer to Sir Florent,
the prince, lord of Morea. And when this Philanthropinos came
to Morea, he sent an envoy to the prince. He sent him answer
from the basileus, that he had come at that time as captain of
Morea and was under orders to meet with him, to parley for the
truce that the prince was asking to make. And the prince sent
word to him by the two knights, written in the form of an oath,[62]
to come to Andravida.

Thereupon, the captain took with him some of the most prudent
archons that he had; with a most honorable company, he went
to Andravida, there where the prince was with his captains who
were in Morea at that time, the most prudent of them. Now,
after the prince and he came together, they parleyed and drew
up such truce as they wanted; in writing, indeed, they put the

[60] P. breaks off at this point with a sarcastic phrase: "but they accomplished
nothing with this truce, as I shall tell you further on, and you will hear."
Ll. 8710-8804 in P. are missing.

[61] See above, p. 261, n. 85. The "twelve houses" were the ancient Byzantine
noble families. Philanthropinos is apparently the same person who later
rebelled and proclaimed himself basileus (M., p. 178). The basileus by this
time was, of course, Andronikos II.

[62] This awkward phrase seems to mean a safe-conduct.

articles of the truce and to these they swore, the prince first, and
then that captain of the basileus. Then, the prince said to the
captain, "I beseech you, my friend, not to take as a reflection
on you what I am going to tell you and disclose to you; you behold
and see that I am a lord and prince in Morea, to do whatever I
wish and it will be firm and unshaken throughout all the years
and times that I shall hold it, and I have need of no one. But
you, your nobleness, brother, have power for a term and cannot,
you are not able, to effect an arrangement that will last any
longer than during your own time. Well, just as I, myself, who
am lord and master in my land, have sworn, so also will the basileus personally swear, and will draw up a chrysobull; that I may
save and hold these things as a guarantee of the truce, just as you
hold my letter, and it bears my seal."

Thereupon, the captain spoke and answered the prince: "It is
true," he said, "my lord, your great nobleness, I admit it and bear
witness, what you said is truly so. Well, if you wish that something
like what you have commanded take place, direct two knights
to go with me, and I will have two young nobles go with them,
and I will write to the basileus, to my holy lord, the affair and
proposal, as your nobleness has expressed it, that he may command
the agreements of the truce be written down and sealed with his
golden seal and that the basileus may swear to this written oath
in the presence of the knights, your envoys."

When the prince heard this, it seemed very good to him; he
directed Chauderon, the grand constable, and Sir Geoffroy d'Aunoy, the lord of Arkadia, to go, the two of them, to the basileus,
there in Byzantion, in the City of Constantine; likewise, Philanthropinos went with them. On seeing them, the basileus received
them well; this truce and peace[63] which he would have with the
prince of Morea seemed very desirable to him because of his heavy
expenses for the armies which he had been sending to Morea and
with which he made war on the Franks. He ordered immediately
that the terms of the treaty be written down, and he drew up an

---

[63] Ἀγάπη καὶ τρέβα. For these words, which appear so often in the
Chronicle, see P. Kalonaros, Ἐθνογραφία Μάνης, pp. 29 ff., and see above,
p. 241, n. 53.

oath and sealed it with the golden seal. On this, the basileus, himself, took an oath in the presence of the knights, and then he presented it to them; they took the oath and went to Morea and they brought it to the prince and presented it to him; the prince received it and it seemed to him very good.

And after the peace and truce was established between the basileus and the prince of Morea, the prince began, like the prudent man he was, to govern his land and to increase his *corvées*; he got along peacefully with the troops of the basileus; all men grew wealthy, Franks and Romans.

And when the basileus saw this and as soon as he was informed that he had a goodly truce with the prince, he wished and desired to renew the war with the despot of Arta, Sir Nikephoros.[64] He hired sixty galleys, which belonged to the Genoese, and directed them to set sail, cross the sea, and by way of the waters of Morea to enter the gulf, and in Xeromeron, there close to Arta, [the troops they carried] to overrun and pillage that whole area.[65] And he likewise ordered armies [to go] by way of the mainland, 14,000 on their horses and 30,000 foot soldiers, so many were they reckoned. And they went from Romania and through Vlachia. And they arrived in Yannina, before the splendid castle; there they encamped in siege of it. The castle is formidable and stands in a lake, for Great Ozeros is all around the castle.[66] The inhabitants enter the castle by a bridge; they bring the supplies into the castle by skiffs. The whole world considers that the castle of Yannina cannot be taken by assault, so long as it has supplies.

Herafter, I close at this point the discussion of the basileus and I am going to tell you the action of the despot. As soon as the despot of Arta heard and learned that the basileus, Palaiologos, I tell you, was getting ready with the armies that he had to come against him by land and by sea, he called his captains and took his counsel; he asked them to counsel him precisely in what manner

[64] This, in fact, was the main reason why Andronikos was desirous of a truce in Morea. The expedition took place in 1291 or 1292.

[65] This passage is somewhat obscure. The gulf is undoubtedly the Gulf of Arta on the western coast of Aetolia-Akarnania. Xeromeron, or Xeromera, is the area around this gulf, and Arta, of course, bears the same name today.

[66] Great Orizos was the medieval name for Lake Ioannina (Pambotis).

and means he might protect his land. Thereupon, the wisest counseled him thus; that he come to an understanding with the prince of Morea, with that Florent, with agreements and to the end that he come with his armies to fight by his side. Therefore, when this advice was given, he sent messengers, two prudent archons, the foremost of his council; he drew up orders for them and gave them in writing his power, giving them authority to effect whatever they could and were able with Florent, the prince of Morea, who had as his wedded wife his niece, who was the daughter of his sister and who was called Isabeau, thus was she named.

The envoys went out thereafter from Arta, crossed over to Morea, went to Andravida, and found the prince holding counsel with his captains over some affairs which he had. They presented the writings which they had; they gave them to the prince and greeted him on behalf of their lord, the despot. In detail, they talked with him and told him by word of mouth the reason and aim wherefore they had come there. Well, I shall omit the details, so that we may get to the end; they came to this agreement: the despot would give the prince, to hold as a hostage, and only so, his son Sir Thomas, until the prince would make his return and get back to the land of Morea with his armies, without fraud and deceit; and the prince with as many armies as he could bring with him would receive the pay of the despot.

And after they had arranged all their agreements, the envoys returned to the despot and told him and related to him that they had arranged for Prince Florent to come with five hundred, the foremost and best of all the principality, to the assistance and aid of his uncle the despot. Thereupon, they outfitted Sir Thomas, the son of the despot, for his journey with great honor and sent him to Morea, to Andravida; they gave him to the prince to do with as he wished. And the prince sent him to the castle of Chloumoutsi, to stand hostage with honor in the castle until the prince should make his return to Morea. And they also brought to the prince the pay for his troops, and they were paid three months' pay only. During those years and times and in those days, when the basileus, the great Palaiologos, began that hot war with the despot of Arta, he set out to destroy him both on land and on sea. Thereupon, in his turn, when the despot heard of it, he determined and resolved with a great will to protect himself from him by every manner and means.[67]

Well, just as he had come to an understanding with Florent, the prince of Morea, who had his niece, so did he do likewise with Count Richard, who was lord and count of Cephalonia at that time, and he gave him as hostage his first daughter to hold her as guarantee, and he himself was to come, in person, indeed, with all his army to the despotate to help him in the war which the basileus had begun with him; he would also have his pay, he and his troops, for the time he would spend in the war.[68] And after they had come to terms, the count made the crossing with one hundred mounted men, soldiers indeed, all choice men and soldiers at arms.[69] And in like manner, the prince of Morea crossed over from Patras, I tell you, and went to Arta. And when the despot then learned and heard that the prince was coming, he went out to meet him; they met at Lesiana[70] and held high celebration; "Welcome, O prince, welcome, my nephew; now I behold and realize the compassion of kinsmen." And when they had had their fill of Roman kisses, they set out and went straightway to Arta; and the count of Cephalonia came from the other direction.

Who could write for you in detail the joy he felt? When the despot saw the Franks that had come at that time, it seemed to him that he had conquered all of Romania. The prince took quarters in the houses of the despot, who, indeed, went into the castle. Then, the captains were given quarters first, honorably, as befitted each one of them, and then the knights and the noble sergeants. And after they had rested that day, on the following morning, the despot went with his captains and all the archons straight to the prince, where he was lodged; and he found him seated with Count Richard and with the marshal de St.-Omer, and also with the bannerets and all the knights. And they were conversing among themselves and taking their counsel as to what

[67] For details of the war, see M., pp. 178 ff., and Lg., pp. 268 ff.

[68] After the war, the son was returned, but the daughter was not. Richard married her to his son John, which enraged her father (L., § 618-19; 652-55).

[69] This last phrase (l. 8876) is taken from P.

[70] Lesiana does not refer to any of the four towns now bearing that name; but I am unable to identify it further.

action they should take with respect to the war in which they
had come to help the despot. And when they saw that the despot,
himself, had come there, they immediately arose to greet him and
they seated one another.

It seemed very good to the despot at that time when he found
the prince together with his council, sitting in counsel as to how
they should act in the war in which they had come to help him.
Now, after they had seated one another, as you have heard, the
despot, himself, began to speak and said to the prince and then
to the count and likewise to the marshal of Morea, and then to
the bannerets, and to the knights, as well, that he thanked them,
as his friends and brothers, for the compassion they had showed
and the sincere love and had come with eagerness to help him
in the war which the basileus had launched against him. Thereupon, he requested them and besought them as soldiers, as noble
and prudent men, to counsel him, that they might take prudent
action and act as soldiers and obtain praise, as they would have
glory. "For if God wills that we be victorious, let no one of you
think nor imagine that the praise will be given to me, by Frank or
Roman, because the undertaking is mine, this war of the basileus;
no, the honor and praise will be given to you, for all men know,
throughout Romania, there are no better in all manner of warfare
than the Franks of Morea, as all the world knows, for you have
prudence and military qualities to the highest perfection."

Now, after the despot had finished what he was saying, the
prince began to answer him thus: "My lord and despot and beloved
uncle, I thank you for your words, the praise which you expressed
for these noble soldiers who are with me today, here in my company.
Be informed of this and hold it as truth, that for love of you and
in answer to your call, these men have come here with me for their
honor. And do not think for a minute that they have come as
mercenaries, to serve you out of need for the pay that you
sent them there in Morea; for the pay that they received suf-
ficed them only to pay for the arms and horses that they bought,
to come here honorably in your need. For I speak for myself, and
hold it as truth, that out of love for you and our kinship, and
because we are neighbors, and it behooves us to help one another,
each the other neighbor in whatever he may have need; and again

because of the custom which the Franks have always to run in
arms to wherever they hear there is need or war or battle, for they
are soldiers and would display and make apparent that they are
soldiers, and they prefer to have honor and the world's praise,
than to be given plunder or money or pay—and, indeed, with
this reasoning have we come to you. And believe it, my good
uncle, I tell you truth, that if they had been able, most of these
that you see have come here, these noble warriors, would have
paid for all their expenses out of their own funds and would not
have taken even a little needle from you; but they have come as
your friends and as noble warriors, to serve you in the need they
see you have. Therefore, we promise you, they and I with them,
not to depart from here, from the despotate, until we give battle
to those armies that have come and are standing in your land,
those of the basileus; either we to taste of death, ourselves, or
they to die, instead."

Thereupon, the despot answered the prince, thanking him warmly, he and his archons, for all that he had said, as the nobleman
he was. Then they took counsel as to how they should act; the
words were many which they said and spoke; but in the end, they
declared that they would get the armies ready, leave Arta very
early the next morning, and go straight to Yannina, for they had
learned the armies were there,[71] and if the Romans, those of the
basileus, stayed there, they would give them battle and God's
will be done.

The marshal of Morea gave orders; and they were proclaimed at
once in the name of the despot, the prince, after him, and his marshal, that the squadrons were to be ready, Franks and Romans,
to follow the gonfalon of de St.-Omer, the marshal of Morea, wherever it might go. Then, on the following morning, the sqadrons
of the army set out and went to Yannina.

Now the grand domestikos, who was the captain in chief of the
basileus over his armies, went and told him and informed him
that the prince of Morea and the count of Cephalonia had come
with all their armies; they had arrived in Arta in the pay of the
despot and were coming straightway against him to give him

[71] This phrase (l. 8979) is from P.

battle. He called his captains, the foremost of his council; they took counsel together as to how they should act. Many were the words that they said to one another; in the end, however, they decided, they declared and affirmed, that if they were to set out from the castle which they were besieging, because of rumors and reports, they would be doing a thing worthy of high reproach; rather, they should stay there to learn the truth.

Later, they were brought truthful reports that the Franks had arrived in Arta and had set out and were coming straight to Yannina. When the domestikos and all his armies heard this, that the Franks had arrived and were in Arta,[72] they tarried not a bit to take counsel; and the most prudent, the foremost of the army, said that the basileus, himself, if he were with them, would not dare to remain to meet the Franks, and that it was more honorable that they leave, rather than that they be overtaken there and murdered. As soon as they heard that the Franks had come to Arta, they did not wait an instant to take any counsel whatever; they immediately struck their tents and broke camp; in a trice, however they happened to be, they set out and left, and neither raised standards, nor formed squadrons, but just as if the Franks were chasing them with their lances, thus and worse did they take to flight over the same road by which they had come from Vlachia.

When those in the castle saw them from within Yannina, they recognized and comprehended that the Romans were fleeing. They sent messengers at once to the despot: "Learn, lord despot, the Romans have fled." When the despot heard and learned that the Romans had set out from the castle of Yannina, he became overjoyed and at a run he went, himself, to where the prince was and told him the news. On hearing this, the prince said to him: "Why are you waiting?" He called the marshal de St.-Omer and he ordered: "Let all our trumpets be sounded and let the squadrons be separated so that they may go quickly straightway to Yannina, so that we may overtake the Romans before they get too far away from us and we have more trouble." They set out, traveled, and arrived that evening in Yannina at the camps of those who had fled, the armies of the basileus. The marshal of Morea ordered

[72] This phrase (l. 9009) is from P.

that they be assigned, and in the camps of the Romans the Franks took up quarters. Now, the despot, and also the bannerets, the leaders of the army, went into the tent of the prince; they took counsel together as to what they should do. In the end they agreed to pursue those who were fleeing, on the chance they might catch up to them and give them battle and take the victory. Even if they did not catch up to them, they would plunder the lands of the basileus there in Romania.

So, on the following morning, they set out and went, and they traveled straightway along the trail of their enemies. The prince called, and the despot came, and he said to him that he should direct some of his troops on light horse to catch up to the Romans and to tell the domestikos, the leader of the army, on behalf of the prince and also the despot, that they called upon them to wait for them to pass some time together in the field; for it was not fitting in such a soldier to come looking for campaigning with the purpose of giving battle, and after he found the battle ready, to run away.

Those who were ordered to go to the Romans made great haste swiftly and they caught up with them in a short time, where they were passing through the territory of Vlachia. They called to them from afar that they were messengers and that they be received to tell what they had been ordered. The domestikos ordered they be given safe-conduct, and they came and approached him and said to him: "My lord, the prince of Morea and also the despot send greeting to your nobility, as their friend and brother. You came from the basileus with the armies that you have, seeking to make war and to fight with others; and now that you have found what you wanted and what you were looking for, they ask you to wait in a suitable place, that they may come with their armies, that you may do battle. And as a prudent and noble man, look to your honor, lest others prevail upon you to abandon your honor and you fall under reproach and the basileus be angry."

He answered and he said to them: "I send many greetings to the prince of Morea, and also to the despot, as brothers and my friends; and inform them in my name that, if the troops of the basileus that I have were at my disposal, I should do what they desire. But, here there are Turks and Cumans, who have their own captains, and they pay no attention to me."

On hearing the answer, they started back; while returning, they found many men whose horses were spent, others whose horses had strayed, and the arms and tents of many others, which those armies had thrown away as they fled. And they took what they could and went to the army and delivered the answer of the grand domestikos. And when the prince and the despot heard that they were going, fleeing as fast as they could, they gave the order to their armies, and they set themselves to plundering and destroyed and laid waste the lands of the basileus, and they won much booty and captured many men. The land was without fear and the men had been emboldened by the armies that had been standing before the castle of Yannina; they fell upon them with a swoop and did great damage.

Now the incursion and the plundering that I am telling you about did not last very long, not even two days, for reports were brought to the despot at that time that there had arrived in the Gulf of Arta sixty Genoese galleys; [the troops they carried] had landed at Prevesa,[73] were plundering the towns, and were preparing to go straight to Arta. On hearing and learning this, the despot was very frightened and was extremely grieved, for he suspected right away that the galleys were the ones that the basileus had hired, those of the Genoese, to come against him, to destroy him. Thereupon, he asked right away: "The prince, where is he?" He set out from his squadron and went to him and he told him and related those reports that the galleys, those of the Genoese, had come and had landed at Prevesa, were plundering the towns, and were getting ready to go straight to Arta, "and I have fear beyond measure that they may capture the town." Thereupon, the prince answered him and said: "Know, uncle, my despot, in truth I tell it to you, for this reason did I come here and left Morea, to be of assistance to you in the war that you have. Well, for as long as I am here in the despotate, order what you need of me and I will do it." Thereupon, the despot thanked him warmly; the prince at once ordered his marshal, and the trumpets

[73] Prevesa lay at the entrance to the Gulf of Arta.

signaled that they were to return.[74] On hearing it, their squadrons came back, and there where they were camped, they separated three squadrons, a thousand mounted men, and they were ordered to go rapidly to get to Arta's assistance "before the fleet of galleys arrives, for we are coming straightway behind you." Thereupon, they set out and traveled without stopping. But the troops of the basileus who were in the ships, in the galleys with the Genoese, went onto the land, captured some men and asked them to tell them where the despot was and if he had any force, any foreign troops with him. And they told them and informed them that the prince of Morea had come, and the count of Cephalonia, with all their armies. And immediately on arriving here and on hearing the reports that the grand domestikos, with the armies that he had, had come and had laid siege to the castle of Yannina, they had made ready and had gone straight to them. And he, on learning of it, had set out and had fled, and they had gone chasing them to overtake them; "and just now some people have told us they cut them all down, and they are coming back, joyful, and will soon arrive."

On hearing this, the archons of the galleys quickly returned again into the tarettes the trebuchets and ladders which they had unloaded to go and assault the castle of Arta. Thereupon, they were brought these reports, also, that the Frankish armies had arrived. They sent for the troops that they had out plundering, and these had overrun the towns and had burnt the lands and the places of Vagenetia which were close to the sea,[75] all these they had plundered and had captured. So, soon after, the followers of the despot arrived, those 1,000 men on horse, who had been sent on, and as many as they caught on the land, Romans and Genoese, they cut them all down and captured certain others.

Thereupon, those of the galleys took counsel how they might in some way damage the despot; and the most prudent, and who

---

[74] After l. 9010, P. becomes rather fragmentary, until in l. 9130 it stops the narrative altogether to record the tale of Geoffroy de Bruyères (H., ll. 8110-8473).

[75] Vagenetia lay close to Arta, in southern Epiros. (La Vegencie, L., § 642, 658).

were experienced, said: "You know well and you must remember the command of the basileus, that he directed the grand domestikos to go with his armies and invade the despotate by land, and we were to go by water and [invade] by sea, they to help us and we, them, insofar as the land might be favorable. Well, since he has fled without giving battle and has taken his armies, in which we had hope—and you see that the prince and count with him have come with their armies and are with the despot—how can we foot soldiers do any damage to the land? You saw that we lost the foot soldiers that were overtaken by the troops of the despot, who are knights. However, let us wait until the despot comes, so that we may also see the prince and what armies he has, to take this information to the holy basileus."

While they were expressing this counsel, the despot and the prince arrived with their armies. And when they heard and learned that the Genoese had not entered the castle of Arta at all, the despot, himself, considered it very good and he paid no attention to the plundering of the towns at all when he heard that the galleys remained in the harbor. On hearing this, the prince said to the despot: "Since the galleys still lie in the harbor, let us not dismount at all, but let us go there together with our armies, foot soldiers and knights, and let us set up our tents across from the galleys, to protect the land lest perhaps they land and do some damage and it be a reproach to us."

As the prince directed, so did it take place; they blew their trumpets and the army set out and went straight to where the harbor was, where the galleys were lying, those of the Genoese. There they set up their tents and took up quarters; on seeing this, the galleys went farther out and drew up the anchors and rode in deep water. Now, the despot asked counsel of the prince as to what he thought should happen and what they should do. And the prince, as a shrewd man, said to the despot: "It seems to me, my good uncle, that we should take our stand here where we have taken up quarters, lest they undertake to land, either to get water, or to do damage. And send armies to the outskirts to protect that land as well, lest they do any damage." As the prince ordered, so was it done.

When the Romans as well as the Genoese who were in those galleys of the basileus saw this, they wondered greatly as to where the despot had found so many handsome troops and the armies that he had, and they praised the prince, in turn, exceedingly and said that the man who had secured the military bearing and conduct of the army was a man experienced in the training of the Franks and the military qualities of the West. Thereupon, those on the galleys took counsel that from then on they could inflict no damage there where the prince and the despot had taken their stand. "But let us turn from here and go to some other place, to Xeromera which is without fear; there perhaps we may win and cause some damage, for it would be unsightly to return to the City without causing some damage to the land of the despot."

As they took counsel, so did they do; they raised the anchors and took up the oars; in a short time they arrived in the territory of Vontiza.[76]

---

[76] Vontiza (la Bondice, or Bondonicce, *qui est sur mer*, L., § 658, 980, 993, 994) is today Vonitsa, a port on the Gulf of Arta. The Chronicle breaks off abruptly at this point.

SELECTED BIBLIOGRAPHY

In the interest of brevity this bibliography has been restricted to those works specifically mentioned in the notes of this book. There are extensive references in the annotations of P. Kalonaros, *Τὸ Χρονικὸν τοῦ Μορέως*, and J. Longnon, *L'Empire latin de Constantinople*. Unfortunately, the usefulness of both is much impaired by the absence of a formal bibliographical apparatus. A lengthy list of books printed in Greece before 1920 may be found in N. Polites, *Ἑλληνικὴ Βιβλιογραφία* (3 vols. in 2), Athens, 1909-20. For the American student, by far the most complete and useful bibliographies are those in the *Cambridge Medieval History*, Vol. IV; D. Zakythinos, *Le Despotat grec de Morée*; K. Setton, *Catalan Domination of Athens*; D. Geanakopolos, *Emperor Michael Palaeologus and the West*; and S. Runciman, *The Sicilian Vespers*.

Editions of the Chronicle of Morea

THE GREEK CHRONICLE

The Chronicle of Morea; *Τὸ Χρονικὸν τοῦ Μορέως*, ed. in parallel texts from the mss. of Copenhagen and Paris by John Schmitt. London, 1904.

Τὸ Χρονικὸν τοῦ Μορέως, ed. Petros P. Kalonaros. Athens, 1940. Most recent edition of the *Codex Havniensis*, based on the edition of Schmitt.

THE FRENCH CHRONICLE

Livre de la conqueste de la princée de l'Amorée: Chronique de Morée (1204-1305), ed. Jean Longnon. Paris, Librairie Renouard, 1911.

THE ARAGONESE CHRONICLE

Libro de los fechos et conquistas del principado de la Morea, compilado, por comandamiento de Don Johan Ferrandez de Heredia, maestro del Hospital de S. Johan de Jerusalem, ed. Alfred Morel-Fatio. Geneva, 1885.

The Italian Chronicle

Istoria della Morea, ed. Charles Hopf. In his *Chroniques gréco-romanes inédites ou peu connues*. Berlin, 1873.

Byzantine Sources

Acropolites, Georges. *Historia*. In *Opera*, vol. I, ed. A. Heisenberg. Leipzig, 1903.

Chronicle of Galaxidi; Χρονικὸν ἀνέκδοτον Γαλαξειδίου, ed. K. N. Sathas. Athens, 1865.

Dorotheos of Monemvasia. *Βιβλίον ἱστορικόν περιέχον ἐν συνόψει διαφόρους καὶ ἐξόχους ἱστορίας*. Venice, 1814.

Gregoras, Nikephoros. *Byzantina historia*, ed. L. Schopen. 3 vols. Bonn, 1830-45.

Michael Choniates. *Τὰ Σωζόμενα*, ed. S. Lampros. 2 vols. Athens, 1879-80.

Niketas Choniates. *Historia*, ed. I. Bekker. Bonn, 1835.

Pachymeres, George. *De Michaele et Andronico Palaeologis*, ed. I. Bekker. 2 vols. Bonn, 1835.

Sphrantzes, George. *Chronicon minus*, in Migne, *PG*, vol. 156, 1025-80. Bonn, 1838. On the longer version of this work, by the "Pseudo-Sphrantzes," see R. J. Loernertz, "Autour du Chronicon Maius attribué à Georges Phrantzes," *Studi e Testi*, CXXIII (Miscellanea G. Mercati, III), Città del Vaticano (1946), 273-311.

Western Sources

Assises de Jérusalem, ed. Comte de Beugnot. (*Recueil des historiens des croisades: Lois, I-II*). 2 vols. Paris, 1841-43.

Buchon, J. A., ed. *Chroniques étrangères relatives aux expéditions françaises pendant le XIIIᵉ siècle*. Paris, 1875. Contains: 1. Anonyme grec; 2. Ramon Muntaner; 3. Bernard d'Esclot; 4. Anonyme sicilien.

—— *Collection des chroniques nationales françaises*. 47 vols. Paris 1824-29. Vols. I and II are Ducange's *History of the Latin Empire of Constantinople*. Vol. IV is 1st edition of Codex Parisinus.

—— *Recherches historiques sur la principauté française de Morée et ses hautes baronnies*. 2 vols. Paris, 1845. Vol. I is *Livre de la Conqueste*; Vol. II is 1st edition of Codex Havniensis.

Hopf, Charles. *Chroniques gréco-romanes inédites ou peu connues.* Berlin, 1873. Contains: 1. Sanudo's *Istoria del Regno di Romania*; 2. Italian Chronicle of Morea.

Innocent III. *Epistolae.* In Migne, *PL*, vols. 214-17.

Jordan, E. *Les registres de Clément IV.* Paris, 1893-1945.

Muntaner, Ramon. *Chronik des edlen en Ramon Muntaner*, ed. K. Lanz. Stuttgart, 1844.

Potthast, A., ed. *Regesta pontificum romanorum (1198-1304).* 2 vols. Berlin, 1874-75.

Recoura, G. *Les Assises de Romanie.* Paris, 1930. For translation, see Topping, *Feudal Institutions.*

Robert of Clari. *Conquest of Constantinople*, tr. E. H. McNeal. New York, 1936.

Villani, Giovanni. *Historia universalis...*, ed. A. Muratori. In *Rerum Italicarum Scriptores*, vol. XIII, cols. 9-1002. Milan, 1728.

Villehardouin, Geoffroy de. *La Conquête de Constantinople avec la continuation de Henri de Valenciennes*, ed. Natalis de Wailly. Paris, 1882.

William, Archbishop of Tyre. *History of Deeds Done beyond the Sea*, trans. E. Babcock and A. C. Krey. New York, 1943.

Secondary Works

Adamantiou, Ad. "Τὰ Χρονικὰ τοῦ Μορέως," Δελτίον τῆς Ἱστορικῆς καὶ Ἐθνολογικῆς Ἑταιρείας τῆς Ἑλλάδος, VI (1906), 453-675.

Alexopoulos, N. K. Μοραΐτου Ἱστορία τῆς Τεγέας. Athens, 1896.

Amantos, C. "Τσακονία-Sclavonia," Ἀφιέρομα εἰς Γ. Χατζιδάκιν. Athens, 1921.

—— "Σαλωνα-Τσάκωνες," Ἑλληνικά, X (1938), 210-12.

Andrews, Kevin. *Castles of the Morea.* Princeton, 1953.

Bees, Nikos A. "Zur Chronik von Morea," *Archiv für Kulturgeschichte*, XIII (1916), 122-24.

Bon, A. "Forteresses médiévales de la grèce centrale," *Bulletin de correspondance Hellénique*, LXI (1937), 136-208.

—— *Le Péloponnèse byzantine jusqu'en 1204.* Paris, 1951.

Buchon, J. *La Grèce continentale et la Morée.* Paris, 1843.

—— *Histoire des conquêtes et de l'établissement des français dans les états de l'ancienne Grèce ...* Paris, 1846.

—— *Nouvelles recherches historiques sur la principauté française de Morée et ses hautes baronnies....* 2 vols. Paris, 1843-45.

—— *Recherches et matériaux pour servir à une histoire de la domination française aux 13e, 14e, et 15e siècles dans les provinces démembrées de l'Empire grec à la suite de la quatrième croisade.* 2 vols. Paris, 1840.

Burns, R. I. "The Catalan Company and the European Powers, 1305-1311," *Speculum*, XXIX (1954), 751-71.

Byrne, Eugene H. *Genoese Shipping in the Twelfth and Thirteenth Centuries.* Cambridge, 1930.

Cambridge Medieval History, ed. J. R. Tanner, C. W. Previté-Orton, and Z. N. Brooke. Vol. IV: Eastern Roman Empire, 217-1453. Cambridge, 1936. Chapter XV, "Greece and the Aegean under Frank and Venetian Domination, 1204-1571" (pp. 432-77), was written by William Miller. See also extensive bibliography, pp. 852-66. (A completely new edition of this volume is now in press.)

Cerone, Francesco. "La sovranità napoletana sulla Morea e sulle isole vicine." *Archivio storico per le province Napoletano*, XLI (Naples, 1916), 5-64, 193-266; XLII (1917), 5-67.

Chapman, Conrad. *Michel Paléologue, restaurateur de l'empire byzantin (1261-1282).* Paris, 1926.

Delpech, H. *La Tactique du XIIIe siècle.* 2 vols. Montpellier, 1855.

Dendias, M. "Ἑλένη Ἀγγελῖνα Δούκαινα Βασίλισσα." Σικελίας καὶ Νεαπόλεως," Ἠπειρωτικὰ Χρονικά., I (1926), 219-94.

—— "Le roi Manfred de Sicile et la bataille de Pélagonie," *Mélanges Charles Diehl*, I, 55-60. Paris, 1930.

Dölger, F. "Chronologisches und Prosopographisches zur byzantinischen Geschichte des 13. Jahrhunderts," *Byzantinische Zeitschrift*, XXVII (1927), 291 ff.

—— "Die neuentdeckte Quelle zur Helenaszene in Goethes Faust. Die Prophyläen," *Beilage zur Münchner Zeitung*, XXVIII (1931), 289-90.

Dragoumis, S. N. "Χρονικοῦ τοῦ Μορέως λέξεις," Ἀθηνᾶ, XXIII, 73-87; XXIII, 363-71; XXVI, 26-32, 223-28.

—— Χρονικῶν τοῦ Μορέως : Τοπονυμικά, Τοπογραφικά, Ἱστορικά. Athens, 1921.

Gay, J. *L'Italie méridionale et l'empire byzantin (867-1071).* Paris, 1904.

Geanakoplos, Deno J. *Emperor Michael Palaeologus and the West.* Cambridge, 1959.

Gregorovius, F. A. *Geschichte der Stadt Athen im Mittelalter.* 2 vols.

Stuttgart, 1889. Ἱστορία τῆς Πόλεως Ἀθηνῶν is a modern Greek trans. and enlarged ed. by S. Lampros in 3 vols., the 3d consisting of new documents. Athens, 1904-6.

Guilland, R. "Contributions à l'histoire administrative de l'empire byzantin: Le dragonaire et le grand dragonaire de la ville," *Byzantinische Zeitschrift*, XLIII (1950), 340-65.

—— "Études de titulature et de Prosopographie Byzantines, Les Chefs de la Marine: Drongaire de la Flotte, Grand Drongaire de la Flotte, Duc de la Flotte, Megaduc," *Byzantinische Zeitschrift*, XLIV (1951), 212-40.

Guldencrone, D. *L'Achaie féodale*. Paris, 1886.

Hatzidakis, G. *Einleitung in die neugriechische Grammatik*. Leipzig, 1892.

—— Γλοσσικαὶ Μελέται. 3 vols. Cairo, 1904-06.

—— Μεσαιωνικὰ καὶ Νέα Ἑλληνικά. 2 vols. Athens, 1905-07.

—— "Περὶ τοῦ ἐτύμου τῆς λέξεως Μεσαρέας," Ἀθηνᾶ, VI, 3-64.

—— "The Chronicle of Morea by John Schmitt, 1904," Ἀθηνᾶ, XVI, 253-54.

Hopf, Charles. *Geschichte Griechenlands vom Beginn des Mittelalters bis auf unsere Zeit*. 2 vols. Leipzig, 1867-68. Published as vols. 85-86 of Ersch and Gruber, *Allgemeine Enzyklopädie der Wissenschaften und Kunste*.

Iliopoulos, K. Τὸ Τοπωνυμικὸν τῆς Ἠλείας. Athens, 1948.

Iorga, N. *Histoire de la vie byzantine*, 3 vols. Bucharest, 1934.

—— *Notes et extraits pour servir à l'histoire des croisades au XVe siècle*. Bucharest, 1915.

Jal, A. *Archéologie navale*. Paris, 1840.

Kalomenopoulos, S. N. Ἡ Στρατιωτικὴ Ὀργάνωσις τῆς Ἑλληνικῆς Αὐτοκρατορίας τοῦ Βυζαντίου. Athens, 1937.

Kalonaros, P. Ἐθνογραφικὰ Μάνης. Athens, 1935.

—— Λουλούδια τῆς Μονεμβασιᾶς καὶ τοῦ Ταϋγέτου (Εἰκόνες ἀπὸ τὴν Πατρίδα μας). Athens, 1936.

Kandeloros, T. Ἱστορία τῆς Γορτυνίας. Athens, 1931.

Kolias, C. Ἱστορικὴ Γεωγραφία τοῦ Ἑλληνικοῦ Χώρου. Athens, 1948.

—— "Σιδεροκάστρο," Ἐπετηρὶς Ἑταιρείας Βυζαντινῶν Σπουδῶν, X, 72-82.

Kontoglos, Ph. Ταξείδια. Athens, 1938.

Koukoules, Ph. Βυζαντινῶν βίος καὶ Πολιτισμός. 5 vols. in 8. Athens. 1948-52.

Krumbacher, K. *Geschichte der byzantinischen Litteratur*. Munich, 1897.

Lampros, Sp. "Ἔκφρασις τῶν ξυλοκονταρίων τοῦ κραταίου ἡμῶν αὐθέντου καὶ βασιλέως," Νέος Ἑλληνομνήμον, V, 3-18.

—— Ἱστορία τῆς Ἑλλάδος. 6 vols. Athens, 1886-1908. Volume VI deals with Frankish period.

—— "John Schmitt, The Chronicle of Morea," Νέος Ἑλλήνομνῆμων, I, 245-50.

Lane, F. C. Venetian Ships and Shipbuilders of the Renaissance. Baltimore, 1934.

Laurent, V., "La croisade et la question d'orient sous le pontificat de Grégoire X," Revue historique du sud-est européen, XXII (1945), 106-37.

—— "Grégoire X et le projet d'une ligue antiturque," Échos d'Orient, XXXVII (1938) 257-73.

Lehman-Haupt, C. "Τζάκωνες," Εἰς μνήμην Σπυρίδωνος Λάμπρου (Athens, 1935), pp. 353 ff.

Lekos, M. Περὶ Τσακώνων καὶ τῆς Τσακωνικῆς Διαλέκτου. Athens, 1920.

Longnon, Jean. L'Empire latin de Constantinople et la principauté de Morée. Paris, 1949.

—— Les Français d'Outre-mer au moyen âge. Essai sur l'expansion française dans le bassin de la Méditerranée. Paris, 1929.

—— "Problèmes de l'histoire de la principauté de Morée," Journal des Savants, (1946) 77-93; 147-61.

—— "Le rattachement de la principauté de Morée au royaume de Sicile en 1267," Journal des Savants (1942) 134 ff.

—— Recherches sur la vie de Geoffroy de Villehardouin suivies du catalogue des actes des Villehardouin. Paris, 1939.

Loray, Terrier de. "Un parlement de dames au XIIIᵉ siècle," Académie des Sciences, Belles-Lettres et Arts de Besançon, 1880 (Besançon, 1881), pp. 205-11.

D. Loukopoulos. Ποιὰ Παιγνίδια Παίζουν τὰ Ἑλληνόπουλα ... Athens, 1926.

Meliarakes, A. "Μεσαρέα," Ἱστορικαὶ ἔρευναι περὶ τοῦ Ὀνόματος τούτου ὡς Γεωγραφικοῦ. Athens, 1893.

—— Οἰκογένεια Μαμωνᾶ. Athens, 1902.

—— Ἱστορία τοῦ Βασιλείου τῆς Νικαίας καὶ τοῦ Δεσποτάτου τῆς Ἠπείρου (1204-61). Athens, 1898.

Meyer, Ernst. Peloponnesische Wanderungen; Reisen und Forschungen zur antiken und mittelalterlichen Topographie von Arkadien und Achaia. Zurich and Leipzig, 1939.

Miller, William. Essays on the Latin Orient. Cambridge, 1921.

—— *The Latins in the Levant: A History of Frankish Greece* (1204-1566). London, 1908.

Millet, Gabriel. *Le monastère de Daphni*. Paris, 1899.

Moravcsik, G. "Zur Quellenfrage der Helenaepisode in Goethes Faust." *Byzantinische-neugriechische Jahrbücher*, VIII (1931), 41-56.

Nicol, D. "The Date of the Battle of Pelagonia," *Byzantinische Zeitschrift*, XLIX (1956), 68-71.

—— *The Despotate of Epiros*. Oxford, 1957.

Nouchakes, I. E. Ἑλληνικὴ Χωρογραφία. Athens, 1901.

Oman, C. *A History of the Art of War in the Middle Ages*. 2 vols. New York, 1923.

Orlandos, A. K. Ἀρχεῖον τῶν Βυζαντινῶν Μνημείων τῆς Ἑλλάδος. 4 vols. Athens, 1936-38.

Ostrogorsky, G. "Agrarian Conditions in the Byzantine Empire in the Middle Ages," *Cambridge Economic History*, I (1941) 194-223.

—— "Le système de la Pronoia à Byzance et en Serbie médiévale," *Comité français des études byzantines. Acts du VIe Congrès International. École des Hautes Etudes*, Sorbonne, I (1950), 181 ff.

—— *Pour l'histoire de la féodalité byzantine*, tr. H. Grégoire. Brussels, 1954.

Paparregopoulos, K. Ἱστορία τοῦ Ἑλληνικοῦ Ἔθνους. New ed. in 8 vols. Athens, 1932.

Petit, E. *Histoire des ducs de Bourgogne de la race Capétienne*. 9 vols. Dijon, 1885-1905.

Phourikis, P. A. "Παρατηρήσεις εἰς τὰ τοπωνύμια τῶν Χρονικῶν τοῦ Μορέως . . .," Ἀθηνᾶ, XL (1928), 26-59.

Polites, N. G. Λαογραφικὰ Σύμμεικτα. Athens, 1920.

Rodd, Ren. *The Princes of Achaia and the Chronicles of Morea: a Study of Greece in the Middle Ages*. 2 vols. London, 1907.

Romanos, I. A. Περὶ τοῦ Δεσποτάτου τῆς Ἠπείρου. Corfu, 1895.

Sarres, I. "Τὰ τοπονυμικὰ τῆς Ἀττικῆς," Ἀθηνᾶ, XL (1929), 129.

Schlumberger, G. *L'expédition des "Almugavares,"....* Paris, 1902.

—— *Récits de Byzance et des Croisades*. Paris, 1916.

Schmitt, John. "La 'Théséide' de Boccace et la 'Théséide' Grecque," *Études de Philologie Néo-Grecque (Bibliothèque de l'École des Hautes Études, XCII)*. Paris, 1892.

Setton, K. M. *Catalan Domination of Athens, 1311-1388*. Cambridge, Mass., 1948.

Soyter, G. *Byzantinische Dichtung*. Heidelberg, 1929.

—— *Byzantinische Geschichtschreiber und Chronisten.* Heidelberg, 1929. See especially pp. 18-28, 51.

Stiernon, L. "Les origines du despotat d'Épire," *Revue des Études Byzantines,* XVII (1959), 90-126.

Tarsoulis, A. *Κάστρα καὶ Πολιτεῖες τοῦ Μωριᾶ.* Athens, 1934.

Topping, P. *Feudal Institutions.* Philadelphia, 1949. Includes a translation of Recoura's *Les Assises de Romanie.*

Trauquair, R. "Medieval Fortresses," *The Annual of the British School of Athens,* XII (1905-6), 258-76; XIII (1906-7), 268-81.

Usseglio, L. *I Marchesi di Monferrato in Italia ed in Oriente durante i Secoli XII e XIII.* Turin, 1926.

Wolff, R. L. "The Organization of the Latin Patriarchate of Constantinople, 1204-1261. Social and Administrative Consequences of the Latin Conquest," *Traditio,* VI (1948), 33-60.

—— "Politics in the Latin Patriarchate of Constantinople, 1204-1261," *Dumbarton Oaks Papers,* No. 8 (1954), pp. 223-303.

Xanthoudides, S. "*Διορθώσεις εἰς Χρονικὸν Μορέως . . .*," *᾿Αθηνᾶ,* XXXII, 205 ff.

Zakythinos, D. *Le Chrysobulle d'Alexis III Comnène.* Paris, 1932.

—— *Le Despotat grec de Morée.* 2 vols. Paris, 1932-53.

—— *Οἱ Σλάβοι ἐν Ἑλλάδι.* Athens, 1945.

Zerlentis, P. *Μηλιγγοὶ καὶ ᾿Εζερίται, Σλάβοι ἐν Πελοποννήσῳ.* Hermoupolis, 1922.

—— *Τάξις ἱεραρχικὴ τῶν ἐν Πελοποννήσῳ ἁγίων τῶν θέων ᾿Εκκλησιῶν.* Hermoupolis, 1922.